Strategies to Achieve a Binding International Agreement on Regulating Cartels

John Sanghyun Lee

Strategies to Achieve a Binding International Agreement on Regulating Cartels

Overcoming Doha Standstill

Springer

John Sanghyun Lee
Global Law Department,
College of Law
Soongsil University
Seoul
Korea (Republic of)

and

Golden Gate University School of Law
San Francisco, CA
USA

ISBN 978-981-10-2755-0 ISBN 978-981-10-2756-7 (eBook)
DOI 10.1007/978-981-10-2756-7

Library of Congress Control Number: 2016954593

Printed on acid-free paper

This Springer imprint is published by Springer Nature
The registered company is Springer Nature Singapore Pte Ltd.
The registered company address is: 152 Beach Road, #22-06/08 Gateway East, Singapore 189721, Singapore

Preface

A cartel, restricting competition among suppliers and getting rid of consumers' welfare, among other things, has been actively regulated mostly by advanced economies. International organizations tried to reach international agreement on competition law and policy, including cartel regulation. In spite of tens of countries in North America and Europe with experiences of serious law enforcement on competition law, such trials have faced hurdles since a multilateral negotiation on Doha Development Agenda (DDA) dropped competition policy from the discussion table in 2003. After dropping the issue, DDA has still produced few, if any, noticeable fruits. A different view between advanced economies and developing countries and its consequential rupture of the discussion are analyzed to be main factors of standstill of DDA.

In order to achieve a binding international agreement on cartels, international community needs to focus on hard core cartel (HHC) activities, narrower than its original definition, because most countries agree with the necessity of regulating such narrowed cartels and because international agreements have been developed with such focuses. Moreover, interstate commodity agreements (ICAs) or intergovernmental producers associations (IPAs) are to be treated differently under the area of international commodity law in light of international law history. Several cases of international cartels, made up of competing private companies, ICAs, and IPAs under suspicion of cartels are to be reviewed with in-depth research.

Four advanced countries, USA, UK, France, and Germany, with experiences of cartel regulations and competition law enforcements are to be addressed in contrast to examples of four developing economies, South Africa, South Korea, People's Republic of China, and Mexico, with less experiences than the four countries. Historic study of international development law and its results will be applied to international agreement on cartel regulation since such study on law sheds light on future international law on cartel regulation reflecting developing countries' interests.

Up until now, international competition law, particularly international agreement on cartels, has grown up centering on soft-law-typed multilateral agreements and binding-powered bilateral agreements. Based upon the observation and research on international law development, two strategies, short-term and long-term approaches, are suggested for achieving a binding international agreement on cartels. By reducing fear of developing countries that international cartel regulation may seriously interfere with their economic interests, international organizations' efforts to have effective international cartel regulation can increase the probability of success.

Meanwhile, distinctive features of commodity led to international commodity agreements under the agenda of sustainable development, formerly defunct, requiring, for adjustment to current trade law system. The following are to be proposed for the adjustment: ①productivity-focused model and ②multilateral cooperation model to reflect multistakeholders' interests.

Seoul, Korea (Republic of) John Sanghyun Lee

Acknowledgments

This book is a work which revised my doctorate thesis originally written in 2008 through reflecting on updated information. A substantial part of the book was influenced by expertise advice from my supervisors, Dr. Sompong Sucharitkul, Prof. Dr. Christian Okeke, Director of SJD International Legal Studies at Golden Gate University School of Law, and Prof. Bart Selden. Professor Sompong had guided me with his wisdom from his rich experience in international law areas until he retired. Professor Okeke encouraged me to pursue this research project, at its initial stage, and suggested several topics for further research. Professor Esq. Selden instructed the foundation of international trade law and business transactions through a series of lectures. This research would have followed a different path without their proper and insightful advice.

I would like to express my thanks to other professors and advisors at GGU. Professor Emeka Duruigbo taught the ways for a young candidate to develop his idea. Professor Michael Daw and Marienne Gerber enriched my research skills through Internet and legal databases. Professor Chris Pagano did not spare her time in giving special advice; she provided me with scholarship when I was admitted at SJD program. Mr. John Pluebell, Senior Academic Advisor, has enabled me to study without being interrupted by any administrative problem. His good works and counsel let me concentrate on researching.

Interacting with good colleagues who have had interest in international law or have sincerely pursued the same degree stimulated me so that I could develop this project seriously and eagerly. Among them, Justin, Nick, Peter, Art Gambell, Huon Thach, Nobert, Franzier Robhert, Joon-Kil Lee, and Patcharang were good friend who shared warm conversation. I would like to express my appreciation to SJD program at Golden Gate University School of Law for the precious opportunity of studying and communicating with students from all over the world.

I am heavily indebted to my two friends, Sorah Kim and Jay Choi, who made comments on my drafts, and public officers at competition authorities in UK. South Africa and South Korea. I reflected their valuable opinions on my study. I would like to extend my gratitude to Mr. Jae-Hoon Jung who edited footnotes sincerely.

I feel thankful and sorry for my wife, Sunhee, who supported my work, and our lovely daughters, Joyce and Eunice, who put up with plays without their father. All the research would be impossible without support from my father, mother, and father-in law and mother-in-law, who cared for my kids and encouraged my research with continuous prayers. Aunt-in-law have spared little efforts in praying for me. Finally, I would like to express my deep gratitude to the Lord Jesus who helped me overcome hurdles whenever I faced difficulties.

Contents

1 Introduction 1
1.1 Hard Core Cartel Against Competition Law 1
1.2 Spreading Competition Laws to the International Community 2
1.3 Hurdles to Leveling Cartel Regulations up to International Laws 4
1.4 Topic Question and Hypothesis of the Research 5
1.5 Structure of the Book 6
1.5.1 Structure of this Book 6
References 8

2 Defining a Cartel and Analyzing Its Effects 9
2.1 A Cartel in Its Historical Context 9
2.2 Definition 10
2.3 Discussions: Advantage and Disadvantage of Cartels 26
2.4 Intergovernmental Agreement for a Commodity Distinctive from a Private Cartel 38
2.5 International Cartels and Their Representatives 50
2.6 Conclusion 58
References 60

3 Legal Status and Historical Background of Cartels in International Law 63
3.1 Opening International Law Era: Infant Stage 63
3.2 Legal Status of International Cartel in International Law 65
3.3 Development of National Cartel Laws and the Necessity of International Law 96
3.4 Development of International Commodity Agreements (ICAs) Separate from Cartel Regime 105
3.5 International Organizations' Endeavors to Achieve Multilateral Agreements Regarding Cartels 118

3.6 Extending Bilateral or Regional Agreement 133
3.7 Conclusion 139
References. 141

4 Conciliation of Conflicts of Opinion Between the North and the South on International Law Regulating Cartel 145
4.1 Introduction 146
4.2 Failure of Further Negotiation on Competition Policy Under Doha Development Agenda (DDA) at WTO Ministerial Conferences 147
4.3 Necessity of Regulating Cartels in Developing Countries. 154
4.4 Different Positions Where Developing Countries Are Placed 159
4.5 International Competition Law Reflecting Development. 167
4.6 Roadmap Toward Binding International Cartel Agreement. 183
4.7 Conclusion 187
References. 189

5 The Regulation of Cartels in Developing Countries 193
5.1 Introduction 193
5.2 Development of Cartel Regulation in the North and the South 194
5.3 Building Consensus to Enforce Cartel Regulation 221
5.4 Securing Institutional Supports for Cartel Regulation 232
5.5 Capacities Building Through International Cooperation 240
5.6 Conclusion 247
References. 250

6 The Need for the Development of International Law on Cartels 253
6.1 Current Stage of International Cartel Regulation 254
6.2 Hurdles to a Binding Multilateral Agreement. 255
6.3 Functions of a Bilateral Agreement Toward a Multilateral Agreement Regulating Cartels 259
6.4 Strategies for Achieving a Binding Multilateral Agreement 265
6.5 Applicability of International Criminal Law as to Cartels. 287
6.6 Proposing a New Approach for International Commodity Agreements (ICAs). 296
6.7 Conclusion 317
References. 321

7 General Conclusion: Summary and Prospect 325
7.1 Compendium of Research. 325
7.2 Moderation of Distinction Between International Competition Law and International Commodity Law 332

Index 335

List of Figures

Figure 1.1	Structure of this Book	6
Figure 2.1	Division of private and public cartels and its respective coverage	25
Figure 4.1	Picture of road map	184
Figure 5.1	Level and strength of competition law enforcement depending on its several bases	200
Figure 5.2	Competition policy and industrial policy	228
Figure 6.1	Export cartels of net exporting nation and net importing nation under international agreement	279
Figure 7.1	Relationship between Int'l competition law and Int'l commodity law	333

List of Tables

Table 2.1 The graphite electrodes cartel investigation of countries 55
Table 2.2 Comparison of penalties in each country (US$ million) 57
Table 2.3 Comparison of market scope: global and Korean Markets (US$ million). 58
Table 3.1 Development of international agreements on nontariff barriers. 64
Table 3.2 Comparison between posteriori and priori allocation 86
Table 5.1 Total cartel cases at KFTC with imposed sanction 215
Table 5.2 Surcharge against collusive behavior (cartel) of KFTC 216
Table 5.3 The application of leniency program at KFTC. 216
Table 6.1 Convergence-harmonization continuum 282

Chapter 1
Introduction

Abstract While competition law and policy has been spread to the international community under the auspice of advanced economies, particularly the U.S. and European Union (EU), there has been obstacles for adopting a binding international law on the area of competition law. A cartel, causing huge loss of consumer welfare, has been rarely under the serious regulatory power of international law. Reasons of such hurdles and delays as to regulate international cartels are to be examined with a clue on standstill of Doha Development Agenda, and research process on their solutions is to be demonstrated.

Keywords Competition law · Cartel · International competition law · International law on cartel · Research process

1.1 Hard Core Cartel Against Competition Law

A free market system based on both freedom of contract and protection of property principles operates challenged by demand and supply. Under the free market system, demand by consumers and supply by producers determine the price and quantity of a product. Competition policy leads suppliers to compete among themselves in sales terms or conditions. Competition toward attracting consumers through lower prices is an important principle for working a free market. Competition law is supposed to protect the functioning of the market.

However, it is against competition law principle for competitors to conspire to fix prices or to limit output. Price-fixing is the artificial setting or maintenance of prices at a certain level, usually higher than the level which would be normal without the price-fixing agreement. Sometimes, the competitors collude to maintain a level of production pre-arranged by themselves. Price-fixing and output restriction are typical to hard core cartels.[1] The hard core cartels cause diverse negative aspects to the economy.

[1] *Refer to* Chap. 2, Sec. 2.2, A for the definition of the 'cartel'.

J.S. Lee, *Strategies to Achieve a Binding International Agreement on Regulating Cartels*, DOI 10.1007/978-981-10-2756-7_1

The hard core cartels take away consumers' benefits that competition among suppliers would have otherwise produced. Consumers in the normal markets purchase products by paying the price set by market mechanisms through the competition of suppliers. However, in a market where the sellers have agreed to set the price or the quantity of the product, consumers cannot avoid paying the higher price than in a market without the collusion.

In addition, cartels cause price-inflexibility regardless of a change in economic circumstances, thereby leading to malfunctions in a free market system. Such malfunction is due to restraining competition among suppliers as an essential element of the free market mechanism.

1.2 Spreading Competition Laws to the International Community

The U.S., as a leader in competition law enforcing countries,[2] has developed sophisticated jurisprudence in competition law since 1890 when it adopted the Sherman Act, the first modern competition law in the world. Price-fixing or output restriction has been treated as illegal under the application of the Sherman Act since *United States v. Trans-Missouri Freight Association* (1897).[3] Through accumulated cases,[4] the judicial branch in the U.S. has developed per se approach to hard core cartels without allowing reasonable justifications for the type of cartel. In addition, in the late twentieth century, especially since the 1990s, the U.S. has pursued the strongest antitrust penalty regime by punishing individuals as well as enterprises with heavy fines and even imprisonment. Moreover, the strict penalty has been strengthened with civil actions under Sec. 4 of the Clayton Act, which provide treble damages for recovery of victimized consumers of the cartels.

The European Union (EU), although some member countries have developed their own competition laws,[5] had not enforced competition law seriously until the Treaty establishing the European Community (EC) adopted a chapter regarding competition law in the late 1950s. EU devoted significant input to its enforcement, which turned out successful. Recently, the Competition Commission of the EU has

[2]Competition law is the law regulating the behaviors of competing corporations in a free market.

[3]166 U.S. 290 (1897).

[4]*Id.* at 333. *Joint Traffic Ass'n v. U.S.,* 171 U.S. 505, 560, 565 (1898); *Socony-Vacuum Oil Co. v. U.S.*, 310 U.S. 150, 60 S.Ct. 811(1940); *U.S. v. Paramount Pictures*, 334 U.S. 131, 68 S.Ct. 915, 92 L.Ed. 1260 (1948); *Northern Pac. R. Co. v. U.S.*, 356 U.S. 1, 78 S.Ct. 514, 2 L.Ed.2d 545 (1958); *U.S. v. General Motors*, 384 U.S. 127, 86 S.Ct. 1321, 16 L.Ed.2d 415 (1966); *Int' Ass'n of Machinists and Aerospace Workers v. OPEC*, 477 F.Supp. 553, 558 (1979).

[5]The United Kingdom created a major competition law principle, rule of reason, in the eighteenth century. Germany also adopted cartel regulations in the late nineteenth century. France also had competition law provisions. But their legislations grew loose or ineffective, so they did not evolve into so sophisticated law principle as the U.S. law. Refer to Chap. 3 for in-detail.

actively investigated cartels, both domestic and international, with the threat of severe punishment.[6] Member states in the EU also have operated effective competition laws, including cartel regulations, under the influence of rigorous EU enforcement.

Other countries, facing domestic and international challenges, have developed competition laws reflecting their respective economic and political situations. More than a hundred countries have antitrust statutes as of 2008.[7]

However, not all the countries with competition laws enforce the laws as seriously as the U.S. or EU. Only eight countries[8] provided criminal liability for both individuals and enterprises as of 2005. Moreover, even these countries had indicated a very short history of major prosecution in numerous cartel cases. Even the EU revealed, there has been no jail sentence against individuals.[9]

In spite of this situation, there has been strong pressure toward widespread regulation against cartels in the international community. The United Nations Conference on Trade and Development (UNCTAD) has held conferences on international competition law since 1980 when the United Nations (UN) passed a recommendation regarding the Set of Multilaterally Agreed Equitable Principles and Rules for the Control of Restrictive Business Practices (the UN Set). On the other hand, the Organization for Economic Co-operation and Development (OECD) recommended that its member countries should adopt criminal sanctions in order to create a deterrent against future cartels and to provide an incentive for cartel participants to cooperate with cartel investigations under the so-called amnesty program.[10] In addition to the OECD recommendation, International Competition Network (ICN) has held regular conferences to discuss diverse topics among which the topic of effective enforcement of criminal penalty against cartels is a heated issue. Moreover, at the 1996 Singapore World Trade Organization (WTO) Ministerial Conference, competition policy was adopted among four main issues[11] that a multilateral agreement should include besides goods and services. The Doha Development Agenda (DDA) has around 20 subjects to negotiate, although now trying to overcome its deadlock after the Hong Kong Ministerial

[6]*Refer to* the international vitamin and graphite electrodes cartel cases under Chap. 2.

[7]International Competition Network has a contact list of 100 competition authorities as of 2008, *at* http://www.internationalcompetitionnetwork.org/pdf/ICN_Contact_List.pdf (visited on Sep. 4, 2008). *See also* Statement by Germany, United Nations Conference on Trade and Development (2005), *available at* http://www.unctad.org.

[8]Austria, U.K, Canada, Ireland, Israel, Japan, Korea, and Norway. *See id.* Baker mentioned only seven countries in 2001. The United Kingdom was added in 2005. Hammond (2006) p. 2.

[9]Baker (2001), at 710; Competition Committee Survey of OECD (2003), at 29; Hammond (2006), at 5.

[10]OECD, *Hard Core Cartel*, 2000 Report by OECD Competition Committee 46, *available at* http://www.oecd.org/competition: OECD, *Recommendation of the Council concerning Effective Action against Hard Core Cartel* (Mar 25 1998), *available at* http://www.oecd.org/competition.

[11]The four Singapore issues are investment, competition, transparency in government procurement, and trade facilitation. *See* 3D/FORUM-ASIA, Practical Guide to the WTO 32, *at* http://www.3dthree.org/en/complement.php?IDcomplement=36.

Conference of 2005, and included competition policy as a major subject to discuss. Still, the WTO has focused on restrictions on cross-border cartels under its directions, one of which proposed to discuss further a multilateral agreement in competition policy.[12]

1.3 Hurdles to Leveling Cartel Regulations up to International Laws

The rigorous approach from the international community leaves much room to be desired. For example, regulatory authorities in South Korea, such as the Korea Fair Trade Commission (KFTC) and public prosecutors, do not frequently apply criminal penalties against cartels although the penalties are available for punishing both individuals and enterprises. The KFTC has treated cartels, in most cases, with imposing administrative fines or surcharges rather than with filing complaints to public prosecutors.[13] Concretely, only 3.6 % of all the cartel cases that KFTC has treated since its establishment are referred to the public prosecutor's office with a KFTC criminal report. The other 96.4 % of cases have been treated under the KFTC with corrective orders, surcharges, recommendations, and warnings.[14] Moreover, officers working for competition-regulating authorities in developing countries, whom the author met during 2006 annual meeting of American Bar Association Section of Antitrust Law, revealed their policies with focus on regulating the monopolization of markets rather than on punishing cartel activity.[15]

Furthermore, competition policy was the first dropped topic out of the four Singapore issues in the DDA multilateral negotiation at the 2003 Cancun Ministerial Conference. Negotiation on the whole DDA discontinued after the 2005 Hong Kong Ministerial Conference due to a disagreement between developing countries and industrialized countries.[16] The different positions reflecting diverse economic situations, such as fears of developing countries that their industries might be negatively affected and hesitancies of industrialized countries to persuade developing countries due to complex internal problems, have barred further negotiations in the competition policy.

---

[12] Dayaratna Banda and Whalley (2005, p. 14).

[13] Without filing the complaint, public prosecutors in South Korea can not prosecute enterprises and their members who violated competition law under Article 71 of the Monopoly Restraint and Fair Trade Act (MRFTA) in South Korea.

[14] KFTC (2004, p. 551).

[15] The author attended 2006 annual conference of antitrust law provided by American Bar Association (ABA), and met officers who worked for competition authorities in developing countries, such as South Africa, Nigeria, Vietnam, etc. They told to me that they had been focusing on regulating monopolization rather than cartels.

[16] Alan Beattie and Frances Williams, *U.S. blamed as trade talks end in acrimony*, FIN. TIMES (FT), July 25, 2006, at 1.

1.4 Topic Question and Hypothesis of the Research

This dissertation will suggest a solution to the challenges of reaching a binding international cartel regulation, which is currently in a standstill. The book started with a question of why competition policy was dropped in WTO DDA negotiation which would be the important chance to adopt binding international law as to cartels. Extending application of cartel regulations in industrialized countries, current extraterritorial application notwithstanding conflict with the comity principle, does and will not satisfy the necessity to regulate international cartels in developing countries as the application undermines cooperation between the North and the South, and does not provide compensation to consumers in the South. Although international organizations achieved soft international laws and cooperation regimes of competition law practices mostly among industrialized countries, efforts to reach binding international cartel regulations have failed.

The reason why efforts have failed is presumably because developing countries, consisting of a majority of most international organizations, did not have the intent to focus on the efficiency-oriented cartel regulation scheme and competition law but focused rather on their economic development. The group of developing countries has endured insufficient financial resource and immature skills and experiences for effective competition policy, let alone the public consensus of damages of the cartels. In order to enjoy rich financial resources and to operate sophisticated institutions, the group of developing countries placed their utmost concern toward economic development rather than creating a competition regime.

After reviewing different positions on cartels of the South, this study suggests that building effective cartel regulations in the South should be the important ground to construct a binding international cartel regulation. With effective domestic cartel enforcement, the multilateral negotiations will have firm basis to obtain an international cartel regulation. By assisting their enforcements, international community can approach with non-treaty agreement an international cartel law. Extending current bilateral or regional agreement can connect the soft law to a binding plurilateral agreement which need to reflect development concern of the South. The plurilateral agreement can have two strategies: narrow focus on hard core cartel in the short term, and cartel regulation under competition regime in the long term.

Since the characteristics of cartels consisting of private companies (private cartels) are different from those of sovereign states (intergovernmental agreement for commodity), the study distinguishes private cartel regulations from intergovernmental agreement for commodity and reviews the development of international commodity law. Such distinction is justified by the fact that developing countries have derived the major impetus for economic development from their major commodities. It is suggested a strategy of differentiated products with high-quality standards to balance market mechanisms with economic development in the South.

The consensus building in the South as to cartel regulations will be achieved through effective enforcements of the cartel regulations supported by international cooperation and assistance from the North. The increased public awareness can reach international cartel regulations as to private cartels while intergovernmental agreements for commodity are left under the different rule.

1.5 Structure of the Book

The book consists of a total of six chapters to answer the research question as the following Fig. 1.1 describes.

1.5.1 Structure of this Book

After Chap. 1 with statement of research purpose, Chap. 2 examines the definition of a cartel, discussion the effects of a cartel, and international agreement for

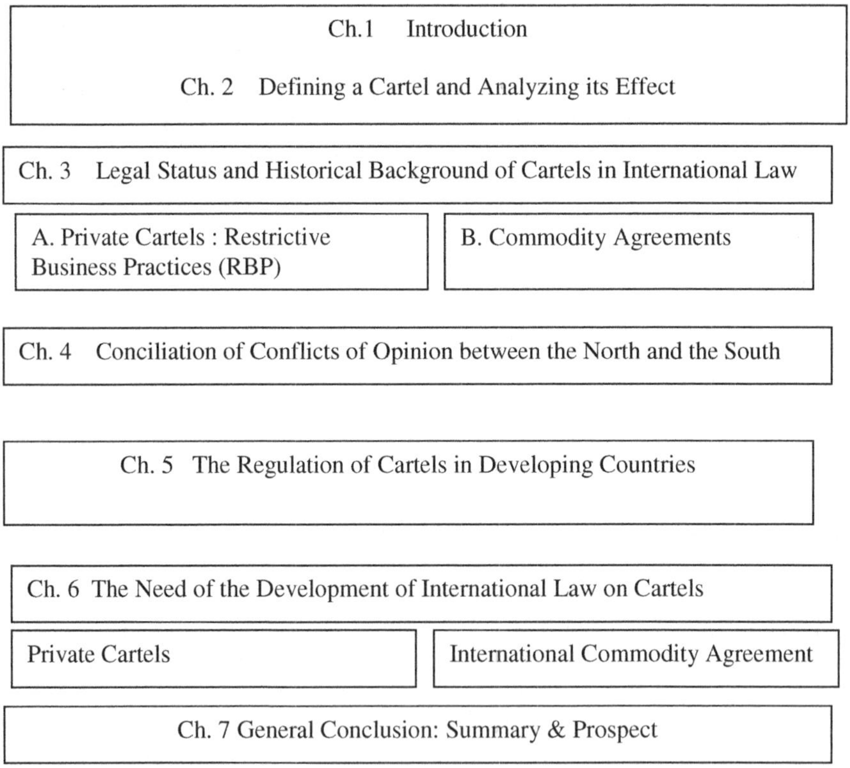

Fig. 1.1 Structure of this Book

commodity distinctive from private cartel, and introduces aspects of international cartels and major exemplary cases from the comparative analysis.

Chapter 3 researches the legal status of international cartels in international law by investigating such international organizations under the doubt of being a cartel. The chapter goes into development of domestic cartel law and of international agreement of commodity. Under the private cartel regulation, trials for achieving multilateral agreements by international organizations and the possibility of extending current bilateral and regional trade agreements including competition law are to be examined.

Chapter 4 analyzes North–South conflicts as hurdles to achieve international cartel regulations. After examining the failure of recent WTO DDA negotiation to adopt cartel law under competition policy, the necessity of cartel regulations in the developing countries is to be asserted with persuasive reasons. The positions of competition policy in developing countries in comparison to advanced countries are to be investigated. The international cartel law reflecting the perspective of international development law is to be considered. The roadmap toward binding cartel law will be proposed.

Chapter 5 starts with a comparative analysis of cartel law in both advanced and developing countries with promising competition law practices. After different types of cartel laws in both the North and South are investigated, consensus-building for active cartel regulations in the South is to be highlighted. Concrete suggestions shall be followed to make efficient institutions with sound foundations in developing countries. Cooperative measures with developed competition authorities shall be suggested as the effective ways to build capacities in developing countries.

Chapter 6 concentrates on suggesting strategies for achieving binding multilateral agreements and advanced models of international agreements for commodities. After looking over current international cartel regulations, the chapter examines the limitation of bilateral agreements as leading measures of international cartel law. It further analyzes the hurdles in binding multilateral agreements. The chapter also proposes a strategy for binding multilateral agreements for cartels, and discusses the possibility of international economic crime. Moreover, reform measures for international commodity agreements will be addressed in light of past failures. Market-related policies, such as price-risk-management, structural policy for economic development, two models reflecting the cause of sustainable development, and eco-label system as a cooperative model between private and public sectors, will be suggested.

Finally, Chap. 7 summarizes all the discussed arguments and summarizes overall assessments and interim conclusions. Then, the future prospect will be added that international competition law and international commodity agreements will have some relationship in the area of international economic law.

References

Baker DI (2001) The use of criminal law remedies to Deter and Punish Cartels and Bid-rigging, 69. Geo Wash L Rev 693

Dayaratna Banda OG, Whalley J (2005) Beyond goods and services: competition policy, investment, mutual recognition, movement of persons, and broader cooperation provisions of recent FTAs involving ASEAN Countries, National Bureau of Economic Research, March 2005

Hammond SD (2006) Charting new waters in international cartel prosecutions, 20 NAT'L Inst. of White COLLAR CRIME 2, available at http://www.usdoj.gov/atr/public/speeches/214861.pdf

Korea Fair Trade Commission (KFTC) (2004) Whitepaper [공정거래백서], KFTC

Chapter 2
Defining a Cartel and Analyzing Its Effects

Abstract A cartel is an agreement or a collective action to restrain reciprocal business activities among plural independent entrepreneurs competing in the same level of a business industry to prevent competition thereby securing extra profit. In order to achieve international law on cartels, the international community needs to focus on hard core cartel (HHC) activities with several types of categories, narrower than the definition, because most countries agree with the necessity of regulating such narrowed cartels and because international agreements have been developed with such focuses. Cartels cause more harms than benefits in markets and societies either domestic or global, so there needs regulations on cartels. Meanwhile, inter-state commodity cartels need to be exempted from such cartel regulation so that they may reduce extreme price fluctuations. The Intergovernmental producers association (IPA) needs to be under international commodity laws different from the law for typical private cartels. To utilize international support for cartel regulations, international cartel law should focus on private cartels with priority since there have been growing research studies on the cartels sufficient enough to reach a consensus among countries.

Keywords Cartel · Hard core cartel · Commodity cartel · Cartel regulation · Intergovernmental producers' association (IPA) · A binding international agreement · International commodity agreement (ICA)

2.1 A Cartel in Its Historical Context

Although a cartel sounds like a recent problem due to the semantics of its language, the phenomenon that it covers dates back to the ancient times when our forefathers earned money by trade and competed so as to have more profits. Competition-restraint measures by suppliers have been maintained with the development of trade throughout human-being's history.

J.S. Lee, *Strategies to Achieve a Binding International Agreement on Regulating Cartels*, DOI 10.1007/978-981-10-2756-7_2

However, modern legislations toward promoting competition based on judicial and economic reasons were not seriously enforced until the 1980s even in industrialized countries. Specifically, up until the 1990s or even the 2000s, there is hardly any anticipation to establish an international organization dealing with competition law issues.

This chapter initiates its exposition through searching the meaning of the term 'cartel' within the context of modern development of its regulatory regimes, either international or domestic. It explores the coverage of cartels by categorizing them. Studying the damages and benefits of the cartels with their effects on the economy, politics, and society helps reduce conflicting views between the countries with strong cartel regulations and those with hesitancy or less skills to investigate the cartels. Examining the possibility of benevolent cartels is an opportunity to investigate arguments of developing countries that do not want to adopt cartel regulations related to international trade negotiations.

2.2 Definition

A. Origin of the Cartel and the Current Meaning

A 'cartel' is thought to come from the **Latin** *charta*, meaning a writing, a paper, or a letter. Before the word was used for a trade jargon, it was used for representing a military agreement between belligerent nations, e.g., the exchange of prisoners.[1] As markets grew expanded and competition became severe among entrepreneurs dealing with the same products, the word arguably changed its usage to the trade term of an agreement for the exchange of sales information, including price or other conditions.[2]

Currently, a cartel is defined as 'an arrangement among supposedly independent corporations or *national monopolies* in the same industrial or resource development field organized to control distribution, set prices, reduce competition and sometimes share technical expertise',[3] or 'a combination of producers or sellers that join together to control a product's production or price' or 'an association of firms with

[1]Stocking and Watkins (1948), p. 3 and footnote 1; Eatwell et al. (1998), p. 372.

[2]Huh (2002), pp. 15–17.

[3]*Refer to* http://dictionary.law.com. Dictionary in the other academic areas includes the public cartel in the similar way to the Law Dictionary. The Britannica Encyclopedia also includes state-monopoly or inter-state cartel, e.g. OPEC. Encyclopaedia Britannica (2007), p. 908. With focus on the element of 'agreement', Friedman (2007), p. 89 explains that a cartel is a group of independent suppliers, which *agree* to restrict trade to their mutual benefit. On the other hand, Greenwald ed. (1994), pp. 136–138 states, with focus on 'anti-competitive acts' rather than the agreement, that a cartel is a group of producers who *coordinate price and output decisions* to increase combined and individual output. If all producers of a good combine, the cartel may seek to imitate the behavior of a monopoly supplier, however, commonly, a fringe of small producers will operate outside the cartel.

common interests, seeking to prevent extreme or unfair competition, allocate market or share knowledge'.[4] All of the definitions have at least two common elements, (i) the gathering of companies and (ii) the purpose of controlling transaction term(s) related to competition.

Compared to its origin, the cartel concept have evolved, under the influence of accumulated economics, to include a type of association consisting of competing entrepreneurs which controls sales or productions or shares knowledge with the purpose of preventing competition. National competition laws and international law have developed regulations of cartel activities which cause severe harm to markets and consumers. Particularly, the laws designated several types of cartel activities, so-called hard core cartels, illegitimate. The cartels are made up of only private companies which are supposed to compete each other. Meanwhile, international law has separated interstate cartels from the coverage of international competition law and thereby placed the public cartel or international commodity agreement under international commodity law. With the increasing number of cartel cases, the concept of a cartel has distinguished itself from the other concepts of business combinations. After reviewing similar concepts and cartel regulations, this research will propose a definition of a cartel distinguished from other concepts.

B. Similar Concepts: Trust, Joint Venture, Syndicate, and Konzern

Competition law in the United States, starting with enacting the Sherman Act in 1890, originally pointed out a trust as the major object of its application since Sec. 1 of the Sherman Act adopted the language, 'every contract in the form of trust or otherwise'. However, a trust is a legal concept different from a cartel. A trust creates binding legal rights that are enforceable in equity for the beneficial enjoyment of a property, the legal title of which a trust settler (settler) transfers to another person (trustee) for the third party (beneficiary)'s benefit.[5] While a cartel is formed among competitors, a trust is created between a settler and a trustee and generates no relationship among competitors. The common law legal tool was used so as to create a strong business combination aiming at restraining competition in the U.S. markets in the late 19t century. Competing companies in the same market, for the purpose of getting rid of competition, transferred their stocks to the third company, which would decide the level of price or production or allocate geographical markets and distribute its profits to the settler companies, usually in proportion of the value of the stocks. The third company controlled the national market with its trustee position while the competing companies, which entrusted their stocks to trustee, took positions of both the settlers, and the beneficiaries. Such trust represented one of legal measures which restricted competition, and Sec. 1 of the Sherman Act explicitly included the trust as one of its targets. Since the competition law in the U.S. is originally designed to prevent anticompetitive business practices, represented by the trust, it has been called an 'anti-trust law' even though the

[4]Garner (2003), p. 86.

[5]Baker (2001), p. 710.

'anti-trust' law covers other aspects of trade restraint such as monopolies, price-discrimination, or anticompetitive mergers.

A joint venture is different from a cartel in terms of the level of business and legal integration and competitive effect. A joint venture is one business undertaking by plural persons engaged in a single project.[6] It has a common purpose but not the one for restricting competition. The U.S. Supreme Court has distinguished a joint venture which set a price from a hard core cartel which fixes a price.[7] As a joint venture in most cases generates pro-competitive effect in markets through cooperation, the pro-competitive effect should be considered for a decision of substantially reducing competition. Meanwhile, a hard core cartel with price-fixing has been treated under per se illegal.[8]

Meanwhile, a syndicate is defined as 'a joint venture among individuals and/or corporations to accomplish a particular business objective, e.g., the purchase, development and sale of a tract of real property, followed by division of the profits, after the completion of which it will dissolve'.[9] Usually, a syndicate means a common sales company established through the common investment by companies in an industry.[10] The syndicate is distinguished from the cartel where independent companies do not establish a common sales company or an association to carry out a transaction but agree to control reciprocal business activities for restraining competition. In the U.S., tight joint ventures including syndicates fall under the merger regulation under Sec. 7 of the Clayton Act and the Celler–Kefauver Amendment.[11]

On the other hand, there were Kozerns or Concerns during World War II in Germany and Japan. The Kozerns were financial combinations of companies that are legally independent. They differ from the cartel which requires no financial

[6]Garner (2003), at 376.

[7]Arizona v. Maricopa County Medical Society, 457 U.S. 332, 356 (1982); Texaco Inc. v. Dagher, 547 U.S. 1, 3; 126 S.Ct. 1276, 1277 (2006). In the Maricopa case, the Court held that the Medical Society was a foundation which did not sell different products but fixed price for medical services, and that it is not analogous to partnership or joint venture. In the Texaco case, the Supreme Court held that it is not per se illegal under Sherman Act § 1 for lawful, economically integrated joint venture to set prices at which it sells its products.

[8]*See* Northern Pacific R. Co. v. United States, 356 U.S. 1, 5, 78 S.Ct. 514, 518, 2 L.Ed.2d 545 (1958).

[9]Law dictionary, available at http://dictionary.law.com. *See* Garner(2003) at 687. The Black's Law Dictionary by Garner defines the syndicate as a group organized for a common purpose, especially an association formed to promote a common interest and carry out a particular business transaction. See also Friedman (2007), p. 655. It defines the syndicate similarly as a group of individuals or companies who have formed a joint venture to undertake a project that the individuals would be unable or unwilling to pursue alone.

[10]Huh (2002), at 21.

[11]U.S. v. Penn-Olin Chemical Co., 378 U.S. 158, 168; 84 S.Ct. 1710, 1715 (1964). The Penn-Olin Chemical Co. case applied Sec. 7 of the Clayton Act, a merger regulation, to the formation by two corporations of a joint venture for production of sodium chlorate and dissolved the joint venture which may substantially reduce competition in a market.

combination or financial dependence but requires the agreement to restrain competition with legal and financial independence.

C. Cartel Definitions from Individual Countries

(1) The United States (U.S.)

The U.S. antitrust law practice has paid little attention to the definition of cartel but developed a per se illegal rule, which determines several types of typical cartel practices as illegal without an analysis of their economic impact on competition.[12] As the main legal foundation to regulate a cartel, Sec. 1 of the Sherman Act does not state a definition of a cartel but states a broad prohibition that 'every contract, combination in the form of trust or otherwise, or conspiracy, in restraint of trade or commerce among the several States or with foreign nations, is declared to be illegal'.This provision has been used to prevent cartel activities. The U.S. Supreme Court has pronounced the cartel aspects as per se illegal under Sec. 1 of the Act, such as agreements for price-fixing, output restrictions, and market allocations among competitors without using the 'cartel' term. The per se illegal rule is distinguished from the rule of reason standard, which determines the anticompetitiveness of the other competition-restraining activities including vertical restraint or other horizontal collusions, e.g., concerted refusal to deal.[13]

The U.S. Supreme Court did not define the concept of a cartel with its own term, but defined the concept of a cartel, in *the U.S. v. National Lead Co.* et al, through the testimony of two people[14] in front of a subcommittee of the U.S. Senate. They stated 'a cartel is, with a protean form, a combination of producers for the purpose of regulating production and, frequently, prices, and an association by agreement of companies or sections of companies having common interests so as to prevent extreme or unfair competition'.[15] Regarding the 'common interests,' one of the testators added that the common interests covers from preventing extreme or unfair competition or allocating markets to interchanging R&D knowledge, exchanging patent rights, standardizing products, and so on. The cited statement, however, does

[12]The Supreme Court explained activities violating Sec. 1 under per se illegal rule as *'agreement or practices which because of their pernicious effect on competition and lack of any redeeming virtue are conclusively presumed to be unreasonable and therefore illegal without elaborate inquiry* as to the precise harm which they have caused or the business excuse for their use.' 356 U. S. 1, 5, 78 S.Ct. 514, 518, 2 L.Ed.2d 545 (1958).

[13]Northwest Wholesale Stationers, Inc. v. Pacific Stationery & Printing Co, 472 U.S. 284, 296 (1985). The case applied rule of reason standard regarding a cooperative activity involving exclusion as a type of concerted refusal to deal.

[14]Sir Mond was the organizer of the Imperial Chemical Industries (ICI) which consolidated competitors in the UK. As the other testator, Sir Pole was the chairman of the Associated Electrical Industries (AEI), a British company which produced and sold light bulbs.

[15]United States v. National Lead Co. et al., 332 U.S. 319, 340; 67 S.Ct. 1634, 1644; 91 L.Ed. 2077, 2096 (1947). The case is as regards the market division agreement of major titanium product manufacturers in the world by providing licenses to each other. It cites Monograph No. 1, Subcommittee on War Mobilization of the Committee on Military Affairs, U.S. Senate, 78th Cong., 2d Sess., Part I, p.1. Quoted also in U.S. v. National Lead Co., 63 F.Supp. 513, 523, note 5.

not address well the anticompetitive effect of a cartel but rather implies its positive effects. It is confirmed by a testimony of the testators that competition is not eliminated but regulated. However, a cartel does not just regulate competition but restrict it, thereby causing a huge inefficiency to the overall economy.[16] The unilateral testimony of the two testifiers come from two testators' background that they were respectively an organizer and a chairman of companies involved in international cartels regarding chemical industry and light bulb manufacturing.[17]

Rather, it is beneficial to look at the categorized types of cartel activities through U.S. cartel-hostile practices in order to have clear understanding of a cartel. The Supreme Court has pronounced the price-fixing, output-restraining, market-allocation cartel as illegal under Sec. 1 of the Sherman Act without inquiring into the reasonableness of the cartel since the middle of the twentieth century under the per se illegal rule.[18] The judicial categorizing of several restrictive business practices into a per se illegal rule has been made under considerable experiences with the RBPs.[19] The judicial body, experiencing a lot of cases with broad business areas, faced an implicit conclusion that typical cartel activities cause severe harm outweighing small benevolent effect and that the judiciary does not need to consider economic impact of the activities. The courts have rarely played roles to justify the typical cartel agreements. Whatever form the agreement or business practice takes, collusive price-rising or output-restriction among competitors has been deemed to violate Sec. 1 of the Sherman Act in the U.S. antitrust practices.[20]

In short, the U.S. Judicial body did not devote effort to define a cartel although Sec. 1 of the Sherman Act has broad language to cover diverse RBPs. However, judicial decisions have distinguished some aspects of a cartel, e.g., price-fixing,

---

[16]Refer to Chap. 1. III.2.

[17]The ICI had been involved in 800 competition-restraining agreements with Du Pont, its American rival company. The 800 agreements ended in 1948 before U.S. antitrust suit regarding its anti-competitiveness produced its result. ICI Plc—Company Profile, Information, Business Description, History, Background Information on Imperial Chemical Industries Plc, available at http://www.referenceforbusiness.com/history2/19/Imperial-Chemical-Industries-Plc.html (visited on 24 Feb. 2008). Meanwhile, the AEI had been a member of the Phoebus cartel consisting of seven competing light bulb companies. The cartel controlled the manufacture and sale of light bulbs for almost 20 years (in 1920s and 30s). It started to be weakened when a Swedish-Danish-Norwegian union of companies launched an independent manufacturing center and sold lamps at a much lower price than Phoebus in spite of economic and legal threats by Phoebus. Phoebus Cartel, available at http://en.wikipedia.org/wiki/Phoebus_cartel (visited on 24 Feb. 2008).

[18]U.S. v. Trenton Potteries Co. 273 U.S. 392, 47 S.Ct. 377, 71 L.Ed. 700 (1927); U.S. v. Socony-Vacuum Oil Co., 310 U.S. 150, 60 S.Ct. 811, 84 L.Ed. 1129 (1940); Chicago Professional Sports LP and WGN Continental Broadcasting Co. v. National Basketball Association, 961 F.2d 667, 674 (Ct of App. 7th Cir. 1992).

[19]Broadcast Music, Inc. et al. v. Columbia Broadcasting System, Inc. et al., 441 U.S. 10, 99 S.Ct. 1551 (1979).

[20]Fox et al. (2004), p. 78.

output-restriction, market-allocation, from the other RBPs by treating them as illegal without looking into its reasonableness. It is because the significant harms of the hard core cartel activities and they have paid little attention to further economic analyses for arguable pro-competitive effects.

(2) United Kingdom (UK)

The Office of Fair Trading (OFT) defines a cartel, using the simple terms, as an agreement, usually secret, verbal and often informal, between businesses not to compete with each other.[21] Section 2(1) of the 1998 Competition Act, by adopting the same language as Art. 81(1) of the EC Treaty, prohibits agreements between undertakings, which, among other things, have as their object or effect the prevention, restriction, or distortion of competition within the UK. Moreover, Sec. 2 (2), parallel to paragraphs of Art. 81(1) of the EC Treaty, enumerated typical activities of a cartel such as agreement to fix prices or other trading conditions (price-fixing), limit production, markets, technical development, or investment (output limitation), share markets or sources of supply (market-allocation), apply discriminatory conditions to other trading parties (discrimination), and make the conclusion of contracts subject to acceptance of irrelevant obligations by the other parties. A cartel enables business people to enjoy higher prices with less effort to offer competitive products or services, which leaves little choice for consumers.[22] As a result, it causes huge damage to consumers and creates inefficiency in the whole economy.

(3) Germany's Federal Cartel Office (Bundeskartellamt)

Article 1 of the Act against the Restraint of Competition (ARC) as the regulation of cartels states, 'agreements between undertakings, decisions by associations of undertakings and concerted practices, which have as their object or effect the prevention, restriction or distortion of competition, shall be prohibited.'[23] The amendment of the ARC for improving compatibility to the European competition regime was made recently which will lead to the identification of five hard core cartel behaviors such as price-fixing, market sharing, production or sales quotas, allocation of customers, and bid-rigging.[24] The hard core cartels are not criminalized but fined under the Administrative Offences Act and the Code of Criminal Procedure.

There are some exemptions from the cartel regulation under ARC although the hard core cartels do not meet the criteria of the exemption. The exemption includes

---

[21]OFT, *What is cartel*, http://www.oft.gov.uk/advice_and_resources/resource_base/cartels/what-cartel. Visited on 24 Feb. 2008.

[22]OFT, *Cartels and the Competition Act 1998: a guide for purchasers*, 3 (2005), *at* http://www.oft.gov.uk/shared_oft/business_leaflets/ca98_mini_guides/oft435.pdf, visited on the same day.

[23]Gesetz gegen Wettbewerbsbeschraenkungen [GWB][Act against Restricting Competition], *at* http://www.bundeskartellamt.de.

[24]Bundeskartellamt, *A Report to ICN Anti-cartel Enforcement*, *at* http://www.bundeskartellamt.de.

the very similar language as Article 101 paragraph 3 of the EU Treaty of Lisbon.[25] Under Sec 2(1), such agreements are exempted from application of ARC as contributes to (i) improving the production or distribution of goods, or (ii) promoting technical or economic progress (iii) without imposing on the undertakings concerned restrictions which are not indispensable to the attainment of these objectives, and (iv) without affording such undertakings the possibility of eliminating competition in respect of a substantial part of the products in question. Additionally, the agreements for the rationalization of economic activities when competition on the market is not substantially impaired and when the agreement improve the competitiveness of small-or middle-sized enterprises are exempted.[26]

(4) Japan Fair Trade Commission (JFTC)

A report to the Asian Pacific Economic Conference (APEC) by the JFTC states that a cartel is a horizontal agreement between competitors to avoid competition.[27] Concretely, a cartel means express or tacit conventions, promises, or agreements among firms to fix the price or limit the volume of production and sales, or select trading partners. Similar to definition of a hard core cartel in the ICN and OECD, they are classified in terms by the object of restriction into four categories: price cartels, volume cartels, market allocation cartels, and bid-riggings.[28]

(5) The Monopoly Restraint Fair Trade Act (MRFTA) of South Korea

Article 19 s. 1 of the MRFTA defines 'improper concerted acts' as certain behaviors which unfairly restrain competition with the other entrepreneurs by agreement, contract, resolution through another method. Not every competition-restraining behavior falls into the category. Article 19 has enumerated eight kinds of improper concerted acts: (i) price-managing, (ii) condition-setting for transactions of goods or services, (iii) restricting production or delivery or transaction, (iv) limiting the territory of trade or customers, (v) restricting the establishment of facilities or necessary equipments, (vi) restricting the specifications of goods or services, (vii) co-managing the main parts of a business or establishing a joint-company, and (viii) any practice that substantially lessens competition in a particular business area.[29]

The Art. 19 adopted so broad a coverage of anti-cartel regulation as the subpara. Seven includes the concept of the syndicate under the improper concerted acts, and the subpara. Eight has a general provision without concrete description of the

---

[25]Compare Sec. 2(1) of ARC to the article of the EU Treaty. Refer to Chap. 2. 4(1) in this book. Although it adopts the almost same language, Sec. 2(2) states that Art. 101 (3) of the Treaty is applicable.

[26]Sec. 3(1).

[27]Japan Fair Trade Commission (JFTC) (2002), p. 1.

[28]JFTC, *What Practices are Subject to Control by the Antimonopoly Act?* (Sec. 3-1, How Does this Apply to Cartels?), *available from* http://www2.jftc.go.jp/e-page/aboutjftc/role/q-3.htm.

[29]English version of Monopoly Regulation and Fair Trade Act (MRFTA) of KOREA is available at http://ftc.go.kr/eng/.

restrictive business practices (RBPs). The subpara. Two (condition-setting), Five (restriction of establishment of facilities), and six (restriction of goods specification) do not fall on the hard core cartel of major international organizations, but can fall on a cartel as they may restrain competition in markets. Korea Fair Trade Commission (KFTC) enjoys discretion to authorize certain collusive behaviors which generate more efficiency-progress than competition-restraint.

D. Cartels in International Law

(1) The EC Treaty

Under the glossary of terms used in the EU Competition Policy, a cartel is defined as 'an arrangement between competing firms designed to limit or eliminate competition between them, with the objective of increasing prices and profits of the participating companies and without producing any objective countervailing benefits.'[30]

For the statute language, Article 101 paragraph 1 of the Treaty of Lisbon prohibits all agreements between undertakings, decisions by associations of undertakings and concerted practices which may affect trade between Member States, and which have as the object or effect of such agreements the prevention, restriction, or distortion of competition within the common market. Particularly, Art. 101(1) considers the following five categories of cartels as anticompetitive: (a) price-fixing, (b) output limitation, (c) market division, (d) discriminatory treatment to equivalent transactions, and (e) making the conclusion of contracts subject to acceptance by the other parties of irrelevant supplementary obligation.[31] However, a cartel is considered as legitimate when such agreement, decision, or concerted practice contributes to improving the production or distribution of goods or to promoting technical or economic progress, while allowing consumers a fair share of the resulting benefit, and which does neither (a) impose on the undertakings the concerted restrictions which are not indispensable to the attainment of these objectives, nor (b) afford such undertakings the possibility of eliminating competition in respect of a substantial part of the products in question.[32] Cartels with net efficiency balance are treated as legitimate and valid.[33]

(2) UN Set and Model Law

The Resolution of the General Assembly of United Nations (UN) to adopt the Set of Multilaterally Agreed Equitable Principles and Rules for the Control of Restrictive Business Practices in 1980 (the UN Set) and the Model Law that the

---

[30]European Commission, *Glossary of Terms used in EU Competition Policy*, 8 (Brussels 2002), *available at* http://europa.eu.int/comm/competition/publications/glossary_en.pdf.

[31]For in-detail statute languages, refer to 1998 Competition Act Sec. 2(2) in the UK., this Chap. II. 3.(2).

[32]Artiicle 101.

[33]*Id.*

UNCTAD drafted for adopting international competition law confine the definition into the agreements to unduly restrain competition among rivals.

The UN Set, using 'restrictive business practices' instead of cartel, states that enterprises, except when dealing with each other in the context of an economic entity wherein they are under a common control, should refrain from the such practices as limit access to markets or otherwise unduly restrain competition through formal, informal, written or unwritten agreements or arrangements with possible adverse effects on international trade and economic development particularly of developing countries. The concrete acts are (a) agreements fixing prices, including as to exports and imports, (b) collusive tendering (bid-rigging), (c) market or customer allocation arrangements, (d) allocation by quota as to sales and production, (e) collective action to enforce arrangements, e.g., by concerted refusals to deal, (f) concerted refusal of supplies to potential importers, (g) collective denial of access to an arrangement, or association, which is crucial to competition. Besides the coverage of the hard core cartel of OECD, the UN Set includes three types of concerted act illustrating from (e) to (g).

Chapter 3 of the Model Law[34] prohibits restrictive agreements or arrangements between rival or potentially rival firms. The restrictive agreements are, almost the same as the UN Set, (a) agreements fixing prices or other terms of sale, including in international trade, (b) collusive tendering, (c) market allocation, (d) restraints on production or sale, including by quota, (e) concerted refusals to purchase, (f) concerted refusal to supply, (g) collective denial of access to an arrangement, or association which is crucial to competition. The Model Law almost follows the UN Set's seven categories although para. 1 of the Model Law added 'other terms of sale' thereby extending its coverage. The illustrated seven examples of RBPs are cartel activities as the agreement among rivals to control reciprocal business activities so as to restrain competition.

The UN Set excludes, from the coverage of its cartel regulation, an economic entity in which the enterprises are under the common control including one through common ownership or otherwise not able to act independently of each other. Commentaries in Chap. 3 of the Model Law confirms the exclusion of one economic entity from the cartel regulation by noting that a prevailing number of jurisdictions have ruled that firms under common ownership or control are not rival or potentially rival firms.

Although the establishment of a common business entity to control independent competitors' behaviors may restrain competition and violate competition law, constructing the common business entity is not under the cartel provision of the Model Law. Establishing a common entity among competitors may be an issue of merger regulation in Sec. I and II of Chap. VI of the Model Law. When it brings about the possibility of lessening competition substantially, it will be prevented or undone under para. 3 Sec. III of the merger regulation.

[34]The Model Law is formally named as The Substantive Possible Elements for articles for a Competition Law.

(3) Hard Core Cartel of Organization for Economic Cooperation and Development (OECD)

The recommendation that the OECD adopted in 1998 defines a hard core cartel with four types of cartel activities. Under the OECD Recommendation, a 'hard core cartel' is an anticompetitive agreement, concerted practice, or arrangement by competitors to (a) fix prices, (b) make rigged bids (collusive tenders), (c) establish output restrictions or quotas, or (d) share or divide markets by allocating customers, suppliers, territories, or lines of commerce.[35] The hard core cartel category, however, does not include agreements, concerted practices or arrangements that (i) are reasonably related to the lawful realization of cost-reducing or output-enhancing efficiencies, (ii) are excluded directly or indirectly from the coverage of a Member country's own laws, or (iii) are authorized in accordance with those laws. All exclusions and authorizations of what would otherwise be hard core cartels should be transparent and should be reviewed periodically to assess whether they are both necessary and no broader than necessary to achieve their overriding policy objectives.[36]

(4) The World Trade Organization (WTO) and the Working Group on the Interaction between Trade and Competition Policy (WGTCP)

The WTO issued a Ministerial Declaration in Doha in Nov. 2001, the Doha Development Agenda (DDA), which launched multilateral negotiations toward legal frameworks regarding agriculture, services, and trade-related issues including a competition policy which had been discussed since the Singapore Ministerial Declaration in 1996. WGTCP which worked for building a multilateral competition legal framework, however, faced a deadlock when the Cancun Ministerial Conference did not reach any consensus on modalities in this area in 2003. The following WTO General Council in 2004 confirmed its failure by deciding that the issue of competition policy would not form a part of the DDA. Therefore, no work toward negotiations on competition policy will take place within the WTO during the DDA.[37] To make things worse, the whole DDA collapsed after the Hong Kong Ministerial Conference in 2005 mostly due to the North–South conflict in agriculture negotiations.

The Doha Declaration did not explain the definition of a cartel but mentioned that further works in the WGTCP would focus on the clarification of provisions on hardcore cartels.[38] By concentrating on hard core cartels, it is implied that the WTO Group tried to limit the topic of multilateral negotiations to the hard core cartel similar to the OECD Recommendation.

---

[35]OECD, *Recommendation of the Council Concerning Effective Action Against Hard Core Cartel*, 921st Sess. C/M(98)7/PROV (Mar. 25, 1998). *See* Art. I Sec. A. para. 2. subsec. a.

[36]I. A. 2. b. of the Recommendation.

[37]WTO, *Competition Policy: History*, available at http://www.wto.org.

[38]Paragraph 25, WT/MIN(01)/DEC/1, available at http://www.wto.org.

(5) International Competition Network (ICN)

The ICN was formed by an original proposal from major advanced competition authorities, the US's DOJ and the International Competition Policy Advisory Committee (ICPAC), for consensus-building on procedural and substantive convergence in antitrust enforcement, along with support from competition professionals, and formerly mentioned international organizations, e.g., WTO, OECD, and UNCTAD.[39] Its main constituents consist of senior government competition officers in both developed and developing countries while the ICN also includes the participation of private experts. The ICN Working Group on Cartels issued a report in 2005 for the 4th Annual Conference of the ICN, which researched extensively on the definition of a cartel. The report agreed with the definition of a hard core cartel in the OECD Recommendation without substantial suggestions for improvement.[40] It suggested the following three common elements of a cartel: (i) an agreement, (ii) between competitors, and (iii) to restrict competition. The 'agreement' need not be formal or written,[41] therefore it includes secret conspiracies. The 'competitors' refer to (private) companies at the same level of distribution channels in direct competition with each other to sell goods or provide services, thereby excluding states or national monopolies. 'To restrict competition' means to target at open competition,[42] whereby placing its focus on the intent or purpose of the agreement.

Further, it categorizes the following four types of conduct commonly identified across jurisdictions: (1) price-fixing, (2) output restrictions, (3) market allocation, and (4) bid-rigging. All four types have the same areas as the OECD Hard Core Cartel Recommendation covers.

(6) Analysis

International law regulating a cartel approaches the consensus that hard core cartel activities with several categories are to be addressed rather than a clear-cut definition of cartel itself. The attitude to derive common denominators from various forms of national cartel laws is not profitable compared to its effort. Some countries adopt a broad provision which applies to vertical restraint as well as horizontal restraint while the other countries treat the former clearly different from the latter. The national cartel laws include exemptions from an anti-cartel provision. The exemptions cover from the one with outweighing competitive effects to the one on the basis of domestic political reason. The standard of analyzing the restraint on competition of a cartel is diverse from the per se rule through quick rule of reason to full rule of reason. Therefore, defining cartel in international competition law

[39]For background of establishing ICN, *see* Harry First (2003), pp. 33–38.

[40]ICN Working Group on Cartels, *Defining Hard Core Cartel Conduct, Effective Institutions, and Effective Penalties*, 11–12, *at* http://www.internationalcompetitionnetwork.org.

[41]*See id.* 10.

[42]*See id.*, 9–10.

appears inefficient as it demand much work to harmonize different national laws with less benefit or promise of reaching a consensus. The approach to a hard core cartel with several categories has proved effective to reach a consensus among diverse interests in individual countries as over all international cartel laws adopt.

E. Assessment

(1) Proposal for a Cartel Definition in the International Law Context

It is not easy to reach the international agreement in light of complicated interests from diverse economic situations, legal systems, and cultural backgrounds. The diverse aspects of cartel activities make the reaching of the agreement more difficult.[43] Rather than adopting the definition covering a broad aspect of cartels, defining a cartel needs to consider its purpose. This thesis pursues the agenda of international cartel regulation, in light of which, the definition of a cartel should start with a narrowed category, in other words, that of a hard core cartel. Since a binding international cartel regulation as the ultimate goal of this thesis is much difficult to obtain accession from countries due to concern about restricted sovereignty, this thesis will confine its discussion into the narrow definition of a cartel.

In light of the distinction of the cartel with the syndicate and the trust, the following elements of the cartel definition are proposed under the narrow focus;

(i) as a subject, more than two independent entrepreneurs or undertakings competing in the same level of business,
(ii) as to conduct, agree to restrain or do restrain reciprocal business activities, e.g., fix price, allocate market, or limit production, and rig a bid,
(iii) as regard to purpose, to prevent competition thereby to secure extra profit.

(2) Subject: Private Companies Reciprocally Competing

Regarding the element (1), a tight combination of competitors, known as a joint venture, has been treated akin to mergers which shall be under merger regulations and not under cartel regulations. An industrial combination in the vertical level from manufactures to distribution to sales invokes the matters of merger, monopoly, and/or vertical restraint rather than a cartel. Particularly, the U.S. practices with persuasive reasoning have developed separate rules and regulations on mergers, monopolies, and vertical restraint from cartel regulation, which focuses on hard core cartels (HCC).[44] However, the combination-operating or forming agreement

[43]Rodger and Macculloch (2000), at 172–173.

[44]While the Sec. 2 of the Sherman Act applies to (attempt) monopoly, Sec. 7 of the Clayton Act, along with merger guidelines and procedural rules applies to merger. The Supreme Court has distinguished a vertical restraint from a cartel. NYNEX Corp. v. Discon, Inc. 525 U.S. 128, 136 (1998); Business Electronics Corp. v. Sharp Electronic Corp. 485 U.S. 717, 730; 108 S.Ct. 1515, 1523 (1988).

needs to be screened by cartel regulation whether it includes competition-restraining activities, particularly HCC activities.[45]

The issue is whether the 'independent entrepreneurs' as member of a cartel include either a country or state-managing company. A country with public interests acts differently from the private company pursuing a profit-interest. A state which receives financial resources from public revenue functions as a market-moderator by taking loss or reducing profit, dissimilar from private companies operating on a maximization principle of profits or market share. Since the U.S. Supreme Court held that the Sherman Act does not apply to a state but persons under Sec. 7[46] in *Parker v. Brown*,[47] the U.S. courts have developed state-action doctrine allowing immunity to state legislations involving the market. Besides such exemption from domestic law, the activities of a state in the international level are protected under the sovereignty immunity which does not allow other countries to intervene in its domestic affairs. The Model Law of the UNCTAD confirms the principle as one of its many examples.[48] In addition, interstate cooperative activities in commodity trade have been acknowledged as legitimate and have been promoted under international commodity laws. The international commodity agreements (ICAs) and intergovernmental producers' associations (IPAs),[49] which are distinguished from a private cartel under competition law, have developed unique regulations under international commodity law. In light of the development of international law and political consideration, the ICAs and IPAs may not be under the same rule as the cartel of private companies only due to the economical perspective that countries restrain competition in the international trade.[50]

---

[45]Consent decree of General Motors/Toyota joint venture case, 103 FTC 374 (1984), includes such orders refraining them from exchanging pivotal non-public information e.g. price, marketing plans.

[46]Section 7 confines the definition of a 'person' under the Sherman Act to corporations and associations existing under or authorized by the laws of the U.S. or any state or any foreign country. The same language of the provision is adopted by Sec. 1(a) of the Clayton Act. The state monopolies or inter-state associations can be exempted from the U.S. competition law.

[47]317 U.S. 341, 351 (1943). At the page of 351, it states that there is no suggestion of a purpose to restrain 'state action' in the Act's legislative history and that the sponsor of the Sherman Act declared that it prevented only business combinations.

[48]*See* Chap. II. Sec. II. para. (c). It stipulates that the Model Law does not apply to the sovereign acts of the state itself, or those of local governments, or to acts of enterprises or natural persons which are compelled or supervised by the State or by the local governments or branches of government acting within their delegated power. Chap. II, Sec. II. para. (c). *See* UNCTAD (2007), p. 3.

[49]The ICA is an international agreement that restrains competition in international trade of a product or raw material with both consuming and producing countries as members while the IPA is one with producing countries only. Refer to 2.4, A of Chap. 2.

[50]Association of states producing natural resources or setting technical standards will be discussed at 2.4 of Chap. 2.

(3) Conduct and Purpose

In terms of conduct, a cartel shall have agreement for restricting or do restrict reciprocal competitive activities in the market among participating companies which are supposed to compete for the purpose of enjoying extra profits. The purpose of restricting competition may be presumed by the contents of the agreement and the impact of cartelistic activities on markets subsequent to the agreement. However, diverse types of business activities may fall under the category of (b) an illegal cartel in the following picture when their anticompetitive effect outweighs pro-competitive effect. For example, concerted refusals to supply to or deal with a competitor fall on the illegal cartel when the cooperative parties enjoy market power or exclusive access which is essential to effective competition,[51] and when the concerted refusals occur horizontally. The decision regarding anticompetitiveness of concerted refusal depends important factors, including (i) the motive of the denial, (ii) the degree to which access to the standard is critical to effective competition, and (iii) the effect on competition from excluding the rival.[52] Vertical restraint, which belong (a) vertical restraint of competition law in the picture, occurs between companies which do not compete each other, so it needs different economic analysis from a cartel regulation to determine its anticompetitiveness.[53] Price-fixing, production-limitation, market-allocation, and bid-rigging, as major four HCC activities, fall under the category of (c) because they in most cases cause much more severe harm than benefit.

As one of the more ambiguous areas, there exists a standard-setting activity which causes both pro-competitive effect, e.g., efficiency enhancement from integration of standards, and anticompetitive effect, e.g., restriction of competition, in a relevant market. The activity may constitute an illegal cartel when it suppresses more than promotes competition.[54] Concretely, it violates cartel regulation when the standard works as an agreement among competitors to fix prices or to exclude another competitor,[55] and when the anticompetitiveness effect should outweigh the efficiency enhancing effect of integration from standard-setting.[56] Even a pool

[51]FTC v. Indiana Federation of Dentists, 476 U.S. 447, 458 (1986). Application of the per se illegal in boycott cases is confined to the case where firms with market power boycott suppliers or customers in order to discourage them from doing business with a competitor. Group boycott has been under per se illegal since the U.S. Supreme Court decision, Klor's, Inc. v. Broadway-Hale Stores, Inc. 359 U.S. 207, 79 S.Ct. 705 (1959).

[52]American Bar Association (ABA) Section of Antitrust Law (2004), p. 65.

[53]Non-price vertical restraints are rarely opposed by competition authorities. UNCTAD (2007), at 26.

[54]National Society of Profession Engineering (NSPE) v. U.S., 435 U.S. 679, 691 (1978).

[55]See National Macaroni Manufacturers Ass'n v. FTC, 345 F.2d 421 (7th Cir. 1965); Radiant Burners, Inc. v. Peoples Gas Light & Coke Co. 364 U.S. 656, 659–660 (1961).

[56]In the U.S., courts which had held the activities derived from standard-setting illegal under per se rule, have relaxed the strict approach. The Standards Development Organization Advancement Act of 2004, Pub.L.No. 108-237, confirmed the shift. ABA Sec. of Antitrust Law (2004), at 31–32 and 34–35.

license agreement as to new technology, where competing patents are pooled,[57] might invoke cartel regulation when anticompetitive effects, e.g., exclusion of non-member competitors or restriction of competition in the area not related to the technology, outweigh pro-competitive benefits, e.g., promotion of R&D.[58] Decisions regarding membership of standard-setting organizations (SSOs) can violate cartel regulations when anticompetitive effect prevails over legitimate interests.[59] Neelie Kroes, the EU competition commissioner, warned more strictly that if voting in the standard-setting context is influenced less by technical merits but rather by side agreements, inducements, package deals, reciprocal agreement, the result of voting may fall foul of EU competition rules.[60] Overall analysis of economic impact and social effect of activities related to SSOs needs complicated studies.[61]

Compared to the major four categories of (c) HCC in the picture, the other category of cartels under (b) needs in-detailed analysis in related markets for the decision of pro- or anticompetitiveness. It is because many cooperative arrangements, designed to increase economic efficiency, can enhance competition in related markets.[62] Although a rule of thumb tells that price-increase and output-reduction actions are mainly evidences of restraining competition, there may be hidden pro-competitive effects, e.g, long-term effects, or outweighing national interests. Each country can place different weights on the national interests or the hidden

[57] ABA (2004), at 73. However, so called blocking patents, in which one party could not practice under its patent without infringing the other party's patents, or complementary patents, which cover different aspects of the same technology, are less likely to be anti-competitive.

[58] U.S. DOJ Antitrust Division, Business Review Letter as to DVD Standards (10 June 1999).

[59] The legitimate interests are proper functioning of the organizations and overall efficiency in related markets. *See* Northwest Wholesale Stationers, Inc. v. Pacific Stationary & Printing Co., 472 U.S. 284, 296 (1985). The decision of a buying cooperative to expel a member would be under the rule of reason unless the cooperative has market power or exclusive access to an element essential to competition. On the other hand, in Pretz v. Holstein Friesian Ass'n of America, 698 F. Supp 1531, 1539 (Kan 1988), the court declined to apply the per se rule to the decision of a cattle registry association to exclude a member even when the association had very substantial market power and membership in the association was essential to effective competition.

[60] Nikki Talt, *Kroes warns on open technology standards*, FT, at 2 (11 June 2008). She made the statement at an OpenForum Europe seminar in Brussels.

[61] ABA (2004), at 44–46, and 47–79. In evaluating the selection and enforcement of standards, courts consider whether the standard creates or enhance the exercise of market power by the SSO or its members and whether the standard has an anticompetitive purpose or effect. The composition of a SSO may be an evidence of the anti-competitive motive. In addition, the non-discriminatory and consistent application of the standards may be another evidence of it. Some types of distortion of the standard-setting process show the anti-competitive effect or purpose.

[62] As to the concerted refusal to deal or boycott issue, refer to Broadcast Music, Inc. v. Columbia Broadcasting System, Inc. 441 U.S. at 20; 99 S.Ct. at 1562 and Northwest Whole Sale Stationeries, v. PSP Co., 105 S. Ct. at 2620. The Supreme Court acknowledges the necessity of careful defining of per se illegal group boycott, by quoting Sullivan, Law of Antitrust, 229–230 (1977), "there is more confusion about the scope and operation of the per se rule against group boycotts than in reference to any other aspect of the per se doctrine."

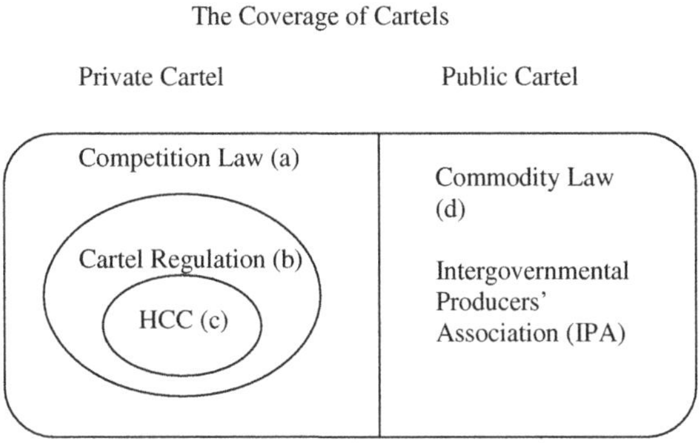

Fig. 2.1 Division of private and public cartels and its respective coverage

effect in light of its unique situation, which works as hurdles to reaching international consensus. The definition of a cartel in this thesis, with the purpose of achieving international cartel law, needs to be confined to the cartel category that clearly causes huge net consumers' loss and market inefficiencies. The narrow definition can conveniently facilitate the achievement of international law on cartels (Fig. 2.1).

(4) The Coverage of the Cartel for International Cartel Law

With the three elements of the cartel, the cartel can be defined as an agreement or a collective action under the agreement to restrain business activities of more than two independent and reciprocally competing entrepreneurs or undertakings so as to restrain competition. The definition matches the (b) plus (c) area in the following picture. The instances of tight business combinations, such as joint venture, do fall on (a) as they are regulated under merger or monopolization regulations within the competition law regime. While the formation of an economic entity with legal personality belongs to merger or monopolization, the formation of a loose combination of companies as an association of competitors to restrict competition falls under the category of a cartel. A vertical restraint can be under the (a) area as it belongs to a different category of regulation.

The IPAs have states or state-monopolies as their members. They are beyond the coverage of competition law but under the commodity law area. However, some usages of a cartel, particularly what is reported on the internet, e.g., dictionary.law.com and Wikipedia,[63] include an interstate cartel under the definition of a cartel with the focus on the economic impact of IPAs similar to a private cartel. It neglects the development of commodity law. Commodity laws regulating international commodity transaction (d) have been developed with the unique characteristics of a commodity.[64] ICAs, although having consuming countries and producing countries as members, have played almost the same roles in the markets as the IPAs. With the

[63]See http://en.wikipedia.org/wiki/Cartel (visited on 27th Feb 2008).

[64]Refer to Chap. 1. IV. and Chap. 2. IV for IPAs and ICAs.

only difference being membership, the ICAs and the IPAs are treated the same way in this thesis. The discussions as to interstate cartels apply to both.

Particularly, for the purpose of achieving an international cartel regulation, the definition of a cartel should have explicit several categories of behaviors with net anticompetitive effects so that they may reduce ambiguity on the effect of the behaviors on competition and reach international consensus for regulation conveniently. The HCC under (c) falls on a representative example. The definition is similar to the OECD HCC recommendation, but narrower than the UN Set, which includes other concerted behaviors such as refusal to deal with a certain partner(s) matching the (b) area. It is noteworthy that the U.S. antitrust law, which has played as the leading competition law in the world, narrowed the (b) area to such a way that its cartel regulation may concentrate on (c) hard core cartel activities. The anticompetitive activities under the (b) have been regulated under the title of horizontal collusive behaviors distinguished from cartel regulation.[65] The reason for such a division comes from a different standard of legitimacy. While a cartel is investigated and prosecuted under a per se illegal rule by the DOJ, other categories are treated under the rule of reason by the Federal Trade Commission. Recent international laws on cartels, particularly from OECD and WTO, have focused on (c) HCC and individual countries have tried to comply with the international laws. Therefore, for the international law perspective, rather than a broad category of cartels with net pro-competitive impact under (b) + (c) or (a) + (b) + (c), the narrow definition of a cartel with four categories of HHC under (c) is more beneficial to reach further international agreement.

2.3 Discussions: Advantage and Disadvantage of Cartels

There are still opinions arguing that some cartels with beneficial effects on the economy should be exempted under the regulations or allowed temporarily. In addition, the public does not know in-detail the damages that cartels cause. After considering the advantages and the disadvantages that cartels arguably have, the alleged exemptions are worthy examining.

A. Advantages of Cartels

(1) Restraining Destructive Competition

The need of using cartels is clearly demonstrated by the ‘brown field economy’ situation where an over-invested facility or capital does not reap as much profit as investors expected but rather goes to chronic deficit due to less demand and decreasing prices. It happens when many competitors participate in the market, who invested a lot of money as a fixed cost, but when the slackened demand cannot raise price. At the moment, an individual entrepreneur in the competitive market cannot

[65]Fox et al. (2004).

help but lower the prices so as to reap profit by increasing sales volume. However, with the other competitors trying to compensate their costs by reducing prices and increasing sales, the entrepreneur ends up with setting prices much below the average cost. This is the situation called 'destructive competition'.[66]

The damage through destructive competition may be quite a large amount of money considering the total investment of the overall number of entrepreneurs in the market. The damage can exacerbate the level of efficiency in society, which competition law tries to protect. The situation needs to be improved with the cooperation among the competitors. A depression cartel is to be facilitated for a temporary period necessary to rescue an industry seriously hurt by an economic depression.

The governments in advanced as well as developing countries have approved this type of cartel in severe economic depressions. Quite a few governments used to operate compulsory cartels under such political pressure as the struggle for existence might wipe out the weak industry. Even the U.S. Supreme Court, in *the Appalachian Coals Incorporation* case, during the Great Depression, acknowledged the coal output limitation cartel without violating Section 1 of the Sherman Act.[67] The Roosevelt Administration used public cartels in several industries.[68] EU member countries have looked for 'cartels' more than once to solve a destructive competition situation.[69] Japan approves depression cartels for one year or less through a specific government agency. Furthermore, Sec. 25 of the Presidential Decree of Korea's Monopoly Restraint Fair Trade Act (MRFTA) has an exceptional approval provision for a cartel aiming to overcome the depression with strict conditions.[70] The Model Law of the UNCTAD is interpreted to allow a cartel in this context since it allows cartels to be authorized by member states when the cartel members demonstrate a 'net public benefit'.[71]

(2) Securing Large-Scale Investment Capital

Joint sponsorship for a project, which costs too much for individual entrepreneurs to take but which is substantially beneficial to all the participants in the

[66]Bower and Rhenman (1985).

[67]*Appalachian Coals Inc. v. United States*, 288 U.S. 344 (1933).

[68]Eatwell et al. (1998), at 373. The National Industrial Recovery Act permitted industries to formulate 'codes of fair competition', which was ruled unconstitutional by the Supreme Court in 1935. However, the U.S. continued to maintain cartels in coal mining, oil production, interstate transportation, and agriculture.

[69]Bower and Rhenman (1985).

[70]Korea's Fair Trade Commission (KFTC) has authority to approve collective behaviors of entrepreneurs when (1) it is clearly expected that demand for a product or a service would continue to decrease and supply would far exceed demand for substantial period, (2) price of the product or service is below average cost for substantial period, (3) substantial number of companies in the industry face possibility of discontinuing their business due to depression, and (4) rationalization of the company can not be a method of overcoming (1) through (3) situation. Huh (2002), 290.

[71]Model Law, Art. 3, paragraph 2.

markets is argued to be another area where cartels can play roles. A research joint venture is a popular phenomenon which academic researchers have analyzed as beneficial.[72] Unless the sharing of information limits the incentive for R&D investment or leads horizontal competitors to engage in monopolistic behaviors, a technology consortium or a technology-exchange agreement produce net consumer welfare benefit.[73] Such cooperation helps innovation efforts of small companies. In Germany and the Scandinavian countries, industrial associations have long helped small companies protect their interests by sharing expenses and promoting technological innovations from larger competitors.[74] Para. 30 and 31 of Chap. IV of Schedule 13 in the U.K. 1998 Competition Act allow joint arrangement between competitors regarding the efficient development and production of petroleum resources.[75] Moreover, Sec. 24-3 of the Presidential Decree of Korea's MRFTA approves a cartel for research and technology development, as an exception to the prohibition of collusive behaviors with restricted conditions.[76]

Developing countries, where companies do not have sufficient financial systems to invest much in research and development (R&D), have more necessity of collecting money for R&D investment than advanced countries. For example, the Colombian legislation, the Lithuanian law, Ukrainian law, and the Hungarian legislation exempt R&D cartels or the agreement that improve investment or technical or economic progress.[77]

(3) Voluntary Regulation by Industry or Professional Associations

When the public requests its government to regulate an industry, autonomous regulation by the industry members before an anticipated government control can be another usage of a cartel. U.S. chemical industries recognized complex problems caused by the toxicity of their products in 1974. Facing public scrutiny of the industry along with the extreme cost of testing the products as well as a scarcely trained workforce, the industry constituted the Chemical Industry Institute of Toxicology to develop the technical strength to win the respect of the government and businesses.[78] Besides health or environmental concerns, voluntary regulation has been used in ethical norms of professional organizations to offer honest and good-quality services by suppressing excessive competition within the professions.

---

[72]Baumol (2001), at 729–731.

[73]*Id.* at 732.

[74]Bower and Rhenman (1985), 126.

[75]Rodger and Macculloch, at 195.

[76]KFTC approves the cartel when (1) the R&D is necessary for increasing industrial competition power and the effect of the R&D on the market is significant, (2) investment for the R&D cost too much to be provided by one company, (3) the cartel is necessary for distributing risk of uncertain result of the R&D, and (4) the effect of R&D outweighs that of restraining competition. Sec. 24-3 of presidential decree of MRFTA.

[77]UNCTAD (2007), at 32–33.

[78]Bower and Rhenman (1985).

Sometimes the ethical standard includes price-fixing[79] or its variations such as a ban on competitive bidding[80] or a maximum medical fee agreement for insurance payment[81] or a boycott to raise fees[82] or a ban on professional advertisements about price and quality.[83] However, the U.S. Supreme Court held per se illegal for all the former cases except the ban on professional advertisement about price and quality. Meanwhile, the U.K. Competition Act allows professional rules, designated and reviewed by the Secretary of State, to be excluded from Chap. I prohibition, cartel regulation.[84] Self-regulating bodies operating under other laws are also excluded from the Chap. I prohibition.[85]

(4) Reducing Price Fluctuation

Cartels are argued to prevent price fluctuations due to its independence from cost and its agreement on fixed prices. The International Coffee Organization (ICoO), arguably functioning as one of the international commodity agreements (ICAs),[86] has set the market share of major global markets and has collected price information

---

[79]Goldfarb et. ux. v. Virginia State Bar et al. 423 U.S. 886, 96 S.Ct. 162 (1975). The Supreme Court held, minimum-fee schedule for lawyers published by the Fairfax County Bar Association and enforced by Virginia State Bar is price-fixing and per se illegal under Sec. 1 of the Sherman Act.

[80]National Society of Professional Engineers v. U.S., 435 U.S. 679 (1978). The Supreme Court granted certiorari for the district court to decide the factual basis of justification and affirmed the trial courts' decision that the ethical rules of the Society violated Sec. 1 of the SA which prohibited members' competitive bidding before an engineer was selected for a specific project by a prospective client.

[81]Arizona v. Maricopa County Medical Society, 457 U.S. 332 (1982). The Court held, the maximum fee schedule is per se illegal price-fixing because (1) strict application of rule of reason standard cost significant money, (2) judges do not have much expertise understanding in the industry and its market structure, (3) a decision of a specific case with different background gives almost no certainty or standard for legitimacy of customs. Per se rule saves courts from the dilemma, and the Court has endured nullity of some customs that would prove to be reasonable if total review is to be done so as to secure procedural economy and conviction of the industry.

[82]FTC v. Superior Court Trial Lawyers Association, 493 U.S. 411 (1990). The Court held, the boycott for raising fee for trial lawyers' representing criminal defendants in Washington D.C. was also price-fixing cartel and illegal per se.

[83]California Dental Association v. FTC, 526 U.S. 756 (1999). The Court held, the association's ban on professional advertising about price and quality requires looking into the circumstances, details and logic of a restraint rather than a quick look analysis for rule of reason.

[84]Schedule 4 exempts designated professional rules. Rodger and Macculloch (2000), at 192–193.

[85]*See* Schedule 2 of the 1998 Act. *Refer to id.* at 193.

[86]The ICoO membership consists of 45 coffee importing countries as well as 32 exporting ones. Under the strict meaning, a cartel is arrangement among producers. The ICoO is not the cartel under the definition. However, it functions to restrain excessive competition in global coffee market and to maintain stable production and price of coffee through allocating market. Refer to ICoO, Rules on Statistics Indicator Price, at 13, Annex I, EB3776/01 Rev.1 (2001), *available at* http://dev.ico.org/documents/eb3776r1e.pdf (last visited on 23 Oct. 2007).

for more than 40 years. The International Tin Agreement (ITA) played a role similar to a cartel by placing a ceiling and a floor price and export quotas.[87] The ICoO and ITA are evaluated high in a point that they achieved price stability during its effective era compared to its demising era.[88] Stable commodity price enables exporting countries, particularly commodity-dependent developing countries (CDDC) to have financial basis for purchasing food for the producers of the raw material and further promoting economic development. Meanwhile, importing countries can enjoy the benefit of predictability from stable price trends, if the price maintains to a reasonable level, regardless of external circumstances such as weather.[89]

B. Disadvantages that Cartels Cause

(1) Inefficiency in Production

Efficiency with low cost and high production quantity can be achieved through a free market mechanism as a result of an individualized rational decision of market participants. However, cartels replace market participants' free exercise of business decisions with a cartel agreement, thereby restricting the free market mechanism or competition. Restraint of the free market mechanism inevitably produces inefficiency of production resources, thereby leading to comparatively a 'high price' and 'low production' because cartels prevent destruction of relatively inefficient high-cost enterprises.[90] The reduced pressure to reduce cost through innovation, although difficult to measure, generates harm to productive efficiency.[91] The inefficient production with high prices directly results in detriments to the consumers.[92]

As to price, the wide margins between costs and high prices caused by cartels were illustrated in the 1930s in the U.S., so called the Great Depression era. In the rubber industry, the international rubber regulation committee was able to maintain prices, yielding a gross profit margin from 50 to 100 % above costs of productions

[87] McFadden (1986), pp. 815–817. The predecessor of ITA was the Int' Tin Committee which had functioned as a producers' cartel with its membership limited to producers from '20s to 40s. The ITA is an outgrowth of the Int' Tin Study Group of 1948–1956, which produced a draft of tin agreement for ITA including consumer states as well as producers in the era of postwar cooperation.

[88] LeClair (2000), pp. 59–61 and Table 3.2. Price variation during ICA functioning period (1976–1986) was from 0.161 to 0.198 while it during non-functioning period (1989–1996) increased up to 0.303. See McFadden (1986), at 819. From the initial Int' Tin Control Scheme in 1931 until the 1985 collapse, the ITA confined price fluctuations to a much narrower range than those in unregulated periods.

[89] Chapter I. Art.1 (2) of International Coffee Agreement 2001, available at http://dev.ico.org/documents/agreeme.pdf (last visited on 23 Oct. 2007).

[90] In the nitrogen cartel agreement of 1930, high cost enterprises were actually given larger relative quotas than low cost enterprises. Edwards (1976), p. 40.

[91] OECD (2002), p. 6.

[92] Edwards (1976), p. 41. It illustrates aluminium manufacturers' cartel involving the Aluminium Corporation of America [Alcoa]. The cartel caused damage to efficiency in the market by price-increase and output reduction.

around its critical shortage period of the 1930s. The copper cartel maintained the price to almost the same level for 20 years while technological improvements of copper production reduced the cost to half during the 1920s and 30s. In addition, methanol price trends in the U.S. from 1926 to 1941, when cartelization of territorial allocation had been progressed in the methanol market by Union Carbide and Carbon, indicated that the synthetic methanol price decreased by only 59 % while output increased by more than 740 %. The Union Carbide and Carbon, the biggest producer of domestic synthetic methanol, did not make much of an effort to reduce the price in loose competition with only output-decreasing wood methanol without other competitors of synthetic methanol.[93]

On the other hand, the limitation of output by a cartel does not necessarily lead to low level of production or high profit. The copper cartel after WWI tried to liquidate the surplus stock, ending up with double the excess stock by the end of 1920. Moreover, after General Electric (GE)'s geographical-market allocation cartel with Krupp Steel Works of Germany in the world tungsten carbide market from 1928 up to 1936, GE's annual sales of the same material with an 800 % price increase was outnumbered by Krupp's monthly sales due to GE's output and demand reduction from the price sky-rocketing. Furthermore, when the Organization of Petroleum Export Countries (OPEC) succeeded in raising oil price per barrel from US$ 2.80 in 1972 to $ 36.68 in 1979, the consumers put effort into substitution and conservation initiatives. The high oil price provoked new producers, e.g., China, to enter the market and non-OPEC producers, e.g., Mexico, to expand their production while the high price caused covet cheating within the organization. The extreme increase of the oil prices turned out to cause severe holdback of sales of OPEC members.[94] All the responses can lead to substantial lessening of pricing power of the OPEC in the long run.

(2) Unfair Treatment: Price-Discrimination

As a cartel agreement has characteristics of exclusiveness against free market mechanisms, it can easily create discriminatory pricing depending on the territory or cartel-affiliation. In a cartel agreement involving the Dow Chemical Company and Alcoa in the magnesium market, Dow provided Alcoa with a discount, averaging 30 to 40 % lower than those quoted to Dow's other domestic customers from 1927 to 1931. Although the price differential between Alcoa and other domestic customers decreased to an average of 28 % from 1931 to spring of 1942 when an antitrust decree broke up the cartel, the price-discrimination was maintained during the time. After the dissolution of the cartel, Alcoa purchased its metal from Dow under price regulations at an average of 5 % below the regular price.[95]

---

[93]Stockings and Watkins (1948), 116–122, 124–125 and 130.

[94]*Id.* at 129–134. LeClair (2000), 14–15 and 67–71. OPEC's share in the world oil market continued to decline from 55.4 % in 1973 to 28.5 % in 1985. The average price per barrel dropped to US$ 14.23 in 1986.

[95]Stocking and Watkins (1948), 138–141.

(3) Inflexibility of Price with Entry Barriers

Cartel prices are not flexible because it does not reflect changing business conditions through the market system. Rather, in most cases, a cartel agreement aims to raise prices and hold it as high as possible without paying much attention to supply and demand in the markets.[96] Some cartels, with their forecasts, fix, and adhere to prices high enough to assure substantial profits to their members, including less efficient companies, even with the minimum output in recession. On the other hand, most cartels advance prices under a prosperous condition up to the point that the reduced quantity of sales may limit profit.[97]

However, although the high-fixed price with maximized profits attract new competitors in the market, new comers do not easily participate in the market because various entry barriers established by cartels create hurdles. The cartels need to bloc entry of new competitors into the industry to enjoy long-term control over price. The major barriers are illustrated as exclusively concerted behaviors, a line of discriminatory distribution, which may be in a collaborated manner among cartel members, unfriendly or even opposed against new comers,[98] technology armed with pooled patents, and a heavy level of fixed capital.

(4) Malfunction of Market Economy Mechanism

Even though it might sound economically sensible in exceptional circumstances to raise prices to improve profits in a distressed industry, the principle applies to limitedly rare cases.[99] Even though the exceptional cases have positive effects on the economy, it is important not to make the exception a main principle to justify the economic harms that most cartels bring about. Noticeably, even in the exceptional cases, cartels might do harm by aggravating the evil circulation of under-investments, under-employment, and decreasing demand power for other products with less incentive to invest.[100]

Rather, imperfect competition, a concept currently popular among modern economists, makes an issue out of the weakness of competition, not the severity of it. They argue that the gentlemanly restraint and mutual deference among competitors rather than competition prevailed in many industries.[101]

Moreover, even though cartel proponents argue that cartels help to restore balanced markets in some fields where overproduction progresses, a temporary restriction of oversupply to take away the current surplus may bring about an expansion of extra-capacity through nonmembers or members' additional and surreptitious investments. The sustained high price sooner or later leads to even more oversupply. On the other hand, the increased price suppresses demand in

[96]Mcfadden (1986), 823–824.

[97]*Id.* at 136. Edwards (1976), 40.

[98]Stocking and Watkins (1948), 136–138. LeClair (2000), 59–60.

[99]Stocking and Watkins (1948), 104–106.

[100]*Id.* at 216–240.

[101]*Id.* at 108.

conflict with a cartel's original goal of securing future consumption. It promotes consumers' substituting efforts with other complementary goods.[102] In the long run, it leads to reducing cartel power. Therefore, cartels can not resolve the initial overproduction problem due to oversupply or reduced demand.[103]

(5) Consumers' Damage

Cartels cause large damages to consumers through fixed prices. Total harm to consumers consists of consumers' loss and consumers' damages. Consumers who would pay the price determined by market mechanism of price-competition will face higher prices in the market where suppliers collude to set price or quantity. Economists agreed that, unless consumers have market power to decrease the price, consumers' collective decisions to purchase less of the product at the cartel-determined higher price means an overall loss of consumers' welfare. As the loss is not easy to calculate, the following concept is used as the basis of calculating consumers' damage.[104]

The consumers' damage (CD) is the sum of expenditure that individual consumers pay additionally beyond the normal price, which amount to unlawful gains of cartel members.[105] In most price-fixing cases, the sum is not easy to quantify since it would require comparing the actual price in the manipulated market to the normal price in a hypothetical competitive market. Moreover, as competition law usually does not require its calculation, it is hard to find out the exact amount of CD. For the research purpose of demonstrating an estimate CD, it is calculated as 'consumed quantity [Qc]' multiplied by the gap between the high fixed price [Pf] and the normal price [Pn] that consumers will pay if there is no price-fixing agreement in the market. The consumers, in other words, are cheated by price-fixing and deprived of the consumer benefit quantified below.

$$\mathrm{CD} = Qc * (Pf - Pn)$$

The amount of CD varies case by case, but usually is large enough to cover the whole scope of a market in light of cartel members' market power. If the suppliers who agreed with the higher price do not have power to affect the market price, consumers can purchase the same product from other suppliers with no higher price, then, the cartel would be ineffective. Individual suppliers are not willing to participate in an agreement when they estimate that a cartel has insufficient market power to affect the market condition. Therefore, once a cartel is formed and has been operated, CD is quite large in light of the scope of the market and the cartel members' power on the market.

---

[102]McFadden (1986), 825 and 830.

[103]Stocking and Watkins (1948), 108–109 and footnote 10: LeClair (2000), 13–14 and 58–61.

[104]Consumers' damage (CD) is used for persuading consumers and policy makers to implement strict policy against cartels, to redress to consumers and to measure appropriate sanctions. OECD (2002), 6.

[105]*Id.*

OECD's survey states that the affected global commerce of just sixteen large cartel cases out of one hundred nineteen cases, revealed from 1996 to 2000, exceeded US$ 55 billion. Considering the insufficient data of cartels' damages, the difficulties of learning about cartel agreements, and under-enforcement in each country, the magnitude of the harm from the cartels will be tens to hundreds billion dollars annually.[106] In the U.S., an international vitamin cartel case reached a US $ 2.4 billion-amount settlement with direct U.S. purchasers in the class action suit, which is estimated as a little more than the total harm that the cartel actually caused. On the other hand, KFTC indicates that while a price-fixing and bid-rigging case among major three school-uniform producers in Korea turned out to cause around US$ 50 million of annual damage for two-and-a-half years,[107] the international electronic-graphite cartel case caused around US$ 37 million of annual damage for 5 years in Korea's market.[108] In light of the fact that the global market scope is around twenty five times larger than Korea's, the annual damage by an international cartel may reach US$ 0.93–1.23 billion. It is noteworthy that, when KFTC and the judicial body of Korea estimated total damages of price-fixing cases, they used the concept of CD, estimated by the total sales of conspirators multiplied by a gap between the fixed price and average price of normal bids.[109]

(6) Loss of Faith in Social Integrity and Honesty

Besides economic harm, a cartel has a negative influence on social justice.[110] When such an agreement as usually secret among competitors brings huge profits to themselves, enterprisers tend to be more concerned about their competitors rather than about their consumers' interests. Social respect toward successful enterprisers and faith in their honesty will be reduced when the public, usually consumers, realizes their cartelistic behaviors, which has the effect of transferring the welfare of

---

[106]OECD, *Policy Brief: Hard Core Cartel—Harm and Effective Sanctions*, May 2002, *available at* http://www.oecd.org/ (visited on 10 Jul. 2008).

[107]Korea's Won 50 billion (the exchange rate is calculated as KW 1000 equal to US $1 in this thesis for its convenience). The school-uniform price-fixing had maintained from the end of 1998 until 2001 for two-and-a-half year, thereby causing 2.5 million students $ 125 million, or $ 50 per purchaser. KFTC, press release: KW 11.5 billion (US $ 11.5 million) surcharge and criminal reference to four corporations and seven individuals involved in price-fixing and interference in consumers' bid (including bid-rigging) among school-uniform producers and distributors [교복제조 유통업체들의 가격담합 및 공동구매 방해 등에 대해 총 115억원 과징금 부과, 법인 4개 및 사업자 7인을 형사고발], 4. para.1 (May 2001), *available at* http://www.kftc.go.kr (visited on 10 July 2008).

[108]The damage calculated by KFTC is KW 183.7 billion for the 5 years which amount to around US $ 184 million.

[109]KFTC (2004). *See also* Ye-Rang Hwang, Seoul District Court Decided that price-fixing damages, US$ 58, should be compensated to individual purchaser [교복값 담합 5만8천원씩 배상하라], The Hankyoreh, 20 June 2005, *available at* http://www.hani.co.kr (visited on 29 Jan 2007).

[110]OECD (2002), 6.

consumers to enterprisers. The sneer attitude toward businessmen might result in the loss of faith in the integrity and honesty of the whole society.

C. Assessment

Although a cartel is effective to prevent the waste of precious resources and the collective destruction of a local economy in a temporary case, it demonstrates that the results of diverse cartels is not good for efficiency but can interfere with a free market mechanism. High or rigidly maintained prices independent from cost or market conditions support producers, especially inefficient suppliers, at the expense of both consumers and new competitors facing entry barriers caused by cartel members. Some examples even indicate the demise of cartels due to oversupply by either non-members or members who cheat by ignoring any restraint of a cartel in response to the high price. In short, the artificial restraint to price or output through a cartel causes conflict with free market mechanism and subsequent inefficiency. The restraint can not maintain its effect in the long run.

However, there are still dubious areas where cartels arguably have some positive effects outweighing their negative effects under certain extreme circumstances during a temporary period. Precedent research have already indicated, notably, in light of the long-term effects, even in the arguably justified cases, that price manipulation eventually turned back to or aggravated the initial problematic situation. As proponents of cartels try to exaggerate very limited advantages of cartels, it is beneficial to investigate exceptional situations with such limited advantages and to find out whether a cartel is justifiable in the context.

(1) Crisis Cartel

First, in destructive competition situations, competitors tend to collude and fix prices or sometimes output levels so that the price level may be maintained. Otherwise, they would compete with each other by lowering prices, thereby ending up with the survival of companies with large financial resources enough to endure price competition regardless of their merit in quality. This result is in conflict with the ideals that competition laws pursue. Although free market mechanisms should allow free entry to and exit from the markets, in the special economic situations, such as severe depression, destructive practices lead to competition not based on merit, quality, or price, but on financial ability to sustain businesses.

Fostering competition needs to be encouraged to maintain ‘merit-based competition’ in a market under an extreme situation. Small- or mid-sized firms with less financial resources but with high quality products should be able to survive the situation. Therefore, lenient approaches against cartels in severe depression may be adopted on the conditions that participants do not have power to control the whole market, and the agreement aims at eliminating destructive practices under a voluntary basis, and not restraining competition. In the Great Depression Era, the U.S. Supreme Court approved Appalachia Coals Inc., established by 137 bituminous coal producers, as an exclusive agent for the sale of all the coal that they produce.[111] In the Sugar Institute case,[112] the U.S. Supreme Court acknowledged that the Institute which used unfair methods of competition was worth not to be dissolved in a depression situation involving destructive practices as well as overcapacity although the methods should be enjoined. The case implied that the Institute was useful, in spite of its anticompetitive practices, and should continue competition in the economic situation. The case further implied that a voluntary agreement among the competitors in the industry could be exempted in light of economic circumstances.[113]

(2) Interstate Cartel or State-Operating Cartel

Second, competition that cartel regulations aim at is supposed to be among private entities, either individuals or enterprises, not a public entity, e.g., state. Regarding interstate or state-operating commodity cartels, the cartel regulation which applies to usual private cartels does not apply in light of unique characteristics of commodities and sovereignty principle. Price fluctuation in commodities, more often than not, is related to poverty, or at least economic development of developing countries. Reduction of poverty, and economic development have been acknowledged as duties of the states in international law with more weight than competition in markets. In addition, excessive exploitation of natural resources from competition intervene with conservation of the natural resources under the states' permanent rights over natural resource and environment protection. The sovereignty of states does not want international regulations over activities of interstate association or the state itself. Developing countries with newly adopted competition laws exclude agricultural commodity and natural resources from their coverages.[114]

Although existent cartel regulations exempt public cartels from their application, such commodity cartels should not totally disregard the competition perspective. Historical inability of cartels to control price or production of natural resources in the long-term proves that cartels do not provide as many advantages as their original intent except in some cases.[115] Cartels usually ended up with generating high price, thereby pushing consumers to alternative source or reducing demand.[116]

---

[111]Appalachian Coals, Inc. et al. v. United States, 288 U.S.344, 53 S.Ct. 471 (1933).

[112]Sugar Inst., Inc. v. United States, 297 U.S. 553 (1936), *aff'ing* 15 F.Supp. 817.

[113]Rudolph (1996), pp. 136–139.

[114]Jamil Anderlini, *Foreign investors fear China law to curb monopolies*, Fin. Times at 5 (31 Aug. 2007). In keeping with the government's commitment to improving the livelihood of more than 800 million rural citizens, China's first anti-monopoly law does not cover the agricultural sector, allowing farms to form cooperatives, such as cartel, that can market their products. The government protects many state-own monopolies by separate regulations in areas including petrochemicals, coal, and power.

[115]LeClair (2000), 81–83. The exceptions are bauxite and petroleum.

[116]International Coffee Agreement (ICA) which specified a price range through export quotas for reducing price and supply fluctuations but ended up with high price lost price control by exporters supplying the excess production over the limit to nonmember countries with cheap price. *Id.* at 58–61. International Cocoa Agreement failed to either stabilize or raise prices due to oversupply of non-participants and entry of new producers. *See id.* at 63–67. Organization of Petroleum

In the interstate commodity cartel, a voluntary guideline without sanction on non-complier need to be acknowledged for output and maximum price fluctuation in the light of special circumstances of producing countries.

On the other hand, as to arrangements or associations of private companies or individuals regarding natural resources, output restriction, or price maintenance can be the object of cartel regulations under competition law. Unless a state drives a public cartel policy with an appropriate legislation, private entities are not under such a duty unlike the states. Private entities can not justify the result that consumers are cheated by the increased price, or the reduced production of a cartel.

(3) Cartels for Research and Development

Third, as to joint research, companies with insufficient financial sources to invest into research or technological innovations in an industry, e.g., small-or mid-sized companies, sometimes need to get together under an arrangement. Benefits from the investment will go directly to consumers if the joint research succeeds in creating a high-quality product with a relatively low price. On the other hand, participants have the high chance of competition-restricting activities, e.g. price-fixing or the suppression of innovation-outlays, increasing because the participants spending a lot of time and money have the same interest in the research.[117]

In light of the conflicting points, a cartel authority may have power to regulate the anticompetitive behaviors of their research in a case where anticompetitive effect outweighs efficiency. Concretely, in exchange of approval, the authority may request that the participating companies should not, during or after their collective research period, conspire or implement an agreement which restrain competition in a market.

However, in light of the characteristics of technology consortia in practice, the possibility of the perversion is low. The negotiation of the arrangements is strictly bilateral rather than multi-lateral convenient for a cartel conspiracy.[118] In addition, the incentives built in a technology consortium lead to the increase of R&D investment. In other words, as a firm only with sufficient technology information may participate in the exchange agreement, the firm needs further R&D investment to maintain the consortium.[119]

(4) Cartels by Professional Organizations

As to the voluntary restraints by a professional organization, there are some necessities for ethical rules of professional services. However, the agreement

(Footnote 116 continued)

Exporting Countries (OPEC) is thought to lose its significant price control back in 70s due to conservation efforts of industrialized countries. Shift to alternative energy sources such as natural gas and coal and the increased number of non-member countries with expanding their output as well as new producers. *Id.* at 67–71.

[117]Baumol (2001), 732.

[118]*Id.*

[119]*Id.* at 732–733.

regarding service fees among member entrepreneurs should not be allowed. Even though the service-fee restraint may lead to competition with more focus on high quality of service by prohibiting fee-decreasing competition, the restriction can not satisfy consumers' desires to have a wide range of services. Although autonomous service quality control is an appropriate policy for professional organizations, price-fixing is never a good method for quality control but is the very measure to restrict a free competition mechanism. Although professional practices have a public-service characteristic, the service is offered to consumers in exchange for money, which falls on commerce. Moreover, the activities of professionals have played an important part in commercial transactions. As a result, their anticompetitive practices impose a restraint on commerce. Since the U.S. Supreme Court in *Goldfarb* et al. *v. Virginia State Bar* et al. case (1975) held that the fee prescribed by a minimum fee schedule issued from the State Bar and County Bar Association fell on price-fixing against Sec.1 of the Sherman Act,[120] the Supreme Court has affirmed a violation of Sec.1 in most cases involving professional organizations' restriction of price competition.[121] Recently, the Omnibus Cartel Repeal Act in South Korea adopted the strict application of cartel regulations against a fee-settlement by nine professional organizations including lawyers, certified public accountants, patent lawyers, customs officers, etc.[122]

2.4 Intergovernmental Agreement for a Commodity Distinctive from a Private Cartel

A. International Commodity Agreement (ICA)

(1) The Meaning

International Commodity Agreement (ICA) is an agreement between governments of both producing and consuming countries to regulate the terms of

[120]Lewis H. Goldfarb et al. v. Virginia State Bar et al. 421 U.S. 773, 95 S.Ct. 2004 (1975).

[121]Price-fixing or its variation restraining price-competition is per se illegal. Goldfarb et al. v. Virginia State Bar et al. 421 U.S. 733 (1975), National Society of Professional Engineers v. United States, 435 U.S. 679 (1978), Arizona v. Maricopa County Medical Society, 457 U.S. 332 (1982), FTC v. Superior Court Trial Lawyers Association, 493 U.S. 411 (1990). In a exceptional case, the Supreme Court requires in-detailed examination under the rule of reason standard for California Dental Association's ban on price advertising. California Dental Association v. FTC, 526 U.S. 756 (1999).

[122]Korea's Omnibus Cartel Repeal Act: Regulating Undue Concerted Activities Exempt from the Application of the Monopoly Regulation and Fair Trade Act (hereinafter OCRA), Law No. 5815 (5 Feb. 1999).

international trade in a specific commodity.[123,124] It is a type of treaty in international law, which provides regulatory measures for the stabilization of prices and supply. It establishes an international organization with an international personality.[125]

(2) Relationship with Intergovernmental Producers' Association (IPA)

The ICA is different from the intergovernmental producers' association (IPA). The IPA includes only producing countries while the ICA needs to admit consuming countries as well as producing countries with an open membership. The ICA is seen as more effective than the IPA in terms of screening the deviation from cooperative measures, e.g., export or production quota, as it requires producing countries to report regular statistics of production and export and consuming countries to limit imports.[126]

The ICA has a similar economic impact on international commodity trade to the IPA. The moderation of price fluctuation of the ICA in a commodity market prevents excessive price changes through market interventions by countries with substantial market power. Free price-setting mechanism of a market is under the control of the agreement. The concrete ways of operation of the ICA include almost the same measures as the IPA. The current demise of ICAs implies that the ICA is not favored by particularly consuming countries. Benefits to consuming countries such as stable prices and participation in commodity policies were considered small while costs to them, e.g., helping DCs under nontransparent artificial market control, were evaluated large.[127] This analysis explains recent resurgences of the IPA.[128] Although the ICA has a bi-partisan membership structure, it has revealed characteristics close to IPA in economic functions in markets. The following characteristics of commodity production apply to both IGA as well as ICAs. In this thesis, ICA is going to be discussed with IGA as there are not big differences between ICA and IGA in terms of its economic impact.

[123] A commodity in the ICAs means a primary commodity, any product of farm, forest, or fishery or any mineral in its natural form or which has undergone such processing as is customarily required to prepare it for marketing in substantial volume in international trade. *See* Art. 56 para. 1. of the Havana Charter.

[124] Christopher Gilbert, *International Commodity Agreements*, p. 2 (14 Jan. 2005), available at http://grade.unitn.it/people/gilbert/file/Attachment_10.pdf (visited on 10 Jul. 2008).

[125] Kabir-ur-Rahman (1982), p. 9.

[126] Gilbert (2005), at 14.

[127] *Id.* at 13–14.

[128] Recently a proposal for the organization of natural gas producing countries, led by Russia, was seriously discussed among major exporting countries. Meanwhile, OPEC demonstrated an increasing influence on global crude oil market. Refer to 2(3).

B. Unique Characteristics of Commodity Production

(1) Economic Perspectives

1) Significant Importance to Domestic Economies of Commodity Dependent Developing Countries (CDDCs)

The interstate commodity cartels have been acknowledged and supported financially by the international community to sustain economic development of developing countries, or the South, and to provide stable and reliable financial resources for the food supplies.[129] In less diversified economies, commodity exports occupy substantial parts of their national income and constitute valuable financial sources to provide foods and other necessities to the public. Particularly, the Least Developed Countries (LDCs), which belong to the CDDCs[130] by Common Fund for Commodities (CFC), have their economic foundations on commodity production. A group of the DCs with specialties in exporting certain demand-increasing commodities do not belong to the CDDCs as they have land-abundant infrastructures and capitals and enjoy a large market share in international trade, most of which have outgrown the level of economic development and simple economic structure of CDDCs.[131] On the other hand, the CDDCs are the other group of the DCs where the export of a commodity facing falling or stagnant demand occupies a significant portion of national income. The commodity export from the CDDCs has stagnant market shares due to poor infrastructure or high-risk investments or low-sized farms. A large part of population in the CDDCs consists of small producers working on a few commodities under less diversified economic structure. The price changes in their major production affect more severely their domestic economies and the poor population than other countries and classes.

2) Instability of Price in relation to Inelasticity of Production

In spite of the close relationship between commodity production and poverty, the actual terms of trade indicated high volatility of the commodity prices. The deteriorating prices of most commodities during the past and recent price surges in food commodities and oil have revealed a wide range of economic impacts on the

---

[129]Common Fund for Commodities (CFC), a UN special agency for financing and supporting commodity trade, was established for supporting commodity development projects, one of which include commodity market risk management or price-management for reliability of supply. See CFC, *Current Trends and the New Development Role of Commodities*, 7–8 (Nov. 2006), *available at* http://www.common-fund.org/download/actualiteit/CT06jelle.pdf (visited on 10 July 2008) and Fig. 3, section of the Decision I of the Governing Council of the Common Fund at its Seventh Meeting in Dec. 1995, Decision I (VII/ 1995). *See id.,* at 24, para. 8 of U.N. General Assembly (GA) Resolution A/57/236 (Dec. 2002).

[130]According to CFC, the CDDCs are defined as the developing countries for which 50 % or more of all merchandise exports are made up of non-oil commodities. Oil is omitted for the following reasonable grounds; (1) most oil exporter meet a qualitatively different challenge from CDDCs and (2) the unique high value of oil can distort export composition. CFC (2006), at 10.

[131]For example, Argentina, Brazil, Thailand, Malaysia and recently Vietnam belong to such Commodity Developers group. *Id.* at 8.

global market. The fluctuation and the deterioration of the prices not only led to lower profits from the international trade of the commodities but also exacerbated the poverty level in the countries that focused on the commodity export.

The sensitivity of the commodity price and its severe impact on the economy is exacerbated by inflexible adjustability of the commodity production to price change. Commodities' outputs respond slowly to increased prices, but once expanded, they are extremely difficult to contract.[132] In addition, a commodity production requires large fixed costs compared to small variable costs for production. As a result, the production tends to be either much larger or smaller than economic equilibrium. As a solution to the insensitivity to market price shifts, a buffer stock, however, requires huge capital to operate in the price-moderating way,[133] which as one major reason led to collapse of the Tin Agreement in 1985.

Meanwhile, agricultural or meat products need a relatively long time from several months to even a decade, to grow up and be processed enough to become commercial products in the market.[134] The storability of agricultural products are limited due to natural decades and consequential cost increase.[135]

(2) Political and Legal Perspectives: State-Involvement

In most cases, states themselves are producers of commodities, particularly natural resources including minerals, or the states are involved in agricultural commodity production with in governmental policies, e.g., subsidies or export quota. The sovereignty issue and public interest from such state-involvements and subsequent rights and obligations is distinguished from the individual entrepreneurs working on the private interest without any public duty or privilege in international law.[136] A state with sovereignty has their unique privileges or duties as a major subject under international law while a private company does not. A government in itself has the right to exploit natural resources as national properties under international law.[137] Even in some cases private companies participate in such productions, as recently growing phenomena, a type of national license or authorization and subsequent government restrictions are needed. The governmental restrictions have the characteristic of sovereign acts, which are protected under international law unless there is a norm of jus cogens, or customary international law, or an international treaty to which the state accedes. It is not easy work

---

[132] *See* Scherer (1994), p. 54.

[133] Edward (1994), 22 Denv. J. Int'l L.& Pol'y 530.

[134] *Id.* at 530. Production cycles limit the ability of an international commodity agreement to control supply. For instance, coffee plants require 10 years to reach full maturity.

[135] *Id.* at 529–530.

[136] Refer to II. 8. of this Chapter.

[137] The right is acknowledged in UN GA Resolution on Permanent Sovereignty over Natural Resources, Art. 31, 33 and 34 of Charter of Economic Rights and Duties of States, Declaration and Program of Action on the Establishment of a NIEO, and UN Conference on New & Renewable Sources of Energy. The economic development of the resource-producing countries has been protected as the principle of UN Charter. Refer to Chap. 3. NIEO.

to persuade a multitude of governments to reach an international agreement for restraining their sovereign powers, which provide a lot of economic benefits to their revenues. For example, governments have provided subsidies to their agricultural producers by supporting their productions while maintaining low prices. Currently, multilateral negotiations for curtailing governmental subsidies under the WTO Doha Round did not create an international agreement due to internal political conflicts. Placing international competition in commodity trades, by cutting subsidies, let the government face risks to deal with strong protests from many laborers who depend on incomes proportionate to the price of their productions.

State interests in intergovernmental cooperation lead states to gather together to manage total production or price level of the commodity and to establish international organizations or associations for the purpose of controlling a respective commodity trade. For instance, developing countries that have significant importance in national commodities launched the Common Fund for Commodities (CFC) which has supported works of individual international commodity bodies.[138] The number of international commodity bodies (ICBs) under the patronage of CFC amount to 25.[139] A recent proposal for the organization of natural gas producing countries as a new IPA, led by Russia, was seriously discussed among major exporting countries.[140] Since the works of such organizations include the management or the setting of the prices or production quantities of commodities, they have similar characteristics to a private cartel.

(3) Different Legal Principles from Private Cartels

The ICA is an international organization with legal personality. It is different from a conventional cartel with nothing but an agreement to restrict competition. The ICA is shielded under the sovereign immunity principle. Additionally, the point that its members are sovereign states enables the ICA to be protected from responsibility through the act of state doctrine in international law. The cooperative behaviors of independent sovereign states do not change their characteristics by gathering together.

International law, moreover, has developed different rules under international commodity law from cartel rules under competition law. Development, right to food, and environmental protection under sustainable development are concerns

---

[138] CFC provided financial support, around total US $ 3.5 million, to price risk managements of cocoa, coffee, cotton and pilot cotton in six cases in 2001. *See id.* at 16, 17, 20, and 21.

[139] International Commodity Bodies (ICBs) are intergovernmental organizations which concentrate on specific commodities through consultations between consumers and producers, and analyses of market developments. Annex IV provides 25 ICBs. See id. 7 and 30–31.

[140] Andrew England, *Gas exporters launch pricing study*, Fin. Times, April 10, 2007, at 2. Russia, Algeria, and Qatar, responsible of 60 % of the world gas exports, reached the decision to operate a committee to study gas pricing policy of the Gas Exporting Countries Forum (GECF). *See also Russia, Qatar eye OPEC-style natural gas cartel: Reserves rich countries seek ways to influence global market,* Associated Press (12 Feb 2007), available at http://www.msnbc.msn.com/id/17116262/.

that the international commodity law needs to address in distinction with competition law. Article XX of the General Agreement on Tariffs and Trade 1994 (1994 GATT) exempts from its general obligations the governmental measures pursuant to the intergovernmental commodity agreement, which is open to participation by both exporting and importing states, and are designed to assure the availability of supplies adequate to meet demand at stable prices.[141]

In addition, the UNCTAD's eleventh session (UNCTAD XI) in 2004 adopted the Sao Paulo Consensus. Para. 74 of the Consensus stipulates that a concerted focus should be directed toward CDDCs, and that efforts by the countries to strengthen the competitiveness of their commodity sectors should be supported by the provision of enhanced market access on a secure and predictable basis and the strengthening of capacity and institutions in both the public and private sectors.[142] The provision placed a legal foundation for an international commodity-managing organization. The subsequent sentence that existing compensatory financing schemes should be reviewed and combined with modern risk management and risk-sharing instruments[143] approves CFC's assistance to ICAs' activities, e.g., quota or buffer system. Moreover, the International Ministerial Conference of Landlocked and Transit Developing Countries, and Donor Countries and International Financial and Development Institutions on Transit Transport Cooperation in Almaty, Kazakhstan, in 2003 (2003 Almaty Conference) urged, for commodity issues, concerted efforts by the landlocked and transit developing countries along with development partners, international organizations, and other relevant regional and subregional organizations.[144]

C. Necessity of Different Regulations in International Commodity Markets

As rapid-increases of the oil price and food price threaten global economies, particularly fuel-importing countries, and less developed countries which need financial resources to purchase food, there are arguments that the currently operating international commodity agreements shall be regulated similarly with private cartel regulations.[145] However, such distinctions of primary commodities as mentioned above necessitate independent regulation under the international commodity law. The following arguments support the independence of commodity law with in-detailed reasonings.

---

[141]Sub-para. (h). Ad Art. XX subpara. (h) extends the exception to any commodity agreement which conforms to the principles approved by the Economic and Social Council in its resolution 30 (IV) of 28 March 1947. However, the exception, although it opened a large loophole, made little practical effects because such agreements were hard to make. Only wheat and sugar agreements had been made effective. Bronz (1956), 69 Harvard L. Rev. 440, pp. 466–467.

[142]CFC (2006), 27.

[143]*See id.*

[144]para. 42 of 2003 Almaty Conference.

[145]Raphael Minder and Joe Leahy, *Asia battles with surging food costs,* Fin Times, at 9 (10 Jan 2008); U.N. General Assembly, Report of the Secretary-General, International trade and development, para. 4 A/62/266 (62nd sess.) (16 Aug. 2007).

(1) Limitations of the Competitive Market Approach

First, the adoption of competition in commodity market can threaten overall economies and economic development of CDDCs. Commodity price competition may suppress stable maintenance of export revenues in most DCs which depend on commodity production for a large part of their economic export. Some countries will prohibit exports of their major commodities at low prices. A research by CFC analyses the distribution of wealth among agricultural-commodity-producing countries through the price-increase of agricultural commodities, thereby distinguishing Commodity Developers[146] from the CDDCs. The research states that the beneficiaries of the increasing demand are Commodity Developers with an economy of scope rather than the CDDCs and that only six commodities out of sixteen agricultural commodities show strong unit price increases.[147]

Second, as commodity price surges throw out the hunger issue,[148] commodity price collapse exacerbate many people's lives in CDDCs where productions and exports of small-farm-produced low-quality commodities occupy a substantial part of national income. The CFC's researches pointed out price-decreases in many traditional agricultural products which the CDDCs depends on while prices surge in some agricultural products. In the CDDCs, the increase of foreign exchange revenues through export growth is unlikely to come true under current situations. Robert Zoellick, the World Bank president, confirmed such difficulties of the CDDCs and states, 'along with high food and energy price, global economic turbulence starting from credit crunch in the U.S. and western Europe poses difficulties to a group of poor countries, mostly in Africa, thereby undermining their recently-built fundamentals for growth and worsening hunger and malnutrition in the poorest sector'.[149]

Third, the rising price addresses the global concern for development of the countries under negative impacts. Countries where the economic structure largely depends on low-quality demand-stagnant commodities need international assistance for profitable agricultural productions and policy guides, which have been provided by international organizations, e.g., the Food and Agricultural Organization (FAO) and the CFC, and industrialized countries, e.g., United States Agency for International Development (USAID).

---

[146]A few developing countries, so-called emerging markets, fall on the Commodity Developers (CDs). They are leading exporters of higher value commodities for which demand is expanding. *See* CFC (2006), p. 8.

[147]*Id.*, at 7. The unit price of commodities from CDDCs had been lower during 2003–2005 than the average world unit price for 12 out of 16 commodities. The reason of such low prices is inferred due to lower quality products. *See also id.* at 10.

[148]FAO Newsroom, *Crop Prospects mixed for low-income food-deficit countries in 2007: 28 countries face food shortages*, *available at* http://www.fao.org/newsroom/en/news/2007/1000628/inde.html.

[149]Krishna Guha and James Politi, *Zoellick calls for fight against hunger to be global priority*,FIN TIMES, 5 (24 Jan. 2008).

Fourth, environmental issues matter when exploitation of natural resources goes competitive. Natural resources shall not be traded without any fetter of environmental protection because excessive exploitation of the natural resources limits the usability of future generations. Under natural resource managements, an increasing number of legislations are reflecting the necessities of agricultural cooperatives and tradable fishing quotas.

(2) Balance of Interests: Bipartisan Membership within the ICA

To effectively work continuously, an ICA should pursue the policy objectives that a majority of the constituents desire.[150] Finding an objective for an organization is important so that the organization may work continuously in a market. Since an ICA is an organization operating in the global market, it needs to obtain correct objectives, which come from resolving conflicting interests among members. Therefore, the ICA needs a political process. If an organization targets an objective, not desired by a powerful faction of the organization, it may lead to its malfunction or destruction.[151]

The conflicting interests within an ICA come from bipartisan membership with different perspectives. First, the conflicting interests within ICAs are the heterogeneous interests of producers and consumers. The producers have more power in most ICAs than consumers as the focus of the organizations is toward production management including a quota. It is noted that some ICAs collapsed due to the difficulty of reconciling two opposite positions between producers and consumers. Second, its members can be divided into two groups, large-and mid-sized economies and small economies. The Commodity Developers (CDs) belong to the former group while the Commodity Dependent Developing Countries (CDDCs) belong to the latter group. As the CDDCs, compared to the CDs, lack an economy of scope, information or techniques for high productivity and high quality, products from the CDDCs tend to be low-quality commodities. Since an ICA needs active participation from large producers, mostly CDs, its objective cannot avoid reflecting the large producers' interests or a reconciliation between large consumers and producers, thereby overlooking the interests of small-scale producers, particularly from the CDDCs.

The proper objective for ICAs is negotiation among different groups and distribution of their interests. Consumers' concerns about food price increases can be negotiated with producers, particularly, in terms of reducing hunger and malnutrition. Particularly, for food commodity agreements, moderation of severe price fluctuation through production management on the basis of output level forecast or increase of productivity of good quality food may be a good objective. However,

---

150 Edward (1994), 532.

151 *Id.* at 531–532. Quill illustrates the collapse of the Int' Tin Agreement (ITA). The ITA was under a severe dispute between consumers from the North, including the U.S. as the biggest consumer, and producers from the South by changing its objective from moderating price-fluctuation and developing efficient production method to a remunerative return to producers. *See id.* at 515–518.

small-size consuming countries or producing countries will still face difficulties in effectively representing their interests on the negotiation table as their contribution to the agreement is less than large economies. The special interests in small economies, particularly CDDCs, e.g., poverty, food shortage, need to be addressed with supplemental law or policy.

(3) Necessity of Supplemental Measures

1) Special and Differential Treatment of International Trade Law

International commodity agreements, prevalent in the 1970s, grew less effective in the 1980s and 1990s when market liberalization policy dominated international commodity trades. Under this liberalization approach, the less competitive low-quality products from the CDDCs faced a reduction of exports under harsh competition, thereby threatening the lives of small-sized producers in the CDDCs. Meanwhile, advanced countries reduced their assistance in ICAs as trade liberalization dominated commodity trades.

One way to solve the problem of less competitive products in less developing countries(less DCs)[152] is for them to learn from trades with advanced countries to produce and develop for themselves.[153] The trade principle of reciprocity, however, as currently illustrated, impedes promotion of international trade between DC groups and advanced countries. Peter Mandelson, the EU Commissioner for Trade, recently stated that the EU could not offer access to the African Caribbean and Pacific (ACP) group unilaterally but on a reciprocal basis under WTO rules.[154] The special treatment of products from the ACP countries in the EU under the Cotonou Agreement (the former Lome Convention) is no longer permitted under the WTO regime. The ACP states cannot help but concede reciprocal trade preferences to the EU in order to have access to the biggest market in the world.[155]

The most-favored-nation (MFN) principle under the WTO regime invokes concerns with less developing countries (less DCs). The less DCs have to offer reciprocal concessions to regionally integrated markets, to which preferential treatment with any trading partner in the future shall be applied equally under the principle, so that the integrated markets may sell their products under the preferential conditions. Out of the concern, Namibia and South Africa refused to sign new

[152]Less DCs are distinguished from the least developed countries (LDCs) designated by the UN. The less DCs are mostly middle-income and low-income developing countries including LDCs. The major petroleum-exporting countries, major exporters of manufacturers and high-income developing countries are excluded from the less DCs. The less DCs are made up of the ACP group. Refer to Chap. 3. III. 1. for the category of countries.

[153]Brown (1994), pp. 369–370. He cites the statement of the former Secretary of State, G. Shultz, in Rio de Janeiro at a conference sponsored by Brazilian business groups.

[154]Mandelson, *Brussels cannot offer ACP unilateral trade access*, FT (12 Dec. 2007).

[155]Andres Bounds and Laura Dixon, *EU to dilute trade deals to avert crisis*, FT (19 Nov. 2007). The literature on preferences highlight.

trade agreements with the EU because they are required to allow future preferential treatments under the MFN principle.[156]

Growing regional market integrations in advanced countries can work against the less DCs as they place more opportunities with products from their member states than the ones from the less DCs.[157] Economic cooperation within the DCs, in response to economic blocs of industrialized countries, has brought less benefits than the cooperation with the blocs because the low level of economic structure in many DCs could not support reciprocal economic development effectively.[158]

The strict application of current international trade law principles, between the less DCs or CDDCs and the advanced regionally integrated markets, neglects the unequal bargaining positions of each group of countries. Supplemental measures for promoting trades between LDCs or CDDCs and advanced countries are in need and thereby necessitate the development of international commodity laws independent from international competition law.

Although the GATT system offered nondiscriminatory quantitative restrictions to further economic reconstruction with strict conditions, which require the prior approval of the contracting parties, the quantitative restrictions have not been used widely to the benefits of CDDCs. Only the Generalized System of Preferences (GSP) under GATT has at least been used in favor of less-skillful products from DCs[159] as the GSP provides permission to have duty-free treatment or non-reciprocal tariff preferences. The point that the GSP operates on a permissive standard rather than on a mandatory one weakens its effectiveness. The CFC has already recognized such practical limitations of currently valid preferential treatments to DC groups.[160]

2) Policy Assistance for Economic Development

Economic development, important for the growth of DCs, does not automatically grow through the trading of commodities which are abundant in DCs. For example, countries where a lot of crude oil exists have achieved less economic growth than expected with profit through their oil-trading and have rarely reached the level of advanced market economy. Economic development requires high-skilled labor forces, diversified economic structures, efficient market systems, transparent financial systems, and competitive manufacturing industries. Neither a

---

[156]Bounds, *Two African nations refuse to join EU trade deal*, FT (4 Dec. 2007).

[157]Edward (1994), 536: Brown (1994), 396. Brown classifies DCs into Newly Industrialized Countries (NICs) and the least developed Fourth World of Asia and Africa, which falls on the LDCs in this thesis. He foresees that, while NICs may join with Japan under a Asian trading bloc, the Fourth World states will be more isolated than ever.

[158]Brown (1994), 169.

[159]Brown (1994), at 362. UNCTAD have been less than satisfied with the scope of the GSP as well as with its ultimate benefit because not all DCs are covered and each advanced country provides too different and complicated schemes to evaluate the closeness to its original goal.

[160]CFC (2006), p. 11.

competitive international market nor the OPEC has provided effective economic development to oil-exporting countries.

3) Concern About Environmental Protection

Commodity production can generate environmental problems. Although economic development through producing commodities requires exploiting natural resources and transforming environments at the cost of future generation's usage, economic development pays more attention to cost reduction than environmental protection. Such market system is difficult to consider environmental issues as an economic analysis of production's effect on the environment remains in the primitive level. For instance, the issue of water shortage is deeply related to the increase in the agricultural production for biofuel, or ethanol which requires a large water supply. The fishery industry can cause derivative killings of marine mammals as the WTO Tuna-Dolphin case illustrates.

A competitive-market-based approach to such environmental issues, however, is short of considerations for future generation. Transformation of an environment takes a very long time to be restored to their original state and, in quite a few cases, they can not be restored at all. The future generation, which does not have a chance to participate in the decision to interfere or alter environment, has to inherit the undesired results and endure the heavy burden of restoration.

International responses sometimes bring about some conflicts with national sovereignty of, particularly, the developing countries which are heavily focused on economic development. The lack of sufficient green technologies and limited economic resources in the developing countries results in another market barrier of 'green protectionism'[161] under the pretext of environment protection. On the other hand, so-called 'eco-imperialism' has something to do with the more direct type of sovereignty intervention. The argument matters when the jurisdiction of a state as to domestic environmental law extends to the territory of another state. For example, the 1972 Marine Mammal Protection Act (MMPA)[162] in the U.S. brought a dispute of fishery trade with Mexico in the Tuna-Dolphin case under the GATT.[163] The MMPA and supplemental regulations placed strict limits on the number of dolphins which can be killed by persons and vessels subject to U.S. jurisdictions,[164]

[161]Brown (1994), p. 382. *See also* Alan Beattie, *Green Barricade*, FT 7 (24 Jan. 2008). The border tax for carbon emission might play the useful role of bargaining strategy in trade negotiation table while the imposition of actual direct tax on imports from under-regulated countries is difficult to be implemented fully due to complexities of global manufacturing system and local regulations in the light of WTO rule.

[162]Marine Mammal Protection Act of 1972 (MMPA), Pub. L. No. 92-522, 86 Stat. 1027 (21 Oct. 1972). Sec.101(a)(2) stated that the incidental kill or serious injury of marine mammals permitted in the course of commercial fishing be reduced to insignificant levels approaching a zero rate.

[163]In the eastern tropical Pacific Ocean where dolphins and tuna are known to swim very closely together and dolphins are encircled with purse-seine nets to catch the tuna underneath, when the nets are withdrawn, dolphins are ensnared in them and/or trapped below the surface where they suffocate.

[164]§ 102(a)(1) of the MMPA.

provided penalties including forfeiture of cargoes,[165] and banned importation of commercial fish, which cause incidental kills or serious injuries of ocean mammals in excess of the U.S. standard.[166] Even the MMPA prohibited the importation of yellowfin tuna from the East-tropical Pacific Ocean (ETP) unless the Secretary of Commerce found that the harvesting country had a program regulating the taking of mammals comparable to the U.S.[167] Mexico argued that the extraterritorial application of the MMPA falls on eco-imperialism. Indonesia in this case argued that the MMPA exploited sympathy for marine mammals to protect the U.S. tuna producers, thereby falling on green protectionism. The GATT panel held that unilateral national legislation, e.g., the MMPA, threatened to undermine the multilateral trading framework of the GATT, and was inconsistent with Art. XI.1.[168] Although the penal decision explicitly declared that basic trade rules are not neglected in the environmental issue of international trade, subsequent environmental critics against the decision implied that the environmental protection issue is an area which multi-dimensional approaches under researches are better to address rather than international trade law. As commodity production is deeply involved with environmental protection, specific regulations for its production and trade are in need. ICAs can be places to discuss the issue of preventing environmental destruction when development-oriented approach is moderated by reflecting the economic evaluation of environmental effect of commodity production. The proclamation of a 'sustainable development' agenda by the international community, which will be discussed in Chap. 6, addresses the necessity for specific regulations.

D. Focus of the International Cartel Law: Private International Cartel

International cartels mostly operating with state-involvement include complicated interests. The member countries of the Organization of Petroleum Exporting Countries (OPEC), currently the most powerful IPA, have argued for sovereign powers to manage the natural resources which have been acknowledged by such international law as the United Nations (UN) General Assembly Resolution on Permanent Sovereignty over Natural Resources, Art. 31, 33, and 34 of the Charter of Economic Rights and Duties of States, the Declaration and Program of Action on the Establishment of New International Economic Order (NIEO), and the UN Conference on New and Renewable Sources of Energy. Independent right to economic development of the OPEC countries has been protected as a principle of the UN Charter. In light of such rights to natural resources, the OPEC member countries will object to any international regulation over OPEC. Even the non-member countries hesitate to accept international regulation regarding interstate cartels with the fear that their sovereign power to produce other natural resources

---

165 § 106(a).

166 § 102(a)(2)(B).

167 § 101(a)(2)(B).

168 GATT Dispute Panel Report, *U.S.-Restriction on Imports of Tuna*, DS21/R, 5.18 (16 Aug. 1991).

may be intervened by the regulation. This thesis, which tries to make a possible international regulation against cartels, places major focus on cartels consisting of private corporations by distinguishing them from IPAs. Countries, free from fear of restriction to their sovereign powers, succeeded in reaching a consensus in regulating cartels of private companies, such as the 1980 UN Set or the 1998 OECD Hard Core Cartel Recommendation. To make binding international law on cartels, it is convenient to root firm international consensus through active practices in the area. Private cartels are to be discussed with priority. As IPAs and ICAs have more weight on economic development and poverty rescue than competition consideration, they need to be regulated under separate laws, and not in the same coverage as private cartels.

2.5 International Cartels and Their Representatives

A. Domestic Cartels versus International Cartels

It is a cartel working across borders rather than the one within a domestic market that quite a few international cartel regulations target. Some cartel conspiracies taking place in one country may affect another country, which belongs to the latter category, the cross-border cartel. The cross-border cartel is defined as an international cartel in this thesis. On the other hand, a cartel conspiracy taking place and affecting one country is defined as a domestic cartel. While the thesis does not neglect the importance of regulating domestic cartels as a basis of consensus-building for international regulation, this thesis plans to devote itself to regulating international cartels with which majority of international agreements deal.

B. Emergence of International Cartels

The phenomena of international cartels took place in the late nineteenth century in Europe where economic trade across national territories had been most in progress in the world. The German–Swiss dyestuffs cartel established in 1880s was one of original international cartels.[169] It set predatory price against competing, usually small, producers from other countries so as to secure dominance over Western European markets. According to a research, no less than 40 international cartels, either public or private, worked in Europe in 1897.[170]

From the occurrence of WWI to the Great Depression, international cartels in the prewar stage were dismantled. When European states tried to recover the broken economy under new frameworks of treaty of Versailles and World Economic Conference in Geneva, one of the objectives of the Conference was to restore economic integration and protect stable equilibrium between production and

[169]Connor (2003), p. 1.

[170]Resch (2005), p. 3.

consumption through international industrial agreements including public and private cartels.[171] However, the Conference reached only a statement requiring close attention to such industrial agreements due to conflicting opinions. The interwar cartels were reestablished in line with agreements on a national level as states did not prohibit cartels.[172] Particularly, an international steel cartel led by France and Germany's steel industries controlled the entire steel production of members under a quota system with penalty payments for excess production. Starting from the international steel cartel, followed by the European Rail Manufacturers' Association (ERMA) in steel industries, international cartels came out in markets of magnesite, carbide, glue, explosives, electric bulbs, bottles, aluminum, and copper. During the Depression, however, most international cartels dissolved.

Although the efforts to achieve market control through international industrial agreements failed, most states did not forsake measures of national intervention, including a public cartel,[173] in disintegrated economies of the Depression era. As quite a few nations adopted favorable or at least accepting legislative attitudes toward cartels, international cartels had prospered supported by the tolerating legislative approaches. International cartels in tin, aluminium, nitrogen, dyestuff, and enamel goods were established with support of national governments through international treaties. The cartels enjoyed their heyday during the 1930s, and affected 40–50 % of world trade with monopolistic pricing.[174] Meanwhile, the U.S. took strict investigations against cartels, thereby causing American companies to be hesitant to participate in international cartels.[175] However, as international cartels covered the American market as well as the European market, the affected commerce in the U.S. during the times amounted to significant rates.[176]

C. Aspects of International Cartels

Although international private cartels appeared in the late nineteenth century and grew popular in the interwar era,[177] the ones uncovered since 1995 are different from the previous ones in terms of scale, multicultural pluralism, refined operational technique, and longevity.[178] Currently discovered international cartels cover

[171] *See id.* p. 6.

[172] Resch, *id*, p. 4; Connor and Helmers (2007).

[173] However, the public cartels were treated by different rules from private cartels under international law. The inter-governmental producers' associations (IPAs) in a clearer term belongs to the public cartel.

[174] Resch (2008), p. 14.

[175] Connor and Helmers (2007).

[176] Stocking and Watkins (1946), pp. 4–5. The tentative results of their research revealed that 87 % by value of mineral products sold in the U.S. in 1939, 60 % of agricultural products, and 42 % of manufactured products were cartelized.

[177] Connor and Helmers (2007), at 48. Hundreds of international cartels operated in the interwar period, affecting nearly 50 % of international merchandise trade.

[178] *See id.* at 1. The 40 international cartels were only the ones involved by Germany. Great Britain was involved in 22 of them.

markets in more no less than two continents, and diverse participants from not only European countries but also Asian countries. They lasted for more than 6 years on average while they worked secretly.

Generally, an international cartel tends to be formed among a few companies competing with a homogeneous product in a high concentrated market where high barriers to market entry block new competitors[179] or an industry trade association exists.[180] Low buyer concentration prevents purchasers from counterveiling against the market power of the sellers in the cartelized market. According to a study, the organic chemical industry had the highest percentage of 283 cartels discovered since 1990, a majority of which are chemicals for food or animal-feed ingredients.[181] The organic chemical market is an area where several conditions for an international cartel are met.

The number of international cartels uncovered and investigated is not large, but they generate enormous damage to not only commerce and consumers' welfare but also to social integrity and industrial efficiency.[182] In terms of commerce, the size of the affected sales is, although not direct, proportionate to the market scope and duration of the investigated international cartel.[183] Compared to domestic cartels, the former research of 283 international cartels demonstrated that global cartels had the highest median sales, $ 2.64 billion while median sales affected by 37 domestic cartels, active in one nation of Western Europe, is $ 1.5 billion larger than domestic cartels in North America.[184] While the average duration of cartels with foreign members was 6.4 years, global cartels last much longer than localized ones.[185] In terms of overcharge, while median overcharges are from 24 to 29 % depending on the geographical area, global cartels have the highest rate at 29 %.[186] This result

[179] *Id.* at 6–8.

[180] OECD (2002), at 7.

[181] Connor (2003), at 10–11. *See* Connor and Helmers (2007), p. 8. Connor and Helmer revealed 22 % of total international cartels came out in the area. *See also* Connor (2003), at 4 and 11. Although Connor defines an 'international cartel' as the cartel of which members include foreign nationality or foreign-based headquarter, he mentions that more than 50 % of the international cartel affects more than two continental market.

[182] *Refer to supra* 2.2 B. Disadvantage of Cartels.

[183] Connor and Helmers (2007), at 12–13. Cartels working in global and West European area occupies 76 % (respectively 37.5) of 40 biggest cartels. The U.S. cartels have 20 %. While none was active only in Asia, 2 cartels were in South America and Oceania respectively.

[184] *See id.* at 3–4. 'International cartel' means a cartel consisting of a member with foreign nationality or foreign headquarter while 'global' means that effect of the cartel covers more than one continent. Connor and Helmers mentioned that 40 North American cartels' median affected sales including those operating in both U.S. and Canada were $ 0.9 billion (900 million). *Id.* at 14–15. On the other hand, Connor's prior research of 55 international cartels indicated, at 11, that the international cartels affected at least 211 billion, thereby causing $ 3.65 billion per cartel in Table 5. *See id.* at 5.

[185] *Id.* at 13. Global cartels lasts for the longest year (6.0 median years), followed by EU-wide cartels (5.5), single nation in EU (3.5). *See id.* at 11.

[186] *Id.* at 21.

nearly matches other research studies.[187] With calculation of Consumers' Damage [CD] under this thesis,[188] median CD of the global cartel is around US $ 770 million ($ 2.64 billion * 29 % = $ 765.6 million).[189]

The global cartels invoked severe sanctions through major competition agencies, particularly U.S. DOJ. The level of enforcement in developing countries is less developed than that in major industrialized countries with strict attitudes. The OECD report, a survey of eighteen nonmembers' anti-cartel enforcements, demonstrates that only four states imposed fines on price-fixing or bid-rigging. Since the report includes domestic cartels, enforcements against, particularly, international cartels, from the developing world would be much trivial in light of the fact that an investigation against an international cartel faces many hurdles.[190] The following is the analysis of representative international cartel cases investigated by several competition authorities.

(1) Graphite Electrodes Cartel
1) Summary of Fact

The UCAR International Inc. (UCAR U.S.) with several subsidiary companies is one of the largest manufactures of graphite electrodes[191] in the world with each subsidiary incorporated under the law of its principal place of business. SGL Carbon Aktiengessellschaft (SGL AG) with many subsidiaries, a corporation of Germany, is also one of the world leaders in manufacturing and trading graphite electrodes. The other significant participants in the manufacture, and trade of graphite electrodes are Showa Denko, Tokai, Nippon Carbon Co., SEC Co. (Japan), VAW Carbon Gmbh (Germany), and the Carbide Graphite Group (USA). The global market for supplying graphite electrodes is concentrated in light of the facts that around fifty areas produced approximately one million tons in the global estimate, and that the UCAR, SGL, and the other companies supplied 80 % of the global need.[192]

Representatives of SGL, UCAR, and other significant manufactures met and reached an agreement to restrict production capacity, to allocate the sales volume

[187] *Id. See* Connor (2003), at 11. Average overcharge in 32 cases with accurate information was around 30 % of sales. Similarly, the average overcharge of 98 international cartels with incomplete data, was 28 % of affected sales. Meanwhile, median overcharges for cartels, both domestic and international, are between 15 and 20 % since a domestic cartel places less overcharge than an international one. *See also* OECD Global Forum on Competition (GFC) (2003), pp. 4–7.

[188] *See* Chap. 2. 2. 2. B(5).

[189] Multiplying affected sales by overcharge rate is CD of a global cartel(s).

[190] See OECD GFC (2003), 7 and Annex C at 27–28. China (6500), Estonia (639), Latvia (0.7 % of annual turnover), and Peru (1800 per each respondent and 900) specified the amount of imposed fines (EUR). For in-detail hurdles, refer to III. 3. (3).

[191] Graphite electrodes are ceramic-moulded columns of graphite used in the production of steel in electric arc furnaces through conducting electric current into a furnace accompanied with high temperature.

[192] The total production is based on 1998 statistics. The market share data comes from the in-house report of SGL in Nov. 1996. KFTC, 심결 [Decision], 1.나.(2)(가)(2002국협0250) (Apr. 4, 2002).

with exports to the graphite electrodes market in each participant's country, to divide the global market, to provide neither rebate nor discount, and to fix prices in the global and regional markets in May, 1992. Since that time until June 1997, meetings among the representatives of the manufacturers continued to convene to discuss in-detail issues and monitoring the enforcement. During the cartel-operating period, the prices of graphite electrodes increased 48.9 % in South Korea,[193] 50 % in the EU,[194] 50–60 % in the U.S.[195] and around 100 % in Canada.[196]

2) Penalty

The cartel was uncovered and prosecuted in the U.S. The investigation was much facilitated by information submitted under its leniency program. The U.S. Department of Justice (DOJ) imposed a fine in the total amount of US $ 290.8 million on seven corporate defendants during the indictment procedure under Sec. 1 of the Sherman Act. The defendants plead guilty and consented to pay the fines, which a court approved. The DOJ indicted former employees of UCAR International, and the president of SGL Carbon, and most of them plead guilty and agreed with the individual fines and jail time.[197] The judicial body approved the guilty pleas.

The EU Competition Commission treated the cartel as a serious infringement of the EC competition rules, and imposed a total of US$ 275.8 million (euro 195.7)[198] fines under Art. 81 of the EC-Treaty and Art. 53 of the EEA-Agreement.

Canada's Court of Justice agreed with imposing a total of US $ 24.95 (Canadian Dollar[CD]$24.95) million on the defendants who pleaded guilty.[199] Two former executives of UCAR International were fined after guilty pleas.[200] The penalties were based on a violation of Sec. 46 (1) of the Competition Act of

---

[193] *See id.*, 2.가.(3).

[194] Europa, *Press Release: Commission Fines Eight Companies in Graphite Electrode Cartel* (July 18, 2001), *available at* http://europa.eu/rapid (visited on 1 Apr. 2008).

[195] OECD, Hard Core Cartels, pp. 35–36 (2003).

[196] Canada Competition Bureau (CB), *New Release: Mitsubishi Fined $1,000,000 for Aiding and Abetting Graphite Electrode Cartel* (12 May 2005), *available at* http://www.competition bureau.gc.ca (visited on 25 Sep. 2007).

[197] Followings are in-detail sentences: former president with US$ 1.25 million and 17 month jail, former employee with $ 1 million and 9 month jail, and president of SGL Carbon with $10 million. KFTC (2004), 1.다. <Table 3>.

[198] Total fine of European Court of Justice was Euro 195.7. Europa, Press release: Competition: Commission welcomes judgments of the Court of Justice in SGL Carbon and Showa Denko Cases (Graphite Electrodes cartel) MEMO/06/258 (29 June 2006). Exchange rate of US$ 1.00 equals to Euro 0.7095 as of 24 Sep. 2007.

[199] KFTC (2004), Table 3; Industry Canada, *News Release: Nippon Carbon Pleads Guilty to Participating in International Graphite Electrodes Cartel* (8 Dec 2005), *available at* http://www.ic.gc.ca (last visited on Sep. 25, 2007); Canada CB (2005). Exchange rate of currency of US$ 1.00 as of 24 Sep. 2007 is CD$ 1.0002, which is almost the same value.

[200] Two individuals were with no jail sentence but fine of a total CD$ 0.12 million. Canada CB (2005).

Table 2.1 The graphite electrodes cartel investigation of countries

	Scope of market (US$ million: from May 1992 to 1997) (ratio to the world market)	Total corporate fines (US$ million)	Individual fines and jails (US$ million/ months)
U.S.		290.8 (48.4 %)	12.25/17 and 9 each
EU		275.8 (45.9 %)	N/A
Canada	440 (high power) (3.9 %)	24.95 (4.2 %)	N/A
S. Korea	450 (ultra high power) (4 %)[a]	9.58 (1.6 %)	N/A
		601.13	

[a]In order to have correct comparison, the work period of the cartel is confined from May, '92 to '97. KFTC-issued data from '92 to '98 was US$ 553 million, but import in '98 was excluded. The cartel-caused harm from '92 to '98 is estimated to be around US$ 139 million, around 25% of the total import. KFTC (2004), 3.

Canada.[201] Private actions in damages were also filed, one of which ended up with a payment of CD$ 29 million to Canadian steel companies.

The Japan Fair Trade Commission did not impose a fine but issued warnings to four companies that were suspected of violating the Antimonopoly Act of Japan. Meanwhile, the Korea Fair Trade Commission (KFTC) imposed a total of around US $ 9.57 million on six defendants in 2002.[202] The cartelistic activities fall on the violation of MRFTA Art. 19 Sec. 1 para. 1 which prohibits competitors from collusively fixing, maintaining, and changing a price (Table 2.1).

3) Assessment

An analysis of the results reveals that the U.S. has strict enforcement records while S. Korea, although its commerce under the influence of the cartel is similar to that of Canada, has a more lenient anti-cartel penalty record than Canada. Korea's under-enforcement against the international cartel is affirmed by the fact that the level of penalty in the graphite electrodes cartel is still the highest among international cartel enforcements in S. Korea during its quarter-century competition law history.

S. Korea, however, hit the international graphite electrodes cartel with a much stronger penalty than any other developing country under the influence of the cartel. It was the global market which the international cartel targeted at through allocating the market and sales volume, restricting production capacities, fixing price, and preventing each member from giving a rebate or discount. The vast majority of the markets in the world did not even know or at least attempt to punish the international cartel after a few advanced countries revealed the conspiracy. Korea, as one of the developing countries, did not notice the cartelistic activities until the competition law enforcement in the advanced countries was announced in public. KFTC could enjoy unprecedented extraterritorial application of MRFTA thanks to

[201]The Attorney General of Canada, Statement of Allegations by the Attorney General of Canada, para. 23 (2005).

[202]KR W 8,812 million equals to US $ 9,567,861 dollar at currency exchange rate (US$ 1 = KRW 921) as of 24 Sep. 2007.

wisely-planned investigation, consensus within the organization, and leadership of KFTC chief.[203]

S. Korea, one of the countries with a relatively short competition law history, found difficulty in dealing with procedural obstacles of an international cartel investigation. It is through international law that international cooperation for reducing the obstacles can be secured. In order to achieve an international law, participation of advanced competition authorities in the creation of a legal frame for international cooperation is very important.

(2) Vitamin Cartel

1) Summary of Fact

Bulk vitamins are used for manufacturing animal feeds, medicine, foods, and cosmetics. In 1989, four major companies dominating the world's bulk vitamin market agreed to allocate the market among themselves, and follow the price increase announced by a cartel member. The producers, through regular meetings, developed a cartel conspiracy and made an in-detail plan. The participants tried to maintain allocated market share by exchanging sales information and managing the quantity of their sales. The meetings progressed with four levels—the top level, heads of marketing, global product marketing level, and regional product marketing level-joined by the remaining seven companies. The arrangement had continued until 1998 when the members noticed the US DOJ investigations starting a year in advance against themselves. In 2 years after the notice, the increased price during the cartel period dropped below the 1989 level.[204]

2) Penalty

The U.S. DOJ prosecuted eleven companies under the violation of Sec.1 of the Sherman Act and imposed an US$ 910.5 million fine with a guilty plea. The judiciary body approved it. Subsequently, the private action from direct purchasers of the vitamin in the U.S. was settled with US$ 2.4 billion.[205]

The EU Competition Commission imposed US$ 1205.4 (Euro 855.2) million on eight companies on the basis that they violated Art. 81 of the Maastricht Treaty on European Union(EU)—currently Art.101 of the Treaty of Lisbon, and Art. 53 of the EEA agreement.

Meanwhile, the DOJ of Canada indicted 12 companies for their collusion under Art. 45 of the Competition Act of Canada. All the companies pleaded guilty and accepted around US$ 96.8 (CD$ 96.8) million in fines.

---

[203] *See id.* at 5.

[204] For example, import price of vitamin E in South Korea increased up by 46 % from 1989 until 1998, but dropped by 52 % to below the original price of 1989. KFTC, *Press Release: KFTC imposing surcharges on international vitamin cartel* [보도자료: 공정위 비타민 국제카르텔에 과징금부과], at 8 (2003).

[205] The private action of foreign direct purchasers was, however, dismissed on the lack of jurisdiction because Foreign Trade Antitrust Improvements Act of 1982 (FTAIA) could not give rise to a claim from foreign injury. Hoffman-La Roche LTC et al. v. Empagran et al., 124 S.Ct. 2359 (2004).

Table 2.2 Comparison of penalties in each country (US$ million)

	Public Penalty (ratio)	Private action	Total (ratio)
U.S.	910.5 (41 %)	2400	3310.5 (71 %)
EU	1205.4 (54 %)	N/A	1205.4 (26 %)
Canada	96.8 (4 %)	0.58	97.38 (2.1 %)
Australia	22.5 (1 %)	N/A	22.5 (0.5 %)
Japan	N/A	N/A	0.0
Swiss	N/A	N/A	0.0
S. Korea	3.7 (0.2 %)	N/A	3.7 (0.08 %)
Total	2238.9[a]		4639.48

[a]OECD revealed that annual worldwide turnover of the vitamin products during the conspiracy period was US$ 3.3 billion. Agreements on some of the products, not all, lasted as long as 10 years. In considering the fact that not all products were under the conspiracy, total affected commerce is less than $ 33 billion. If conservatively presumed, 50 %, 16.5 million, is affected, total fine, around 2.24 billion, is 13.6 % of the affected commerce. Since the median cartel mark-up in 14 cases ranged from 15 to 20 %, the conservative presumption, 13.6 %, indicated that total public penalty is a little less than harm. *See id.*, n.13

The Australian Competition Committee prosecuted three companies for price-fixing and market-allocation of animal-feeding vitamins. All the defendants plead guilty and received a fine of US$ 22.5 (AU$ 26) million. For cases of other developed countries, Japan issued a warning without a penalty while Switzerland rendered a consent order without a fine.[206]

3) Developing Countries' Enforcement

The KFTC, after hearing of the advanced countries competition law enforcements, launched an investigation against the cartel with the presumption that the cartel affected the market in S. Korea in 2002. With data shared by the advanced competition enforcers, the KFTC revealed the effect of the cartel on Korea's market and imposed a total of US$ 3.73 (KRW 3433) million in fines against six companies under Art. 19. 1. para. 1 of the MRFTA. The following table compares the ratio of vitamin sales and monetary penalties against the cartel (Table 2.2).

The under-enforcement of a monetary penalty against cartels in South Korea is demonstrated by the comparison of the ratio of the scope between Korea's market and the global market. As Table 2.3 indicates, the ratio of the vitamin market in South Korea to the global market and the ratio of cartel members' profits in S. Korea to their profits in the global market are around 1.5 %. Meanwhile, the ratios of penalties between S.Korea and the other advanced countries are 0.2 % in criminal (including administrative) fines and 0.08 % in monetary sanctions including private actions. Provided the damages of the cartel accrue in proportion to the ratio of market scope or profits, the penalty remains much below the ratio of

[206]OECD (2002), 35.

Table 2.3 Comparison of market scope: global and Korean Markets (US$ million)

	All defendants' total profits for 10 years of the cartel operation	Their sales of cartelized vitamins (A, E, D3 and AD 3) in 1998
The whole markets in the world	18,000	1687
South Korean market	185	26.5
Ratio (S. Korean/Global)	**1.5 %**	**1.5 %**

See Brief for Certain Professors of Economics as Amici Curiae Supporting Respondents, Hoffmann-La Roche Ltd. v. Empargran, 542 U.S. 155 (2004) (No. 03-724), 2003 U.S. BRIEFS 724, 9—11. Compare it to KFTC Decision, 제 2003—098호 [case number 2003-098] (2003 국협 0396), 2003년 4월 29일 [April 29, 2003], Korean version at http://www.ftc.go.kr. When the numbers on the second line are divided by those on the first line, the ratio is around 1.5 % which reveals the scope of Korea's market to the global market

harms. It means that penalty regimes, both public and private, are less active in South Korea than advanced countries.

The other developing countries, except Brazil, did not even launch an investigation or seriously punish the cartel participants even though the cartel had a negative impact on their countries.[207] Procedural hurdles, which the developing countries might experience in investigating foreign companies with no branches in the countries as well as their immature capacities, contributed to the barren results.[208] International cooperation to support competition law enforcement in the developing countries, as well as their own efforts to entrench in a competition culture, is necessary to balance the level of anti-cartel law enforcement with the cartel-causing damages.

2.6 Conclusion

A cartel is an agreement or a collective action to restrain reciprocal business activities among plural independent entrepreneurs competing in the same level of a business industry to prevent competition thereby securing extra profit. Domestic competition laws have adopted this definition under their cartel regulations. However, the coverage of this definition is less appropriate in achieving effective international cartel regulation because some cartels in the definition cause more

[207]The Brazilian eight-year-long investigation under the hardship of gathering information led to the imposition of fine, total US$ 4.3 million or 15 million Brazilian reais. Although the conspiracies affected many regional markets in the world, the penalties were issued mostly from developed countries. OECD (2003), at 37–38.

[208]*Id.* at 34–35.

pro-competitive effects than anticompetitive ones and individual nations have developed different rules on cartels with hybrid effects. In order to achieve international law on cartels, the international community needs to focus on hard core cartel (HHC) activities with several types of categories, narrower than the definition, because most countries agree with the necessity of regulating such cartels and because international agreements have been developed with a narrow focus. Recent activities of regulating cartels in the OECD and ICN have concentrated on cartels under the narrow HHC definition.

Cartels function to control competition in the markets, which brings inefficiencies to whole industries, harm to consumers, a loss of consumers' surpluses, and undermines both the trust in social integrity and sincere entrepreneurship.

On the other hand, cartels can save the waste of financial and personal resources through harsh competition. Severe competition in an economic depression era could not save the related industry or economy in light of past experiences of even advanced market economies. According to economic analyses, mass unemployment and bankruptcies of companies during an extreme financial crisis came from an ineffective financial system, which did not produce sufficient funds, rather than from productive inefficiencies which a competition law aims at eliminating through cartel regulations. Particularly, in economic depressions, emerging or developing economies under an immature financial system have resorted to industrial policies, instead of newly adopted or young competition policies. In an extremely severe economic depression period, it is unexpected for young economies to apply cartel regulations to the same level under normal situations. In order to gather wide participation from emerging markets or developing countries, the international cartel regulation needs to exempt so-called crisis cartels. Even the industrialized countries with an advanced competition law system have approved this type of cartel in their histories.

In addition, although collecting money for investments is necessary in developing market economies, the developing countries usually face insufficient funds for investment. There is a greater chance to raise enough money for innovation and investment when so-called investment cartels are exempted with strict screening procedures.

Moreover, interstate commodity cartels need to be exempted from cartel regulation so that they may reduce extreme price fluctuations. The Intergovernmental producers association (IPA) needs to be under international commodity laws different from the law for typical private cartels. The ICAs under bipartisan membership of consuming countries as well as producing countries operate similar to the IPA under a unilateral membership of producing countries. Except membership and its derivative rules, placing both IPAs and ICAs under the same regulation does not interfere with the development of international commodity law. The IPAs and ICAs share a common concern between them that certain developing countries, particularly CDDCs, have heavily relied on commodities production in exchange of which small-sized producers may manage to earn money for food. International law has developed independent commodity laws for the IPAs and ICAs.

International private cartels, which have prevailed since the 1990s, generate bigger average damages, US$ 2.64 billion per cartel, than average damages of domestic ones, $ 1.5 billion per cartel. The international cartels are formed in a highly concentrated market with a few companies with a homogenous product where entry barriers exist. The graphite electrodes cartel and the vitamin cartel are main examples of international private cartels. In a comparison of anti-cartel enforcements in the industrialized countries under the Table 2.1, South Korea as well as other developing countries demonstrated much lower level of public and private enforcements against two cartels. Such under-enforcements are due to less experience, insufficient support, and procedural hurdles. The international support for cartel regulation enforcement needs to be promoted.

To utilize international support for cartel regulations, international cartel law should focus on private cartels with priority since there have been growing research studies on the cartels sufficient enough to reach a consensus among countries.

References

Book

American Bar Association (ABA) (2004) Section of Antitrust Law, Handbook on the antitrust aspect of standard setting

Competition Committee Survey of OECD (2003) Hard Core cartels: recent progress and challenges ahead. OECD

Connor JM (2003) Private International Cartels: effectiveness, welfare & antitrust enforcement. Purdue Univ

Encyclopaedia Britannica (2007) The New Encyclopaedia Britannica, vol 2 Micropaedia, 15th ed. Encyclopaedia Britannica Inc

Edwards CD (1976) Economic and political aspects of international cartels. Arno Press, A New York Times Company, New York

Eatwell J, Milgate M, Newman P (1998) The new palgrave: a dictionary of economics, vol 1. Stockton Press Ltd., Houndmills

Friedman J (2007) Dictionary of business terms, Barron's, 4th ed

Fox E, Sullivan L, Peritz R (2004) Cases & materials on U.S. Antitrust in Global Context, 2nd ed. West Pub., New York

Garner BA (2003) Black's Law Dictionary, 2nd pocket ed

Greenwald D (ed) (1994) The Mcgraw-Hill encyclopedia of economics, 2nd ed. R.R. Donnelley & Sons Co., Chicago

Harry First (2003) Evolving toward What? The Development of International Antitrust. In: Drexl J (ed) The future of transnational antitrust-from comparative to common competition law. Kluwer Law Int'l, Alphen aan den Rijn, pp 33–38

Huh C-H (2002) Korea's Monopoly Restraint and Fair Trade Act [MRFTA] & Cartel Regulation [공정거래법과 카르텔규제], Bi-Bong Pub, Seoul, Korea

Kabir-ur-Rahman K (1982) The Law & The organization of international commodity agreements. Martinus Nijhoff Pub., Leiden

Korea Fair Trade Commission (KFTC) (2004) Whitepaper [공정거래백서], KFTC

LeClair MS (2000) International commodity market and the roles of cartels. M.E. Sharpe Inc., Armonk

Rodger B, Macculloch A (eds) (2000) The UK competition act, at 172–173. In: Rodger, Macculloch (eds) Hart Pub., The Rocks
Rudolph JRP (1996) Competition policy in America, history, rhetoric, law, rev. ed. Oxford Univ. Press, Oxford
Scherer FM (1994) Competition policies for an integrated world economy. Brookings Inst., Washington
Stocking GW, Watkins MW (1948) Cartels or competition? The Twentieth Century Fund
Stocking GW, Watkins MW (1946) Cartels in Action, The Twentieth Century Fund
UNCTAD (2007) Model law on competition. United Nations

Thesis, Papers

Baker DI (2001) The use of criminal law remedies to Deter and Punish Cartels and Bid-rigging, 69 Geo. Wash. L. Rev. 693 (2001)
Baumol W (2001) When is inter-firm coordination beneficial? The case of innovation. In: 19 International journal of industrial organization, p 727
Brown B (1994) Developing countries in the international trade order. 14 N.Ill.U.L.Rev. 347:369–370
Bower JL, Rhenman EA (2003) Benevolent Cartels, 63. Harvard Bus Rev 4:124–132
Bronz G (1956) An international trade organization: the second attempt. 69 Harvard L Rev 440:466–467
Connor J, Helmers G (2007) Statistics on modern private international cartels: 1990–2005. The American Antitrust Institute (AAI) Working Paper No. 07-01
CFC (2006) Current Trends & the New Development Role of Commodities, Nov. 2006, available at http://www.common-fund.org/download/actualiteit/CT06jelle.pdf. Visited on 10 Jul. 2008
Edward Q (1994) The failure of international commodity agreements: forms, functions, and implications, 22 Denv. J Int Law Policy 530
Gilbert C (2005) International Commodity Agreements, Jan. 14, 2005, available at http://grade.unitn.it/people/gilbert/file/Attachment_10.pdf. Visited on 10 Jul. 2008
JFTC (2002) Capacity building to Combat Cartels in Japan, at http://www.jftc.go.jp/eacpf/05/APECTrainingProgram2002/Japan1.pdf. Visited on 25 Feb. 2008
McFadden EJ (1986) The collapse of tin: restructuring a failed commodity agreement, 80 A J I L 811:815
OECD (2002) Report on the Nature and Impact of Hard Core Cartel and Sanctions against Cartels under National Competition Laws, DAFFE/COMP(2002)7
OECD Global Forum on Competition (2003) How enforcement against private anti-competitive conduct has contributed to economic development, CCNM/GF/COMP(2003)7
Resch A (2008) Phases of competition policy in Europe, Inst. of European Studies Paper 050401, 2005, available at http://repositories.cdlib.org/ies/050401/. Visited on Jul. 10, 2008

Chapter 3
Legal Status and Historical Background of Cartels in International Law

Abstract International cartels are categorized into two types, an agreement among competing companies to restrict competition and a loose association, often with legal personality, established by such agreements consisting of competing companies. As international organizations under suspicion of allegedly an international cartel, there are OPEC, ITU, and IATA. OPEC is not fit to a cartel under competition law but international commodity agreement among states with sovereignty since element, such as no penalty against cheating, oil as nonrenewable natural resources, and the necessity of sustainable development, are not fit to characteristics of a cartel under competition law but international commodity agreement. The ITU as a standard-setting organization is not an international cartel which violates competition law. The IATA consisting of private airlines, on the contrary, has the possibility of cartel because it provides practices of passenger rate or air cargo fee setting. The counterargument of nonbinding recommendation is weak. Although international competition law has experienced failures of reaching concrete codes, cartel regulation of international competition law, currently, has grown up with multilateral agreements as well as bilateral agreements. By reducing fear of developing countries that international cartel regulation interfere with their domestic economic policies, among other things, including industrial policy, international organizations' effort to have effective international cartel regulation can increase the probability of success.

Keywords International cartels · International commodity agreement · OPEC · IATA · International competition law

3.1 Opening International Law Era: Infant Stage

The international community's effort to institutionalize free trade and to liberalize cross-border commerce since the end of WWII has resulted, during the last decade of twentieth century, in the establishment of the European Union (EU) in 1993, the Word Trade Organization (WTO) in 1995 as a result of the Uruguay Round, and the Doha Declaration proclaiming that competition policy, along with around 20 issues

J.S. Lee, *Strategies to Achieve a Binding International Agreement on Regulating Cartels*, DOI 10.1007/978-981-10-2756-7_3

Table 3.1 Development of international agreements on nontariff barriers

Title of the round	Its period	Major issue(s)
Kennedy round	1964–1967	Special-rule-based tariff reduction, Development, and nontariff barriers
Tokyo round	1973–1979	Negotiation on nontariff barriers
Uruguay round	1986–1992	Binding Nontariff rules, launching WTO, binding trade dispute settlement procedure

beside goods and services, should be negotiated in a multilateral agreement. Such achievements are contrasted with the failure to ratify the Havana Charter for an International Trade Organization (ITO) after World War II, an attempt to launch a comprehensive set of rules and procedures with detailed rules covering restrictive business practices or competition law. The failure was due to domestic opposition of American protectionist groups to the exceptions to free market principles that were established in order to facilitate the negotiation of diverse economic levels.[1] However, the commercial policy sections of the Charter were implemented in 1948 as the General Agreement on Tariffs and Trade (GATT), which played an important role in promoting free trade legislations and policies in the world especially by the launching of several free trade rounds, such as Kennedy Round, Tokyo Round, and the Uruguay Round (Table 3.1).[2]

The ongoing trend toward establishing free trade trend challenged competition laws and policies in individual countries with an attempt to promote the level of domestic competition up to the global business standard. The European Community (EC)'s efforts to integrate members' markets under competition law led to the EC Treaty of 1957 Article 85, later Maastricht Treaty (1992) Article 81 and Treaty on the Functioning of the EU (2007) Article 101 as a main cartel law of little change. Since the following treaties did not make substantial changes to the competition provisions of the EC Treaty in 1957, competition law on a cartel originally dates back to the EC Treaty with Article 85. Besides the EU's competition law, the WTO adopted competition policy as one of the multinegotiation subjects in the Singapore Ministerial Conference in 1996. The Doha Declaration urged further negotiation to take place regarding competition policy although the Doha Agenda has been at a standstill since 2003. Furthermore, there are bilateral agreements and multilateral agreements to contribute to international competition law. Among industrialized countries, bilateral agreements for cooperating enforcement of competition law include methods to alleviate conflicts arising from divergence of competition laws and different national interests. Multilateral agreements are currently in progress to achieve binding regulations.

This chapter treats the issue of the legal status of international cartels in relation to three cases, where it will be investigated whether the cases fall within the realm

[1]Baldwin (2004), *at* 3.

[2]*See id.* at 4–7 for the in-detail achievements of the Rounds.

of cartel. This chapter will also deal with the development of domestic cartel regulations and the necessity of international legal measures in response to the emergence of international cartels, as well as shifting its focus toward the development of international commodity law. Finally, this chapter will return to the issues of competition law, examining past efforts to achieve multilateral cartel regulations by international organizations. The discussion will soon be followed by the development of cartel regulation in bilateral or regional agreement.

3.2 Legal Status of International Cartel in International Law

A. Necessity of Examining Legal Status

It is important, in the process of regulating an international cartel, to characterize it in terms of international law. According to the configuration of legal status, the international cartel can have different legal treatments in terms of rights and duties under international law.

Some international organizations, such as OPEC, ITU, and IATA, have been suspected as international cartel. The Organization of the Petroleum Exporting Countries (OPEC) has managed to limit crude oil output in its member countries, thereby affecting oil price in the global crude oil market. The International Telecommunication Union (ITU) has had to endure accusations that it had restrained competition in the telecommunication industry by allocating radio frequency spectrum (RFS) and settling account rate in international call. The International Air Transportation Association (IATA) has been charged as a cartel, regulating prices, allocating schedules and routes in order to promote its members' profits. All the cases involve international organizations, respectively, consisting of states (OPEC), private companies (IATA), and both (ITU). Investigating the legal status of each organization will affect analysis of the cases.

B. Legal Status of International Cartel

(1) Elements of International Organization

International organizations are formed and governed by its constituent international agreement, its charter, and laws pertaining to such an agreement and international organization.[3] International organizations, for the most part, have legal personalities. A legal personality requires three elements, duties which incur legal responsibility, rights which allow the claiming of benefits through related laws, and the capacity to enter into a legal relationship with other legal persons.[4] As the International Court of Justice (ICJ) stated at reparation for injury suffered in the

[3]The American Law Institute (ALI), Restatement (Third) of Foreign Relations Law of the United States, Part II, Chap. 2, Introductory Note (1987).

[4]Okeke (1973), at p. 19.

service of the UN case, the rights and duties of an organization must depend on its purposes and functions as specified or implied in its constituent document as well as practices in light of the needs of its community.[5] Otherwise, members (consisting mostly of states that agreed to become members with expectation that the organization's activities would remain active in constitutional provisions in spite of its sovereign limitation) would refuse to collaborate.[6] Although the power to enter into relationship with other international persons has been considered necessary to international organizations, it needs to be examined whether a particular treaty or agreement is relevant to the purposes and competence of such international organizations,[7] which indicates the limitation of capacity of international organizations compared to states.

(2) The IGCs, IPAs, and ICAs as International Organizations

Intergovernmental producers' associations (IPAs) or intergovernmental companies (IGCs) were generally established by treaties which stipulate that they shall be under respective municipal law rather than international law including international arbitration or generally accepted principles of law. Judge Lauterpach's opinion in the report on the Law of Treaties is noteworthy in deciding whether such an association falls on an international organization; in a case when parties selected one of the municipal laws as governing law but the constituent agreement met elements of a treaty, he stated that the applicable municipal law is transformed into conventional international law and subsequent transactions are still under principles of international law and rules interpreting treaties.[8] IGCs, IPAs, and intergovernmental commodity agreements (ICAs) can have rights and take duties under international law with distinction to a private cartel. They can make international agreements under their constituent agreements. As a result, such companies or agreements fall on international organization as they fulfill the requirement, and thereby fall under the international organization law.

(3) An International Cartel as an International Organization?

On the other hand, a cartel defined by (i) an agreement among private companies to restrict competition itself or (ii) a loose association of private companies established by such agreement, is rarely qualified for an international organization. The association-typed cartel may be qualified for a limited legal personality, but the agreement-typed cartel without establishing an independent entity does not have a legal personality at all although its members of private competing companies are acknowledged to have limited legal capacity to do transactions in international

[5]Advisory Opinion, 1949 I.C.J.,174 (April 11), at 178–179.

[6]It is called 'implied powers doctrine.' *See* Rama-Montaldo, 44 Brit. Y.B.I.L. at 123–124 (1970).

[7]Article 6 of the UN Convention on Treaties Concluded between States and International Organizations or between two or more international organizations. *See* Fitzmaurice, *The Law and Procedure of the International Court of Justice*, 30 Brit. Y.B.I.L. 2 (1953).

[8]Lauterpacht, Report on the Law of Treaties, UN (AC/4/163); Okeke (1973), 219.

law.[9] In light of the three elements of legal personality, an independent duty, the possibility of claim to enjoy benefit of right or law, and an independent capacity to do legal and valid affairs related to its purpose,[10] the agreement-typed cartel does not meet any of the three elements. On the contrary, an association established under a cartel agreement can fulfill all the elements.

First, the agreement-typed cartel does not take any responsibility itself. Rather, the participating companies will abide by a legal obligation such as restriction of competitive business practices. It reflects the same principle in contract law that a contract between individuals does not incur liability on the contract itself but on the individuals. On the other hand, the association-typed cartel can incur a duty pursuant to the objective of constituent agreement.

Regarding a claim conferred on the cartel, associations accept legitimate claims under their constituent agreements or an organization-related law when the associations are acknowledged as legitimate and valid under standard of cartel regulations. However, the agreement-typed cartel without establishing any entity allows few, if any, claims.

The element of a legal capacity to do something valid and legitimate independently from members invokes a sensitive issue of validity and legitimacy of cartel. A cartel operating as an association of private competing companies may have an independent legal capacity if it meets the standard of legitimacy under cartel regulation and other provisions of competition law. In addition, the association-typed cartel should pass tests of validity including restraint of competition so that the cartel may be acknowledged to have a legal capacity. On the other hand, the agreement-typed cartel does not have any legal capacity as an agreement itself does not remain active independently in public relations from its members which act for their own interests.

In short, the association-typed cartels, acknowledged as legitimate and valid, fall under the realm of international organizations. However, the agreement-typed cartels do not satisfy any of the elements of international organization regardless of the result of legitimacy and validity tests.

(4) International Cartel as International Agreement

The agreement-typed international cartels may be categorized as international agreements among private companies with limited legal personality. The international agreements are not treaties because a treaty covers the agreements between subjects of international law pursuant to international law. Although the Vienna

---

[9]*See* Okeke (1973), 215. Okeke states, "though they (private corporations and nongovernmental organizations) can not be said to enjoy international personality as ascribed to international governmental organizations, nonetheless, they conduct activities on the international plane with often significant political importance and with little or no governmental control. Their status is different from that of public international organizations." He acknowledges international legal personality of private companies although the personality is more confined than intergovernmental organizations.

[10]Okeke (1973), 19.

Convention on the Law of Treaties in 1969 is limitedly applied to treaties between states only, a treaty may be extended to cover international agreement between a state and an international organization as a subject of international law.[11] In light of the U.S. Constitution Art. 6 that a treaty has the same power as legislation of Congress and need to go through constitutional procedures, a treaty may not be extended to cover the international agreement among private companies. Private companies, conspiring to restrict competition, enjoy no legal personality under international law as their activities are not treated as legitimate; a cartel agreement among competing private companies does not fulfill the requirement.

Moreover, the agreements must be governed by international law regardless of the intents of parties. However, the cartel agreement falls under the realm of domestic competition laws tending to enjoy currently extraterritorial application. The jurisdiction of domestic competition law has been acknowledged through laws of advanced countries without respect to intents of participating companies. As a result, the international cartel agreement is a kind of international agreement, not a treaty, among competing private companies because the companies usually represent diverse nationalities. The cartel agreement has been treated as illegal and void in countries with advanced competition law practices.

C. Some Intergovernmental Organizations under Suspicion of Cartels

Practices of some international organizations are condemned as cartel activities which arguably restrict competition in markets in relation to their works. It is suspected that under the category do fall the organizations representing countries with commodities such as nonrenewable natural resource and organizations setting international standards.

The international organizations consisting of commodity-producing sovereign countries are often the objects of blame since their activities have a similar effect on the market as do those of international cartels. Nonmember countries argue that these organizations set high prices amidst low production levels, thereby causing a transfer of wealth from consuming countries to producing countries. Among other organizations, the OPEC has been suspected to be in charge of a competition-restricting cartel for decades. The impact of the OPEC with 13 members[12] on the global oil market is expected to increase in the near future as the accelerated levels of consumption in emerging countries much outweighs the lagging supply due to the delay of production projects in new provinces and the limited production in mature areas of non-OPEC member states.[13]

---

[11]ALI, Restatement (3rd) of Foreign Relations Law, Sec. 303 comment (a) (1987) explains the authority of the U.S president to make a treaty on the premise that any treaty to which the U.S. is subject needs the participation of the U.S. president. *See* Damrosch et al. (2001), at page 455, which states that an international agreement between international organizations may be treated as a treaty when they are qualified as subjects of international law.

[12]Ed Crooks and Javier Blas, *Angola joins cartel: OPEC expansion increases US dependence*, Fin. Times, January 3, 2007, at 4.

[13]Javier Blas, *World will face oil crunch 'in five years'*, Fin. Times, July 10, 2007, at 1.

In addition, international standard-setting organizations, particularly the ITU, regulate the development of technology by settling a single global standard. Nonmember countries argue that the standard-setting of the ITU has created an entry barrier to newly developing technologies and that it supports the maintaining of the market power of existent member states in the global telecommunication market, thereby falling under the category of a cartel activity.

(1) Organization of the Petroleum Exporting Countries (OPEC)
1) Decisions of the U.S. Courts

American judicial body has had a chance to decide whether the activities of the OPEC had violated Sec. 1 of the Sherman Act as cartel activities. A labor union, as a plaintiff, filed a suit by arguing that it had endured the injury of paying higher price for gasoline at the gas stations because of the anticompetitive actions of OPEC and its member countries. The suit for damages and injunctive relief against the OPEC and its 13 member states[14] was decided by the U.S. District Court of Central Division of California and Court of Appeals for the Ninth Circuit.[15] The District Court dismissed the suit on the basis that OPEC could not legally be served either under the Foreign Sovereign Immunities Act of 1976 (FSIA) or under the International Organizations Immunities Act (IOIA).[16] With regard to the suits against the other 13 nations, the District Court dismissed the plaintiffs' claim for damages, designating them as the indirect purchasers under the *Illinois Brick* rule.[17]

For the remaining injunctive relief against the 13 countries, after allowing the plaintiffs as indirect purchasers to maintain the suit,[18] the District Court held that the subject-matter jurisdiction of the action against the member states could not be

---

[14]International Association of Machinists and Aerospace Workers (IAM) alleged that price-setting activities of OPEC and its members violated Sec. 1 of the Sherman Act, and brought injunctive relief under 15 U.S.C. Sec. 26, Sec. 16 of the Clayton Act, and a default judgment against OPEC along with 13 foreign nations in an action for damages under 15 U.S.C. 15, Sec. 4 of the Clayton Act in December 1978.

[15]International Association of Machinists and Aerospace Workers (IAM) v. OPEC, 477 F. Supp. 553; 1979 U.S.Dist. LEXIS 9713;1979–2 Trade Cas.(CCH) P62, 868 (U.S.Dis.Ct, C.D. CA, 1979), *aff'd by* 649 F.2d 1354, 1981–1 Trade Cases P 64,143 (C.A. 9th Cir. 1981).

[16]FSIA applies only to foreign sovereignties, not international organization, and IOIA applies only to those international organizations with the U.S. as the member, which is not a case of OPEC. The plaintiff admitted the hurdle for legal service to OPEC. *See* 477 F.Supp.560.

[17]In the damage action, the court disallowed indirect purchasers from bringing damage action under Illinois Brick Co. v. Illinois, 97 S.Ct. at 2068, and the suit from falling on exceptions. *Id.* at 560–563.

[18]The District Court cites Mid-West Paper Products Company v. Continental Group, Inc. 596 F.2d 573, 591–2 (3d Cir. 1979). *See id.* at 564. The test for standing under Sec. 16 of the Clayton Act (injunctive relief) has been framed under a proximate cause standard that is less constrained than that under Sec. 4 (the treble damage action) and which might in fact be no more rigorous than the general rule of standing.

allowed when the sovereign immunity[19] applies to the alleged cartel activities of the countries.[20] The District Court dismissed the case by stating that the activities of alleged price-fixing or output reduction did not fall under the commercial activity exception to the sovereign immunity, thereby resulting in the lack of jurisdiction on the basis of the sovereign immunity principle.[21]

As to the 'commercial activity' exception of the sovereign immunity, especially, the Court further analyzed the pricing mechanism of the members of the OPEC. The pricing involved the so-called 'government take' through levying a tax on foreign oil-extracting companies or charging a royalty for the extracted oils, which the Court characterized as governmental rather than commercial in nature under Sec. 1603(d) of FSIA.[22] With the basis of an expert's testimony, the Court pointed to control of supply as a major mechanism of crude oil pricing which, instead of the alleged price-fixing, actually allowed the management of price.[23] With the foundation of various resolutions from the UN General Assembly,[24] the Charter of Economic Rights and Duties of States (CERDS),[25] and the Declaration on the Establishment of a New International Economic Order (NIEO Declaration) in

[19]The sovereign immunity, under which domestic courts must refrain from jurisdiction over a foreign state, is an international law doctrine recognized since the Schooner Exchange v. M'Faddon, 11 U.S. (7 Cranch) 116, 3 L.Ed. 287 (1812) and evolved by the restrictive theory of sovereign immunity adopted in U.S. Foreign Sovereign Immunities Act in 1976. *Id.* at 565.

[20]District courts only have jurisdiction to hear actions against foreign states when the foreign state is not entitled to sovereign immunity either under Sec. 28 U.S.C. 1605(a)(2) or under any applicable international agreement according to Sec. 1330(a) of this title. The question of sovereign immunity is the main question for determining jurisdiction issue. 477 F.Supp. 553, 564; 1979 U.S. Dist.LEXIS 9713, 23. Moreover, 28 U.S.C. sec 1605 (a)(2), by adopting the restrictive sovereign immunity theory, provides that a foreign state shall not be immune from the jurisdiction of courts of the United States or of the States in any case, in which the action is based upon an act outside the territory of the U.S. in connection with a commercial activity of the foreign state elsewhere and that act causes a direct effect in the U.S.

[21]Lastly, the District Court cited the lack of causation between the alleged act and the damage, even with the assumption of the jurisdiction. It further opined that even if the activities were not sovereign but commercial, the evidence did not support the granting of an injunction due to lack of proving the causal connection between the injury and the anticompetitive conduct. 477 F. Supp.553, 553; 1979 U.S.Dist.LEXIS 9713, 9713.

[22]Section 1603(d) defines 'commercial activity' as either a regular course of commercial conduct or a particular commercial transaction or act. The commercial character of an activity shall be determined by reference to the nature of the course of conduct or particular transaction or act, rather than by reference to its purpose.

[23]Dr. Morris A. Adelman, Prof. of Economics at Massachusetts Institute of Technology, was appointed as one of the experts in the field of World Petroleum Economics by the Court. *Id.* at 566.

[24]Resolution 1803, G.A. Res. 1803, Sec. I(1), 17 U.N.GAOR, 2d Comm. 327, U.N.Doc. A/C 2/5 R 850 (1962); Resolution 3171, G.A.Res. 3171, 28 U.N.GAOR 30 (Vol. 1) at 52, U.N.Doc. A/9030 (1973); Resolution 2158, G.A.Res. 2158, Sec I(1), 21 U.N.GAOR, Supp. (No. 16) 29, U. N.Doc. A/6316(1966).

[25]Chap. II, Art. 2(1), U.N. Doc. A/RES/3281 (XXIX) (1974).

1974,[26] along with the U.S. Congress sole power to make rules pertaining to the development of resources under Art. IV, Sec. 3, Cl. 2 of the Constitution, the Court stated that the control over natural resources of a nation stems from the nation's sovereignty.[27] Activities such as the 'government take' and production control were not considered to be commercial activities, but as sovereign activity by establishing the terms and conditions for removing a prime natural resource from its territory. The reasoning on the part of the 13 member states was due to the recognition by the judicial branch of the international law principle that the right to control the production of natural resources belongs to the sovereign power, which must be exercised in the interest of both its national development and its people.

Moreover, the U.S. Court of Appeals for the Ninth Circuit held that, due to the act of state doctrine, a federal court did not have jurisdiction to judge the legality of the sovereign acts of the foreign states. The act of state doctrine, similar to the political question doctrine, reveals the passive nature of the U.S. judicial branch within a structure based on the separation of power, because further examination into the acts of foreign states may intervene with the executive body and the legislative bodies' international diplomacy.[28] Since the Ninth Cir. Court agreed with the significant sovereign nature of OPEC's competition-restriction, it applied the action of state doctrine to the acts of OPEC, thereby leaving no decision on the merit of the case, a decision distinct from that of the lower court. Finally, the Ninth Cir. Court stated, under the proposition that the greater the degree of codification or consensus concerning a particular area of international law, the more appropriate it is for the judiciary to render decisions regarding it, but that there is no international consensus condemning cartels and production agreements although conspiracies in restriction of free trade are explicitly illegal under the U.S. law. Rather, it added that the international community has supported the principle of supreme state sovereignty over natural resources.[29]

2) Collective Acts of Nations Producing the Natural Resource

Although control over natural resources has been declared as a permanent sovereign act, it appears difficult to maintain the sovereign immunity when countries producing the most important energy resource, crude oil, made collective efforts to control over it with result in significant influence on the global market.[30] The sovereign nature of production control is diluted by its strong commercial nature when petroleum-exporting countries work together to curb the global market.

---

[26]G.A.Res. 3201 (S-VI), Sec. 4(e), U.N.GAOR, 6th Spec.Sess., Supp. (No. 1) 3, U.N.Doc. A/9559.

[27]477 F.Supp. 553, 565–67.

[28]*See* IAM v. OPEC, 649 F.2d 1354, 1358–59. *Refer to* this chapter, footnote 14.

[29]*See id,* at 1361.

[30]The IMF Research Department (2000), at p. 8–12, Chap. III. It argues five major changes from higher oil prices, (i) transfer of income from oil consumers to oil producers, (ii) a rise in the cost of production of goods and services in the economy, (iii) impact on the price level and on inflation, (iv) direct and indirect impact on financial markets, and (v) incentives for energy suppliers to increase production and investment, and for oil consumers to economize.

As collective price-fixing or output restriction or market allocation among private multinational companies competing in a global market is proclaimed against international law under the Declaration of the U.N., the collective setting of target price range or output range among major petroleum-exporting countries with a significant portion in the global petroleum market cannot avoid influencing both crude oil market and global market mechanism. The relative price increase of crude oil as major energy input has influence on the whole price level in national economies of oil-importing countries regardless of developing or industrialized.[31]

3) All People's Right to Use the Natural Resource

The unhealthy rent-seeking that so-called the People's Fund proposal[32] tried to reduce is stepped up by the collective practice. The argument that a right to permanent sovereignty over natural resources (PSNR) is vested in the entire population of a country[33] needs to reflect the interest of the whole population who uses the natural resources, including the people of the country. Art. 1 Sec. (2) of the both Human Rights Covenants[34] states that all people's free disposal of natural wealth without prejudice to any obligations is arising out of international economic

(Footnote 30 continued)

See id, 11. Although the impact is larger for industrial countries than for developing countries due to the fact that net oil exporters belong to developing countries, the impact on individual countries which import oil from developing countries is often large.

See also Crooks and Blas, *supra* note 12, at 4. OPEC supplies more than 54 % of the oil imports of industrial countries in 2007 when Angola joins the organization.

[31]The IMF Research Department (2000), at 11 and 18. Even 30 of the 40 Heavily Indebted Poor Countries are among the most seriously affected by higher oil prices. *See also*, Hyundai Research Institute (2004), at 2–3. Economy of South Korea totally depending on import of oil was under two oil price hikes.

(%)	1971–1973	1974–1976	1977–1979	1980–1982
Oil Price (US$ per barrel)	2.5	11.0	14.1	31.2
Economic Growth	8.6	8.4	8.7	3.9
Inflation	9.1	14.8	22.2	38.9
The Trade Balance	−10.8	−18.8	−27.7	−40.2

Data: Korea Central Bank and the National Statistical Office

[32]The proposal targeted to reduce collusive acts within the governments managing natural resources through movement of public assets including natural resources from governments to citizens. *See* Duruigbo (2006), at 68–75. Nobel Economics Laureate Vernon Smith proposed a new geopolitical-economic paradigm on the principle that public assets belong directly to the public.

[33]*See id.*, 38–67.

[34]They are the International Covenant on Civil and Political Rights (ICCPR), G.A. Res. 2200 (XXI), at 52, U.N.Doc. A/6316 (December 19, 1966), and the International Covenant on Economic, Social and Cultural Rights (ICESC), G.A. Res. 2200 (XXI), at 49, U.N.Doc. A/6316 (December 19, 1966).

cooperation, based on the principle of mutual benefit and international law. Art. 25 of the International Covenant on Economic, Social, and Cultural Rights (ICESC) states, "nothing in the present Covenant shall be interpreted as impairing the inherent right of *all people* to enjoy and utilize fully and freely their natural resources." In the provisions, free disposal of all people over their natural resource should not get rid of any duty under international economic cooperation under the principle of mutual benefit. 'All people' cover not only the population of the country with natural resource but also that of the other countries using the natural resource because international economic cooperation under mutual benefit and international law can be interpreted as reflecting the interest of the consumer class utilizing the natural resource.

4) Price Increase in the Global Market

The decision of the Central District Court of California, moreover, adduced major reasons of gasoline price increase during 1973–1974 and 1978–1979 in failures of several federal administrative policies.[35] Although the OPEC was not a cause of oil shortage and gasoline lines in the U.S., the oil price increase during the period was a global phenomenon[36] and affected Gross Domestic Production (GDP) of oil-importing countries.[37] Moreover, the reasons for the gasoline price increase in the other countries did not altogether come from the failures of their government policies.

5) No Penalty

Noticeably, there has been no penalty against a member country which does not comply with production quota of OPEC. OPEC and its member country have adjusted its production quota according to shifting price and supply of oil market.[38] The cartel has maintained despite the lack of penalty against cheating the output quota because Saudi Arabia, as the most oil producer, has kept its production quota and placed weight on the quota of OPEC assigned for its own interest.[39] The absence of the penalty makes OPEC distinguished from the other typical cartels functioning under penalty threat to a potential cheating member.

---

[35]The decision enumerate such federal regulations as (i) Federal Energy Administration regulations preventing refiners from recovering costs of the additional capacity thereby leading to a shortage of refinery capacity, (ii) federal allocation regulations establishing a series of priorities for different users and set-aside requirements for government supply of gasoline, and (iii) two federal regulations of the Environmental Protection Agency leading to shortages in crude oil at domestic refineries. *See* 477 F.Supp. 553, 573–574.

[36]The IMF Research Department (2000), figure A1: Oil Market (1972–2000) in Annex.

[37]For impacts on world GDP, *see id.*, figure A2: Macroeconomic Aggregates (1970–2000) in Annex. For those on OECD countries' GDP, *see id.*, Table A1: Impact of Nominal Oil Price Hikes in Annex.

[38]Dr. Adnan Shihab-Eldin, *OPEC on Oil Supplies and Prices*, Wash. Post, June 18, 2004, *at* http://www.washingtonpost.com/wp-dyn/articles/A48713-2004Jun17.html.

[39]Benjamin Zycher, OPEC, Concise Encyclopedia of Economics, at http://www.econlib.org/library/Enc/OPEC.html.

6) Assessment

The international organization with sovereign state as members, OPEC, should be treated differently from an international cartel with private entities as members. However, OPEC has operated as an IPA moderating production of oil under the common production plan in the global market. The IPA can impose severe economic harms on consumers. For example, although failures of domestic energy policies exacerbated its price surge, the sudden price rise of crude oil in 1973 and 1979 illustrates the power of OPEC to control the world oil market with restriction of quantity of production in the context of shifting political circumstances in the Middle East.[40] In case the OPEC works against the principle of mutual benefit under international economic cooperation, its production manipulation can be beyond the protection of Art. 1 Sec. 2 of the ICCPR and ICESC.

It is very hard to condemn OPEC's plan of production managements as violation of competition law. First, the regime has no penalty regime against a potential cheating member country. As a voluntary guideline, the production control of OPEC lacks of a characteristic of a condemned cartel which screen member's free activity. Moreover, crude oil, as the most important nonrenewable resource of energy currently, needs to be preserved as balanced against fluctuated market demand. The limited resource needs stable management: volatile price and subsequent impacts on the global economy does not generate benefits to both the advanced and developing countries. In terms of less diversified economic structures of its exporting countries, their rights over it to promote their economic development have been acknowledged as permanent sovereignty of producing countries under international law.

However, in case OPEC member countries directly breach obligation for international economic cooperation on the basis of mutual benefit, e.g., significant infringement on consumers' interests, their rights of PSNR should be limited in a way that international economic cooperation can be secured. As an IPA has more limited availability for reflecting opinions of consuming countries than an ICA, its collective enjoyment of PSNR should be under more restraints. Several factors can mislead OPEC into suspicious areas beyond coverage of PSNR: price-fixing, production limitation regardless of oil price surge, and penalty for maintaining collective production plan.

(2) The International Telecommunication Union (ITU)

It is questioned whether the ITU of standard-setting organization restricts competition as a cartel. In order to discuss the question, first, the structure of the organization is to be addressed because its membership for a country is difficult to invoke the violation of international competition law due to the state immunity doctrine. In considering the merit, the characteristic of standard-setting of the organization with regard to competition is to be examined from competition law perspective. Concretely, its account rate-setting practices invoke the doubt of price-fixing. On the other hand, radio frequency spectrum (RFS) allocation is

[40]Leclair (2000), at 67–71.

argued to restrict competition by allocating markets or to create monopoly within the allotted range.

1) Purpose and Structure of ITU

The ITU is the UN Specialized Agency responsible for the regulation, standardization, and development of worldwide telecommunication. For researching both purpose and structure of the ITU, it is important to note that the International Telecommunication Convention (ITC) as constitution of the ITU establishes its structure and set forth its purposes. The ITC is divided into two parts: (1) Basic Provisions and (2) General Regulations.[41]

In the light of the Basic Provisions and the General Regulations, the purposes of the ITU are (i) the promotion of efficiency and (ii) that of equitable usage in technology and network. The Basic Provisions have efficiency-oriented purposes implying equity concern, such as the maintenance of an efficient worldwide telecommunication network, and the constant upgrading of the techniques and procedures in the network. To achieve the purposes, the General Regulations enumerate eight kinds of activities of the Union.[42] Among them, related to equity promotion are using radio telecommunication among countries in harmonized ways, and assisting in development of telecommunication technology in developing countries (DCs). Offering telecommunication service at the least rate in the light of public interest contributes to both efficiency and equity.

While cartels have characteristics of increasing price and reducing production, the ITU has its purpose to foster collaboration so as to offer service at such a rate as low as possible within a range consistent with efficiency.[43] The cause of collaboration among members is not to seek rent[44] but to use telecommunication services in a harmonious way between public interest and private profits. To make a long story short, the ITU promotes downward price competition while price cartels usually try to abolish it.

While conferences, plenipotentiary or administrative, take prerogative for decision-making, International Radio Consultative Committee (CCIR) and the International Telegraph and Telephone Consultative Committee (CCITT) are in charge of studying innovations in telecommunication and making standards. The two committees are composed of specialists from government and industry.[45]

---

[41]Codding Jr. et al. (1982), at 205.

[42]*Id.* at 206. *See also* ITU, International Telecommunication Convention, Art. 4 (November 6, 1982), at http://www.austlii.edu.au/au/other/dfat/treaties/1984/35.html (last visit on June 19, 2007).

[43]Article 4. 2 (e) of the ITC.

[44]Rent-seeking is defined as incorporating "efforts, both legal and illegal, to acquire access to or control over opportunities for earning rents". Particularly, with reference to countries largely depending on oil revenue from the export of the commodity, it states, rent-seeking refers to widespread behavior, in both the public and private sectors, aimed at capturing oil money through unproductive means. Karl (2004), at 661.

[45]*See* Codding et al. (1982), at 59 and 84.

The CCITT under the auspice of the ITU was attacked as a virtual cartel of Postal Telegraph and Telephone (PTT) due to its recommendations. Until recently, the CCITT rules for international commerce in telecommunications services had been treated almost absolute. The recommendations concerning telecommunications services used to function fairly smoothly for relatively slow changing technology, homogeneous and vertically integrated services, and the same basic range of services under more or less the same regulatory conditions.[46] Since the telecommunication technology recently changes fast and new services grow diversified, the effects of the recommendation are currently not so absolute as in the past in the light of differentiated services and differently corresponding regulations in each country.[47]

2) Members of the ITU

(A) Countries under the Doctrine of Sovereign Immunity

Countries' sovereign acts do not provoke cartel violation under the doctrine of sovereign immunity established as international customary law unless they concern real property or the disposition of the property of a deceased person.[48] According to the U.S. Foreign Sovereign Immunities Act (FSIA) of 1976, adopting the 'restrictive form' of the sovereign immunity doctrine, states are not absolutely immune from the jurisdiction of foreign courts when they are involved in 'commercial activities,' and their commercial property may be levied upon for satisfaction of judgments against them in connection with their 'commercial activities'.[49] The 'commercial activity' is defined as ① a regular course of commercial conduct or ② a particular commercial transaction or act. The commercial character of an activity shall be determined by reference to nature of the course of conduct or particular transaction rather than by reference to its purpose.[50]

Critics might argue that the organization's standard-setting is, in its nature, a commercial activity not immune from the sovereign immunity doctrine. The standard-setting of such sector as CCITT or CCIR by its nature, however, is not a commercial conduct but *putting in place a regulatory framework in order to foster commercial activity and competition*. Efficient telecommunication needs normal standard to ensure compatibility of technology. Unlike the production of goods, the standard-setting to make the trade of goods effective does not belong to the regular course of commercial conduct in international trade but to a regulatory function such as that of the works of administrative bodies of related countries. Concretely, the allocation of the radio frequency spectrum (RFS)[51] has the characteristic of regulatory

---

[46]Aronson and Cowhey (1988), pp. 45–48.

[47]Savage (1989), p. 25–27.

[48]The Schooner Exchange v. McFaddon, 11 U.S. (7 Cranch) 116, 3 Led. 287 (1812). Damrosch et al. cite, as a commercial exception, Letter of Acting Legal Adviser, Jack B. Tate, To Department of Justice, May 19, 1952, 26 Dep't State Bull. 984 (1952). *See* Damrosch et al. *supra* note 11, 1204–1206.

[49]28 U.S.C. § 1602.

[50]28 U.S.C. § 1603(d).

[51]The RFS means an electromagnetic wave of frequencies propagated in space used to transmit information. *Refer to infra* (5).

activities in the telecommunication industry between sovereign powers. Rate-setting, however, arguably has something to do with a commercial conduct, as discussed later.

In sum, the ITU or its sectors have limited jurisdictional basis for any cartel investigation because its member states are immune from the jurisdiction of foreign courts under the sovereign immunity doctrine; its standard-setting does not fall under the commercial activity exception.

(B) Sector Members: Private Entities

The ITU has private entities as its constituents besides sovereign states, as CCITT or CCIR, a sector of the ITU, includes the private entities under its association. Besides 193 member states, around 800 sector members including ICT companies, universities and regional organizations, and associates[52] comprise the ITU as of 2015. Since the ITU is organized into three sectors such as development (ITU-D), radio communications (ITU-R), standardization (ITU-T), an interested entity or organization, either private or public, may join any sector of the ITU as a sector member provided they meet certain qualifications. Particularly, the chance is more prevalent in the Standardization (ITU-T) sector. The sector members do various activities,[53] among which standard-setting is noteworthy in terms of relationship with competition. Concretely, a sector membership may be endowed on the following entities: Recognized Operating Agencies, and other entities dealing with telecommunication matters.

(A) Recognized Operating Agencies (ROA),[54] scientific or industrial organizations,[55] and financial or development institutions, which should be approved by the Administration of the Member State concerned,

[52]Any interested entity or organization may join an ITU sector as an Associate and be entitled to take part in the work of a selected single Study Group or Working Group thereof. Associates may have access to documentation required for their work and may serve as rapporteur or editor.

[53]Besnier (2003), at 6–8. Sector members are involved in paying its annual contribution, influencing the evolution of global telecommunications networks, increasing the awareness of business priorities among the representatives of global telecommunication, promoting network contact, participating in sector members' works, holding positions within study or working groups, and having access to invaluable information such as access to ITU working documents, or free or discounted ITU publications.

[54]The ROA is the operating agency that operates a public correspondence or broadcasting service and upon which the obligations provided for in Art. 6 of the ITU Constitution are imposed by the Member State in whose territory the head office of the agency is situated, or by the Member State which has authorized this operating agency to establish and operate a telecommunication service on its territory. Any individual company, corporation, or governmental agency which operates a telecommunication installation intended for an international telecommunication service or capable of causing harmful interference with such a service falls on the ROA. The ROA covers *multinational telecommunication corporation dealing with international telecommunication service and governmental regulatory authorities in international telecommunication.*

[55]The scientific or industrial organization in category 1 is private organization other than a governmental establishment or agency, which is engaged in the study of telecommunication problems or in the design or manufacture of equipment intended for telecommunication services.

(B) Other entities dealing with telecommunication matters,[56] which should be approved by the Administration of the Member State concerned, and regional and other international telecommunication, standardization, financial or development organizations.[57]

As the category (B) allows private entities to become sector members, the possibility of cartel activity among private entities exists.

(C) Standard-setting of the ITU as Restraint to Competition?

To discuss whether ITU standardization restricts competition, several factors are to be analyzed, such as ① efficiency, ② entry barrier to new competitors, and ③ the consumers' benefit. Suspicion regarding cartel's sanction, review of activities of International Consultative Committees (CCIs), and restriction of public availability.

As to ① efficiency, the ITU's global standardization of both telecommunication equipment and the means of delivering telecommunication services ensure the continuity of technology and service, cuts manufacture costs, and provides telecommunication authorities with international compatible equipment as the ITU has its objectives in promoting the global development of telecommunication technology and in assisting in the ever-advancing integration of communication media.[58] All these benefits increase the efficiency of the telecommunication service by saving time and money which would be spent in adapting equipment to multistandards.[59]

Regarding ② entry barrier, global standard under the ITU might arguably interrupt the free placing of diverse standards by late comers in the telecommunication industry. However, ITU recommendations for standardization without binding power cannot restrict member countries which stick to their own standards. The standardization, rather, has contributed to promoting the ability of countries or competitive private companies with technological advantage to obtain their access to export markets with the global standard.[60]

In addition, the technology developed by a single large firm, often with the global use in mind, might arguably lead to a global monopoly. However, there are such procedural barriers to the alleged global monopoly conspiracy because the approval of International Consultative Committees (CCIs) as specialized committees, and the consensual approval from members at the ITU Plenary Assembly are necessary. Rather, the advanced technology is used to generate multistandards

[56]This category includes private entities in telecommunication-related industries as sector members. Many telecommunication companies, e.g., Alcatel-Lucent France, Sony Corp., and Nokia Corp., are actively working as sector members.

[57]ITU, *ITU Telecommunication Standardization Sector (ITU-T) Membership*, available at http://www.itu.int/ITU-T/membership/_page.pr.

[58]ITU, CCITT Document, AP VII-No. 110 (1980).

[59]The experts comprising International Consultative Committee (CCI) delegations under ITU universally recognize the desirability of the standardized telecommunication. *See* Savage (1989), 25–7.

[60]*Id.*

instead of a monopoly in an industry where global standardization threatens the political or economic strengths of a nation.[61]

From the perspective of ③ consumers' welfare, the global standard protects the users from facing incompatibility in the world where diverse standards from different countries interfere with consumers' usages of the same standard. The ITU-T recommendation generates a unique multilateral forum which allows competing interests to harmonize in an atmosphere of constructive debates, providing a framework for companies to mediate their differences for the benefit of consumers.[62]

Opponents of the ITU argued that the longstanding ITU-supported system, on the contrary to such short life span of most cartels as in an economic theory, was due to legal sanction which helped in monitoring and enforcing the competition-restricting activities of the ITU as a cartel.[63] The argument does not consider the nonbinding characteristics of the recommendations of the ITU or its sector, as well as the lack of legal sanction against noncompliant entities. The main reason why the ITU survived and functioned for more than 130 years comes from the necessity for countries facing new technologies to have international standards for promoting cooperation and increasing the efficiency of the technologies. The standards are committed to achieving equitable access in the technological development and fostering global competition on equipment pertaining to compatibility.

Although the ITU achieved many successes in the late nineteenth century,[64] it is noteworthy to examine the CCIs under the ITU since they have issued recommendations influential to global standardization through continuous studies. The CCIR issues the recommendations for all wireless services of radiocommunication, while CCITT[65] does the same for wired telephone services. Although a global commitment to standardization for improved telecommunication might arguably conflict with recognition of a country's sovereign right to exercise control over its technology standards,[66] the standardization efforts of CCIs cause no, if any, serious conflict with a

---

[61] *See id.* at 184. Six incompatible cellular car telephone systems of EU in 1987, for example, maintained their different standards because the cellular car telephones were distributed by monopolies which employ 'buy domestic' policies. National administrators who seek to protect their interests barred creation of a single standard of the cellular car telephones in the Western European market where the international standard would have promoted consumers' welfare much more.

[62] ITU, supra note 58.

[63] Aronson and Cowhey, *supra* note 46, at 218–220.

[64] The major achievements are the establishment of both European telegraphy network through the standardization of Morse code, along with the setting of an acceptable rate structure and periodic meetings, and International Bureau of Telegraph Administration, as the first global permanent bureau of telegraph, publishing rate tables, statistics, and journals besides the gathering of the information in the nineteenth century.

[65] *Id.* at 46. the International Consultative Committee on Telegraphs (CCIT) and CCIF later merged into CCITT.

[66] Efforts to strengthen the CCI recommendations by giving them power of international law might be seen as one way of promoting international standardization, which is a mistaken perception. As most CCI decisions have great effect on domestic telecoms services and equipment procurement, it

state's sovereignty since they issue nonbinding recommendations. Although the CCIs' recommendations have no sanction against noncompliers, they are respected as the global codes of conduct and technical criteria set by the CCIR are vital to international communication and as global telephone linkage is possible through specific recommendations of the CCITT. The voluntary nature of the recommendation bears little resemblance to the characteristic of cartel.

Efficient telecommunication based upon global standardization by means of delivery, moreover, is one of the main objectives to which CCIs, particularly CCIR and CCITT, have made a commitment. Art. 4(b) of the 1982 Nairobi ITU Convention points to promoting the development of technological facilities and their most efficient operation with a view to improving the efficiency and public availableness of telecommunication services. Specifically, the International Consultative Committee on Long-distance Telephones (CCIF) and the CCITT have played important roles in issuing recommendations as to the standardization of telephone and telegraph equipment and interstate circuits and system.[67] For example, in 1939, the overall standardization of the EU telephone networks by the CCIF allowed any EU subscriber to communicate to any other subscriber with a generally highly satisfactory condition of audibility without having to wait for a connection. Inspired by the success, its proponents empowered the CCIF's plan for a single standard global network in which national and international systems would be technically indistinguishable, enabling the CCIF to aid and to advice newly independent and developing countries in studies related to establishing and maintaining domestic national networks. The role of the CCIs to make international network feasible have not changed since the time, and the enormous growth in telecommunication technology afterward has enhanced the importance of the CCIs.[68]

Regarding priority between efficiency and universality, it is argued that most CCI recommendations promote technical efficiency over universality of access to new technology or affordability, which contributes to the LDC perception of being caught in the wrong end of an increasing technology gap.[69] However, the argument is not related to violation of competition law because the competition law perspective focuses on fostering technical efficiency rather than on universal access. Moreover, the argument acknowledged that given the CCI's recommendatory roles, it must be at the cutting edge of new technological developments.[70] The availability of the access

(Footnote 66 continued)

would be unacceptable to even the most diminutive ITU member to relinquish national standard-setting discretion to the international CCI level if the international process was anything stronger than recommendatory. Legally binding standards can only be set domestically by national standard-setting agencies. *See id.* at 168.

[67] *Id.* at 31.

[68] *Id.*, at 48.

[69] Savage (1989), at 181.

[70] *Id.*

to market or RFS is ensured by an extension of membership in the Plenipotentiary Conference and the growing influence of the New World Information Order.

Global standardization has contributed to fostering competition. Through its standardization efforts for more than 130 years, the ITU has helped the telecommunication industry growth to become the world's third-largest business sector with an annual value of over USD one trillion.[71] The international standards, in addition, provide manufactures with a solid basis for competition in the global market without the hindrance of technical barriers. The convergence among Internet Protocol (IP), public switched telephone network (PSTN), digital subscriber line (DSL), cable television (CATV), wireless local area network (WLAN), and mobile technologies is a task which would have been impossible without the development of the global standard.

3) Rate-setting: Price-fixing?

There are strong arguments that rate-setting on the part of the ITU might restrict competition in reducing the rate.[72] Major targets of the complaints are (i) the accounting rate[73] system that resembles that of a cartel with both an arcane sharing of the revenue from international calls which secretly distributes the spoils of telecommunication business among major members,[74] (ii) a method that penalizes companies that cut their prices, and (iii) restrictions on private circuits which were designed to keep noncartel members out of the market and enshrined on the CCITT's recommendations.[75]

Concretely, the complaint about the accounting rate system was supported by price for phone call set by the CCITT at three times as high as the cost.[76] The inculpation against the accounting rate system, not closely reflecting actual cost, is exacerbated by the fact that countries with a monopoly approach, or developing countries, have shared revenues of those with liberalized approach, or the industrialized countries. As the latter have to pay half of its revenue for international calls terminated in the former, the international call price cannot be decreased in spite of

[71]ITU, *Overview-Standardization Sector*, available at http://www.itu.int/ (last visit on June 20, 2007).

[72]Aronson and Cowhey, *supra* note 46, 218–220.

[73]The 'accounting rate' is the internal price agreed between public telecommunication operators (PTOs) for carrying international traffic between two points. Usually one half of the accounting rate, so-called settlement rate, is used to determine the price charged to the originating PTO by the terminating PTO. ITU, *Trade in Telecommunications: A Glossary of Technical Terms*, available at http://www.itu.int/newsarchive/press/WTPF98/Glossarytechnterms.html (visited on April 15, 2008).

[74]Dixon, *Reconnecting Charges with Costs*, Fin. Times (April 3, 1990).

[75]*Id.* It mentioned D-series of its Blue Book as well as the CCITT recommendation.

[76]Hugo Dixon, *Phone club days are numbered: Change is on the line for global cartel,* Fin. Times (May 15, 1990). "There is little pretense that payments for international calls begin to reflect the underlying costs of the infrastructures used," Mr. Jonathan Solomon, cable and wireless' director for corporate business development and a former senior civil servant at the UK's Department of Trade and Industry, argued. Artificially high accounting rates for international calls deter companies from cutting their international prices.

price competition in industrialized countries. The research of the Federal Communications Commission (FCC) in the U.S. confirmed that the U.S. balance of payment (BOP) deficit for international telephone traffic grew from US$ 40 million in 1970 to US$ 2 billion in 1988, and insisted that accounting rates substantially above the cost of network go into excess profits by international carriers because the profits are to subsidize domestic and local services in their country.[77]

From the opposite point of view, DCs rather complained about the problem of equal division of the accounting revenue to compensate for the higher unit cost for their telecommunication facilities. The complaint proposed a resolution attached to new regulations that countries should agree to a split of the accounting rate other than a half and half in the light of the ITU's further research on real costs.

Considering the rate-setting structure as well as the complaints, the current ITU activity or structure does not resemble the typical characteristic of cartel for the following reasons.

First, carriers of international call in an originating country and a terminating country are placed in the opposite position with reciprocally conflicting interests under accounting settlement arrangement of bilateral relationship. It demonstrates sharp distinction with a cartel agreement of multilateral arrangement where competitors are in the same position with competing interests. A carrier in a destination country can be remunerated by a flat-rate price per circuit on the basis of the traffic units carried, or through a procedure whereby accounting revenue is shared between terminal operators.[78] The carrier which experienced the BOP surplus would maintain such a current situation so that credit from incoming calls outweighs the debit of outgoing calls. On the other hand, its partner in BOP deficit would mitigate the deficit by negotiating for the reduction of the accounting rate and by assisting the carrier to have more frequent outgoing calls.[79]

The developing countries (DCs)' proposal on the revenue division reflecting real costs can be repudiated in the following way. Although, in theory, it is possible to split the accounting rate in other ways besides 50/50, there is extreme difficulty in obtaining reliable data supporting splits in different ratios due to the absence of sophisticated accounting and administrative infrastructure among countries. Therefore, a universal agreement on the calculations and accounting procedure with equal division such as 50/50 is more practical unless a new infrastructure of accounting and administration in telephone industry becomes available.

Second, the price-fixing conspiracy of accounting rate standard is seriously doubted with several persuasive bases. Among other things, the setting rate is the maximum rather than the minimum as the ITU-T Recommendation D.600 R,[80]

---

[77]Stern (1990), at 3–4.

[78]The CCITT Recommendation D. 150 and D. 155.

[79]*Id.* 5–7.

[80]ITU-T Recommendation D.600 R, Charging and Accounting in International Telecommunication Services: Determination of Accounting Rate Shares and Collection Charges in Telephone Relations between Countries in Africa (1994).

clause 2.4.1 indicates. It verifies that the purpose of setting maximum rates is to decrease rate under a certain level.[81]

As to the second point, it matters whether the accounting system has any penalties against noncomplier to maintain the alleged cartel regime. Its standard is recommendatory rather than binding. As a result, noncompliance does not cause any punishment. The agreement in summer 1998 through the accounting rate reform in the context of ITU-T Study Group 3 allowed a departure from the global limit on the total accounting rate. Works of the World Telecommunication Policy Forum and its Focus Group related to the ITU-T Study Group provide flexible means of establishing target rates in a way tailored to the specific situations of individual countries.[82] Moreover, ITU-T Recommendations for regional application[83] specifically mention that, for the accounting rate shares for each country, illustrated standard rates are recommended.[84] For collection charges, the recommendations allow diversified collection regimes by asking each country to settle its unique charge by establishing different charges for each method or a single collection charge weighted in light of the volume of each type of traffic.[85]

At last, it matters whether the restriction on private circuits to keep noncartel members out of the market falls as an entry barrier to new competitors. The World Administrative Telegraph and Telephone Conference (WATTC) in 1988 limited the application of the restriction, faced by contestants who argued that the existent international organization was outdated. Its limitation resulted in the removal of the potential regulatory barrier in the entry into new competitive enhanced services including basic international services and international transport means.

Actual price shifts in real markets do not align with the cartel charge. Accounting rates have successfully been reduced in compliance with the expectation of ITU-T recommendations.[86] Prices of international commercial services provided by international carriers, such as Teleglobe, have been reduced by as much as 35 % over the last few years and have been accompanied by a continuing trend of reduction in accounting rates through the negotiating mechanism which is

---

[81]With the maximum rate level, recommendatory remuneration standards on the basis of a flat-rate price for a transit country and a destination country are stated in clause 2.4.2.1. and clause 2.4.2.2. of D.601 R has very similar recommendations regarding accounting rate and collection charges.

[82]ITU, *Accounting Rate Reform: the Current Debate, opening remarks prepared for Dr. Henry Chasia* (September 29, 1998), available at http://www.itu.int/ITU-D/ict/papers/accrates/_page.printrl.

[83]ITU-T Recommendation D.301 R (Recommendations for Regional Application), Standards Rates Applicable in the International Telecommunication Services: Determination of Accounting Rate Shares and Collection Charges in Telex Relations between Countries in Europe and the Mediterranean Basin (1995).

[84]*See also id.*, clause 2.3.1.1 fn b. It adds that recommended accounting rates may not be appropriate to some small capacity submarine cables, in which cases the rates should be fixed by agreements among the parties concerned. This implies the flexibility of recommended rates.

[85]*Refer to* Clause 3.3.2 of D.600 R. The collection charge is the price charged by the PTO which originates a call to a customer. *See* ITU, *supra* note 73.

[86]D.140 of Study Group 3 on accounting rates principles for the international telephone service.

afforded by the current arrangements. Although the global accounting rate decline was only 4 % per year from 1992 to 1996, it reached up to a decline of 12 % between 96 and 98, reaching 20 % per year after 1998 while actual costs have been declining at a faster rate.

In the majority of the ITU's 189 member states unwilling to adopt competition policy in international telecommunication service, such ITU recommendations can work as rules restricting extraordinarily high price. Price-setting regulations can be necessary in light of the public characteristics of telecommunication since pricing in the telecommunication industry can be viewed from a public service perspective. It is argued that pricing policy in telecommunication must consider at least eight basic goals: (i) universal service, (ii) static efficiency, (iii) equity for different kinds of users and services, (iv) financial self-sufficiency, (v) prevention of uneconomic entry, (vi) consistency with expected technological change, (vii) administrative simplicity, and (viii) historical continuity. The policy goals indicate that the interests of the public, e.g., universal service, administrative simplicity, and continuity, should be taken into account besides economic or private interests. The utilization charges are made at a level generating the revenue required for its operation, maintenance, and advertisement of the system as well as the amortization of and compensation for the use of capital.

In the member states with effective competition, which account for more than three-quarters of total traffic, telecommunication service is becoming more and more considered as a tradable commodity. With the advent of competition for transit traffic,[87] carriers began in the late 1970s to offer Transit Remuneration Plans whereby the transit facilities were offered to terminal operators at competitive rates. The fierce competition among carriers to attract the transit traffic is not a characteristic of a cartel any more than their behaviors in negotiating accounting rates are. The pressure to liberalize the global telecommunication service market continued to be furthered when the Uruguay Round adopted a new General Agreement on Trade in Services (GATS) with a provision that prices should reflect costs.

In short, the ITU or ITU-T has no high price-fixing arrangement, as a key characteristic of a cartel. In light of the accounting rate system of the ITU without any binding provisions for international carriers to enter into agreements to set prices and without penalties against violators, the actual price trend, the public interests, and the pressures to liberalize from the industrialized countries, it is evident that the existent international organization and its practices contain no formal traits of collusion. An argument with the pro-competition stance of the ITU opines that the ITU Constitution and the Convention and Administrative Regulations acknowledge the sovereignty of each nation to regulate its telecommunications depending on their interests. The treaties are the result of difficult compromises made between the liberalization request from the industrialized countries and the championing of the sovereign principle from DCs. The present

[87]'Transit traffic' means telecommunications traffic that an originating carrier delivers to a transiting carrier or carriers for delivery to a terminating carrier.

international settlement procedure contains an inner commercially driven dynamism toward cost reduction in all the instances where traffic imbalances occur.[88] Domestic communication agencies have contributed their efforts to reducing price to a certain level for a decade.[89]

4) Radio Frequency Spectrum (RFS) Distribution: Market Allocation?

Radio Frequency Spectrum (RFS) is an electromagnetic wave of frequencies propagated in space used to transmit information through signals.[90] A frequency is not an entity but the number of cycles that an electronic carrier wave diffuses in a second. Within a designated frequency spectrum range, electronic wave carries sound or picture from a broadcaster to recipients. If incorrectly operating, radio waves can interfere reciprocally and nullify their benefit since allocation of the RFS proceeds independently in individual countries. The ITU holds World Radiocommunication Conferences (WRC) every 2 years to debate the allocation of spectrum so that the technology used in an individual country works effectively without any technical problems.[91]

Arguments that the allocation of RFS falls on market allocation or monopoly come from a misunderstanding of the RFS. The RFS allocation is inevitable for countries that use telecommunication technology without reciprocal interference. The RFS is a limited resource with a characteristic of inelasticity.[92] It vests exclusive rights to assigned entities to send the RFS within the designated spectra. In order to avoid conflicts with the other electronic waves, each broadcaster requires the range of RFS designated for its exclusive use. A global consensus is effective in solving technical problems such as harmful interference among countries and the impossibility of global roaming.[93] The ITU-R ensures the rational, equitable, efficient, and economic use of the RFS by all radiocommunication services, including those using the geostationary satellite orbit, and carries out studies without limit of frequency ranges.[94] As technology needs a certain range of RFS for global roaming, the WRC has led the discussion for allocating the RFS to the technique for roaming.[95]

---

[88]Stern, *supra* note 77.

[89]Sarah Laitner and Andrew Parker, *EU to cap price of mobile calls*, 3 Fin. Times (Th. May 24, 2007). EU decided to impose price caps on international telephone call charges despite fierce opposition from operators. *See also* Stern, *supra* note 77, 5. The FCC in the U.S. issued a notice of proposed rule to bring international accounting rates closer to the cost of providing international telecommunication services and to reduce US prices by as much as 50 %. OFTEL in BK made inquiry after the two FT articles about the BT's international rates, not included in the basket of prices subject to the UK price cap formula.

[90]*Refer to* Recommendation ITU-R V.662-3 (2000) and V.575-3 (1990).

[91]Lin (2004), at 245.

[92]Inelasticity means the characteristic of goods or service which cannot be produced so sufficiently to match the increasing demand.

[93]Lin, *supra* note 91, at. 252.

[94]CS Art. 12.1.1.

[95]Email from Dr. Seung-Joon Park, Researcher at LG Electronics (June 27, 2007 5:56 PM) (on file with author).

Table 3.2 Comparison between posteriori and priori allocation

Posteriori (unplanned bands)	Priori (planned bands)
Protecting vested rights	Concerning equity
Flexibility	Rigidity
Case-by-case approach (first-come first-serve)	Principled approach
Often used in domestic level	Used in international level

Moreover, the global standard for the RFS allocation has changed toward promoting competition in light of equity concern. The equitable access to RFS is requested by DCs. With several international agreements, radio frequencies and the geostationary satellite orbit regarded as limited resources become affordable so that countries may have equitable access to each other.[96] The concrete ways of the allocation indicate interests in both equitable access as well as efficiency. They are categorized as posteriori and priori. The following is a comparison between the two ways of allocation (Table 3.2).

Through the posteriori allocation standard, rights to use a specific radio channel in a geographical area are vested on first-come first-serve basis. The posteriori standard was a success of the International Radio Conferences (IRCs) held in order to assign the existing RFS and to avoid interference with existent stations in the early twentieth century. However, the rate tables negotiated at the Conferences were not accepted by the U.S. and Canada where private companies set telegraph rates and the government only supervised them with nonspecific guidelines. After World War II ended, which destroyed many parts of international telecommunication systems but made the radio technology central, the priori spectrum, or the planned system for registration of frequency list was adopted as an international standard in the 1947 Atlantic City Convention[97] to distribute the usable radio frequencies among the members with a basis on sound engineering principles.[98] The new standard reflected equitable access, fairness, and technical efficiency of operation, and was applauded by DCs with the belief that the priori planning would achieve just distribution and technical feasibility for new RFS, such as orbit allotment.

The attitudes of the European Commission (EC) and the European Court of Justice (ECJ) are compatible with the opinion that RFS allocation does not restrict competition. The EC issued a directive asking member states to open telecommunication services and equipment markets to competition by withdrawing an exclusive right to supply telecommunication service under Art. 82 and 86 of the Treaty of Rome.[99] Several member states with the Postal Telegraph and Telephone (PTT) monopolies contended the directive and caused a legal dispute. The holding

[96]ITU CV. Art. 44.

[97]Savage (1989), p. 28–44. Codding et al. (1982), 11–26.

[98]A full a priori allocation plan was scheduled to take effect on September 1, 1939, but, due to the outbreak of WWII, the plan failed in being effective. Savage (1989), 37.

[99]Commission Directive 90/338/EEC of 28 June 1990 had its foundation on former Art. 86 and 90 of the Treaty.

of the ECJ was that only in opening telecommunications services and terminal equipment market, but not in RFS distribution, free market principles should be enforced.[100]

The monopoly argument was made by countries or enterprises without favorable frequency bands because most areas had been occupied by advanced countries. The ITU, however, counterargues by pointing out the equity-concerned 'Table of Frequency Allocations (TFA)', which states that an individual country in the designated geographical areas had an equitable access to a frequency band. The TFA was included in the Radio Regulations (RRs) so as to avoid interference between certain stations.[101] Thus, the equity-based approach to solve technical problems in the light of the distinction of RFS with competitive equipment market is so persuasive as to outweigh the monopoly argument.

The RFS of the ITU does not constitute a market-allocation cartel, either. From a technical viewpoint, the ITU, with the RRs covering wider spectra and more radio services, needed an effective coordination among countries to make their radiocommunication effective and noninterfered. The international coordination through RFS allocation is indispensable to radio broadcasting. When the coordination is fairly managed with concern for equity, it enhances consumers' benefit rather than restricts it.

Moreover, individual countries do not face any penalties, unlike cartels, although they do not abide by its international agreement.[102] They are totally free to distribute RFS allocation in ways different from the allocation of the ITU or the WRC. The international standard is only for avoiding technical problems and making telecommunication effective in the global level.

5) Conclusion: the ITU is not a cartel

The ITU does not violate competition laws with either accounting rate-setting or its RFS allocation. The rate-setting works on the voluntary basis with the maximum rate standard. The actual market price trend for international phone call indicates a downward trend in terms of the telephone service fee. There is an international pressure to liberalize service trade under the GATS. It is also noted that rate-setting should reflect public interests such as equitable access, universal service, and static

---

[100]ECJ, Judgment of 17 Nov. 1992, Case C-271/90, C-281/90, and C-289/90, ECR I-05833, para. 36 (1992). Kingdom of Spain, Kingdom of Belgium, and Italian Republic intervened by French Republic were in position of applicant for requesting annulment of the Directive. Regarding withdrawing 'special right' in the terminal equipment directive, the court held that the directive to the extent of the 'special right' must be annulled due to the lack of specific information about the type of special rights. The directive applied to telecommunication services except telex, mobile radio telephony, paging and satellite services, as well as telephone equipment.

[101]Vacancy Notice, No. 17-1998 ITU, 253(August 13, 1998). The stations are the following: aircraft, control towers, car telephones, ships at both sea and coast stations, radio stations, spacecraft, and earth-based stations.

[102]Email from Dr. Seung-Joon Park, *supra* note 95.

efficiency. The concern for public interests provides the justification for a recommendatory accounting rate-setting.

The RFS allocation is inevitable in order to have effective cross-border radio broadcasting without interference in different radio spectra. Judicial bodies in advanced countries, on the other hand, hold that establishing monopolies in the telecommunication industry violates competition law. However, the decision does not apply to the RFS allocation because the act of allocation is not within an industry where private companies compete to sell products. The RFS allocation in the ITU is not a restriction of competition but a management practice to ensure its fair distribution and effective use. The standards of the TFA and the RR have reflected the consideration for equity among DCs.

(3) The International Air Transport Association (IATA)
1) Origin and Legal Status

The less-developed international commercial aviation industry, where carriers were satisfied with uncoordinated and informal negotiation, prior to WW II, had grown sufficiently enough for many nations to convene at the Chicago Civil Aviation Conference (CCAC), and thereby establish the International Civil Aviation Organization (ICAO). However, the ICAO, although an intergovernmental organization, was not empowered to engage in economic regulation due to conflicts of interests mainly between the U.S. and the UK governments.

With a need to cooperate in economic matters of the international civil aviation industry, 31 scheduled airlines, private companies which participated in CCAC as observers, organized the IATA in Havana, Cuba in April 1945. The nongovernmental organization was given a corporate charter by an Act of the Canadian Parliament in December.[103] Subsequently, in January 1946, the UK, under the threat of price-cutting by the U.S. airlines, engaged the U.S. in disagreement with regard to economic regulation at CCAC, only to reach a compromise in Burmuda, through which the U.S. Civil Aeronautics Board (CAB) allowed antitrust law immunity to airlines participating at IATA rate-setting conferences by the late 1970s while the UK allowed U.S. airlines to fly transatlantic routes.[104]

2) Structure and Works

IATA works to coordinate the diverse differences in airlines, currencies, policies, and laws regarding international air transportation so as to create a global air transport system among users, airlines, and governments. Important achievements of the IATA include: lobbying for lower taxes, monitoring fuel prices, compiling information from members, providing data-processing equipment and programs, studying airmail conveyance rates of various governments, operating a clearing

[103]Hannigan(1982), 112–113.

[104]Peterson (1990), at 65–66 and 71.

house for controlling interline accounts among carriers, and disseminating public relations materials to governments, civic groups, and the general public.[105]

The IATA operated a two-tier mechanism of the organization itself and the conferences which discussed and agreed on such issues as rights to carry traffic on routes, prices to be charged, and standards for various services. Among other things, Traffic Conferences and Tariff Coordination discussed, respectively, the international coordination of international fares, fare-related conditions, and procedures along with governments, as well as fares and commissions on sales among members only.[106] The agreements from such conferences included recommendations subsequently delivered to individual governments by company representatives or as bilateral agreements dispatched to reciprocal national congresses for ratification.

While the Traffic Conferences, with open membership including governments, mostly focused on coordinating international fares and on establishing their conditions and procedures, the organization treated a wide range of aviation policies from in-detailed techniques, e.g., communication procedures, to coordination of services, e.g., a centralized ticket clearing house. The highest authority of organization itself was on the annual general meeting consisting of representatives of the members. The administrative functions including policy direction and execution were up to the IATA secretariat, an executive committee headed by the director general and aided by five standing committees in the technical, legal, financial, and medical areas of traffic advisory.[107] The administrative body has sought to achieve multilateral agreements among the national governments of its members for cohesiveness and cooperation in ITAT policy enforcement.[108]

Since 1980, in response to the condemnation of cartel led by the U.S., the organization has been transformed to the Trade Association for the coordination of matters other than rate and the Tariff Coordination for rate-setting. Up until 2007, activities of the Tariff Coordination had been under exemption from national antitrust laws.[109] The main intent of such restructuring is considered to be to protect the IATA from accusations against cartel-like behaviors.

---

[105] *Id.* at 69.

[106] *Id.* at 69–70.

[107] Hannigan (1982), 114.

[108] Two successful models, EU agreement for opening aviation industry among EU member states and APEC agreement for creating a single aviation market, are likely to be affected by such efforts.

[109] Peterson (1990), at 73 and 77. IATA confirms such analysis at its website by the following statement: in the late 1970s when the US Government, which had first given IATA Traffic Conferences immunity from national antitrust law in 1946, began its own review of air transport regulation, and the international dimension of the US review resulted in a 'Show Cause Order' in 1979 by which IATA was called upon at the hearing of U.S. Congress to show cause why antitrust immunity should not be removed from its Tariff Coordination activities. Eventually, IATA restructured its organization as such two-tier system. The IATA still argues that all Tariff Coordination activities continue to be protected. IATA, *History-a Two Tier IATA: part 4*, available at http://www.iata.org/about/history (visited on August 13, '15).

3) Membership

In its launching era, 57 international air carriers from 31 countries, mostly leading airlines in Europe and North America, belonged to the IATA. Currently, 260 members from 117 countries are members of the IATA.[110] As IATA is voluntary, nonexclusive, democratic, and a nonpolitical organization, any airline can be a member of it if it has been able to provide scheduled air service under license by a government with qualified membership in ICAO.[111] While the participation in Traffic Conferences was not required, the Tariff Coordination has more than 100 members. Observers from governments, although not members, were allowed to attend IATA conferences.[112]

4) Debate on Cartel Suspicion

There have been disputes as to whether the IATA is a cartel in need of competition law regulation, a reconsideration of the formerly provided antitrust or competition law exemptions with regard to its conferences. As backgrounds for such disputes, the current aviation industry has met increasing market competition compared to the initial stage of the IATA. The national authorities which pursued an airline industry deregulation policy in major countries, particularly the U.S.[113] and the EU,[114] blamed conferences of the IATA for restricting competition. Particularly, the points of disputes are whether tariff coordination falls under the category of a price-fixing cartel and whether slot allocation and airport scheduling restricts new competitors' entry into the market as the result of a collective refusal to negotiate.

First, opponents against the IATA's fare setting, e.g., the U.S. CAB, argue that the coordination of air fares in traffic conferences and the issued recommendations has restricted an otherwise competitive process of reducing airfares.[115] Discussions

---

[110]IATA, *History-Introduction: part 1*, available at http://www.iata.org/about/history. (visited on August 13, '15).

[111]Peterson (1990), at 68.

[112]*Id.* at 74.

[113]The Air Cargo Deregulation At of 1977, the Airline Deregulation Act of 1978, Order to Show Cause on IATA Conference Agreement (June 9, 1978), and the International Air Transportation Competition Act (IATCA) of 1979 are major four official policies for deregulating airlines in the U.S. For in-detailed U.S. Air Transport Policy shift, *refer to* Peterson, *id.* at 70–75.

[114]European Competition granted Art. 81(3) exemptions, cartel provision exemptions to certain IATA conferences with Council Regulation 3876/87 and 1617/93 which applies to June 2005. However, the coverage of block exemptions has been narrowed only two consultations, consultations on passenger tariffs on intra-Community scheduled air services, and slot allocation and airport scheduling in terms of intra-Community airport services. *See* EU Competition Commission (CC), Director General (DG) Competition Consultation Paper: concerning the revision and possible prorogation of Commission Regulation 1617/93 on the application of Art. 81(3) to certain categories of agreements and concerted practices concerning consultations on passenger tariffs on scheduled air services and slot allocation at air ports (DG CCP), 4–5.

[115]Peterson (1990), 73–74; Hannigan (1982), 123.

at IATA meetings were allegedly aimed more at harmonizing and adjusting airfares than sharing price information, thereby obtaining a uniform price.

In response to the criticism, the DG of the IATA argue that its pricing agreements were merely recommendations to governments, not binding orders to airlines, and further, that the participation in Traffic Conferences is not mandatory to any carrier while observers from governments are allowed to attend. Such characteristics of international air carriage as a perishable commodity which cannot be stocked, as well as indispensable frequent contacts with diverse domestic laws and policies, make the air transport industry a market which necessitates careful coordination among airlines and governments.[116] The IATA, rather, requested an intergovernmental approach to deal with price coordination and interlining. The direct negotiation of national governments as an alternative to that among individual airlines was not a popular one, as it was not welcomed by the major dominant powers in international civil aviation.[117] It looks as if the airlines with strong market power do not want to dispose off their bilateral negotiations with national governments as to market entry or international fare or rate.

The IATA further argues that such improvement of production or distribution or promotion of economic progress results from increased market access, access to coordinated implementation, access to market knowledge, efficiency through one-time multilateral meetings, through tariff information dissemination, and through development of standards, equality from the unanimity rule, and worldwide antitrust immunity.[118] Moreover, it adds consumer benefits attributable to the IATA interlining system.[119]

Second, airport scheduling and slot allocation may treat arguably in an unfair way new carriers or carriers who request more slots and thereby bloc their access to the market. Entry has been denied for many years to new supplemental carriers while remaining open to scheduled carriers in similar circumstances.[120]

On the other hand, it is argued that the possibility of unfair discrimination or blocking entry by collective boycott is eliminated. IATA Worldwide Scheduling Guidelines provide that all air carriers can participate in the discussions and negotiations for allocating slots and that the allocation at congested airports is made on a nondiscriminatory and transparent basis. It added that the entry to congested airports will remain possible for the purpose of securing competition.[121]

---

[116]Peterson, *id.* 74–75.

[117]Hannigan (1982), 133.

[118]EU CC, *supra* note 114, 16.

[119]The 'interlining service' provides passengers with convenient options with their purchased tickets, e.g., changing airlines for the return portion of a round trip ticket, or taking the other airline to destination with a single ticket issued from the airline taken on leave, baggage transfer without repetitive checks, and the establishment of through fare. *See id.* at 17.

[120]*Id.* at 116.

[121]EU CC, *supra* note 114, 10.

5) Assessment

(A) Tariff Coordination Conference under the Category of Price-fixing Cartel

The conferences for tariff coordination as themselves have a high probability of falling under the category of a price-fixing cartel. Since they offer pivotal information regarding passenger fare and cargo rate which can restrict competition in the air transport industry, the conferences at the very least promote price-fixing activities and lead to the forming of hardcore cartels among competing airlines, which need to be strictly regulated.

Of the two categories that comprise cartel acts,[122] the IATA falls under the category of the association-typed cartel consisting of competing private companies. The IATA is the association which consists of majority of the competitors in a horizontal market because the majority of competing airlines which cover the world air transport industry are their members.

The IATA at least offers a forum, e.g., the Traffic Conference, where the settlement of international passenger fare or cargo rate and the dissemination of fare or rate information are allowed in spite of competition-restrictiveness. Even non-binding recommendations of the IATA have revealed their anticompetitive impacts on the markets by preventing fare-reducing competition.[123] For example, IATA's Special North Atlantic Tariff Conference (SNATC) in the first half of 1990 agreed to increase fares between the U.S. and most European countries, thereby raising fares from 4 to 15 % depending on areas.[124] In contrast to the IATA argument that services would be disrupted,[125] in markets where carriers are non-IATA members, services and fares have been improved and lowered.[126] In light of such circumstances, the settlement or dissemination of such price-related matters has the effect of restricting competition. In terms of 'purpose' of the agreement, this element is presumed by circumstantial evidences including the result of a sustained high level of fares/rates. According to the CAP reports, the main purpose of tariff coordination is to agree on price among direct competitors to the maximum extent.[127] While fuel costs increased throughout the enforcement of the deregulation policy,[128] the international passenger fares which increased under exemption regulation decreased

[122]*Refer to* Chap. 1.II.1.

[123]U.S. DOJ, *Comments of the DOJ before the U.S. Department of Transportation*, Doc. 46928, at 9 (August 7, 1990). U.S.DOJ, Reply Comments of the DOJ, at 7 (May 14, 1992).

[124]US DOJ, *supra* note 123, 11–12 (1992). Each 1 % of fare increase from ITAT fare coordination activity costs U.S. consumers nearly $ 60 million annually in the North Atlantic market alone. *Id.* at 16.

[125]Peterson (1990), 74. He cites CAB Final Order Terminating Proceeding 81-5-27.

[126]US DOJ, *supra* note 123, 10 (1990). It cites DOT's study of the U.S. airline industry, a study of Morrison and Minston (1989), and that of OECD.

[127]U.S. DOJ, *supra* note 123, at 6–10 (1990); U.S.DOJ *supra* note 350, at 7 (1992).

[128]The rates of increase are, respectively, 42 % from '77 to '79 and 82 % from '79 to '81. Peterson (1999), at 77, which cites Statistical Abstract of the United States, selected issues, 1975 to 1984–5, 88 (Washington, DC: U.S. Department of Commerce, Government Printing Office).

after deregulating U.S. airline.[129] In addition, due to the agreed mileage rules,[130] overall costs reflecting such uncertainty will possibly be increased, which may produce competition-restricting effects in relation to the increased fare.[131] The analyses indicate that tariff coordination on the part of the IATA is for raising fares, thereby restricting competition, which the European Commission approved in reviewing exemption of cartel law application to passenger tariff conference as to intra-Community routes.[132] In 2006, the European Commission decided to withdraw all exemption to IATA tariff consultations for intra-Community interlining starting from January 1, 2007 for interlining between EU and the U.S.A. and Australia from July 1, 2007, and between EU and the other countries from November 1, 2007.[133] The evidences indicate the goal of raising fares of IATA's tariff coordination.

An efficient interlining service as a benevolent institution to customers and an important public benefit justifying IATA's tariff coordination, can be offered without the horizontal price-fixing. Although the IATA argues that the IATA interlineable fare has been customarily used as a benchmark fare by airline corporate agreements,[134] and that the Multilateral Interline Tariff Agreement (MITA) and the multilateral prorate system as main pillars sustaining IATA Interlining System have the effect of settling the IATA's interlineable fare to the same level without imposing any legal obligation, the sophisticated mechanism for facilitating interlining has not revealed the indispensable dependence of the interlining system on IATA's multilateral tariff coordination. Large U.S. domestic carriers, e.g., U.S. Air, and Alaska Air, international carriers wishing to offer interline service to internal points in the U.S. found no difficulty in interlining with the majority of the U.S. carriers which were not a member of IATA tariff coordination conferences.[135] Without anticompetitive tariff coordination, benefits of the interlining system can be provided through fare publications, bilateral prorate agreements, the developed

[129]The following are shift of average passenger-mile rate.

1973	1977	1979	1983
0.040	0.045	0.042	0.034

See id. 77; Statistical Abstract, *supra* note 128

[130]The agreed mileage rule, inherent institution to the IATA interlining system, provides passengers with flexibility to change routes and to add or delete intermediate stopping points.

[131]EU CC, *supra* note 114, at 9.

[132]Maastricht Treaty Art. 81(3) and TFEU Art. 101(3). *Id.* at 22–23.

[133]Article 4 of Commission Regulation No. 1456/2006 of 28 Sept. 2006.

[134]IATA, DG-Competition Consultation on Regulation 1617/93: IATA Observations on Third-Party Comments, 5 (December 22, 2004). It is because signatory airlines that issued the ticket and received payment need to conform to the settled fare so as to compensate the airline which actually carried passengers at the prorate agreed in the IATA passenger tariff conferences.

[135]US DOJ, *supra* note 123, 21–22 (1992).

computerized fare quote system which enables airlines to search for complex fare changes, and an efficient clearing house mechanism for partners to exchange compensation. In addition, the MITA has been under oversight of the IATA Passenger and Cargo Services Conferences and a joint IATA/Air Transport Association group, different from the Tariff Coordination Conference. The custom of settling the interlineable fare does not justify tariff-coordinating activities.[136]

The coordination requirement of the specific characteristics of the air transport industry, e.g., exposure to diverse national laws and currencies, may well be negotiated in the IATA. However, the settlement of fare, rate, or its floor level has a very high possibility of meeting the standard of competition-restriction as price-fixing HCC in spite of its recommendatory nature. Although it is acknowledged that there is a unique necessity in the industry to lead to an intergovernment or multilateral agreement among governments, the fare/rate settlement among competitors restricts competition as the fair/rate is the pivotal point of competition which can attract consumers. The proposal of the U.S. Department of Transportation (DOT) to withdraw the antitrust exemption as to IATA tariff-coordinating conferences has its background of U.S./EC Air Transport Agreement of 2007 signed for cooperative competition law enforcement.[137] Such proposal of the withdrawal by U.S. DOT demonstrates that the IATA conferences have restricted fare-reducing competition although there may be benefit for travelers from interlining fare coordination. The EU Commission and Australia's competition authority had already withdrawn the exemption from cartel regulation.

(B) Slot Allocation and Airport Scheduling

As to slot allocation and airport scheduling, the measures are considered as necessary to the arrangement of congested airports because the coordination has such advantages as improving efficient utilization of scare airport capacity, facilitating air traffic control, and helping to maximize the benefits of air transport service to airport users. So as to avoid the restriction of competition, the allocation and the scheduling require (i) an open entry into negotiation and (ii) nondiscriminatory and transparent consultation.[138] The use of 'historical precedence' of the IATA[139] can point out necessity of competition-based rule. The IATA allowed an airline with a series of slots allocated for regular scheduled services, e.g., one operating not less than 80 % of the slots, to have priority over other airlines in the next equivalent period. Competition in air transport services can be lessened through the historical

[136]EU CC, *supra* note 114, 8–9.

[137]DOT, *DOT Proposes Revoking IATA's Antitrust Exemption for Transatlantic and U.S.-Australia Fare and Rate Coordination*, available at http://www.dot.gov/affairs/dot7506.htm (visited on March 4, '08).

[138]The European Commission acknowledged the standards in a preamble of official regulation. *See* EC (2006), at I.272/4. On the other hand, IATA states that activities of agencies in charge of scheduling and allocation should be neutral, transparent, and nondiscriminatory. IATA (2007), at 7, 11, and 12.

[139]IATA, *id*, at 22.

precedence. The intent of the use of the historical precedence is analyzed to secure foreseeable scheduling for existent large airlines in the same period and encouragement for them to use as more airport slots as possible. In terms of the convenience for airport users, the historical precedence can provide familiarity to users. The possibility of abusing the institution, e.g., intentional interference with competing airlines operations through exchange of slots, is screened by coordinator, and coordination committee or slot performance committee.[140]

However, the historical precedence can impede a new airline competing with the existent airlines from using slots or having schedule in the similar times. More efficient usage of slots can be made with preference to airlines willing to pay more airport fee with longer effective operation period rather than airlines maintaining a large portion of slots. While the unilateral focus of the historic precedence on large airlines with market power may lead to inefficiency from monopoly, competition among airlines can improve services and decrease fare. In EU, the protection for the IATA Guidelines by the block exemption of Art. 81 (3) expired.[141] The nonrenewal of the application of the block exemption implies a strict attitude of eliminating competition-restricting activities of slot allocation and airport scheduling.

As an alternative institution, the slot auction system, which U.S. DOJ suggested for O'Hare (Chicago) or LaGardia (New York) airport, is a market-based model for preventing the restriction of competition through slot allocation in air service markets.[142] However, the auction system may shrink airlines' investment plan because it significantly reduces the foreseeability of schedule and usable slots. The over-ten-year spectrum license system which the U.S. Federal Communications Commission has used at auctions reduces the uncertainty of the auction.[143] The preference for an airline with effective longer operation can be provided through a kind of loyalty program, loyalty discount, or special slot allocation.

The EU Council Regulations have illustrated concrete measures to increase competition in slot allocation in an open, nondiscriminatory, and transparent way. Art. 2 para. 1 states (a) openness to all new carriers with interest, (b) establishment of nondiscriminatory rule of priority, (c) 50 % share allocation of available slots to new enterers in EU airports, (d) significant share in third country airports, and (e) securing of open access to the rule of priority, slot information, and allocation criteria, and (f) reason for refusal of slot request.[144] The historic precedence did not

---

[140]*See id.* at 29.

[141]It did expire from 2007. Art. 4 of the Regulation No. 1456/2006.

[142]U.S. DOJ, Comments of the DOJ: Before the Federal Aviation Administration Department of Transportation (DOT), Notice of Alternative Policy Options for Managing Capacity at Laguardia Airport and Proposed Extension of Lottery Allocation, Doc. No. FAA-2001-9854, at 14–15 (2002); DOJ, Comments of the DOJ: Congestion and Delay Reduction at Chicago O'Hare Int' Airport, Doc No. FAA-2005-20704, at 19 (2005).

[143]U.S DOJ, *supra* note 142, at 13 (2005).

[144]EC, *supra* note 138, at 32. It stated that Council Regulation 95/93 as modified by Regulation 793/2004 of the European Parliament brought the Community system to the practices in scheduling guidelines.

allow sufficient openness to all new carriers or the rule of priority. 50 % share allocation of remaining slots as a pool to new entrants under the Guidelines will occupy only a tiny portion of the whole slot allocation. The new entrant status can be endowed on an airline holding fewer than only five slots at an airport on the day of request. A modified slot allocation rule with administrative procedure of the U.S. FAA at LaGuardia airport has provided only a limited portion of slots to a pool for small community service, and the impact on new carriers was small.[145] Similarly, the pool of slots for new entrants under the IATA historic precedence will not solve the problems of inadequate access to new carriers, monopoly inefficiency, and efficiency use of congested airport.

In short, although the other aspects of slot allocation under IATA Scheduling Guidelines do not indicate competition-restrictive practices, the historic precedence rule has discriminatory characteristics in favor of existent large airlines.

3.3 Development of National Cartel Laws and the Necessity of International Law

A. Cartel Regulations in Ancient and Medieval Times

In the ancient times, when international trade started to grow, there were regulations against illegal price-fixing and collective boycotts for profits. In several centuries B.C., there was a law regulating profits earned through boycotts in India. In the latter part of the Roman Empire era, there were laws against raising food price or imposing monopoly prices on grain; Diocletian's Edict on Maximum Prices in 301 A.D. and the Constitution of Zeno in 483 A.D. imposed fines or even physical punishment on illegal attempts to raise the price of food or commodity. In 737 A.D., the Tang Dynasty of the ancient China issued a prohibition on price-fixing under Art. 33 of the Tang Code.[146]

In the Medieval times, however, there were no records regarding regulation against cartels. Guilds, as a basic unit of commerce, had operated under the merchants' association with power to restrict competition in commerce in the early stage. A craft guild, under manufacturers' association with exclusive power to manufacture and sell the goods, replaced the merchants' association. Both the guilds enjoyed its monopoly powers, in wholesale and retail areas, acquired from local governments.

As the industrial revolution led to mass production and the demand for labor attracted the population into the cities in the eighteenth century, guilds gradually lost their powers. Although the guilds afterward disappeared, individual enterprises began to collaborate with competitors by reducing production or maintaining price

---

[145] A withdrawal of 3 % or less every year or every 2 years from the air carrier existent slot category would provide a pool for new entrants, which means at most two slots, e.g., one landing and one departure, would become available in any given hour. US DOJ, *supra* note 142, Notice, at 13 (2002).

[146] Taylor (2006), at 74 and footnote 8.

when they faced an economic panic which led to falling prices and decreasing demand on the part of the public. Individual nations developed unique legal treatments regarding collusive activities among competitors. Such legal developments reflected economic, political, and legal backgrounds in each country.

B. Cartel Regulation in Modern Times

(1) The U.S.: The Sherman Act and Effect Doctrine

The U.S. was the only country with a serious push to promote competition in its domestic market starting from the late nineteenth century, when it faced serious economic situation. While major companies colluded to create a trust to raise profits by fixing prices and allocating market and large companies grew through continuous mergers, small and middle size companies were threatened by growing conglomerates. Consumers complained about the high prices fixed by major cartel members in the industry. The unique position of the U.S. with strict competition policy continued up to the end of WW II when European countries adopted effective competition law as a method to economic recovery. Since 1890 when the U.S. Congress enacted the Sherman Act, U.S. courts have developed a literal interpretation of it, as regards to Sec. 1 of the Act covering cartels, rather than following the rule of reason in common law. Through subsequent case laws, the Supreme Court adopted a per se illegal approach by stating that unrestricted competition ensures reasonable prices and consumer welfare.

Extending the subject-matter jurisdiction over national border is the other aspect of cartel regulation related to international law. The initial extraterritorial application of the U.S. competition law to a foreign cartel came out in 1945 with confidence of having the most developed competition law scheme in the *U.S. v. Aluminum Co. of America (Alcoa)*, where the U.S. Court of Appeals for the Second Circuit stated that the Sherman Act does not cover agreements abroad unless it intended to affect imports or exports and its performance is actually shown to have had some effect upon them.[147] The *Alcoa* doctrine faced harsh criticism from other nations, especially Great Britain, which, by adopting a blocking statute, Chap. 11 of the British Protection of Trading Interests Act (1980), prevented documents in the UK from being produced for foreign litigation and allowed a British firm to recover penal damages paid pursuant to a foreign judgment. In response to the retaliatory legislations, some cases adopted approach of balancing foreign interests with national interests by holding that courts should refrain from exercising jurisdiction if the interests of foreign nations and their nationals in the nonenforcement of U.S. law outbalance the U.S.' interest in enforcement.[148] In the context of the balancing

[147]United States v. Aluminum Co. of America, 148 F.2d 416, 444–445 (CA2 1945) (L. Hand, J.). The Aloca doctrine was accepted by Matsushita case. Matsushita Elec. Industrial Co. v. Zenith Radio Corp., 475 U.S. 574, 582, n. 6, 106 S.Ct. 1348, 1354, n. 6, 89 L.Ed.2d 538 (1986).

[148]Timberlane Lumber Co. v. Bank of America, N.T. and S.A., 549 F.2d 597, 614 (C.A. Cal. 1976); Mannington Mills, Inc. v. Congoleum Corp., 595 F.2d 1287, 1297–98 (3rd Cir. 1979); Industrial Inv. Dev. Corp. v. Mitsui & Co. 671 F.2d 876, 884–5 (5th Cir. 1982); Montreal Trading Ltd. V. Amex, Inc. 661 F.3d 864, 869–70 (10th Cir. 1982). In the Timberlane case, the 9th Cir.

principle, other courts refused to apply it due to incommensurability between American interests in antitrust enforcement and British interests against it.[149] In the midst of conflicting opinions, the extraterritorial application of the U.S. antitrust laws achieved, as a result of the Foreign Trade Antitrust Improvement Act (FTAIA) of 1982, the legislative basis of expanding their subject-matter jurisdiction to anticompetitive conduct of foreign companies that occurs in a foreign country in so far as the conduct has a direct, substantial, and reasonably foreseeable effect on U.S. domestic commerce, and such effect gives rise to a claim under the provision of Sec. 1–7 of the Sherman Act.[150] Finally, the U.S. Supreme Court resolved existent conflicting opinions, in *Hartford Fire Insurance Co. v. California* (1993), by holding that the Sherman Act applies to foreign conduct that was meant to produce (and did, in fact) some substantial effect on the U.S.[151] The following 'implementation approach' in the judicial branch of the EU had similar results to that of the developed 'effect doctrine' in the U.S.

(2) European Countries: the United Kingdom (UK), France, and Germany
(A) UK

The British Kingdom with strong industrial competitiveness from the medieval era did not have to focus on cartels due to its common law tradition that any restraint of freedom of commerce had been considered as illegal in public.[152] As the English courts recognized justification of trade restraint, when 'reasonably' limited in time and space, the earlier strict rule grew weakened. In *Mitchel v. Reynolds* (1711), the English

(Footnote 148 continued)

suggested a balance approach in determining extraterritorial effect of antitrust laws, which illustrated elements to be weighed such as (i) degree of conflict with foreign law or policy, (ii) nationality or allegiance of parties, (iii) locations or principal places of business of corporations, (iv) extent to which enforcement by either state can be expected to achieve compliance, (v) relative significance of effects on the United States as compared with those elsewhere, (vi) extent to which there is explicit purpose to harm or affect American commerce, (vii) the foreseeability of such effect, and (viii) the relative importance to violations charged of conduct within the United States as compared with conduct abroad.

[149] Laker Airways Ltd. v. Sabena, Belgian World Airlines, 731 F.2d 909, 948–49 (D.C.Cir. 1984); In re Uranium Antitrust Litigation, 617 F.2d 1248, 1255 (7th Cir. 1980).

[150] 15 U.S.C. Sec. 6a; Sec. 6a (1)(A) and (B), and (2) of the Sherman Act; Sec. 402 of the FTAIA of 1982.

[151] 509 U.S. 764, 796; 113 S.Ct. 2891, 2909 (1993).

[152] The English courts held *unenforceable a promise not to compete,* which was ancillary to a lawful transaction. The reason for such prohibition was not that they might limit competition but from the fear *that skilled workmen deprived of his trade due to the restriction to their freedom of commerce would become a burden upon the public.* In those times, when trade was controlled by the guilds and towns, the promise not to compete in the locality meant by far severer restriction on practicing one's trade than the current meaning of competition-restriction, thereby reaching his inability to practice anywhere. Phillip Areeda, Antitrust Analysis: problems, text, and cases, 45 (3rd ed., 1981).

court enforced a provision not to compete for 5 years in the immediate locality using 'reasonable' standard. It held that trade restraints may be justified as 'reasonable' if ancillary to some principal transaction and if limited in time and space.[153]

In *Nordenfelt v. Maxim Nordernfelt Guns and Ammunition Co.* (1894), although the court acknowledged the traditional rule, it loosened its antirestraint policy by expanding the 'reasonable' standard and holding that the restraints may be justified if the restriction is reasonable (a) in reference to the interests of the parties concerned, (b) in reference to the interests of public, and (c) so framed and so guarded as to afford adequate protection to the parties without injuring the public.[154] Moreover, the 'reasonableness' standard was decided mostly on the basis of the related parties' interests because the courts accepted prima facie presumption in favor of public interest unless evidences of negative economic conditions outweigh those of positive conditions. The Court of Appeals, in 1889, dismissed an action against an agreement among shipowners of the low fee fixing to dispel competitors and the discontinuance of rebate on the condition that shippers would use the competitors' ships. The holding of the majority drew a delimitation of illegality of an agreement for combining competitors to drive outsiders away from markets by stating that the agreement could not secure judicial aids, e.g., relief or action on its basis. It opined that, unless they injured rival business through fraud, intimidation, or molestation, making the agreement itself is not indictable or actionable.[155] As an economic analysis was in a less-developed stage to reflect a predatory pricing or a monopoly attempt, Queen's Bench Division pointed out that damage caused to competitors' rights to trade by the agreement was so strictly limited that it could not form an unlawful act.[156] The holding implied that moral culpability against the agreement is weak, which was in contrast to a dissenting opinion that the agreement is one intended to interfere with the free trade of nonparty and a wrongful act against both an individual and public welfare if carried out.[157]

A shift of the loosening policies toward the stringent one took place after WW II when a whitepaper was published warning that the attainment of postwar full employment objectives might be jeopardized by the price-fixing practices of cartels and monopolies.[158] Pursuant to the whitepaper, 1956 Restrictive Trade Practices Act (RTPA) prohibited restraints of trade among suppliers of goods with specified exceptions, and required registration of trade-restricting agreements with the Office of Fair Trading (OFT) under its rebuttable presumption that such formal agreements impede public interest. RTPA of 1956 created a Restrictive Practices Court

---

[153]*See id.* 1. P.Wms. 181, 24 Eng. Rep. 347 (K.B. 1711). The attitude of common law was imported in the U.S.

[154]Areeda (1981), 45–46. [1894] A.C. 535, 565.

[155]Mogul Steamship Co. v. McGregor, Gow & Co. et al., 23 Q.B.D. 598, 626–27 (1889). *See also* Scherer (1994), at 26–27.

[156]*Mogul Steam Co.* case, at 613–615 and 624–625.

[157]*See id.* at 606. Lord Esher mentioned that an illegal act against the public welfare seems to have the necessary elements of a crime (at 606) and that the agreement was an indictable conspiracy done with malice to obstruct plaintiffs (at 608–610).

[158]George (1990) at 105.

(RPC) to adjudicate contested cases. The RPC decisions caused more than 50 % of formal restrictive agreements under its review to be abandoned between 1956 and 1965. The UK was considered as a country with the most serious enforcement against formal cartels by 1960s.[159]

(B) France

In France, the earliest cartel dates back to the Marseille Cartel in soda industry, 1838. Subsequently from 1840s, it was followed by cartels from raw materials, e.g., iron, coal, sugar, and petroleum, to artificial products, e.g., chemicals, glass, porcelain, and textiles.[160] Although a number of cartels came out, their control over market competition is analyzed as very limited as foreign competition beyond the coverage of such cartels challenged national markets. Meanwhile, internationalization of cartels grew under the facilitation of nation-level agreements, e.g., the federation of Luxemburg-Lorraine crude iron works in 1879.[161] The international cartels were mostly dissolved during the great depression starting in the late 1920s.

France, similar to countries in the European Communities which adopted anti-cartel provisions had shown rare effective cartel regulations before 2000, had not actively applied, by the end of WW II, Art. 409 of the Napoleonic Penal Code, which prohibited collective action to raise or lower prices artificially for the purpose of acquiring profits. Restraint on competition under gentlemen's agreement was acknowledged in French culture. Moreover, strict level of burden of proof on artificiality or abnormality of the desired price under the criminal statute, along with war-time tolerance of cartels, led to loose enforcement.[162] As a result, cartel formation was allowed in practice under the ineffective law.[163] During the postwar era when economic recovery was in progress and when the legal foundation of economic development including competition law was set, still the tolerant attitude had prevailed.

(C) Germany

On the other hand, Germany neither regulated cartels like the U.S. nor had such strong freedom-oriented public opinion like France let alone common law tradition of UK. When cartels regulated raw material supply according to economic ups and downs in the late nineteenth century, the German Empire Court, the highest court of Germany, even held, in 1897 in a case involving wood pulp manufacturers, that a cartel agreement falls on freedom of association accorded workers and businesses and is binding unless a cartel led to an actual monopoly or extreme exploitation of consumers.[164] In

---

[159] *See* Scherer, *supra* note 155, 32: Harding and Joshua (2010), pp. 108–110.

[160] Resch, *Phases of Competition Policy in Europe*, Working Paper AY0504, 3Institute of European Studies: UC Berkeley, April 2005), available at http://repositories.cdlib.org.

[161] *Id.* at 3–4.

[162] Edwards (1964), at 32–33.

[163] Id; Resch (2005) at 2.

[164] Scherer, *supra* note 155, 24.

1908, representing public opinions,[165] the Court pronounced that the members of a construction cartel adhere to their agreement by focusing on such a benefit of the cartel as the mitigating of the damage of unrestrained competition from dishonest underbidding. As to offense to public moral by secret bid agreement, it stated that agreements whose purpose is to mitigate the damage and maintain appropriate prices offends public morals so little that they deserve approval, and that a public official, actually mislead by such secret understandings, has only his own negligent comprehension of how business is done to blame.[166] Through the formal approval of cartel from the court, cartels grew popular in diverse industries.[167] Internationalization of cartels developed to such a level that 40 international cartels involving Germany existed in 1897.[168]

German government even took advantage of cartels so as to secure materials for warfare during WW I. Under the suffering of political turmoil and postwar hyperinflation,[169] Germany's legislative body enacted the German Cartel Ordinance of 1923 that adopted abuse principle, in other words, made illegitimate only abuse of restraint of trade among collaborating competitors under the national supervision of a new administrative agency that could request the correction of abuses before a new Cartel Court. However, the Ordinance was sparingly enforced.[170] Subsequently, when Nazis government's trial to solve high price and inflation by destructuring cartels failed, the government made such compulsory cartels as Marktvergand (market groups) and supervised food business groups through which the government intervened in economy for securing war-time capacities.

After the WW II, Germany adopted competition law in 1957 with focus on administrative corrective sanctions. The academic community grew positive to its enforcement, thereby offering foundation for revisions of German competition law. Informal collusion or concerted practices among competitors was illegalized in 1970s.

C. Necessity of International Legal Measures

(1) Rationales for International Agreement as regards Cartels

[165]*Id.*, 24–25. Although it is not sure whether judicial decisions reflected scholarly opinions, the leading contemporary economist in cartel, Robert Liefmann considered unrestricted competition as inherently unstable and the advantages of cartelization compelling thereby stating that State only needs to hinder the unfavorable effects as much as possible. Gustav Schmoller, the most eminent German economist, shared the same judgment in 1905.

[166]*See id.*

[167]*Scherer, id.* at 23.

Year	1875	1887	1896	1905	1911
Number of Cartels	8	70	250	395	600

[168]Resch, *supra* note 161, 3.

[169]There were Hitler's coup in Bavaria, crisis in Saxony, and the conflict in the Ruhr area. *Id.* at 5.

[170]Scherer, *supra* note 155, 26; Voigt (1962), at 170–74.

Why have countries strived to achieve bilateral and multilateral agreements in competition policy, particularly cartel regulations, although there are suspicions regarding such efforts?

First, without international agreements for controlling cartelistic behaviors, each country will have a narrow perspective on maximizing its national interests regardless of the harm that consumers and competitors in other countries will have to endure. The case of the free trade dilemma applies in competition law and anticartel regulations. A country may have benefit through allowing by lenient application or legalization, or by stimulating cartel activities among domestic firms which affect mostly foreign countries, but the restrictive business practice produces a negative effect on the global economy, such as high-price low-quality goods, entry barrier for new enterprises, and a disincentive to invest in innovative technology. Widespread export cartel exemptions are the examples. In order to promote total economic welfare through fair competition on the global level, a binding agreement on the serious enforcement of competition law as well as cooperation in its enforcement is necessary.

Second, the agreement can let member countries overcome hurdles in the investigation and enforcement of international cartels. Its major advantages are that competition authorities can collect evidence located in other member countries, share confidential information, and make foreign-based companies comply with judgments under the agreement. Domestic competition laws may be difficult to effectively enforce against overseas cartels, such as obstacles in investigating overseas meeting of foreign companies, collecting substantial (confidential) evidences located outside domestic territories, and pertaining to the delivery of documents to foreign participators, and collection of surcharges from them. Insufficient cooperation from the other competition authorities may be added in case bilateral agreements lack or do not cover sufficient substances for cooperation.[171]

Diverse kinds of international law can reduce the obstacles substantially. A bilateral agreement as to the cooperation of competition law enforcements is the most important basic cooperative measure to substantially reduce such investigatory difficulties as collecting evidences, delivering documents, enforcing surcharges, and sharing confidential information during the procedure. The competition authorities from DCs where an international cartel member usually do not have an affiliate need international cooperation to secure evidence against international cartel members. A multilateral agreement or a treaty may address these issues when many countries make bilateral agreements and widely use them. The multilateral agreements, such as the current OECD-level recommendation, will contribute to the building of competition capacities in countries with insufficient experiences and immature skills regarding cartel enforcement.

A governmental authority of a country involved with a cartel participant may object to penalties imposed on the participating company because the economic damage to the company caused by the penalties may negatively affect the country's economy and industrial competitiveness. The widespread competition cultures, the

[171]KFTC (2004), at 8–9.

establishment of the effective cooperation among the competition authorities, and the understanding of the risks and damages of the cartel under international law can reduce the intergovernmental conflicts.

Third, the international agreement is a legal foundation for DCs which lack the resources and experience in anticartel law enforcement to improve their capabilities. Developed countries can assist the promotion of anticartel enforcement in the DCs with their skills, experiences, and the sharing of information. Currently, UNCTAD, OECD, and ICN are the main institutions devoted to assisting DCs in competition law and cartel norm enforcement. Advanced countries need to be aware that building a competition culture in emerging markets help multinational corporations from the markets to abide by competition laws in their countries with growing competition law awareness. As regional markets grow integrated and consumers are treated as a whole regardless of territories, widening competition norms in the less-developed areas can prevent the enterprises in the South from unintentionally violating competition laws in the advanced markets. In addition, potential cartel members in the North will face the utmost deterrence when DCs, where the members neither leave important evidence nor have head offices in most cases, are ready to enforce their anticartel regulations seriously.

Fourth, it can reduce jurisdictional conflict of extraterritorial application of domestic competition laws and disputes over defining relevant markets in the light of the global impact beyond national territories. When a cartel with cross-border effect is prohibited in a country but allowed in the other country, the strict application of the former country's anticartel law as to the cross-border cartel may intervene in the other country's jurisdiction. On the other hand, a weak jurisdictional basis to extraterritorial applications to overseas conduct might lead to a reluctance to investigate or apply competition laws to overseas cartels. Stipulations in advance as to extraterritoriality with clear guidelines of negative and positive comity principles can reduce such possible conflicts regarding the sovereign principle. Currently, the issue has been dealt with bilateral agreements. In near future when a consensus as to the extraterritorial application of cartel regulations is reached, a multilateral agreement is able to be enforced regarding this issue.

In addition, although defining a relevant market is an important process in competition law, and the market scope is widened to regional or global level through regional/global free trade agreement; in reality, competition law enforcers frequently examined it within national borders. The international agreement is expected to contribute to defining sophisticated relevant markets in the light of the global market beyond national territories.

Fifth, the fact that harms on DCs' economy imposed by international cartels are quite substantial that should be duly noted. The Working Group on Competition Policy (WGCP) under WTO, addressed the importance of regulating cartels in DCs. In the light of necessity of developing certain economic sectors and industries in DCs, UNCTAD IV conference in 1976 provided special treatment to DCs, which eventually led to the UN Set in 1980. Since then, a variety of harmful activities on the part of international cartels have been researched in the global scope, resulting in a consensus for international cooperation against cartel activities. By the consensus, the 1998 OECD Recommendation against Hard Core Cartel, a non-binding recommendation, has been reached. So, as to reduce the damages from international cartels, with more reports from sophisticated researches and recommendations, binding international laws shall address international cartels. The binding international law will promote international cooperation through international laws that would contributes to eliminating cartels, thereby bringing positive effects to advanced countries and DCs.

(2) EU: Competition Chapter under 1957 Treaty and Implementation Approach

The Treat establishing the European Community (the 1957 EC Treaty) as a single market includes a chapter of rules on competition under Title VI (ex. Title V) and promotes a high degree of competitiveness through a system ensuring that competition in the internal market is not distorted under Articles 2 and 3. Concretely, Art. 81 (1) (ex. 85 (1)), as regarding cartels, prohibits all agreements between undertakings, decisions by associations of undertakings and concerted practices which may affect trade between Member States, which have as their main object or effect the prevention, restriction, or distortion of competition within the common market unless they satisfy the justifying conditions of para. 3 of the same article.[172] Art. 81 (1) enumerates five particular activities: (a) price-fixing, (b) production control, (c) market sharing, (d) application of discriminatory condition, and (e) placing the conclusion of contracts subject to acceptance of unrelated supplementary obligations. The Competition Directorate has published annual report on competition policy, although major politicians tried to remove the competition policy from the EC Treaty.[173] An adamant attitude against price-fixing and market-sharing cartels is reflected in the representative competition policy of the Community.[174] The EC Council adopted Council Regulation 17 (1961)[175] as an initial implementing measure on anticartel and antimonopoly pursuant to Art. 83 (ex. Art. 87) to be substituted by Council Regulation (2002).[176]

Regarding extraterritorial application of its competition law, the ECJ held that an infringement of Art. 81 (ex. 85) consists of a conduct of two elements, (i) the formation of the agreement, decision or concerted practice and (ii) the implementation thereof, and that if the applicability of prohibitions under competition law were made

[172]Any agreement or decision or concerted practice which contributes to improving the production or distribution of goods or to promoting technical or economic progress, while allowing consumers a fair share of the resulting benefit, and which does not (a) impose on the undertakings concerned restrictions which are not indispensable to the attainment of these objectives, and (b) afford such undertakings the possibility of eliminating competition in respect of a substantial part of the products in question in light of Article 81 (3) of EC treaty.

[173]*Sarkozy Scraps Competition Clause From New Treaty*, SMD/Reuter (June 22, 2007), at http://www.spiegel.de/international/europe/0,1518,490136,00.html (visited on February 12, '08).

[174]XXIXth Report on Competition Policy, ¶ 2 (1999). XXVIth Report on Competition Policy (1996) states generally, as Commission's policy, promoting the competitiveness of European industry as a whole by strict enforcement of the competition rules, Art. 81, 82, and 86, applicable to Member States and those applicable to undertakings 8.

[175]Council Regulation No. 17 of 6 Feb. 1962.

[176]Council Regulation (EC) No. 1/2003 of 16 Dec. 2002.

to depend on the place where the agreement, decision, or practice was formed, the result would obviously be to give undertakings an easy means of evading those prohibitions.[177] As a result, the ECJ placed focus on the place of the implementation of a formed agreement.[178] In terms of import trade, the 'implementation approach' of the ECJ has a high possibility of producing the same result as American 'effect doctrine' because cartel abroad cannot have a substantial effect on a domestic market without implementation of its conspiracy within the market.[179]

3.4 Development of International Commodity Agreements (ICAs) Separate from Cartel Regime

A.Initial Treatments

(1) A Period of National Interest (1921–1933 World Monetary and Economic Conference (WMEC))

In this period, governments had relied heavily on national regulations for their national interests. Their representative regulatory measures were export levies under the Rubber Restriction Scheme and a buffer stock and a quota system as export quantity control under the Tin Scheme 1931.[180] Whatever forms the control measures took, the measures were justified on a strong public interest basis. State-owned profits from primary commodities constituted a large portion of governmental revenues.[181] In countries where a mining industry has created the majority of their wealth, stable and fair remunerations for mining were considered necessary to prevent social and economic crises. Opposition against national control was not against the scheme itself but against the rigidity of its operation. The U.S., however, as major importers of rubber and tin, changed its attitude from acquiescence to governmental control to the condemnation of it, by deeming it as an attempt to set up private monopolies.[182] Aware of such criticism, the British government invited representatives of consuming countries to voice their interests at a committee; which controlled the global scheme, so as to protect their interests from excessive price fluctuation. Protection of the consumers became the principle of organization, which distinguished its commodity organization from that of a private cartel. As wide participation was necessary for the operation of the organization, consideration was given to low-end producers by setting a two-tier

[177] Ahlstrom Osakeyhtio et al. v. Commission of the European Communities, cases 89, 104,116–117, 125–129/85 [1988] ECR 5193, ¶ 16 (EU). This case is called as Wood pulp case.

[178] *Id.*

[179] Flynn et al. (2005), at 172 footnote 52.

[180] Kahn (1982), at 53–54.

[181] *See id.*, at 52.

[182] *See id.* at 54.

negotiation process in control. After the first negotiation amongst high-end producers took place regarding international obligations and rights, the second negotiation among low-end producers decided on imposing less or no obligations.[183]

(2) The League of Nations Period (1933–1948)

The concern about national interests in the Anglo-Dutch phase was shifted to that of the global economy in this period in the context of economic depression. The League of Nations developed international economic law principle based on Article 23 (3) stating that Members will make provisions to secure and maintain the freedom of communication and transit, as well as the equitable treatment for the commerce of all Members. With acknowledgement on the importance of economic policies to international security, promotion of international economic cooperation was accepted widely as a general principle. At the World Economic Conference of 1927, there were advocates of farmers interests who had encouraged farmers to organize themselves in order to deal with the saturated market through an agreement among governments. The final resolution of the WMEC of 1933 reflected such a necessity, by including the statement that, in the exceptional conditions of the present world crisis, concerted action should be required for the purpose of increasing the purchasing power of the producers of primary commodities to a reasonable level, and that plans should be adopted for the coordination of the production and marketing of certain commodities.[184] The possible conflict that would arise from preferential treatment for commodity-producing countries was reconciled as organs of the League, e.g., Economic Committee, acknowledged that cereal surpluses were a global economic issue to be dealt seriously with priority and that such preferences would be a temporary and limited exception. The WMEC actively supported the formation of commodity agreements by enunciating certain principles as to the organization of the commodity agreements, declaring its favor of the agreements complying with the principles, and inviting the participating countries to negotiate agreements. The principles included: the participation of producing countries and assent of the majority of producers as well as their states, fairness to both producers and consumers for securing a fair price level, and the cooperation of consuming interests of importing countries.[185] The 'consuming interests' were considered to be on equal footing to those of governments of importing countries. Commodity agreements, during and after the WMEC, adopted these principles. The International Sugar Agreement of 1937, in its preamble, mentioned the League principles of the orderly relationship between supply and demand of sugar in the world market and of fair and equitable

[183] *Id.* at 55.

[184] *Id.* at 57. He also cites the statement of the President, J. Ramsay MacDonald of the World Monetary and Economic Conference 1933 who stated that international cooperation is our best way to national recovery.

[185] Section (d) of the WMEC resolution. C.435.M.220 (1933). *See id.* at 61 to 62.

treatment of consumers as well as producers.[186] However, the representatives of the consumers worked in an advisory function as the International Rubber Regulation Committee under the International Rubber Agreement 1934 and the International Tin Agreement 1937 illustrated. An accurate reflection of consuming interests in the settling of price levels was not possible. The International Tea Committee confirmed the concern of importing countries and mentioned, with a focus on consuming countries' assurance for the reasonable operation of governmental regulatory schemes as to raw materials, that such schemes should have adequate provisions for the effective representation of consumers and be subject to governmental supervision so that the controlling body can take immediate action in the event of an unreasonable rise of prices or other effects prejudicial to the consumers.[187]

B. Distinctive Legal Treatment from Conventional Cartel

(1) International Law

1) Chapter VI of the Havana Charter and its Survival

(A) The Principles and Rules governing ICA

Although the Havana Charter of 1948 with a design of a complex legal framework of international law in the post WW II era failed to be in effect, Chap. VI of the Charter dealing with ICAs came into existence. The particular chapter was intended to address the difficulties unique in primary commodity trade such as the tendency toward persistent disequilibrium between production and consumption, the accumulation of stocks, and pronounced fluctuations in prices. The special difficulties may cause adverse effects on the interests of both producers and consumers accompanied by widespread repercussions jeopardizing the general policy of economic expansions. As a result, such special difficulties request special treatment of international trade in such commodities through intergovernmental agreements.[188] The general principles governing ICAs are: open participation, equitable treatment between participating countries and nonparticipating countries, and the most-favored-nation (MFN) principle to overall nonparticipants, bipartisan participation from both consuming countries and producing countries, and the full publicity of the statements of consideration and objective of the proposing member, and the nature and development of the corrective measures of the ICA.[189]

Particularly, the commodity control agreement regarding price regulation or quantitative control of production, export, or import needs to be subject to additional principles with the parity of vote between importing and exporting countries, the offer of increasing opportunities for satisfying national consumption and world market requirements, and internal economic adjustment program to ensure as much

[186] *Id.* at 61.

[187] *Id.* at 66; ILO, IGCA, 137–139.

[188] Article 55 of the Chap. VI. Of Havana Charter.

[189] Article 60.¶ 1.

progress as practicable.[190] The control agreement may be entered into only in the circumstance (i) when a burdensome surplus of a primary commodity has or is expected to develop, which would cause serious hardship to producers, particularly small producers in charge of a substantial portion of the total output, and the surplus could not be corrected by normal market forces, or (ii) when widespread unemployment or one in relation to a primary commodity due to its unique difficulties has or is expected to develop which could not be corrected by normal market forces in time to prevent widespread and undue hardship to workers.[191]

(B) Art. XX (h) of GATT and 1947 Resolution of Economic and Social Council

The survival of the chapter was due to the supports from both the Economic and Social Council (ECOSOC) and the General Agreement on Tariffs and Trade (GATT), as well as subsequent state practices. The ECOSOC resolution 30 (IV) of March 28, 1947 recommended that Members of the United Nations (UN) adopt the principles in Chapter VI as a general guide in intergovernmental consultation or action with respect to commodity problems. Pursuant to ECOSOC's request for the UN Secretary General to launch an interim coordinating committee for international commodity agreements (ICCICA), the committee started to work to stay informed of and to facilitate intergovernmental consultation as to commodity surplus problems. The GATT accepted measures in pursuance of obligations under the ICA as an exception to trade law principles under Art. XX (h). The exception applies to the one which conforms to the principles approved by ECOSOC in the resolution in 1947 as well as the one which conforms to criteria submitted to the contracting parties and not disapproved by them.[192] State practices, reports and findings of ICCICA, and subsequent ICAs, e.g., 1954 International Sugar Agreement and International Tine Agreement, maintain the validity of the Chapter VI.[193]

(C) Assessment

Although Chap. VI of the Charter contributed to the organization of ICA and built regulations of supplies separately from private cartel regulations in competition law, it did not address the positive points of the ICAs toward economic development and special treatment to LDCs.[194] The resolutions, negotiations, and recommendations of UN conferences, as mentioned later, extended the limited functions of the international ICA law.

---

[190] Article 63 (b), (c) and (d) of Chap. VI.

[191] Article 62 (a) and (b) of Chap. VI.

[192] Article XX (h) and ad. Article XX(h) of GATT 1947.

[193] Khan, *supra* note 180, 67. The principles of parity of votes have been applied almost consistently.

[194] *Id.* at 73.

2) UN Conferences

(A) Trade and Development (UNCTAD)

UNCTAD, since its first conference, has contributed to supporting the work of the international commodity bodies for promoting cooperation between producers and consumers, which, however, have functioned similar to cartels. The New International Economic Order (NIEO) principle proposed by UNCTAD and passed by UN General Assembly as Resolution 3201 and 3202[195] has operated as the legal foundation for operating such interstate commodity agreements.

São Paulo Consensus adopted at UNCTAD XI in June 2004 confirmed its mission to continue to help build effective partnerships among relevant stakeholders, aiming for viable solutions and sustainable approaches to commodity problems. The São Paulo conference established an independent international task force on commodities which is to review the contribution of ICAs. Recently, UNCTAD adopted a new agreement on olive oil and table olives in the context of increasing demand from advanced countries with an interest in health benefits, by transferring advanced cultivation technologies to DCs.[196]

(B) Environment and Development (UNCED)

The so-called 'Stockholm Declaration' adopted by the United Nations Conference on the Human Environment stated that natural resources of the earth must be safeguarded for the benefit of present and future generations through careful planning or management as appropriate.[197] Similarly as to nonrenewable natural resources, sustainable development through managing the exploitation of nonrenewable natural resources requires careful concerns to the danger of their future exhaustion and equitable sharing of their benefits by all of mankind.[198] A commodity price management by an ICA or an IPA has its legal foundation concretely in principle 10, stating that, for the DCs, the stability of prices and adequate earnings from primary commodities and raw materials are essential to environmental management since economic factors as well as ecological processes must be taken into account.[199]

UNCED adopted the RIO Declaration on Environment and Development in 1992 which stipulated that while states have the sovereign right to exploit their own resources under their own environmental and developmental policies, the right to

---

[195]Declaration on the Establishment of a New International Economic Order (NIEO), GA Res. 3201, (1 May 1974); Programme of Action on the Establishment of a NIEO, GA Res. 3202, (1 May 1974).

[196]Ostensson, Press Release: New Agreement On Olive Oil And Table Olives Record rise in demand for this commodity, UNCTAD/PRESS/PR/2005/01529/04/05, *available at* http://www.unctad.org/Templates.

[197]Principle 2.

[198]Stockholm Declaration of the United Nations Conference on the Human Environment, Principle 5, UN Doc. A/COF.48/14 (June 16, 1972).

[199]Principle 10.

development must be fulfilled so as to equitably meet developmental and environmental needs of present and future generations.[200] In the case of nonrenewable natural resources, exploitative competition in producing the resources under the sovereign right might cause exhaustion at a premature stage, thereby conflicting with interests of future generations. Management in producing exhaustible commodity is required because states should reduce and eliminate unsustainable patterns of production and consumption to achieve sustainable development and a higher quality of life for all people.[201]

Moreover, the 2002 Johannesburg Declaration on Sustainable Development and a Plan of Implementation for the further implementation of Agenda 21 (2002 Johannesburg Declaration) under the World Summit on Sustainable Development (WSSD) requested the international community to address the instability of commodity prices and declining terms of trade and suggested international assistance for sustainable resource management.[202]

3) UN

(A) Resolutions of General Assembly

Although the Havana Charter included provisions pertaining to ICAs under Chap. VI, separately from the competition provisions of Chap. V, neither provisions nor the whole Charter came into effect. The UN adopted a series of General Assembly (GA) Resolutions,[203] clearly approving of permanent sovereignty over natural resources (NR) since 1950s, some of which foundered the so-called New International Economic Order (NIEO).[204] Under the NIEO principle, subsequent resolutions recognized the relationship between the economic development of NR-producing DCs and the permanent sovereignty principle over NRs;[205] the promotion of international cooperation for economic development was considered to have its basis on respect for the right to sovereignty over national wealth and resources.[206]

[200]Principle 2 and 3.

[201]Principle 8.

[202]Item IX, The Plan of Implementation, Means of Implementation, ¶ 8.

[203]UN General Assembly (GA) Resolution 523(VI) of 12 Jan. 1952, 626(VII) of 21 Dec. 1952, 1314(XIII) of 12 Dec. 1958, 1515(XV) of 15 Dec. 1960, 1803(XVII) of 14 Dec. 1962, 2158 (XXI) of 25 Dec. 1966, 2386 (XXIII) of 19 Nov. 1968, 2625 (XXV) of 24 Oct. 1970, 2692 (XXV) of 11 Dec. 1970, 3016 (XXVII) of 18 Dec. 1972, and 3171 (XXVIII) of 17 Dec. 1973, particularly Chap. VIII of 3202 (VI) of 1 May 1974, 4(e) of 3201 (VI) of 1 May 1974, and Chap. II Art. 2(1) of 3281(XXIX) of 12 Dec. 1974.

[204]They are Declaration on the Establishment of a New International Economic Order (NIEO), GA Res. 3201 (1974) and Programme of Action on the Establishment of a NIEO, GA Res. 3202 (1974).

[205]One of them is preamble ¶ 6 of Res. 3171 (XXVIII) of 17 Dec. 1973.

[206]Chap. I.6. of 1803 (XVII) of 14 Dec. 1962, 7 of Res. 3171 (XXVIII) of 17 Dec. 1973, and Chap. I.1.(b) of Res. 3202 (VI) of 1 May 1974.

The ICAs have a firm justification under the NIEO. As a method to develop economic cooperation among commodity-producing states, interstate cartels are not only allowed but also encouraged as a state's economic right,[207] or even required[208] as a duty which the other states should respect.[209] Since such commodities include agricultural products as well as natural resources, associations, or long-term multilateral agreements of primary commodity producers (IPAs[210]) have been approved with concern on the sustained growth of world economy, particularly, the economic development of DCs.[211] For example, OPEC, as the model for IPA successfully operating during the era, has been working under such concrete legal provisions as 4(t) of Declaration of the Establishment of a NIEO, Chap. VII.1(a) of Program of Action on the Establishment of a NIEO, and Chap. II Art. 5 and 28 of Charter of Economic Rights and Duties of States (CERDS).

Concretely, stable pricing of the commodity trade is considered as essential to secure the global economy's continuous growth. Excessive competition in producing commodity is regarded as a threat to global economic development, including the economic development of DCs, particularly, the survival of LDCs, where commodity trade occupies a considerable portion of the gross domestic product (GDP).[212] When decreasing commodity price threatens LDCs' capability to procure foods, states need to cooperate to sustain the decreasing price with non-reciprocal and special treatments.[213] The necessity to provide food, recognized as the individual's urgent right to food, is to be met with adequate priority in countries' development strategies and expenditure.[214] The duty of states to end the waste of natural resources, including food product, and the request for their collective actions for mutual economic cooperation among the DCs resulted in the approval of production or price management since the trade of natural resources is directly related to economic development, an urgent mission of the developing world, particularly the LDCs.[215]

---

[207]Chap. I.1.(b) of Res. 3202, 3.(a)(iii),(viii),(xi), and 4(f) of Res. 3202, and para.4(t) of Res. 3201.

[208]Chap. I.6. of Res. 3171.

[209]Chap. II. Art. 5 and Art. 28 of Res. 3281.

[210]An Intergovernmental Producers' Association (IPA) works in the similar way to an ICA. Under the large category of a cartel, it belongs to a public cartel subject to international commodity law rather than competition law. *Refer to* Chap. 1.II.8.

[211]Chap. II. Art.5, 6, and 14 of Res. 3281.

[212]Among 141 DCs with data, 68 depended on nonfuel commodities for more than 50 % of their export earnings in 1990–1992. The number of the countries, so-called Commodity-Dependent Developing Countries (CDDCs) had fallen to 62 by 1998–2000. Sophia Twarog, *New Insights on Opportunities and Problems in World Commodities Trade*, UNCTAD/DITC (2004), at http://www.unctadxi.org/templates/Page____957.aspx (last visited on Oct. 24, '07).

[213]4.(j) (m), and (n), Art. 9, 14, 18 and 19 of Res. 3201.

[214]UN GA Res. On the Right to Food, GA Res. 56/155, UNGAOR, 56th Sess., Supp. No. 49, at 348, UN Doc.A/RES/56/155 (February 15, 2002). *See* para. 1, 2, 4, and 6.

[215]4. (q)(r) and (s) of Res. 3201.

Notably, the interests of consuming countries are not to be disregarded but to be balanced to achieve the equitable development of the world economy.[216] The surging of basic food or cereal price has the potential of generating more social tension as a major political issue in industrialized countries as well as DCs, more so than the energy price surge, e.g., oil shock, does in transitional economies.[217] Although the LDCs' interests in primary commodity are urgent, the NIEO's emphasis on DCs' interests was to balance the interests of both producers and consumers for the sustained economic growth of the global economy. Stressing regional and international cooperation to deal with the global food security issue, the UN GA Resolution on Right to Food urged each country to adopt a strategy consistent with the resources and capacities, which gives priority in their development strategies and expenditures to the realization of the right to food.[218] The Declaration on World Food Security adopted by heads of state and government at 2002 World Food Summit confirms the importance of the efficient use of resources and sustainable management of natural resources in responding to the challenge of globalization—particularly with respect to agriculture and food security. The Declaration urges cooperation and solidarity to consolidate FAO activities.[219]

In order for the declarations of UNCED to result in success, the necessity of managing natural resources and all living species pursuant to sustainable development in light of the future generation should be noted by changing current unsustainable patterns of production and consumption.[220] UN GA members are aware of the insufficiency of the resources in our earth,[221] and commodity management is permitted in the interests of environmental protection.

By reflecting the principles which justify public cartels consisting of ICAs and IPAs, the resolutions have been treated separately from cartel regulations aiming at private companies in international law. Noteworthy are the other causes that international law pursues as to public cartels in distinction with private cartels such as development and reduction of poverty in LDCs and the protection against the wasting of natural resources. However, the recent surges in commodity prices demonstrate that a better strategy in regulating commodity trade can be drafted on the basis of an association of consuming and producing countries (ICA) rather than an association of producing states only (IPA).

---

[216] Chap. II. Art. 6 of CERDS, GA Res. 3281 (1974).

[217] Guy Dinmore, *Italians spurn pasta in price protest*, Fin Times (September 14, 2007). *See* Javier Blas, *Agriculture Commodities:Political Sensitivity over food price rises*, Fin Times (Oct. 17, 2007). For instance, wheat price has hit an all-time high of more than $9 a bushel.

[218] UN GA Resolution on the Right to Food, GA Res. 56/155, UN GAOR, 56th Sess., Supp. No. 49, at 348 (February 15, 2002). *Refer* to 4 and 6.

[219] ¶ 20, 21, and 26. Rome, June 11–13, 2002, at http://www.fao.org/worldfoodsummit/english/index.html (visited on April 1, 2008).

[220] ¶ 6 and 22 of UN Millennium Declaration (MD) A/55/L.2.

[221] ¶ 21 of UN MD.

(B) Treaties under the UN

There are 46 multilateral treaties regulating commodity trade registered to the Secretary General of the UN, among which 30 treaties expired or were replaced by subsequent treaties. Quite a few commodity agreements ended or broke down in the 1980s. The reasons were because their decision-making mechanism did not harmonize the requests of exporting countries to limit their export with the interests of consuming countries unwilling to cooperate to the export control, and because its members failed to treat the market force flexibly under their short-sighted concerns.[222] In addition, the U.S., as a major trading country which has maintained its domestic agricultural subsidies even during the DDA negotiation for correcting unfair trade practices, has, ironically, displaced a negative attitude toward ICAs, particularly for agricultural commodity, on the basis of competition.

Except the International Tin Study Group, not yet active, all 15 treaties registered under the UN are effective. While two treaties, such as the International Coffee Agreement and the International Cocoa Agreement, consist of producing and consuming member states, the other 11 treaties, such as the Terms of Reference to International Copper Study Group, have producing countries only as their members. Although a public cartel, in strict meaning, covers the latter type, the functional aspects of the former type of treaties have been very similar in restricting competition in the global market.[223] In terms of a regulatory purpose, it will make little, if any, difference between treaties with hybrid membership and those with producing countries only.[224]

(2) The U.S. Law

Since a commodity agreement is made up of states rather than private companies, an antitrust review of activities of the states has brought out legal issues in front of courts, such as act of state doctrine and sovereign immunity.

1) Act of State Doctrine

Since the decision of the U.S. Supreme Court in *Underhill v. Hernandez* that every sovereign state is bound to respect the independence of every other sovereign state, and that a judicial body of one country will not sit in judgment on the acts of the government of another done within its own territory, 'act of state doctrine' has been applied as a valid judicial rule.[225] As a rule for judicial abstention, the legal

---

[222]MacFadden (1986), at page 824–827.

[223]*Id.*, at 811 and 815. While producers, mostly developing countries, argued that fair-level commodity price should work for transferring wealth from the developed countries consisting of mostly consumers, consumers contended that the goal of the organization should be to restrict short-term price fluctuations and to secure an orderly supply of the commodity. Regardless of the internal dispute, the commodity agreements operated on export control or buffer stock or price maintenance to regulate market.

[224]For in-detail explanation, refer to Chap. 1.II.8.

[225]The 3rd Restatement of U.S. Foreign Relations Law confirms the effectiveness of the rule by stating that, in the absence of a treaty or other unambiguous agreement regarding controlling legal

theory does not allow a judicial body to intervene in foreign affairs related to an executive body, even when the validity of the act of a foreign government is an unavoidable issue in trial. Although the act of state doctrine is originally a domestic rule made by the U.S. judicial body[226] and accepted by competition authorities,[227] it is worthwhile to review it because the limitation of the judicial body in foreign policy matters is widely acknowledged by other countries.[228] In the OPEC case with an alleged cartel conspiracy in violation of the U.S. Sherman Act Sec 1, the U. S. Court of Appeals for the Ninth Circuit declined to acknowledge states' responsibility in being involved in the cartel under the 'act of state doctrine.'[229] In the U.S., however, the doctrine does not have a constitutional founding so it can be modified by national legislations.[230]

As explained above, commodity agreements, in particular, have been historically approved by international law.[231] Moreover, a commodity agreement itself is a treaty registered under the UN as a major source of international law. In other words, the states operate through the ICA on the legitimate basis of international law. Although the ICAs and IPAs look to be in conflict with competition laws regulating cartels, the cartel regulations themselves derives their legitimacy from legislation on the same level as treaties, not from the constitution. In short, the operation of the public cartels is a legitimate act subject to international commodity law.

(Footnote 225 continued)

principles, courts in the United States will generally refrain from sitting in judgment on acts of a governmental character done by a foreign state within its own territory and applicable there.

[226]Among other case, the original one is Underhill v. Hernandez, 168 U.S. 250 (1897). The controversial one is Banco Nacional De Cuba v. Sabbatino, 376 U.S. 398, 84 S.Ct. 923, 11 L. Ed.2d 804 (1964). Along with Sabbatino case, Republic of Iraq v. First National City Bank, 353 F.2d 47 (2d Cir. 1965), *cert. denied*, 382 U.S. 1027, 86 S.Ct. 648 (1966) was challenged by the Second Hickenlooper Amendment stating that no court should decline to make a determination on the ground of the federal act of state doctrine in the situation. 22 U.S.C. Sec. 2370(e)(2). However, the coverage of the 2nd Hickenlooper Amendment was interpreted as limited by further decisions thereby developing act of state doctrine.

[227]Department of Justice Antitrust Division and Federal Trade Commission, Antitrust Enforcement Guidelines for International Operations, 3.33 (1995).

[228]*See* American Law Institute (ALI), Restatement (3rd) of Foreign Relations Law, Sec. 443, Reporter's Note 12 (1987); Callejo v. Bancomer, S.A. 764 F.2d 1101, 1114 fn 13 (C.A. 5th Cir. 1985). The 5th Cir Court of Appeals states that although the act of state is not prescribed by international law, most other nations have shown a similar solicitude for the felling of their fellow states. The Note indicates actual cases of expropriation by foreign states, but in the light of its wide coverage, the competition law area will be under the same treatment.

[229]*See OPEC*, 649 F.2d 1358–59 and 1361–62: Clayco Petroleum Corp. v. Occidental Petroleum Corp., 712 F.2d 404 (9th Cir. 1983).

[230]Vertigan (2007), at page 175.

[231]IV.1. and IV.2.(1) of this chapter, Chap. 2, have concrete examples.

2) Foreign Sovereign Immunities Act (FSIA) from Sovereign Immunity Principle

Sovereign immunity of international law, originally providing absolute immunity irrespective of the nature of state activities, has developed an exceptional area, mostly, of states' commercial activities or the area of *ius gestionis* under the relative doctrine. It is a result of the consideration of balancing the potential damage to private parties who otherwise would lose their opportunity for judicial remedy with the self-restraint of the judiciary body, often a result of the separation of power within a government. States,[232] according to the converging opinions, enacted domestic legislations approving the restrictive doctrine of sovereign immunity, such as the 1976 FSIA of the U.S. Under the Sec. 1603(d) of the FSIA, the exception of commercial activity is to be decided by reference to the 'nature' of the course of conduct, or a particular transaction, the standard of which had been adopted by the Italian Court of Cassation and the State Department of the U.S.[233] Subsequently, the nature standard of the FSIA was adopted by the U.S. Supreme Court.[234]

In terms of setting a range of production level of a primary commodity by a nation, it has the characteristic of a sovereign decision for national development rather than of private transaction. International law, as reviewed later, approves a state's right to produce natural resources as well as agricultural products.[235] Additionally, interstate cooperation to produce food or natural resources under the auspice of international law allows an association of commodity producers to develop their national economies or a long-term multilateral commodity agreement reflecting the interests of both producers and consumers.[236] Particularly, in light of instances of environmental management or economic development in DCs, a measure, either domestic or interstate cooperative, for maintaining the stability of prices and adequate earnings for primary commodities and raw materials is considered to be essential.[237] Although the functioning of commodity agreement affects international commerce, a commodity agreement itself has a perspective that the sovereign operation of states fall under sovereign immunity rather than falling under the commercial exception.

---

[232]The UK, Canada, Australia, Pakistan, Singapore, and South Africa. *See* U.N. Doc. ST/LEG/SER.B/20(1982).

[233]Governo degli Stati Uniti di America c. Soc. I.R.S.A., [1963] Foro Ital. 1405, 47 Revista de Diritto Internazionale 484 (May 13, 1963): Letter to Argentine Embassy (April 19, 1962), concerning Mirabella v. Banco Industrial De La Republica Argentina, 38 Misc.2d 128, 237 N.Y.S.2d 499 (1963).

[234]Republic of Argentia v. Weltover, Inc. 504 U.S. 607, 112 S.Ct. 2160 (1992).

[235]Principle 21 of Stockholm Declaration of UN Conference on the Human Development (June 16, 1972): Principle 2 of Rio Declaration on Environment and Development, UNCED (June 13, 1992): Para. 4 (e) of Declaration on the Establishment of a NIEO (NIEO Declaration) (May 1, 1974): para. 1 of UN GA Resolution on PSNR (December 14, 1962).

[236]Para. 4 (J), (m), (q), (r), (s), and (t) of NIEO Declaration: Art. 3, 5, 6, and 28 of Charter of Economic Rights and Duties of States (CERDS) (December 12, 1974).

[237]Principle 10 and 13 of Stockholm Declaration: Art. 5 of CERDS.

By respecting the legitimacy of commodity agreements, all states have duty to respect the right by refraining from applying economic and political measures that would limit it.[238] Sovereign immunity is a legal principle which shields states' right to have commodity agreements on a domestic level from each country's law. Under the concept of sovereign immunity, commodity agreements are protected in domestic courts from penalties or remedies.

C. International Organizations for Securing Stable Commodity Trade

(1) Development Agenda of the Common Fund for Commodities (CFC)

The UNCTAD, under a strong movement toward the NIEO, negotiated the Act establishing the CFC in 1970s, and reached its conclusion in 1980. The intent of launching the CFC was to establish a large fund which could link the finances of various commodity agreements which buy and sell a particular primary commodity in an attempt to alleviate the short-term price fluctuations.[239] However, in the '80s, a lot of commodity agreements started to fall apart[240] due to the failure of its management, e.g., the famous collapse of the Tin Agreement, although they had succeeded for several decades. In spite of the declining power of commodity agreements, the proposal from UNCTAD to institutionalize intergovernmental financial organizations for supporting stable commodity trade has worked and brought about the creation of the CFC in 1989. It represented international efforts to moderate the more declining terms of trade for commodity exports due to the falls of commodity agreements.[241] The CFC currently have more than a hundred member states with several institutional members, e.g., the EC, African Union (AU), the East African Community and the Common Market for Eastern and Southern Africa (COMESA).[242]

The main objective of the CFC is securing efficiency in commodity market and their development, aiming at the socioeconomic development of commodity producers.[243] Concretely, the CFC has supported the diversification of commodity production and trade and the improvement, thereby alleviating poverty in commodity-dependent developing countries (CDDCs). The CFC took actions in order to alleviate the constriction of supply in commodity production, such as vertical diversification into producing value-added products and exporting them, or horizontal diversification of supplying niche markets. The technical assistances for

[238] Art. 5 of CERDS.

[239] Brown (1994), at p. 364.

[240] *See id.*

[241] *Id.*

[242] *Refer to* http://www.fao.org/DOCREP/MEETING/004/Y2655E.HTM. Statement of Rolf W. Boehnke, Managing Director, at the International Conference for Financing for Development, Monterrey, Mexico (March 18, 2002), *available at* http://www.un.org/ffd/statements/cfcE.htm.

[243] Boehnke, *supra* note 242.

raising productivity and human resources for enhanced work are provided by its funds. Its 5-year action plan, in light of the experiences through previous plans, throws out development projects in the commodity market. The CFC issues yearly reports as to ongoing projects.[244]

(2) Right to Food and Food and Agricultural Organizations (FAO)

Established in October 1945, the FAO with more than 190 members has been working on reducing hunger due to insufficient food production or unwise distribution. Its focus is on the food security issue rather than food trade. Its argument to invoke the right to food as an international human right, although originally acknowledged in the Universal Declaration of Human Rights in 1948,[245] has not been effectively adopted by subsequent laws.[246] The growing threat of increase in food prices needs to be dealt in the context of human rights issues of impoverished people. Its approach to food not as a product of trade but as the object of a basic human right implies that the international private cartel law for promoting competition in a free competitive market is not an appropriate law in regulating international agricultural commodity trades.

Besides providing know-how, expertise, information to less-developed countries regarding agricultural production, fishery, and livestock, as a special agency on the food issue, the FAO convenes regularly in order to reach a common understanding between the industrialized and the less-developed countries. As a result, it has 16 ICAs approved and effective under its Constitution, including the Constitution on the International Rice Commission (1948) and Agreement for the Establishment of the Indian Ocean Tuna Commission (1993). In spite of recent criticisms, e.g., its bias in favor of the donor group of countries and inefficient usage of its budget,[247] its strenuous invocation for securing food for food-insufficient countries has raised the issue of human right in the context of the food commodity trade. The FAO's works, at least, call for the insufficient access to food in poor areas to be relieved by assistances from the international community.

---

[244]For instance, *see* CFC, 2007 Basic Fact, *available at* http://www.common-fund.org/download/content/CFC_BF_English.pdf.

[245]Article 25 para. 1 states that everyone has the right to a standard of living adequate for the health and well-being of himself and of his family, including food (infra omitted).

[246]Alison Small, FAO insists on food as a human right, FAO press release (2007), *available at* http://www.fao.org/newsroom/en/news/2007/1000680/index.html.

[247]Recently credibility of FAO's works is undermined. FAO's research on genetic production provoked strong dissent from the less-developed countries. Meanwhile, its large budget mostly from donations from the industrialized countries has been under pressure to curtail due to inefficiency.

3.5 International Organizations' Endeavors to Achieve Multilateral Agreements Regarding Cartels

Through international organizations, the international community has succeeded in making a few multilateral approaches out of several trials to reach an agreement. The major substantive rules that nations have agreed with are (i) the Set of Multilaterally Agreed Equitable Principles and Rules for the Control of Restrictive Business Practices (hereinafter the UN Set) that General Assembly of the UN has adopted as resolution with nonbinding recommendatory characteristics in 1980 after the UNTAD initially recommended it to the UN, and (ii) a recommendation against hard core cartels adopted in 1998 by the OECD, even though it does not have an enforcement mechanism or a dispute resolution system.

A. Failed Attempts of International Agreement as to Restrictive Business Practices (RBPs)

(1) The Havana Charter

The initial trial for a multilateral agreement in competition policy was made with the Havana Charter,[248] which failed to have sufficient ratification, resulting in its abandonment by the International Trade Organization (ITO) after WW II. The Charter, acknowledging the UN Charter in contrast to the WTO, adopted full employment and development as its objectives,[249] and allowed special assistance in the form of protective measures to promote the development of a particular industry of agriculture as an indigenous primary commodity industry.[250] It allowed, through ICAs, governmental measures to stabilize commodity price, e.g., price control, and the measures to preserve exhaustible natural resources, e.g., quantity control in severe economic situations.[251] It even encouraged conferences and studies among member states producing commodities, implying that an OPEC-like arrangement of producing countries for primary products be desirable.[252] All of the commodity agreements or related disputes were supposed to be reviewed at a regular interval or ultimately decided under the ITO.[253]

---

[248]Havana Charter for an ITO, March 24, 1948, Art. 46, U.N.Doc. E/C.2/78, reprinted in Dep't St., Pub.No.3206, Commercial Policy Series 114, 86–87 (1948), *available at* http://www.worldtradelaw.net/misc/havana.pdf (last visited on September 20, '07). The Economic and Social Council (ECOSOC) convened the UN Conference on Trade and Employment in Havana in 1948, and approved the Charter for an International Trade Organization (Havana Charter).

[249]Article 1. particularly, para. 6.

[250]Article 13. para. 1., Art. 14. para. 1, 2, and 3, and Art. 55.

[251]Article 57 (c) and (d), Art. 61, para. 2, (a) quantity control agreement, and (b) regulation of price, Art. 62, and Art. 63.

[252]*See* Art. 58, para. 3, and 59 para. 1. Art. 55–70 were adopted as Art. XX, para. (h) of GATT. *See*, for more details, Bronz (1956), at 465–467.

[253]Art. 65–66.

On the other hand, the Charter adopted, under Chap. V, concrete rules on both the substance and the enforcement of competition law including cartel regulations.[254] Art. 46 para. 3 enumerates the following cartel activities as restrictive business behaviors (RBPs): (a) fixing prices, terms, or conditions, (b) dividing any territorial market or field of business activity, excluding enterprises from the market or field, allocating customers, or fixing quotas of sales or purchase, (c) discrimination against a particular enterprise, and (d) limiting production quotas. It further stipulated that consultation, investigation, studies to RBPs and member's obligations were necessary in taking every measure to prevent RBPs.

A member state negatively affected by RBPs may seek an investigation procedure or consultation regarding the member concerned. In the former procedure, the ITO was supposed to be a judge to decide on the complaint from a member state and to request the member concerned to take every possible remedial action.[255] To start an investigation by the ITO, members should agree that complaints need to be subject to investigation under the articles whenever (i) such a complaint is presented to the ITO, (ii) the practice falls on the enumerated RBP, and (iii) they possess the power to effectively control trade among a number of countries.[256] A RBP in service trade is dealt with in an appropriate intergovernmental organization with priority.[257]

The Charter, drafted as one of the instruments establishing the postwar global economic order with the World Bank and the International Monetary Fund,[258] was initially supported by the U.S. but later refused to be ratified due to the concern that it, particularly Chap. V in regard to competition, would place restrictions upon the U.S. sovereignty, not to mention such concerns as the presence of complex domestic political pressures and foreign diplomacy.[259] Out of the entire set of rules concerning overbroad circumstances, only one chapter was made effective, as the General Agreement on Tariffs and Trade (GATT). The competition provisions under Chap. V were not mentioned with the implication that GATT members would not consider the competition issues.[260] Although it did not come into existence, this attempt is considered to be at least a precious lesson for future multilateral agreements on international competition policy.

---

[254] *Id.* at Art. 46 –53.

[255] Article 48.5.

[256] Article 46.2.

[257] Article 53. 3.

[258] Waller (1997), at 350.

[259] The main reasons for failure to ratification are (i) weakened political support, e.g., death of Keynes as originator and retirement from office of Cordell Hull, a main political supporter, (ii) opposition from the U.S. business community fearing that its strong antitrust law would place them in disadvantage, and (iii) distraction of national interest by other diplomatic issues, the cold war, the Marshall Plan, and reciprocal trade agreements. After the reelection of President Truman, he proposed the Charter to Congress in 1950, but the legislators never bothered to vote on it. George (2007), at 2; Paasman (1990), at 30; Malaguti (1999), at 615; Scherer, *supra* note 155, 38.

[260] *See* Waller (1997).

(2) Draft Agreement of ECOSOC

Subsequently, another attempt to revive the competition rules of the Havana Charter was made in 1953 in the United Nations Economic and Social Council (ECOSOC), constituted of six industrialized countries and four DCs.[261] The draft agreement as to competition policy, similar to Chap. V of the Charter, enumerated cartelistic activities as RBPs.[262] It allowed an international agency to investigate complaints, to provide nonbinding recommendation of remedial measures to the member state concerned, and to publish a report of decisions, reasons, and recommended measures.[263] The member could undertake a corrective action if it considers it appropriate according to its legal system.[264] It failed to be effective, however, due to bipolarized international politics during the cold war[265] and the U.S. passive stance.[266] The U.S. hesitated to adopt the draft agreement because its business community strongly opposed the draft due to the fear that American companies might be at a relative disadvantage because of strong domestic antitrust policies.[267]

(3) Recommendation for Consultations of GATT

Afterward, the last trial to focus on competition issues in the middle of twentieth century came from the GATT. The group of experts appointed by the Executive Secretary of the GATT gathered in Geneva in 1959 to discuss competition issues during the postwar period. They noted that, on the contrary to the goal of the GATT, international cartels harmed the growth of the global economy and economic development in individual countries, and recommended further consultations of related states on bilateral or multilateral basis and the convention of experts.[268] However, after discussion among the experts, they could not come to a multilateral agreement to control the RBP due to the difference of opinions with regard to

---

[261]India, Mexico, Pakistan, and Uruguay belonged to the developing group. Scherer, *supra* note 155, 39.

[262]Article 1 para. 3 of the Draft articles of Agreement, Annex II of Report of the Ad Hoc Committee on Restrictive Business Practices to the ECOSOC, U.N. ESCOR, 16th Sess., Supp. No. 11, U.N. Doc. E/2380 (1953).

[263]Article. 3 para. 1,3,5.8, and 10.

[264]Article 5 para. 1 and 4.

[265]Ironically, former Union of Soviet Socialist Republics (U.S.S.R.) which strongly objected to the Havana Charter supported the necessity of a universal approach, reviving the Charter, to problems of developing international economic relations. Bronz, *supra* note 252, 443 and n.10.

[266]The draft required the accumulation of ratifications from nations accounting for around 65 % of world imports and exports. Scherer, *supra* note 155, 39.

[267]Paasman, *supra* note 259, 30; Malaguti (1999), 615; Scherer, *supra* note 155, 39–40. U.S. politics was under pressure to reject it from business community. American enterprises understood that a law against restrictive business practice had never been witnessed by a majority of 60 UN members, and worried that the one-signatory one-vote provision would stimulate vote-participating nations to instigate harassing complaints against the U.S.

[268]GATT, Restrictive Business Practices: Arrangements for Consultations, Report of Experts, Chap. I. para. 1, 4 and 5, and para. 1 of Recommendation, L/1015, BISD 9S/170(June 2, 1960), *at* http://www.worldtradelaw.net/misc/rbp2.pdf.

insufficient practice experiences and a lack of consensus regarding RBPs regulation among member states.[269] As a result, the majority's recommendation was to encourage direct consultations between member countries and studies among experts so as to eliminate harmful effects of RBPs rather than through multilateral agreement.[270] The failed trials revealed divergences of viewpoints regarding the RBPs, including cartels.

B. The United Nations Conference on Trade and Development (UNCTAD)

(1) The UN Set

The DCs in the 1960s made efforts to come by political power through an international organization. It was through the UNCTAD that DCs insisted in implementing developmental agenda against the free market approach from advanced countries. They urged the advanced countries to grant preferential treatment on goods from DCs. As regards competition law enforcement, the UNCTAD has focused on the developmental dimension of the international competition agreement, thereby promoting an international consensus of regulating RBPs, supporting DCs' efforts to establish and operate competition law, and assisting their young competition authorities' practices with technical support, education, and training. It has held seminars with competition experts from countries that were experienced and skilled in these matters, to share their knowledge and experiences.[271]

The matrix of concrete rules regarding competition in UNCTAD was the UNCTAD III Conference in 1972 which established an expert group on the competition policy with instruction to formulate a set of multilateral rules and principles to control RBPs and to outline a special consultation procedure. Finally, the expert group produced a draft regarding international competition rules, so-called the UN Set. Subsequently, the UNCTAD and the UN General Assembly passed the draft in 1980.[272]

While the UN Set reflected the objective of protecting less DCs[273] from the restrictive business practices (RBPs) of multinational corporations, insufficient experiences and low interests of less DCs in competition law impeded effective reflection of their objective into final provisions and its implementation. Seemingly radical opinions from some less DC groups at that time were assuaged to a more conventional aspect of competition law[274] because the North, with experience in

[269]*See id.*, at Chap. I. ¶ 6. Malaguti (1999), 616.

[270]*See id.* at Chap. II ¶ 7 and 9.

[271]Statement by Germany 5th UNCTAD Conference on reviewing the UN Set, *at* http://r0.unctad.org/en/subsites/cpolicy/english/cpissues.htm.

[272]Resolution adopted by the UNCTAD 22 April 1980, and Resolution 35/63 of 5 December 1980, UN GA 35th Sess.

[273]The Group of 77 was a representative of the less DCs. Sell (1998), at 146–147.

[274]Taylor (2006), 130–131.

competition law, brought their drafts to final provisions.[275] The Code did not adopt an effective dispute resolution system or binding powers on the contrary to the requests of less DCs.[276] The Set with status of nonbinding recommendation stated, "in the performance of its functions, neither the Intergovernmental Group nor its subsidiary organs shall act like a tribunal or otherwise pass judgment on the activities or conduct of individual governments or of individual enterprises in connection with a specific business transaction."[277] Meanwhile, the consultation procedures in the UN Set[278] have never been used. The lack of usage of such consultation procedures was analyzed to be due to a reason that DCs were aimed at controlling domestic activities of foreign MNEs rather than RBPs themselves.[279]

Although the UN Set was less effective than expectation, it perpetuated its further development. The Set requested a UN conference to be convened by the Secretary General of the UN under the auspices of the UNCTAD for the purpose of reviewing all the aspects of the Set, thereby keeping its attention to further steps of the states which accept the Set to meet their commitment.[280] Every 5 years since the adoption of the Set in 1980, according to the request, UN Conferences to Review All Aspects of the Set have taken place regularly.[281] The 2000 UN conference recommended that all UN nations should implement the provisions of the Code while UNCTAD should develop similar versions adjusted to regional characteristics particularly for small developing nations. The conference explicitly pointed out the importance of development of sophisticated legal instruments and analytical capabilities by less DCs and acknowledged its role in assisting such less DCs' pursuit of competition policy in relation to developmental issues.[282]

Among all the substantive provisions, the UN Set has a provision with regard to restriction on cartels. The provision prohibits enterprises from doing such practices as (a) price-fixing agreements including as to exports and imports, (b) collusive tendering, (c) market or customer allocation agreements, (d) allocation by quota as to sales and production, and such diverse boycott activities as (e) concerted refusals

---

[275]Sell, *supra* note 273, 141.

[276]Taylor mentions that the fact that the Code was approved by the UN General Assembly without dissent carries considerable authoritative weight. *See* Taylor (2006), at 131, fn 43. However, no subsequently established multilateral instrument in existence since 1980, which Talyor acknowledged, limited impact of the UNCTAD code with limited fame, at 132, and lack of international consensus exploded in 2003 Cancun Ministerial Conference indicates that the authoritative weight is trivial. *See id.* at 131.

[277]*See* Part VI. Sec. G. Art. 4 of the UN Set.

[278]If a country suspects that another country's enterprise is involved in RBPs, it can place a formal complaint to the UNCTAD. In response to it, the accused country is to submit a report with regard to the activities of the enterprise to the UNCTAD. *See* Sell, *supra* note 273, 163.

[279]*See id.* Sell cites Davidow (1980), at 393–394.

[280]*See* part IV, Sec. G, Art. 2.

[281]*See* part I. For reference, the UNCAD IX conference in 1996 made a resolution which confirmed UNCTAD's mandate in the research and cooperation on the RBPs.

[282]*See* Taylor (2006), 132.

to deal, (f) concerted refusals of supplies to potential importers, and (g) collective denial of access to an important arrangement or association, when they limit access to markets or unduly restrict competition, having or likely to have adverse effects on international trade, particularly the trades of DCs, and on their economic development.[283]

The UN Set adopted preferential or differential treatment to DCs, particularly the least developed countries (LDCs), by considering their needs to develop domestic industries and other economic sectors and to encourage economic development through international arrangements among DCs.[284] Moreover, the UN Set imposed, under principles and rules for states, a duty of operational assistance to DCs on the part of the states with more expertise in controlling RBPs.[285] However, the level of technical assistance under the UN Set F (6) did not satisfy the expectation of the DCs group after its passage. The director of UNCTAD's Manufacturers Division stated, by rejecting the argument from the North that extensive technical assistance had been provided, that while some bilateral activities existed, multilateral assistance would unlikely go forward within the present institutional and financial environment, which reflects dissatisfaction of the South.[286]

(2) Model Law

When, pursuant to Sec. F(5) of the UN Set which requests elaboration of a law on RBPs, the UNCTAD discussed the adoption of a model law, a major issue was whether the purpose of the law may include development as well as competition as a separate and independent criterion for determining a RBP. The Group of 77, representing the less DCs, argued that Sec. E(2) of the UN Set included "having or being likely to have adverse effects on international trade or economic development" as an additional element of the RBP besides the unduly restraining of competition. It further argued that the goal of the model law may be to exert control over RBPs negatively affecting trade and development of the particular country in question, not to protect competition which is only one means to the goal.[287] On the other hand, the Group B, representing the North, insisted that the model law should be consistent with the principle of promoting competition and not adopt the effect on development as an independent standard for actions against RBPs.[288] Regarding the incorporation of the rule of reason standard into the model law, the South preferred an absolute

[283]*See* part IV, Sec. D, paragraph 3.

[284]Paasman, *supra* note 259, 30. *See* Part IV, Sec. C (iii).

[285]Part IV, Sec. E ¶ 8 and 9, e.g., sharing their experience, providing technical assistance, and supplying publicly available information necessary for its effective control of RBPs to other countries, particularly DCs.

[286]Sell, *supra* note 273, 164–5. The argument from the North was that technical assistance was provided on a bilateral and multilateral basis outside the framework of the UN Set in spite of lack of funds from UN Development Program (UNDP).

[287]*See id.* at 167.

[288]*Id.* at 166–7.

prohibition of practices enumerated in the UN Set while the North favored a rule of reason approach which leaves the decision whether individual cases violate competition law to the evaluation of domestic competition authorities.[289]

Despite the controversial disputes, UNCTAD published a model law on competition under the name of 'Draft commentaries to possible elements for articles of a Model Law or Laws (hereinafter Model Law)' in light of the recent development of competition law among states. Chapter II, subchapter II of the Model Law confines the coverage of the object of its application to enterprises and natural persons, thereby excluding sovereign acts of the state, local governments, or acts of enterprises or natural persons within the delegated power compelled or supervised by the state or local governments. Chap. III. Subch.I. of Model Law prohibits almost the same competition-restricting agreements, as illustrated under the UN Set, between (potentially) rival firms, regardless of formality, since the elements of the chapter have basis on Sec. D(3) of the UN Set under a prohibition approach.[290] The commentaries on Chap. III states, the agreements or arrangements under the chapter include any agreement, whether written or oral, formal or informal, or whether it has the intent to be legally binding or not. A list of RBPs from (a) to (g) in Chap. III Subch. I are not exhaustive acts but exemplary ones, thereby making the chapter a general clause covering the other RBPs.

On the other hand, Chap. III Subch. II allows the authorization of a cartel or its exemption.[291] The subchapter stipulated that, properly notified in advance, and engaged in by firms subject to effective competition, practices in the competition-restrictive agreements may be authorized or exempted when competition officials conclude that the agreement as a whole will produce 'net public benefit.' The policy that requires the agencies to determine 'net public benefit' rather than 'no public harm' shifts to the firms their burden of proofs to produce the net public benefit, thereby making the authorization process quite strict.[292] Major exemplary reasons for the net public benefit are (i) promoting technical or economic progress, (ii) reasonably organizing production or distribution, (iii) overcoming crisis, (iv) developing small or medium-sized entrepreneurs that would not result in the substantial restriction of competition, (v) relating to the sovereign function of government, and (vi) optimizing the export or import of products. Enlarged efficiency and applicable defense in (i) and (ii) cartels may be proved in cartel regulations of both developing and developed countries. Meanwhile, net public interests through restricting competition, e.g., (iii) and (iv), may be different, depending on the level of the competition policy and economic development.

Export or import cartels are to be considered under special treatment for DCs, particularly LDCs, so as to further their economic development, despite their possible negative effects upon consumers' interests in advanced countries. Although some countries exempt export cartels on certain conditions, such as notification and

---

[289]*Id.* at 168.

[290]UNCTAD (2007), at 22, ¶ 21.

[291]Article 3 ¶ 2.

[292]UNCTAD, *supra* note 517, at 27, ¶ 47.

registration, Chap. III Subch.I.1. prohibits price-fixing agreement in international trade.[293] In contrast to a cartel with impact on a domestic market, an export cartel has been acknowledged by most national laws because the export cartel does not affect the domestic market. In light of the fact that the export cartel has direct anticompetitive effects on a foreign market, regular reviews of such exemption under strict standards need to be taken by a country where the export cartel works. The authorization or exemption provision is to be reasonable and inevitable in each country's context.[294] Otherwise, cartels might prevail with colorable pretexts.

Although Chap. III Subch. II mentions competition officials or agencies as a determiner with the discretion to allow exemptions, the determiner does not need to belong to the administrative branch. As a result of attempting to reflect the diverse competition laws of the member countries, the authority to approve exemption of cartel regulation is provided to judges,[295] or administrative officers in charge of trade or competition.[296]

C. A Trial of a Plurilateral Agreement: Draft International Antitrust Code (DIAC) Proposed by the Munich Group

While a multilateral agreement includes all of the members of international organizations, a plurilateral agreement may consist of a few or many nations whether inside or outside of an international organization. In case a plurilateral agreement is established within a large international organization, members have the option to become contracting parties. The plurilateral agreement of international competition law, introduced by the Munich Group consisting of major competition scholars for further consideration of WTO, obligates contracting parties to respect its standards of competition law as a part of their domestic competition legal systems, nonobservance of which, similar to WTO system, causes an international dispute between states as violation of international law.[297] The Munich Code was an ambitious attempt in its broad scope of coverage, including all potential RBPs from horizontal and vertical restraints to a regime for public undertakings and state authorizations, to remedies covering administrative, criminal, and private actions, and to a plan of an international antitrust agency. The jurisdictional criterion of the Code is to deal with only cross-border cases thereby leaving domestic cases to domestic legislations. The agreement was not adopted by the WTO or any other international organization under the criticism that nations would not accept overbroad regulations along with a wide limitation of its sovereignty at the time when the convergence of competition law had not been maturely discussed.

---

[293]Joint ventures under the U.S. Export Trading Company Act is not treated as export cartel as they do not possess market power in domestic or foreign markets. UNCTAD, *supra* note 290, 24 n.67.

[294]Article 81 (3) of the Treaty of Rome of European Community, Germany, Japan, Lithuania, Spain, Sweden, Venezuela, Colombia, Hungary, India, Slovakia, Turkey, Austria, Algeria, Chile, Ukraine, Zambia, Tunisia, and Russian Federation. *See id,* 27–33.

[295]The U.S. and EU.

[296]Tunisia, Algeria, Norwey, Turkey, India and South Korea.

[297]*Refer* to Art. 20 DIAC. Drexl (2003b), at 315–316.

The trial, however, left valuable lessons for future international competition rules. Among other things, the DIAC, at least, produced efforts from a private area to create international competition rules in line with free trade law. Although rules over such unfair practices, as antidumping, cover the phenomena similarly as competition law does, and although their ultimate goal of free and efficient resource allocation is the same, they caused conflicts in short-term objectives as well as in their measures to achieve them.[298] The convergence of domestic competition policies and the reduction of such measures which can be replaced with the enforcement of competition law, as antidumping duty with respect to monopoly restraint or predatory pricing, can be a solution to conflict between trade law and competition law. Moreover, a plurilateral agreement as an alternative to a multilateral agreement can prove to be a method to achieve cooperative relationships in international competition law since it offers the option to accede, and countries with common interests could reap benefits from the plurilateral agreement. Annex IV of the WTO Agreement indicates the example.[299]

Moreover, the DIAC brought light on the international procedural initiatives (IPI). While the EU system requires the referral of national cases to ECJ under Art. 234, the principle of IPI allowed the International Antitrust Authority the right to ask national authorities to initiate investigations and to bring cases to national courts under national law.[300] The reason behind the unique procedural initiative, juxtaposed to the international dispute settlement, is that in considering such characteristics of competition law as reflecting the policy considerations and the economic reasoning of the respective country, jurisdiction of individual competition cases can match domestic courts rather than the international dispute settlement body.[301]

D. Organization for Economic Cooperation and Development (OECD)

OECD, originally established to coordinate postwar financial assistance in Europe in 1960 but now working as a global organization of intergovernmental discussions and informal peer review system, has addressed competition law issues.

[298]The dumped price, arguably, is not unfair but due to high price in home market where the exporter has a dominant position, which matches the area of competition law rather than that of trade law. When the dumping case is treated with antidumping provision of trade law, it often causes export cartels, price-fixing arrangements, as well as voluntary export restraints. On the other hand, the Art. 11 (1) of the Agreement on Safeguards under exceptions allows unilateral measures to implement protectionist policies, e.g., antidumping measures. The background of adopting the art. is that competition policies permitting export cartels would damage trade policy, but the unilateral methods without considering competition law application do not solve the conflict with competition law. *See* Malaguti (1999), at 659–662.

[299]John and Matsushita (2002), at 251–252. Agreeing with Annex IV consisting of the following four plurilateral trade agreements is optional to WTO accession: (i) agreement on trade in civil aircraft, (ii) agreement on government procurement, (iii) international dairy agreement, and (iv) international bovine meat agreement. They are referred to as the TRAMS (Agreement on Trade-Related aspects of Anti-trust Measures).

[300]Article 19s. 2 of DIAC.

[301]Drexl, *supra* note 297, 316–7.

An OECD report urged member states to utilize information exchange and consultation procedures for resolving disputes over multinational-enterprise (MNEs)-regulating matters. The 1973 OECD recommendation proposed that members notify each other in any antitrust enforcement actions and exchange information between interested parties, while the 1973 amendment adopted a voluntary conciliation procedure within the OECD on disputes as to such law enforcements.[302] The concerns about MNEs' RBPs generated the 1976 OECD Guidelines for MNEs with cartel regulations.[303] Such attitudes were appreciated as support for a simpler code reflecting parties in similar economic situations than resolving the North–South conflict.[304]

The OECD have enacted competition policy outreach program since planned economies in East Europe and other communist countries shifted to market economies in 1989. So as to work market economy and get integrated into the global economy, the countries needed basic framework policies under rule of law, including competition policy and sustainable development.[305] OECD's outreach program facilitated assisting in the design and implementation of competition law and competition policy through providing the experience and expertise of advanced competition regimes in short-term events to other members and interested nonmembers.[306]

Apart from the outreach program allowing access to nonmembers, OECD's main activities regarding competition issues came from the Competition Law and Policy (CLP) Committee, which has succeeded in achieving a convergence in competition law enforcement over the last 40 years without binding rules. The nonbinding rule principle encouraged members to accept international agreements regarding competition law with less difficulty. The most beneficial instruments to OECD members of the CLP are a series of recommendations regarding RBPs affecting international trade.[307] Among other things, recently OECD revised the Recommendation on Antitrust Cooperation in 1995[308] which, initially aiming at reducing conflict among OECD members, emphasized and facilitated mutual assistance of competition law

---

[302] Sell, *supra* note 273, 74–75.

[303] Under competition, Chapter 3 states that enterprises should refrain from participating in international or domestic cartels or restrictive agreements which adversely affect or eliminate competition and which are not generally or specifically accepted under applicable national or international legislation.

[304] *Id.* at 75.

[305] The conclusion of OECD Ministerial meeting in July 1999. Winslow (2001), at 236.

[306] *Id.* at 236–7.

[307] *See* Recommendations of the Council Concerning Co-operation between Member Countries on Restrictive Business Practices Affecting International Trade, OECD Doc.C(67)54/final (Oct. 5, 1967); C(86)44(Final), 21 May 1986, (1986) 25 ILM 1629; C(95)130/Final, 28 July 1995. The OECD has revised the recommendations three times since 1967, respectively, in 1973, '86, and '95.

[308] *See* Revised Recommendation of the Council Concerning Co-operation Between Member Countries on Anticompetitive Practices Affecting International Trade, OECD Doc.C(95)130/final (July 27 and 28, 1995), *available in* 35 I.L.M. 1314 (1996) [hereinafter the Revised Recommendation]. Waller (1997), 361–62.

enforcement through the notification and exchange of information, coordination of action, consultation, and conciliation.[309] Subsequent cooperation agreements among OECD members resembled the Revised Recommendation.[310]

Before the year of 2000, the OECD Council's Recommendation Concerning Effective Action Against Hard Core Cartels adopted in 1998 (1998 OECD Recommendation) began focusing on cartel regulations. The 1998 OECD Recommendation, even though exempting its application to the cartels evaluated as reasonable under cost/benefit analyses or those excluded from the legislation of a member country or authorized under domestic law, is important in that it urges member countries to provide effective sanctions and enforcement measures with powers adequate to detect and remedy hard core cartels[311] and that it develops a concrete cooperation method on the basis of the positive comity principle.[312] In addition, it requires the exemption process to be transparent and to be reviewed periodically so as to limit its coverage not broader than necessary.[313] Moreover, it includes the definition of a hard core cartel, as illustrated earlier.[314]

Subsequently, the CLP of OECD published three comprehensive reports. The reports are the result of demonstrating how member states' practices have complied with the 1998 Recommendation by investigating its progress in jurisdiction of member states and observers. The third report (2005) indicated that efforts of member states and observers to fight against cartels and to cooperate among competition authorities to investigate international cartels were at a very high level.[315] The nonbinding recommendations and peer review of members' reports have contributed to the successful frame work for cooperation in enforcing competition law.[316]

On the other hand, exchanging confidential business information has been less successful in light of its importance in attacking international cartels, although there are a few if any achievements. Most OECD countries have banned the exchange of

[309]Preamble of the Revised Recommendation.

[310]Even the cooperation agreement among the competition authorities of the three Baltic countries is modeled on the OECD Recommendation. *See id.* at 241–42.

[311]1998 Recommendation [C/M(98)7/PROV], ¶ 1 of Sec. A of Art. I.

[312]*Id. See* ¶ 1–3 of Sec. B of Article I. The positive comity, on the request of the other country, invokes the one country to apply its domestic competition law so as to remove anticompetitive practices that occur in its jurisdiction and that adversely affect the other party. This principle is a way to control anticompetitive activities that adversely affect a party without resorting to an extraterritorial application of its competition law that may result in a conflict of jurisdiction, which is useful for making international agreement for cooperation of competition law enforcements. *See* Mitsuo Matsushita, *supra* note 299, at 254.

[313]*See*Art. I, Sec. A. para. 2 subsec. b.

[314]*Id. See*Art. I. Sec. A. para. 2 subsec. a. *Refer to* Chap. 2. 2.2 of this book.

[315]OECD, *Hard Core Cartel: Third Report on the Implementation of the 1998 Recommendation*, 3 (2003).

[316]Waller (1997), at 362.

much information even not confidential.[317] To challenge the restriction and raise the level of awareness to the potential damage inflicted by cartels, the CLP issued a report on approximate cost and economic harm resulting from activities of international cartels. It argued the necessity of legal mechanisms for cooperation in international cartel investigations, particularly the sharing of information among national offices.[318]

OECD has provided the Global Forum on Competition (GFC) annually to officials of member states, the European Commission, and some nonmember states[319] since 2001. The GFC has supported member states and some nonmembers to build competition-law-operating skills by leading a peer review on the competition law and policy of those states. Although broader consensus against cartels and capacity-building measures among its members through the OECD extend the benefit to nonmembers,[320] in the light of the nature of the OECD as an organization of a total of thirty countries with an advanced economy, accessibility of nonmembers has been limited with the exception of those with big regional markets.[321] It needs to enhance intergovernmental cooperation in anticartel and competition law enforcement beyond the OECD scope.

E. International Competition Network (ICN)

Countries gathered for facilitating robust competition law enforcement, which resulted in the International Competition Network (ICN) in 2001. The ICN has provided places for senior officers of competition law agencies in both developing and developed countries to discuss convergence issues in their competition law enforcements. Although the ICN has no authority to make decisions or to issue binding rules, it has been operating as a global forum to announce nonbinding recommendations, harmonizing all the participating competition-enforcing officials. Recently nongovernmental advisers comprising of lawyers, scholars, and international organizations have actively taken part in its work.

The network has its aim at assisting DCs in promoting competition cultures based upon sound economic principles. Its membership started with 14 founding members, including both developing and developed countries. In 2009, its members reached 104 agencies from 92 countries.[322] The enlarged membership was thought

[317]*See* Winslow (2001), at 243.

[318]*See id.,* at 244.

[319]Such countries with big regional market as Brazil, China, Russia, Indonesia, and South Africa.

[320]*See* Winslow (2001), at 246–7.

[321]Drexl (2003a), at 321–322; Taylor (2006), 135. OECD website offers information about member countries, *available at* http://www.oecd.org/countrieslist/0,3351,en_33873108_33844430_1_1_1_1_1,00.html (last visited on Jul. 15, 2008).

[322]Initial founding Members countries are the following: U.S.A., EU, Canada, Mexico, Australia, France, Germany, Israel, Italy, Japan, Korea, South Africa, United Kingdom, United States, and Zambia. FTC, *U.S. and Foreign Antitrust Officials Launch International Competition Network, at* http://www.ftc.gov/opa/2001/10/icn.htm. Statement of Germany, *available at* www.unctad.org.

to be a result of the DCs' sympathy and expectation of benefits with the activities of the ICN.

The ICN has its focus on several topics of competition laws, one of which is the issue of cartel enforcement. The Cartel Working Group established in 2004 has worked on facilitating cooperation and convergence of anticartel enforcements. Annual meetings of enforcement officers in charge of cartel regulation have discussed and shared the latest enforcement techniques against cartels since 1999. The ICN's effort to combat cartels has offered non-OECD member countries precious opportunities to learn the expertise of anticartel enforcement skills in the most experienced countries.[323]

F. Cartel Regulation in World Trade Organization (WTO)

(1) Doha Development Agenda (DDA)

In December 1996, the WTO decided to discuss competition policy by adopting one of their negotiation agendas and to establish the Working Group on the Interaction between Trade and Competition Policy at the Singapore Ministerial Conference. In 5 years, in November 2001, WTO Ministerial Conference in Doha announced that further negotiation would take place on the basis of explicit consensual decision regarding the establishment of a multilateral framework to enhance the contribution of competition policy to international trade and development as well as the need for enhanced technical support and capacity building in the area.[324] Of the three projects,[325] the Working Group had been focusing on, it was the 'provision of hardcore cartels' that requested full consideration of the needs of DCs and LDCs.[326]

(2) Rupture While Trying to Renegotiate

However, so-called the Doha Agenda has been in a deadlock through failures to reach a consensus in the successive ministerial conferences. At the Cancun Ministerial Conference in 2003, participants dropped competition policy issues in further negotiation. After the Hong Kong Conference in 2005, the Doha Agenda went underground without producing any positive result. In spite of the standstill, there have been, from time to time, endeavors by politicians or trade representatives mostly from industrialized countries to revive the Doha Round,[327] which turns out with no visible accomplishment.

---

[323]OECD, *Hard Core Cartel: Third Report on the Implementation of the 1998 Recommendation*, 17 (2005).

[324]Para. 23 of the Doha Ministerial Declaration.

[325]The following are the three projects: (i) the clarification of core principles including transparency, (ii) nondiscrimination and procedural fairness, and (iii) provisions on hardcore cartels, modalities for voluntary cooperation, and support for progressive reinforcement of competition institutions in DCs through capacity building.

[326]WTO, Doha Ministerial Declaration, para.23 to 25 (November 14, 2001).

[327]In July 2007, India and Brazil did not reach an agreement to revive further negotiation with the U.S. and EU mostly due to conflicts such as elimination or reduction of agricultural subsidies in the industrial countries and tariff reduction on products in emerging economies. See ICTSD, *G-4*

(3) Limitation of Anticartel Rules within the WTO

Since Art. III.2 of the Agreement establishing the WTO provides the forum for negotiating matters dealt with in the Annexes to the Agreement including RBP, and Art. IX of the Agreement on Trade-Related Investment Measures (TRIMS) requires the Council for Trade in Goods to consider adopting provisions on competition policy, the WTO has sufficient legal foundation to carry out further multilateral negotiations on this issue.[328] Confining of the scope of prospective competition rules in relation to international trade within the legal foundation of the WTO is necessary because the international rules regulating cartels within the WTO may intervene in each member's sovereignty over competition policies. The members eventually agreed to limit their sovereignty only to the extent that their domestic policies could jeopardize international trade.[329] The coverage of the rules includes not only domestic practices or measures that directly restrict imports or exports to those that foreclose the market, but also those that indirectly affect international trade which are considered to circumvent obligations of opening up a member state's market.[330] Hence, any foreclosure cartels with aim of driving existing and potential competitors out of the market, as well as other market-allocating or any price-fixing cartels with the same effect on the market, can be prohibited by the WTO.

The above-mentioned coverage, however, may be remedied only when autonomous state responsibility is proved, in other words, members have a duty under the specific provision of the Marrakech Agreements to ensure that private undertakings will not engage in certain RBPs.[331] An opinion places weight on the obligation to guarantee market access under Art. XVI of the GATS as complementing major legal principles of Marrakech Agreements by arguing that it may be construed as the basis for the duty, that member states should prevent market barriers by means of either private or public anticompetitive restraints.[332] Although such market foreclosure by private undertakings causes a negative effect on both competition and trade, the article of the GATS does not have sufficient foundation to restrain the sovereignty of a member engaging in trade of 'goods', not 'services'. Since rules on competition currently in the Marrakech Agreement do not impose a direct and general duty on members, prohibition of RBPs in trade of 'goods' has no legal basis from international law perspective. While active measures of a member state could be nullified and impaired under Art. XXIII, para.1 (b) of GATT, anticompetitive

(Footnote 327 continued)

Talks in Potsdam Break Down, Doha Round's Fate in the Balance Once Again, 11 Bridges Weekly 23 (June 27, 2007), available at *http://www.ictsd.org/weekly/07-06-27/story1.htm*.

[328]Malaguti (1999), 619 and 622.

[329]*Id.* at 624–625.

[330]A vertical restraint with exclusive arrangement needs positive proof of foreclosing market in contrast to merely making entry more costly but still economically feasible. *Id.* at 625–6.

[331]*Id.*, 639.

[332]*Id.* at 645–652.

damages caused by private undertakings and omission by a member state does not assign such duty to the member state under the current WTO regime. The scope of the WTO needs to be extended to regulate whole private entities' RBPs, particularly in trade of 'goods'.[333]

G. Assessment

The efforts to make competition law, including cartel regulation, as a part of international law produced precious fruits represented in the UN Set, Model Law, the 1998 OECD Recommendation, and the Doha Agenda. There have been conflicting interests, however, between proponents and contestants of international competition law and cartel regulation, which contribute to the current collapse of the Doha Agenda. The proponents groups, mostly consisting of EU and its member countries, failed to dissuade DCs from having the fear that international competition law might intervene in their legislation and shackle business activities of relatively weak domestic companies. Even the U.S., considered as a proponent, was hesitant to devote itself to ensuring the success of the negotiation, stating to the effect that the application of its competition law, with the most experience and the longest history, may be limited by the international law and that potential benefit under the negotiation could be obtained through bilateral or trilateral agreements.[334]

The decision to revive the multilateral framework looks to be up to the persuasive powers of leaders with interests in promoting a global economy toward free trade and competition, to the benefit of DCs. It is no wonder that the leaders of the countries with large local market announced that the Doha Agenda should be rediscussed when they meet.[335] Although the OECD urged resumption of the Doha Round, there are still disagreements from DCs.[336]

In light of the point that international law has been working through the consensus of the global community, the majority of which DCs and LDCs occupy, it is important to persuade DCs and LDCs to agree with international competition law by assisting in their adopting of competition law and as well as assisting in their practicing with the skills, experiences, and theoretical foundations of developed competition law. Cartels can be active in DCs with less sophisticated competition regimes, where the possibility of facing severe sanctions is very rare.[337] As a result, the cartels impose much harm on these countries. However, cartel members who can have influence on politicians in DCs are likely to lobby against competition

---

[333] *Id.* at 641–643. Malaguti argues that adopting an international competition code or inserting a duty to prohibit RBPs hindering market access would be the solution. *See id.* at 643–645.

[334] Chang, Seung Wha, *Interaction between Trade and Competition: Why a Multilateral Approach for the United States*? in Matsushida, M, and Ahn, D, eds. (2004), at 329–330.

[335] Bertrand Benoit and Ralph Atkins, *G7 'committed' to Doha trade deal*, Fin. Times (February 11, 2007 15:58), *available at* http://www.ft.com.

[336] *OECD tries to revive Doha talks,* BBC NEWS (October 11, 2006 17:39:15 GMT), *available at* http://news.bbc.co.uk/go/pr/fr/-/1/hi/business/6041930.stm.

[337] UNCTAD, Cross-border Anti-competitive Practices: the Challenge for DCs and Economies in Transition, TD/D/C.I/CLP/, p. 9 (2012).

law. The general public in DCs, not fully aware of the damaging effect of cartels, might not have the sufficient power to support competition law enforcement against cartels. Industry promotion policies which DCs usually focus on would try to make exemptions to cartel regulations such as cartels under depression or export cartels. So as to overcome such hurdles in DCs, sound foundations of legal reasoning and economical theories for establishing competition cultures are indispensable. International law on cartels will require such sound theoretical support and development of practices, along with the gaining of experience in DCs to further their progress.

3.6 Extending Bilateral or Regional Agreement

A. Advantages and Role of Bilateral Agreements

A bilateral agreement is the most popular form of international agreement on competition policy. It has been effectively enforced beside a regional agreement of the Treaty of Rome establishing the EU not only because it is easier for two parties to reach an agreement than many parties but also because it enables two parties to discuss such issues as only the two parties have a special interest. Moreover, the accumulation of successful bilateral agreements and international cooperation in competition law can function as major building blocks to the creating of a multilateral agreement.[338]

Noticeably, there is a distinction between the role of bilateral agreement and that of multilateral agreement in competition policy. While multilateral agreements regulating RBPs were negotiated in terms of supplementing loopholes of international trade law or suggesting universal anticartel and other competition codes, bilateral agreements in competition law addressed the issues of cooperation between competition authorities, extraterritoriality, and conflicts of domestic competition laws. In light of the respective role, bilateral agreements have operated as supplements rather than as alternatives to multilateral agreements.[339]

B. Treaties regarding Mutual Legal Assistance (MLATs) for Competition Policy

Bilateral agreements, particularly regarding competition matters such as cartels, had not come up frequently until the 1990s when a large number of countries adopted competition laws. Anticartel enforcements between competition authorities, except the one between the U.S. and West Germany,[340] had been treated similarly as other criminal law matters among countries penalized cartel activities. By 2012, the U.S., the foremost country in terms of seriously dealing with cartels as

[338]Evenett et al. (2001), at 1237–1240. They mentioned that confidential information sharing is major hurdle.

[339]Malaguti (1999), 651–52.

[340]West Germany does not criminalize a cartel activity.

criminals, had enforced 56 treaties regarding mutual legal assistance (MLATs) on criminal matters. The U.S. and EU, in 2010, signed MLAT for every member country of the EU to either supplement MLAT in effect or create new one.[341] Although the MLAT was a powerful method to support investigation as to cross-border cartels, most of them were considered to be ineffective against cartels because the effective usage of the MLAT necessitates a level of capability of cartel regulation and enforcement as well as political will to penalize cartels along with anticartel penalty. Successful examples of MLAT usages occurred between the authorities, which have already, under the developed market system, accumulated considerable cartel practices in investigation practices, and between advanced countries which have criminalized cartels and the other anticompetitive activities imposing harm on consumers. The 1985 MLAT between the U.S. and Canada in criminal matters[342] and the 1995 MLAT between the U.S. and the UK on criminal matters,[343] for examples, respectively, state that the treaty should be an effective tool in prosecuting modern criminals, including members of drug cartels[344] and those who commit antitrust crimes in violation of consumer protection law,[345] and that the definition of offense includes an offense in the category of consumer protection.[346] Especially, the U.S.–Canada cooperation in anticartel enforcement under the 1985 MLAT was evaluated as remarkably successful in the point that coordinated searches between the U.S. and Canadian cartel investigatory institutions[347] as well as the search by one party on behalf of the other party produced more increased prosecutions of cross-border cartels and subsequent fines.[348]

[341]Stark, Charles S., *Improving Bilateral Antitrust Cooperation*, in Jones, C. and Matsushita, M. ed. (2002), at 84.

[342]March 18, 1985, U.S.-Canada, S. Treaty Doc. No. 100-14 (1988). The treaty came into effect 5 years later in 1990.

[343]Jan. 23, 1995, U.S.–UK, S. Treaty Doc. No. 104-2 (1995).

[344]Letters of Transmittal to the Senate of the United States in both treaties.

[345]*See* MLAT between the U.S. and Canada, Annex. *See also* Waller (1997), at 366 and n.131.

[346]Annex (4) of the 1985 Treaty.

[347]In the thermal facsimile paper cartel case, the U.S. and Canada cooperated in their first joint criminal antitrust investigation with a result of guilty pleas and substantial fines for Japanese firms and their American subsidiaries. *U.S. and Canadian Prosecutors Attack Cartel Behavior by Fax Paper Distributors*, 67 Antitrust & Trade Reg. Rep. (BNA) 108 (July 21, 1994): Waller (1997), at 368 n.141.

[348]Stark, *supra* note 321, 84–85. For instance, Canadian prosecutions of international cartels, first uncovered by the U.S. Antitrust Division, have lead to the imposition of fines in Canada for violation of Canadian antitrust law of nearly US $ 100 million in late 1990s and 2000. *See also* Waller (1997), n. 140. In the U.S. investigation into price-fixing in the plastic dinnerware industry, the U.S. obtained the assistance of Canadian authorities in executing search warrants and transmitting the evidence. *Plastic Dinnerware Price Fixing Probe Nets Indictment, Guilty Pleas Agreement*, 66 Antitrust & Trade Reg. Rep. (BNA) 661 (June 16, 1994).

C. Bilateral Agreements regarding Enforcing Competition Law

As countries came to grips with the nature of interdependent economic relationship in the globalization era, they grew aware of the necessity of cooperation, particularly in enforcing competition law to deal with cross-border anticompetitive behaviors of multinational corporations, foreign or domestic companies expanding their business over national markets. Challenged by conflicts of competition law in some cases,[349] competition authorities in industrialized countries have narrowed the divergence of their competition laws through discussion and have adopted bilateral agreements to cooperate in enforcing their competition laws. Since the U.S. had made an antitrust accord[350] with West Germany in 1976, it has resulted in eight bilateral agreements regarding enforcement of competition laws.[351] Especially, the 1991 Agreement between the Government of the U.S.A. and the European Communities regarding the Application of Their Competition Laws (hereinafter 1991 Agreement), consisting of eleven articles, became the model of subsequent bilateral agreements. The concrete cooperative measures are, among other things, mutual notification in case a party's enforcement may affect interests of the other party, the exchange of information on general policy or specific action, and assistance by one party in the other's enforcement actions. The agreement does not have binding power but provides reciprocal options to demur. Subsequently, the U.S. expanded the number of partners in the agreement regarding cooperation of

---

[349]*In re* Uranium Antitrust Litigation, 480 F. Supp. 1138, 1154 (N.D.Ill. 1979), *aff'd*, 617 F.2d 1248, 1256 (7th Cir. 1980). The controversy of the Uranium case delayed bilateral efforts for formal agreement of cooperation until 1984 when Canada and the U.S. entered into a Memorandum of Understanding (MOU) regarding notification, consultation, and cooperation with respect to the application of national antitrust laws (March 9, 1984), *available at* 23 I.L.M. 275 (1984). *See* Boeing's merger with MacDonald Douglas. While the U.S. FTC approved the merger by stating that the merger would not substantially lessen competition in any relevant market, European Commission (EC) decided that the proposed merger would lead to strengthening of Boeing's dominant position in aircraft markets. FTC, Statement, 5 CCH Trade Reg. Rep. (CCH) [Transfer Binder 1997–2001], para. 24,295 (1997); EC Decision, Case IV/M.877 O.J. L 336/16 (1997). *See also* Hartford Fire case, and GE/ Honeywell merger case.

[350]The formal title of the bilateral agreement in 1976 is Agreement Between the Government of the United States of America and the Government of the Federal Republic of Germany Relating to Mutual Cooperation Regarding Restrictive Business Practices. Its full text is available at http://www.ftc.gov/bc/international/docs/agree_germany.pdf.

[351]Competition Agreements of the U.S. with other countries are available at http://www.ftc.gov/oia/agreements.shtm (last visited on Sept. 14, 2007). The countries are Germany ('76), Australia ('82), EC ('91), Canada ('95), Israel ('99), Brazil ('99), Japan ('99), and Mexico ('00).

competition enforcement from just Canada in 1995,[352] to Brazil, Australia, and Israel in 1999,[353] and to Japan in 2000.[354,355]

Particularly, the 1998 Agreement between the Government of the U.S.A. and the E. C. on the Application of Positive Comity Principles in the Enforcement of their Competition Laws (1998 Positive Comity Agreement) supplemented Art. V, the so-called positive comity, of the 1991 Agreement[356] between the two parties. The languages of the 1998 Agreement succeeded to the same agreement between Canada and the U.S.A. in 2004.[357] The positive comity principle, distinguished from extraterritorial application of domestic competition law, imposed the duty to investigate anticompetitive business practice on a party when the activities were occurring in whole or in substantial part in the territory of the party and were adversely affecting the interests of the other party, and when the activities were impermissible under the competition law of the former party. Major purposes of the agreement were to establish cooperative procedures of the most effective and efficient international competition law enforcement and to avoid allocating enforcement resources to dealing with anticompetitive activities occurring principally in and directed toward the other party's territory.

D. Cartel Regulations in Regional Trade Agreements

(1) The Adoption of Competition Issue in Free Trade Agreements (FTAs)

Most free trade agreements have a chapter or provisions regarding competition. Although they do not address, particularly, a cartel, one or some of them in fact apply to cartel regulations. For example, the North American Free Trade Agreement

---

352 Agreement between the Government of Canada and the Government of the U.S.A. Regarding the Application of Their Competition and Deceptive Marketing Practices Laws, August 1, 1995, 35 I.L.M. 309 (1995). *See* Waller (1997), 365–66. Waller explains characteristics of the 1995 Agreement such as binding version of 1984 MOU, inclusion of FTC and DOJ, mechanism for cooperation in both transborder consumer protection enforcement and competition matters. *See* the 1995 Agreement, Art. III and VII.

353 Agreement between the Gov. of the U.S.A. and the Gov. of the State of Israel Regarding the Application of their Competition Laws, March 15, 1999. Agreement between the Gov. of the U.S. A. and the Gov. of Australia on Mutual Antitrust Enforcement Assistance, April 27, 1999. Agreement between the Gov. of the U.S.A. and the Gov. of the Federal Republic of Brazil Regarding Cooperation between their Competition Authorities in the Enforcement of Their Competition Laws, October 26, 1999. They have very similar structures consisting of 13 articles. Full text of both agreements are available at http://www.ftc.gov/os/1999/03/usisrael.pdf.

354 Agreement between the Government of U.S.A. and the Gov. of Japan Concerning Cooperation on Anticompetitive Activities, October 7, 1999, *available at* http://www.ftc.gov/oia/agreements.shtm.

355 Stark, *supra* note 341, 89–91.

356 *See preamble and Art. VI of the 1998 Agreement*. The 1998 Agreement shall supplement and be interpreted consistently with the 1991 Agreement, which remains fully in force.

357 Agreement between the Government of Canada and the Gov. of the U.S.A. on the Application of Positive Comity Principles to the Enforcement of Their Competition Laws (October 5, 2004), *available at* http://www.ftc.gov/os/2004/10/0410comityagreeenglish.pdf (visited on July 16, 2008) The 2004 Agreement had exactly the same languages as the 1998 Agreement.

between the Government of the United States, the Government of Canada, and the Government of the United Mexico (NAFTA), in general terms, includes the promotion of conditions of fair competition in the free trade area as one of the objectives of the Agreement although it does not have specific regulations regarding cartels. The Free Trade Agreement between the U.S.A. and South Korea (KORUS FTA) adopted an article with regard to competition law and anticompetitive business conduct. Although KORUS FTA did not address specifically the cartel regulation, it urged cooperation and coordination for effective competition law enforcement between two authorities in charge of its enforcement.[358] KORUS FTA includes an article, particularly, dealing with cross-border consumer protection, which highlights cooperation with respect to the protection including prevention of fraudulent and deceptive commercial practices against consumers. The cooperation requirement through the mutual assistance, notification, consultation, and exchange of information will apply to cartel investigations.[359]

(2) Cooperation Agreement regarding Competition Law

Besides FTAs, there are cooperation arrangements between competition authorities. The cooperation agreements focus on the issue of competition law enforcements. Although not specifically mentioning ‘a cartel’ in languages, the provisions apply to cartel regulations in the same way as other regulatory areas within the competition law. One of the arrangements is “Cooperation Arrangement between the Commissioner of Competition (Canada), the Australian Competition and Consumer Commission and the New Zealand Commerce Commission regarding the Application of their Competition and Consumer Laws.” Important provisions related to cartel enforcement are (i) notification requirement when one’s enforcement may affect the other party’s interests in the application of its competition law, and (ii) cooperation through sharing information and coordinative efforts when parties enforce the laws to the same or similar matters.[360]

The notification requirement under (i) should be fulfilled when any RBP subject to penalties under the one party’s competition law was carried out in the other party’s territory.[361] The sharing of the information under (ii) in light of domestic interests in the application of competition law needs to accompany the securing of the confidentiality of shared information[362] for the sound function of an authority that shared the information. The sharing of information under confidentiality requirement can work essentially for balancing cooperation in cartel investigation

[358] Article 16.1 (7) of Chap. 16 of FTA between the South Korea and the U.S.A (KORUS FTA). The KORUS FTA was effective in 2012 through renegotiation after the first draft.

[359] Article 16.6 (1) and (2) of KORUS FTA.

[360] *Id.* III.1 and 2.

[361] Cooperation Arrangement between The Commission of Competition (Canada), the Australian Competition and Consumer Commission and the New Zealand Commerce Commission regarding the Application of their Competition and Consumer Laws, II.1.b. (Oct. 2000), *available at* http://strategis.ic.gc.ca/pics/ct/euro-agree_e.pdf (visited on July 18, 2008).

[362] *Id.* VI.2 and 3.

with operation of leniency program. Periodical meeting among competition officials[363] enables parties to discuss application of competition law and strengthen cooperative investigation, particularly, against international cartels.

(3) Asian Pacific Economic Cooperation (APEC)

As a broad regional economic cooperation, APEC has acknowledged the importance of developing competition principles and contributed to the promotion of overall competition law and policy through issuing agenda, action plan, declaration, and principles.[364] APEC Principles to Enhance Competition and Regulatory Reform does not mention a cartel specifically, but urges member economies to address anticompetitive behaviors by implementing competition policy for protecting the competitive process.[365] Confidence and capacity building in DCs and effective cooperation on competition policy through APEC,[366] particularly operating database on competition policy as a concrete measure,[367] facilitate cartel law enforcement.

On the other hand, APEC allows members to have exemptions and exceptions of competition law as long as they are no broader than necessary to achieve an objective of APEC through competition policy.[368] The sustainable development[369] and the peculiarity of food system[370] are the areas where APEC has paid attention besides competition. Cartels not only for environmental protection but also for primary commodity can be permitted. APEC, particularly, acknowledges the importance of Small and Medium Enterprises (SMEs) to economic activities within the region under Manila Action Plan for APEC, thereby implying that the SMEs-related exceptions to cartel regulations, e.g., crisis cartel and R&D cartel among SMEs, are acceptable.

E. Hurdles to Cooperation in Investigation and Enforcement

It is noted that although the U.S. and the EU have developed their cooperation in competition law enforcement, member states are usually unwilling to share confidential evidence, which they had obtained through their respective cartel investigation. The lack of cooperation is analyzed to be due to the reluctance of the member states that need to protect domestic business sectors and to secure the cooperation of the investigated companies with fear that their confidential business information may spread to authorities of other countries. Facing the problem, most

[363] *Id.* V. d and e.

[364] APEC, Principles to Enhance Competition and Regulatory Reform, preamble; The Auckland Challenge, APEC economic leaders' declaration, para. 6 (Sept 13, 1999); Osaka Action Agenda (OAA), Implementation of the Bogor Declaration, 8. Objective (1995).

[365] APEC, *id.* Implementation 3). The Osaka Action Agenda, 8 Guidelines b.

[366] Principles, 6 –10. The Agenda, 8. Collective Actions a (iv) and e.

[367] The Agenda, 8.Collective Actions, a.(iii).

[368] OAA, 8.CA.a.(iii).

[369] Manila Action Plan for APEC (MAPA) para. 5 to 7 (Jul. 11–12, 1996).

[370] The Auckland Challenge, para. 15–16.

member states in the EU, institutionally, have acknowledged the support under their national laws and the U.S. has enacted a legislation to facilitate antitrust cooperative investigation and enforcement in 1994.[371] Under the new legislation, the International Antitrust Enforcement Assistance Act (IAEAA), the U.S. has tried to overcome the difficulty of sharing confidential information.[372]

Although accumulated bilateral agreements will be the foundation for international competition law, bilateral agreements are not direct contributors to achieving international cartel regulation but act as complementary building blocks. The bilateral agreements, still, have focused on cooperation of competition law enforcement rather than harmonization of the competition law itself only with the exception of New Zealand and Australia.[373] In addition, bilateral agreements have their limitations in that participating countries were usually the most industrialized countries. Countries with underdeveloped or developing economies with inexperienced competition authorities not yet actively participate in bilateral agreements. MLATs on criminal matters may cover cartel regulation but, in the light of the current situation that DCs rarely employ criminal penalty against cartel members, they are likely to produce few, if any, practical results. International organizations try to build multilateral agreements by issuing recommendation or launching negotiation toward multilateral agreements in the circumstance where the number of bilateral agreements is increasing.

3.7 Conclusion

International cartels are categorized into two types, an agreement among competing companies to restrict competition and a loose association established by such agreements consisting of competing companies. The agreement-typed cartels have legal characteristic of international agreements among private companies with limited legal personality. Meanwhile, the association-typed cartels, such as IGCs, and IPAs, can have limited legal personality and a legal characteristic of international organization.

---

[371]Stark, *supra* note 341, at 87. In 1994, the U.S. enacted the International Antitrust Enforcement Assistance Act (IAEAA), 15 U.S.C. Sec. 6201–6212 (1994), under which through bilateral agreement confidential information can be shared, and antitrust authorities can use their investigative powers on one another's behalf. *See id.* at 90: Waller (1997), 371–72. Waller analyzes in detail the IAEAA in terms of antitrust mutual assistance agreement, and its legislative background with focus on restriction of confidential information as to premerger notifications under Hart–Scott–Rodino Act.

[372]The U.S. has made an agreement with Australia under the IAEAA. *See* Agreement between the Gov. of the U.S.A. and the Gov. of Australia on Mutual Antitrust Enforcement Assistance, *at* http://www.usdoj.gov/atr/international/usaus7.htm.

[373]New Zealand and Australia substantially harmonized their national competition laws, replaced antidumping law with true competition provisions, and amended domestic competition laws to facilitate competition enforcement under a free trade area agreement, Closer Economic Relations-Trade Agreement (March 28, 1983), 22 I.L.M. 945. Waller (1997), 355–356.

As international organizations under suspicion of allegedly an international cartel, there are OPEC, ITU, and IATA. First, the OPEC, as one of the long-existing IPAs, is not a private international cartel. The characteristics of the agreements among states with sovereignty, no penalty against cheating, oil as nonrenewable natural resources, and the necessity of sustainable development are not fit to a cartel under competition law but international commodity agreement subject to economic cooperation on the basis of mutual benefit under commodity law as a distinctive area of international law.

Second, the ITU as a standard-setting organization is not an international cartel infringing competition law. Its practice of rate-setting without binding power or penalty indicates downward price trend and reflects public interests, e.g., equity, static efficiency, and universality. The RFS allocation is an inevitable way to achieve effective cross-border radio broadcasting under the current technical level unless it severely limits new competitive comers' accesses.

Third, the IATA consisting of private airlines, on the contrary, can violate competition law as a cartel because it reveals practices of passenger rate or air cargo fee setting. The counterargument of nonbinding recommendation is weak because the interlineable fare system of IATA has worked as a factor of settling fares to the same level. EU and US DOJ, which withdrew the immunity of competition law conferred on IATA, have investigated anticompetitiveness of such rate coordination. On the other hand, slot allocation and airport scheduling are acknowledged as necessary procedures for relieving congestion in airports, unless the practices of 'historical precedence' work as exclusive behaviors impeding new competitors' participation.

Cartel regulatory regimes have developed in the late half of twentieth century in industrialized countries although there were laws prohibiting profiteering through HCC activities from the ancient to the medieval to the modern ages. However, the occurrence of international cartels necessitated international law with respect to cartel activities, thereby developing international agreements regarding competition.

In distinction with a cartel made up of private companies under competition law, ICAs have been treated under international commodity law. The separation is due to unique characteristics of commodities. International organizations have issued declarations, resolutions, and made treaties registered. Such separate treatment of commodity under international law was accepted into domestic laws. As a result, the international commodity law has pursued a different path from competition law.

Although international competition law have experienced failures of reaching concrete codes, cartel regulation of international competition law, currently, has grown up with multilateral agreements as well as bilateral agreements. The 1947 Havana Charter with a chapter focusing on competition was not effective due to insufficient ratification. Trials to revive the chapter came in a deadlock due to conflicting opinions in UN ECOSOC in the 1950s. International organizations such as the UNTAD and the OECD have devoted their efforts to secure multilateral agreements, thereby achieving the 1980 UN Set and the 1998 OECD Recommendation. In addition to these endeavors, the ICN has worked for promotion of competition law and practical support for competition authorities without sophisticated enforcement experiences. The WTO included the issue of competition law under DDA, although dropping at 2003 Cancun conference due to severe objection from less DCs, currently in standstill. As a result, the recognition of the importance of cartel regulation has widened to DCs and less DCs recently.

Bilateral agreements with characteristics of an international agreement on cartels have not been many until the 1990s when a large number of countries adopted competition laws. The bilateral agreements have advantages over multilateral agreements in some points, e.g., the negotiation of specific interests between countries, much less costs. MLATs occurred centering the countries with accumulated cases and practices and treated competition law and cartels along with other criminal matters. Following the MLATs, bilateral agreements addressing the issues of competition law, e.g., 1991 Agreement between U.S.A. and the E.C. regarding the Application of their Competition Laws, came out from 1990s. However, the bilateral agreements have the following weak points: such as the unwillingness of member states to share confidential information, limitation as foundation for international cartel law, and a confined scope of participating countries, or mostly industrialized countries.

Therefore, on the way toward binding international law, a multilateral agreement has still its importance and unique role. Multitude of bilateral agreements cannot replace the role for building a binding international cartel law of a multilateral agreement, through which the harmonization of domestic cartel regulation can effectively come true. In light of the former failures to achieve multilateral agreements of competition law including cartel regulation, it needs to place the priority in solving the dispute of opinions, particularly between less DCs and relatively industrialized countries, as regards international cartel regulation as the 2003 Cancun Conference indicated in 2003. Since the cartel regulation defends consumers' rights to have products through price mechanism of merit-based competition in markets and punish anticompetitive business activities curbing competition, it has much reciprocal benefit for DCs as well as industrial countries. By reducing fear of DCs that international cartel regulation interfere with their domestic economic policies, among other things, including industrial policy, international organizations' effort to have effective international cartel regulation can increase the probability of success. The next chapter will discuss how to reduce conflicts between DCs and industrialized countries.

References

Books

Aronson JD, Cowhey PF (1988) When countries talk: international trade in telecommunications services. Ballinger, Cambridge

Codding GA Jr et al (1982) The international telecommunication union in a changing world. Artech House, Dedham

Damrosch LF et al (2001) International law: cases and materials, 4th edn. Westgroup, St Paul

Davidow J (1980) The seeking of a world competition code: quixotic quest? In: Schachter O, Hellawell R (eds) Competition in international business law and policy on restrictive practices. Columbia University Press, New York
Drexl J (ed) (2003a) The future of transnational antitrust—from comparative to common competition law. Staempfli Pub. Ltd, Berne
Edwards CD (1964) Cartelization in Western Europe. U.S. Department of State, Washington
Flynn J, First H, Bush D (2005) Antitrust statutes, treaties, regulations, guidelines, and policies 2005–2006. Foundation Press, Eagan
John CA, Matsushita M (eds) (2002) Competition policy in the global trading system. Kluwer Law International, Dordrecht
Kahn KR (1982) The law & the organisation of international commodity agreements. M. Nijhoff Pub, The Hague
Leclair MS (2000) International commodity market and the roles of cartels. M.E. Sharpe Inc, Armonk
Lin C-H (2004) International telecommunication regime and its influence on Taiwan's telecommunication regulations. SJD thesis, Golden Gate Univ. School of Law
Matsushida M, Ahn D (eds) (2004) WTO and East Asia: New Perspective. Cameron, Houston
Okeke CN (1973) The expansion of new subjects of contemporary international law through their treaty-making capacity. Universitaire Pers, Rotterdam
Savage JG (1989) The politics of international telecommunications regulation. Westview Press, Boulder
Scherer FM (1994) Competition policies for an integrated world economy. Brookings Institution, Washington, DC
Sell S (1998) Power & ideas: north-south politics of intellectual property and antitrust. State Univ. of New York Press, New York
Taylor MD (2006) International competition law: a new dimension for the WTO?. Cambridge University Press, Cambridge
United Nations (2007) Conference on trade and development (UNCTAD), model law on competition: UNCTAD series on issues in competition law and policy. UN, New York

Journal Articles and Papers

Baldwin RE (2004) Failure of the WTO ministerial conference at Cancun: reasons and remedies. http://www.fordschool.umich.edu/rsie/Conferences/CGP/May2004Papers/Baldwin.pdf
Besnier J Y (2003) Membership benefits-ITU-D overview, seminar on standardization and ICT development for the information society. http://www.itu.int
Bronz G (1956) An international trade organization: the second attempt. Harv Law Rev 69(3):465–467
Brown B (1994) Developing countries in the international trade order. N Ill Univ Law Rev 14:347
Drexl J (2003) Do we need "courage" for international antitrust law? Choosing between supranational and international law principles of enforcement. In: Drexl J (ed) The future of transnational antitrust—from comparative to common competition law. Staempfli Pub., Berne
Duruigbo E (2006) Permanent sovereignty and peoples' ownership of natural resources in international law. Geo Wash Int Law Rev 38:68–75
EC (2006) Official Journal of the European Union. http://ec.europa.eu/transport/air_portal/competition/doc/ec_2006_1459_en.pdf. Visited on 4 Mar 2008
Evenett S, Levenstein M, Suslow V (2001) International cartel enforcement: lessons from 1990s. World Bank policy research working paper no. 2680
Fitzmaurice (1953) The law and procedure of the international court of justice. Br YBIL 31:2
George K (1990) UK competition policy: issues and institutions. In: Comanor WS et al (eds) Competition policy in Europe and North America: economic issues and institutions. NY Harwood Academic, New York

George S (2007) Alternative finances: the world trade organisation we could have had, 2. http://www.zmag.org/content. Visited on 14 Sept 2007

Hannigan JA (1982) Unfriendly skies: the decline of the world aviation cartel. Pac Sociol Rev 25 (1):107–136

Harding C, Joshua J (2010) Regulating Cartels in Europe, 2nd edn. Oxford University Press, Oxford

Hyundai Research Institute (2004), 3차 오일쇼크는 오는가 Does the third oil price shock comes? http://www.hri.co.kr/upload/bbs_file/publication/BSR20040809_2_1.PDF

IATA (2007) Worldwide scheduling guidelines, 15th edn

Karl TL (2004) Oil-led development: social, political, and economic consequences. In: Cleverland CJ (ed) The Encyclopedia of energy, vol 4. Elsevier, Amsterdam, p 661

Korea Fair Trade Commission (KFTC) (2004) KFTC's experience in dealing with international cartels, APEC Training Program, 8–9. http://www.jftc.go.jp/eacpf/05/APECTrainingProgramMarch2004/KE.experience.Jand.pdf. Visited on 18 Aug 2008

MacFadden EJ (1986) The collapse of tin: restructuring a failed commodity agreement. AJIL 80:811

Malaguti MC (1999) Restrictive business practices in international trade and the role of the World Trade Organization, 615. In: Paolo Mengozzi, Int'l trade law on the 50th anniversary of the multilateral trade system, 615 (A. Giuffre, 1999)

Paasman BR (1990) Multilateral rules on competition policy: an overview of the debate, 30 (U.N. Economic Commission for Latin America and the Caribbean, Division of Trade and Development Finance, 1999)

Peterson RD (1990) The CAB's struggle to establish price and route rivalry in world air transport. Am J Econ Sociol 49(1):65–80

Resch A (2005) Phases of competition policy in Europe. Working paper AY0504, Institute of European Studies: UC Berkeley http://repositories.cdlib.org/cgi/viewcontent.cgi?article=1049&context=ies. Visited on 17 Mar 2008

Stern PA (1990) The international telecommunications settlement process: what's needed? Destroy and replace it or adjust it? IIC Telecommunications Forum (Washington). http://www.itu.int/

The IMF Research Department (2000) The impact of higher oil prices on the global economy. http://www.imf.org/external/pubs/ft/oil/2000/#annex

Vertigan KE (2007) Foreign antitrust injunctions: taking a lesson from the act of state doctrine. Geo Wash Law Rev 76:155

Voigt F (1962) German experience with cartels and their control during the pre-war and post-war periods. In: Miller JP (ed) Competition, cartels and their regulation. North-Holland, Amsterdam

Waller SW (1997) The internationalization of antitrust enforcement. Boston Univ Law Rev 77:343

Winslow WT (2001) OECD program for international responses to global competition issues. In: Chao Y-C et al (eds) International and comparative competition laws and policies. Kluwer Law International, Dordrecht

Chapter 4
Conciliation of Conflicts of Opinion Between the North and the South on International Law Regulating Cartel

Abstract International competition law cannot avoid considering the development-perspective of competition law since the majority of the constituents of international organizations which tried to adopt competition law experience or experienced developing market economies or least-developed economies. As the 2003 Cancun Ministerial Conference for Doha Development Agenda demonstrated, the unilateral market-oriented competition policy from the advanced countries was not welcomed in the developing countries' context even though competition law produces legal guidelines to business activities among competing companies along with providing much benefit in increasing consumers' welfare and efficiency. In light of the development-approach, there need to be flexible rules acknowledging exceptions to cartel regulations and assistance in operating cartel regulations in developing economies. Major aspects of international development law, e.g., differential treatment, non-reciprocity, and convention of commodity-producing and consuming countries in markets, need to be adopted by international competition law since the international competition law is currently in the initial stage and the wide gap of experiences in practice between advanced countries and developing countries cannot be regulated under a single standard. As binding international cartel law can help foster competition policy in less-competitive markets, it will support MNEs or companies from advanced countries which want to expand their market. On the other hand, it can also proffer benefits to developing countries where the level of economic development outgrows its low level and international trade occupies a growing portion of Gross Domestic Product.

Keywords Doha development agenda · Development approach · Non-reciprocal principle · Special and differential treatment · International development law · Binding international cartel agreement

J.S. Lee, *Strategies to Achieve a Binding International Agreement on Regulating Cartels*, DOI 10.1007/978-981-10-2756-7_4

4.1 Introduction

International law regarding cartel regulation has evolved with the support of the developing countries in 1970s and 1980s and produced the UN Set, while in 1990s and the 2000s it developed under the industrialized countries' auspice and created OECD Hard Core Cartel Recommendation. The effort to achieve a binding international agreement failed in 2003, due to developing countries (DCs)' opposition to the inclusion of competition policy into the Doha Development Agenda (DDA). It appears ironic that the UN Set regarding restrictive business practice (RBP)s of transnational corporation was adopted by DCs but that the proposal of multilateral agreement to adopt the competition policy was rejected by the same group 20 years later. It should be noted that the languages of the UN Set and Doha Declaration are similar in terms of cartel regulation. Therefore, it is worthwhile to research the reason for dropping competition policy out from the negotiation of DDA because the regulation, once accepted by developing countries, was abandoned by the same group.

The two regulations originate from different perspectives. The major differences between the two are the objectives of regulation and the ideological motive to introduce the regulations. The UN Set was introduced to the UN General Assembly as a result of the United Nations Conference on Trade and Development (UNCTAD) resolution. It was for regulating restrictive business activities of multinational corporations (MNCs), most of which have their headquarters in the industrialized countries. It was a part of the New International Economic Order (NIEO) with a significant impact on the international community that supported UNCTAD's adoption of the resolution. The UN Set, consisting of recommendations without binding power, has requested to hold regular conferences for reviewing each country's effort to comply.

On the other hand, the DDA was introduced by the World Trade Organization (WTO). It was for achieving binding multilateral agreements with such ambition of setting global trade that the DDA included competition policy under a broad coverage of discussion agenda. The effort towards an international free trade regime originated from the New Liberalism that has predominated the international economy since the collapse of communist regimes in the 1990s.

The conflict between the two groups invokes the question whether cartel regulation is necessary in international law. It is important that the benefits of international cartel regulation to DCs and less DCs should outweigh the cost of the regulation. If so, the group which currently disagrees with adopting international cartel regulation will be more willing to accord approval to it. With persuasive researches added, its fear for the regulation can also be reduced.

This chapter analyzes the failure of negotiating the DDA in Cancun due to distinct positions of industrialized countries and DCs. Subsequently, different theological backgrounds with which each group of countries under the North–South dialog holds their positions are to be researched in-detail. In spite of the different placements in which each group is located, the necessity of cartel regulation in international law is to be demonstrated in terms of benefit derived to DCs.

4.2 Failure of Further Negotiation on Competition Policy Under Doha Development Agenda (DDA) at WTO Ministerial Conferences

A. Standstill of DDA Negotiation

(1) Collapse of the Negotiation at Cancun, 2003

A chair of the Ministerial Conference called an end to the Conference by dropping the Singapore issues under multilateral negotiation for DDA. It was even before foreign ministers at the site proceeded to a discussion of agriculture, the most controversial issue. Although the reasons for the sudden end are arguably analyzed as a strong objection to Singapore issues from developing countries' groups such as African Caribbean Pacific group (ACP),[1] advanced countries' insincerity,[2] WTO decision-making procedures,[3] and a judgment by the chair to end the talks early, which was motivated by the unwillingness of developed countries to discuss agricultural reforms,[4] the most serious reason looks to be the first one: the strong opposition from the majority of DCs.

EC Trade Commissioner Lamy, on the last day of negotiation, agreed with the chairman's position that the EC would be willing to remove investment and

---

[1]The ACP grouping consists of over seventy countries that are beneficiaries of the European Union's preferential market access programs, originally provided by the Lome Convention and later renewed by the Contonou agreement. White and Case LLP (2003), at 3.

[2]EC's concession to drop two issues including competition policy was criticized for being too late. *See id.*

[3]The procedure is criticized from two conflicting perspectives. The one from advanced countries argues that although the consensus-based system is democratic, it is exposed to abuse from anti-trade or anti-liberalization groups and inefficient to produce any substantial result with further negotiation. *See* White and Case LLP, *supra* note 1, at 9; Baldwin (2008), at 3 and 10. The other one from developing countries insists that WTO's untransparent and nonparticipatory decision-making process which invoked developing countries' rage led to the collapse of the negotiation, whereby criticizing WTO's bias in favor of minority of developed countries rather than majority of developing countries. The informal drafting custom by chairmen, since 1996 Singapore Ministerial Conference, urged every member to adopt the last draft on the last day of schedule, which accumulated anger from members with limited access to decision. Khor (2003), at 3–6.

[4]The chairman's closing announcement was considered as surprise since quite a few WTO members were absent at the meeting where the EC concession was presented. Arguably, the motives of the chairman might have been driven by other factors, not related to Singapore issues, such as developed countries efforts to thwart agricultural reform. *See* Khor, *supra* note 3, at 1–5; White and Case LLP, *supra* note 1, 2–4.

competition from the agenda, too late in the light of the strong positions of DCs.[5] The EC's concession invoked a gust of responses. After an-hour-long discussion among ministers, Botswana, on behalf of the ACP, expressed the rejection for all four issues. The ACP had held the strong position in requesting the cotton initiative and an end of subsidies.[6] On the other hand, South Korea argued that it could not accept the dropping of any issue.[7] The strong stand by the ACP group invoked a sudden halt to the negotiation on any issue.

The G-21+,[8] a group of developing countries with a middle level of income or with a big domestic market, were upset at the sudden closure of the negotiation by stating that the group was a negotiating force that must be dealt with seriously, and that WTO discussions should move forward in order to achieve agriculture reform.[9] Its member countries blamed the ACP grouping in particular for the collapse.[10]

The United States Trade Representative (USTR) Zoellick shifted the responsibility indirectly to the African and Caribbean countries, by stating that the talk failed after the countries walked out on the efforts to launch negotiations on trade facilitation as a necessary modernization process in order to foster customs and other procedures. On the other hand, the US reproached Brazil, the leader of the G-21+, by arguing that the demands of the group, which was unwilling to engage in constructive talks, were based on an insincere attitude.[11]

---

[5]Khor, *supra* note 3, at 2 and 9. However, Khor states, the Chairman proposed that the two issues, investment and competition policy, would be dropped out from the agenda but that for the other two issues, trade facilitation and procurement, negotiations could begin. In response to the proposal, the EC Commissioner agreed to it, giving impression that these would be removed from the WTO altogether, not just from Doha mandate. Khor, *id.* at 2.

[6]*See* White and Case LLP, *supra* note 1, at 2–3. The article states that the second draft Ministerial Declaration reflected the U.S. proposal regarding the cotton initiative in conflict with the initial pleading of four West African cotton producers, Burkina Faso, Benin, Chad and Mali, for the consideration of a sectoral initiative to reduce and eliminate cotton subsidies. *Id.* 5–6. Especially the text language inflames the African countries, saying that international bodies direct existing programmes and resources toward diversification of the economies where cotton accounts for the major share of their GDP, because the African countries recognized the wording as suggestion of stopping growing cotton. JOB(03)/150/Rev.2, at para. 27. They asked the ACP group of support for the initiative, and the group requested to end all export subsidies in 3 years, production subsidies in 4 years starting in 2005, and to remit payments of maximum $300 million annually to African countries affected by subsidies. The situation appeared to have spiraled out of control. *See id.* at 6.

[7]Khor, *supra* note 3, at 2–3.

[8]The G-21+, led by Brazil, China, and India, also includes Argentina, Bolivia, Chile, Colombia, Costa Rica, Ecuador, El Salvador (later withdrew), Guatemala, Mexico, Pakistan, Paraguay, Peru, Philippines, South Africa, Thailand, and Venezuela. At the start of the Cancun Ministerial, Egypt, Senegal and Turkey joined, Indonesia and Nigeria joined toward the close of Ministerial. *See id.* at 3 fn 3.

[9]The G-21+ group had taken a hard line on agriculture negotiation.

[10]*See id.* at 3.

[11]*See id.* at 4.

(2) Assessment

The tension between the North and the South grew exacerbated through discussion and negotiation. DCs' groups, ACP and G-21+, focused on the 'development' cause of DDA by addressing their demands. The developing countries, in addition, have manifested their dissatisfactions with the current balance of trading concessions since the conclusion of the Uruguay Round. For instance, they resisted holding the Ministerial Conference in Qatar that launched the Doha Agenda due to the lack of significant progress on some implementation issues of the WTO agreement under the Uruguay Round. They have also complained about the tardy process of agricultural trade system reform and of removing quantitative restrictions on textile imports in the developed countries.[12] The initiative for immediate reform of the cotton sector, however, was difficult for the U.S. and other developed countries to accept because it was closely related to agricultural reform as one of the most controversial domestic political issues.[13]

Besides the objection from the groups, diverse opinions within the developing countries turned the whole negotiation into a standstill. While the G-21+ group held a position to continue to negotiate on the Singapore issues with an interest in agricultural subsidy reduction, the ACP group strongly objected to further discussion of all Singapore issues. Some developing countries with high-level incomes insisted on keeping the issues on the table. It was difficult to have a consensus-based decision made because of diverse conflicting interests within the South.

Developed countries, on the other hand, not ready to adopt a unilateral liberalization approach alone, failed to persuade the developing countries to acknowledge that adopting new trade-related rule issues, such as competition and investment, can proffer more gains in terms of development than cost.[14] It looked as if major developed countries had underestimated the developing countries' complaints and had believed, from their past experiences, that developing countries would not be brave enough to thwart the on-going multilateral negotiation of the Doha Agenda and remain open to criticism if the major trade powers formed a unified voice.[15]

Although reforms of the existent procedure of WTO decision-making are proposed by both the North and the South groups, the problem consists in the mistrust in each other because of the lack of an opportunity to understand reciprocal positions. The continual failure to revive the DDA among the group of advanced countries, like the EU and the U.S., and the leaders of emerging economies with big local markets, such as India and Brazil, can not be explained but by the

[12]Baldwin, *supra* note 3, 9–10.

[13]U.S. General Accounting Office [GAO] (2004), at 2–3.

[14]*See id.*

[15]Less than a month before the meetings, the U.S. and the EU jointly presented a broad framework for improving market access for agricultural products and joined with Canada in presenting a proposal aimed at reaching an agreement on negotiating modalities for nonagricutlural products. Baldwin, *supra* note 3, at 10.

misunderstanding of reciprocal positions despite tenacious proposals to further DDA negotiation.

The argument for the chairman's biased closure in favor of the unwilling developed countries does not provide persuasive supporting evidences. On the contrary, while developed countries, e.g., the U.S. and the EU, put their efforts to revive the Doha multilateral negotiation afterwards, the ACP group cheered the collapse. The subsequent failures of WTO Ministerial Conferences indicate that the collapse was not from faults of individuals, e.g., the chairman, and delegates, but from structural conflict of interests among the groups of countries. Some observers agreed with this analysis and evaluated the decision of the chairman as wise and timely in advance of the situation worsening due to the hardened positions of the developing countries.[16] The grounds of the argument regarding his biased judgment should be carefully examined in order to eliminate possible prejudices of subsequent chairmen.

B. The Competition Policy Issue Under the GATT/WTO

(1) Insufficient Consensus in Competition Policy

Competition policy among the Singapore issues, although not the very topic so controversial to lead to the failure of Cancun Conference, was the issue that some developed countries[17] put aside for future negotiation rather than prioritizing. Developing countries, which had diverse positions in the negotiation of the Singapore issues, mostly agreed that the competition policy should be dropped out of the current negotiation table.[18] The point that the second draft Ministerial Declaration at Cancun relegated competition policy to further study reflects this reality.[19]

The position of the majority of the DCs was on the opposite side when the countries spearheaded the passage of the UN Set at the General Assembly in 1980. In the DDA negotiation, which is supposed to include development concerns of the South, the majority group of the DCs, or ACP 77, perceived the competition policy including cartel regulation as a method to press the domestic markets' opening, to restrict national economic development policy, and to curb cooperation among domestic companies. On the contrary, the South in the UN Set had considered cartel provisions

[16]White and Case LLP, *supra* note 1, at 2; Khor, *supra* note 3, at 5.

[17]Canada's trade minister Pierre Pettigrew facilitated the discussions on the Singapore issues at Cancun and proposed a compromise that would have allowed the two less controversial issues to proceed, public procurement and trade facilitation, along with eventual negotiations on investment, but not competition. On the other hand, the EU and Japan had been the main supporters for negotiation on investment and competition since at the Singapore Conference in 1996. However, the EU made concession to remove the investment and competition at Cancun.

[18]Malaysia, an opponent of all the issues, however, suggested to agree to trade facilitation and competition, not in public procurement. On the other hand, South Korea, traditional supporter of all the issues, kept on its position in spite of the EU's concession. *See id.* at 2–3.

[19]JOB(03)/150/Rev.2, at para. 15.

as a shield to prevent multinational or foreign corporations from the North from exploiting consumer welfare through anticompetitive business behaviors.

The different views came from the distinction of respective major objective and negotiating attitudes of proposed multilateral agreements. Although the economic development issue was one of the major goals set by both agreements, the DDA in WTO was for promoting free trade by reducing or eliminating trade barriers while the UN Set was intended for control over RBPs of MNCs. ACP 77 countries, which approved the launching of DDA negotiation under the commitment of the Uruguay Round and international pressure, gradually lost trust in the benefits of the WTO-leading trade liberalization approach to themselves, because their main trade interests in cotton and agricultural product were not reflected in in-detailed negotiations. While the North's concern for intervention into sovereignty was reflected in the UN Set with a nonbinding characteristic, the South's request for negotiation with a narrow range of topics was rejected in the DDA under coercion of a wide range of trade topics toward international binding rules. Rough or seemingly hesitant attitudes to such requests from advanced countries, e.g., EU or U.S. generated much anger in the ACP 77 group. The cause of development, particularly the necessity of DCs and LDCs' for enhanced support in competition policy, proclaimed in the DDA, was suspected as an excuse for opening domestic markets in almost all aspects of trade, covering services, agricultures, and trade-related laws. If cartel regulation in competition policy within DDA negotiations had placed its basis on the UN Set and expressed a sincere attitude for respecting the accumulated resources of competition policy of the UNCTAD, as the Declaration states,[20] such a sudden deadlock could have been avoided. A minimum consensus could have been reached as to the maxim principles, e.g., restriction against hard core cartels and international cooperation.

(2) Reflecting Fairness Principle Within GATT

The regulation of so-called 'unfair trading practices' has constituted an integral part of GATT/WTO rules.[21] Article XX of the GATT, for promoting fair competition, prevents products of free economic systems with a choice of employment options and wages, from competing with the products of forced prison labor. Art. VI para. 1 addresses the prohibition of dumping[22] which causes or threatens to cause material injury to an established industry. Para. 2 permits governments to

[20]Para. 24 of Doha Ministerial Declaration states that the ministers shall work in cooperation with other relevant intergovernmental organizations, including UNCTAD, and, through appropriate regional and bilateral channels, to provide strengthened and adequately resourced assistance to respond to the needs of DCs and LDCs for competition policy.

[21]Baldwin, *supra* note 3, at 12.

[22]Dumping means that the price of a product which is introduced into the commerce of an importing country is less than (a) the comparable domestic price, in the ordinary course of trade, for the like product in the exporting country, or (b) in the absence of such price, either (i) the highest comparable price for the like product for export to any third country, or (ii) the cost of production plus a reasonable addition for selling cost and profit. GATT (1947), Art. VI para. 1.

impose a limited amount of anti-dumping duties not greater than the margin of dumping. Para. 3, similarly, allows a limited amount of countervailing duties if a foreign exporting government provides subsidies to the production or export of a product in the country.

Moreover, developmental concerns under the GATT/WTO scheme imply that formal reciprocal and nondiscriminatory treatment of DCs can produce unfair results. The 1955 GATT amendment for substantial reduction of tariff and nontariff barriers on a reciprocal and mutually advantageous basis announced that multilateral negotiations should afford adequate opportunities to take into account 'the need of less-developed countries for a more flexible use of tariff protection to assist their economic development'.[23] An agreement among GATT members in 1971 to temporarily waive Art. I, stipulating nondiscrimination principle, allowed advanced countries to accord preferential tariff treatment to products from DCs. So-called the Enabling Clause of 1979 extended the time and scope of the waiver to an indefinite level and by covering nontariff measures. Ministerial declarations in both the Uruguay and Doha Rounds had urged the developed countries[24] to grant special and differential treatment to developing countries, especially the least-developed countries (LDC).[25]

'Fairness' principle, on the other hand, has operated in favor of industrialized countries in pressing the negotiation agenda. Besides quite a few cases of dumping and foreign governmental subsidies, there have been an increasing number of unfair trade cases regarding lax or ineffective environmental and labor standards of DCs. While developed countries pressured DCs to insert such rules into bilateral and

[23]Baldwin, *supra* note 3, at 12.

[24]Although UN does not have any established convention for the designation of 'developed' and 'developing' countries or areas, UNCTAD considers 'developed' such countries as Israel and Japan in Asia, Canada and the U.S. in northern America, Australia and New Zealand in Oceania and most countries in Europe. Meanwhile, it treats as a separate group South-East Europe including countries of former Yugoslavia as well as Commonwealth of Independent States (CIS), former U.S.S.R. All the other countries fall on 'developing countries'. Countries are categorized under such classification. Definition of Developed, Developing countries [code 491], *at* http://unstats.un.org (last visited on 14 Sept. 2007); UNCTAD (2005), at 10.

[25]Baldwin, *supra* note 3, 12–13. The LDCs are defined by low-income, human resource weakness, and economic vulnerability. The low-income criterion is under $ 750 for inclusion and above $ 900 for graduation based on three-year average estimate of the gross domestic product per capita. The human resource weakness criterion is indicated by nutrition, health, education, and adult literacy. The last criterion is based on the instability of agricultural production, instability of exports of goods and services, the economic importance of nontraditional activities, merchandise export concentration, and the handicap of economic smallness (excluding large economies with more than 75 million people), and the percentage of population displaced by natural disasters. 50 countries are categorized as LDCs by the UN. The list of LDCs is reviewed every 3 years by the Economic and Social Council, *available at* http://www.un.org/geninfo/faq/factsheets/FS20.HTM (last visited on 14 Sept. 2007).

regional trade agreements, new rules under the WTO as to cartel and competition policy have not been introduced. Competition law, although widely adopted by DCs, looks to be the last area where wide international consensus results in a multilateral treaty.

(3) Understanding DCs' Situations

The relatively low expertise and knowledge, along with a lower priority in competition law on the part of developing countries (DCs), caused the drop-out of the competition policy from the DDA negotiation. With current institutions, human and financial resources, and the level of experience, DCs have the difficulty in actively enforcing competition law and cartel regulations. They have kept their focus on economic development.[26]

An important concern of DCs in multilateral negotiation for competition law is the disruptive domestic adjustment problem of a new competition law, such as economic, political, and social implication, coming from the potential negative domestic effect of the new rules.[27] Cartel regulation possibly affects the economic situation in the repression period, industrial cooperation in R&D, management on nonrenewable natural resources of developing countries, traditionally accepted business activities, national industrial policy, and so on. Reaching a binding international agreement as to cartel regulation with developing countries on the basis of current non-binding recommendatory rules necessitates the understanding of their arguments and concerns as well as the proposition of persuasive solutions. Researches on the concept of the b and the NIEO are beneficial for the further understanding of their positions.

Researches and investigations regarding cost and benefit of competition law enforcement in DCs must be promoted so that the countries can make a commitment to negotiation on the topic. Compared to mergers and acquisitions as well as market dominant behaviors, cartels cause direct harms to consumers by raising prices and reducing outputs. As the benefits of cartel regulation are clear, cartel regulation is an area where consensus among the members can be achieved without a strong objection. Further in-depth research will be beneficial in reaching a broad range of countries' consensus—in appropriate penalties or remedies, some exceptional types of cases of justifying cartels, and the costs and funding of the enforcement.[28]

---

[26]Refer to III of this chapter.

[27]Baldwin, *supra* note 3, at 22 and 24.

[28]Baldwin has the same opinion. *See id.*, at 16. He requests immediately to set up Working Groups to investigate on the matter and the adjustment problems among various competition rules besides enforcement costs and possible means of funding.

4.3 Necessity of Regulating Cartels in Developing Countries

A. Damages of Cartels in Developing Countries (DCs)

Companies are exposed to the temptation of a collusive behavior, the formation of a cartel, more in the DCs under loose regulations. The representative harmful effect of such a collusive behavior is price increasing, which transfers consumers' welfare into suppliers' surplus. The rate of the price increase of international cartels in the DCs is much higher than the average price increase in overall countries. Representative international cartel cases in the 90s, such as Citric Acid and Graphite Electrodes, indicated that developing countries were overcharged for their imports in a range from 20 to 45 %.[29] The level of overcharge in developing countries overwhelms the median price increase between 14 and 20 % in overall countries.[30]

The damages caused by the price increase under a cartel reach a considerable amount. Although it is not easy to measure the exact amount of damage that a cartel has caused,[31] it is estimated that, conservatively, it exceeds many billions of US dollars annually.[32] A research of OECD demonstrated that, in 1997, total goods imported by developing countries, worth more than US $ 81 billion, were from suppliers involved in price-fixing conspiracies in the 90s.[33] The other research (Levenstein and Suslow) showed that US $ 51.1 billion were from industries in international cartel activities during the same period.[34] The amount outnumbers official development assistance (ODA) to all the developing countries, $ 39.4

---

[29] Levenstein and Suslow (2003–2004), at 801–818.

[30] Estimated price effects in 14 cartel cases under the survey range from 3 to 65 %. *See* OECD (2002), at 9.

[31] The reasons are following. First, most competition authorities, first, do not require calculation of the damage as an element of prosecution, but focus on the unlawful gain accruing to cartel operators for sanctions because it is easy to figure out. Due to lack of formal record or data, the work of quantifying the total damage is interesting academic researchers. Second, the result of quantifying the total damage may not be correct because it comes under assumption for a competitive price, a predicted price in the affected market, so as to determine the unlawful margin. OECD, *id,* at 6–7.

[32] *Id.* at 5 and at 9.

[33] *Id. See also* UNCTAD (2003), at 16. The UNCTAD report introduced a bid-rigging case on the United States Agency for International Development (USAID) in Egypt, filed on Aug. 11, 2000, in the U.S. District Court in Birmingham, Alabama. The defendant, American International Contractors Inc. (AICI) pleaded guilty to participating in a conspiracy involving bid-rigging from Jun. 1988 until at least Jan. 1995, and was required to pay US$ 4.2 million fine for the bid-rigging for wastewater treatment facilities construction contracts funded by the USAID in Egypt. Philipp Holzmann AG, a construction company based in Frankfurt, Germany, pleaded guilty to its participation in the cartel and was ordered to pay $ 30 million fine. As a result of such bid-rigging, the procurement market in Egypt became less-competitive and the competitive lowest price was unavailable.

[34] Levenstein and Suslow, *supra* note 29, 804.

billion, in 1997.[35] It should be noted that the illegal cartels that are actually detected and prosecuted are nothing but the tip of a large iceberg.[36]

The exploitation of consumers' welfare in DCs by cartel members has the actual effect of taking away foreign assistance since the cartels transfer wealth from consumers in DCs to the suppliers mostly working in industrialized countries. In a conservative calculation, the former OECD research indicates that, in 1997, 20 % price increase of the whole imports influenced by cartels (a minimum level) equals 41.1 % of development assistance. Meanwhile, a 45 % price increase (a maximum level) equals 92.5 %.[37] Meanwhile, the latter research (Levenstein and Suslow) indicates that damages caused by the price increases of international cartels in DCs reaches from 25 to 58.4 % of ODA.[38] In short, the results mean that participants from industrialized in discovered international cartels countries took away from at least 25.9 % up to 92.5 % of foreign development assistance in 1997.[39]

Moreover, international cartels provoke equity problems, particularly exacerbating the poverty inherent in developing countries where a large number of the world population lives.[40] Concretely, the international vitamin cartel regime caused price increase for nearly a decade for vitamins sold in developing countries. The estimated damage to consumers in six developing countries, or India, Pakistan, Kenya, South Africa, Tanzania, and Zambia are about $ 200 million.[41] The reduced production would impede distribution of the vitamins to poor consumers living in rural areas.

A cartel hinders the world trade from growing in the pro-competitive way by bolstering up market power, waste, and inefficiency in the countries which

---

[35]*See id.*, at 816. It cites World Development Indicators for 2001 of World Bank. The series used was 'official development assistance and official aid'.

[36]Evenett et al. (2001), at pp. 1237–1240.

[37]Levenstein and Suslow, *supra* note 29, at 813–818. Their calculation is based on the conservative approach. First, it included only products with available narrow Standard International Trade Classification (SITC) rather than those with broader SITC which might contain goods with the cartelized product. The latter standard was used only when the narrow level standard was not available. Second, it excluded service trade. Third, it considers only international cartels, not domestic cartels which might affect negatively developing countries. Fourth, it used only known cartel conspiracies.

[38]*See id.* at 816–818. Even a narrower approach of the two researchers demonstrates that the average annual amount of trade in the cartel-affected industries from 1990 to 1997 was $ 18.5 billion, and that wealth-transfer due to international cartels equals 9.4 % (minimum price-increase) or 21 % (maximum price-increase) of development assistance.

[39]*Id.*, at 816. According to an average calculation, international cartels have kept taking the amount from 9.4 to 21 % of development assistance during the 8 years when the average 10 % price increase in overall countries is applied for the conservative approach.

[40]In Asian Pacific region where many LDCs as well as a few developed countries are located, 800 million live out of the 1.2 billion poor people of the world who live on less than a dollar a day. Mehta (2003), at 79.

[41]Consumer Unity and Trust Society (CUTS) (2003).

otherwise would be competitive.[42] Since an anticompetitive business activity deprives the consumers' welfare, it interrupts the maximizing of efficiency in a national market, thereby aggravating static and dynamic inefficiency. In addition, the efforts of suppliers to innovate quality of products and to reduce price lessen.[43] Concerns about maintaining collusive behaviors among competitors tend to establish market barriers such as exclusive transactions to new enterprises or potential entrants, majority of which come from developing countries.[44]

Cartel members use anti-dumping action as a WTO-approved legal trade remedy to screen the international cartel and to establish barriers to nonmembers. The abuse of the trade remedy means that the international cartels have reduced the opportunities of developing countries' exports besides consumers' welfare. In addition, such an advantage of exporters in developing countries as relatively low costs does not lead to a greater market share because the cartel agreement has shut new members out of the market to maintain predetermined allocation terms.[45] For instance, after an international citric acid cartel was broken up in the U.S. in 1997, exports from China, although falling at first, dramatically rebounded.[46] A cartel scheme causes stagnancy in the market share during its operating time. An international lysine cartel of five producers, operating between 1992 and 1995 with control over 97 % of the global capacity, fixed prices, allocated sales quotas, and monitored the volumes. The production shares of two Korea's producers as cartel members, at a standstill during the period, afterwards increased at the expense of other companies' market shares. Potential competitors from developing countries have been blocked to entry through price discrimination under market allocation agreement. China's new joint ventures began operation in 1993 with a small market share, but, by 2000, its productive capacity occupied 13 % of the global sale.[47]

B. Benefits of Cartel Regulation to DCs Group

(1) Consumer

Consumers, as a result of successful enforcement of competition law, can enjoy lower prices for the same or high-quality products since price increases (the most common effect of cartel) are to be removed and suppliers should compete to

[42]Conclusion from the 1998 Recommendation of the OECD Council Concerning Effective Action against Hard Core Cartels. OECD GFC (2003), at 4.

[43]OECD GFC, *id*, at 6. It states, the harm to productive and dynamic efficiency is no less real than that to allocative efficiency if even more difficult to measure.

[44]UNCTAD, *supra* note 33, 16.

[45]*See id.* at 11.

[46]The reason for the first drop is analyzed by Mathew Lerner who pointed the fact out that the Chinese government has stopped giving export tax credits to Chinese citric acid producers. Levenstein and Suslow, *supra* note 29, 822–824.

[47]UNCTAD, *supra* note 33, at 13–14.

increase their profits. Most of the cartel investigation cases reveal price decreases after the breaking-up of cartels.[48]

The choice of products, decreased by an exclusive market barrier, will expand in width. Since cartel members blocked new competitors from entering the market with collaborative behaviors, consumers used to have limited access to new products with better quality.[49] The product innovation and technological improvement, either at a slow rate or at a standstill, will be faster.[50] Marketing skills will be more consumer-friendly as competition increases.

(2) Government: The Reduction of Bid-Rigging

Strong anti-cartel enforcement against governmental procurement contracts or public bids can reduce governmental expense caused by bid-rigging. Bid rigging cases uncovered by competition authorities demonstrate that the damage from bid-riggings amounts to more than US$ hundreds of millions, which could even possibly increase depending on the scope of the duration and the contract. Although many countries penalize bid rigging with criminal law, an immature practice and a low level of public awareness in many DCs and LDCs have prevented a successful investigation into the cartels.[51] When the push for cartel regulation grows more active and attracts more public attention, bid rigging cases will be revealed through more investigative experiences and financial support from their governments. Particularly, in developing countries where transparency in terms of governmental contracts is insufficient, cartel regulation can contribute to the reducing of bid rigging.

(3) Economic Development

Anti-cartel enforcements contribute to promoting competition and opening market structure similar to other areas of competition policy. The break-down of a cartel discontinues the extension of damages caused by the continued cartel. If the

[48]For example, a report from Ukraine states that revisions of prices for electricity and water supply, formerly set by another regulator, in 2 years have reduced consumers' costs with a total amount more than US$ 200 million. OECD GFC (2004), Sess.IV., at 3.

[49]Although monopolist or a competitor restrained entry into a market, enforcement of competition law opened the market, thereby generating much wider choices for consumers. For Russian money transfer system case and Jamaica's communication interface of bank case, *see id.* at 4.

[50]Lithuania's privatization of telecommunication could succeed with active enforcement of competition law to prevent existent operator's anticompetitive behaviors. Currently, network digitalization reaches 88 % while ADSL services are available 85 % of the telecom operator's customers. Pakistan's two merger cases were approved on the condition to introduce improved technology. *Id.* at 3–4. The similar principle can apply to a cartel case.

[51]Bid rigging is widely prevalent in Nepal, especially in the construction and supply sector. A conspiracy among manufacturers and suppliers of polythene pipes to the Napal Drinking Water Corporation, and one among suppliers of rations to the Royal Napalese Army and Nepal Police are reported. Due to prevalent bid rigging, even municipalities in Nepal have refused to follow the guideline which requires the awarding of a contract to the lowest bidder at the time of execution of the development project. UNCTAD (2004), at 64–65.

threat to potential conspirators and the affected commerce are taken into account, a cartel regulation may promote the related industries by more than the amount of calculated damages. As similar to the case of liberalization trade policy, although increasing efficiency can not be measured in a quantifiable number, competitive culture brought upon by the anti-cartel regulation will provide more benefit in the long term to the whole economy.[52] Producers will devote their efforts to producing high-quality products with lower price so as to survive competition. With an open-market structure, potential enterprises with innovative techniques will enter the market where merit-based competition prevails. The good products which win in domestic competition can be exported to other countries, thereby strengthening the economic development of a home country. Concrete data from a transitional economy, e.g. Ukraine, prove that industries under the competition system can grow by far more than the industry at large, for example, by six times in transportation.[53]

There is a counter-opinion that non-cartel participants from developing countries may have increased their prices in parallel to the cartel price. However, non-cartel producers with a small portion of the market share cannot charge the cartel price due to inferior quality, insecure supply and contract terms, or different transportation costs. The price increase of nonmembers in a graphite electronic cartel in South Korea was only around 9 % during the cartel period compared to a 48.9 % increase of cartel prices.[54]

On the other hand, cartel members collectively attack promising producers from DCs with predatory pricing. During the cartel's activity, the price of graphite electrodes in India was 68 % of the world price where the Indian Graphite Electrode Manufactures Association was established and exports had increased.[55] Cartel members, moreover, use another method of attacking nonmembers such as technical barriers or patent pooling. A cartel of graphite electrode producers from 1992 to 1997 collectively restricted non-conspirator companies' access to their graphite electrode manufacturing technology.[56] Profits from the exclusive behaviors that cartel members employ against nonmembers usually outweigh profits from the paralleled price increase. Private market barriers, including the exclusive behaviors, can be reduced or removed by active anti-cartel enforcements.

---

[52]OECD GFC (2003), at 6.

[53]In those industries in Ukraine where there is competition in at least half of activities such as the food, forestry, and light industry sectors, growth is between 1.2 and 2 times higher than in the industry at large. In the road transportation for passengers, opened for competition in the last 3 years, growth of the transportation volume has been 6 times higher than in the railway transport sector, still under monopoly. *See id.* at 5.

[54]Levenstein and Suslow, *supra* note 29, at 839–840; KFTC Decision [공정거래위원회심결] 2002국협0250, Table 2 and 10–11 (2002), *at* http://ftc.go.kr/data/hwp/case/20020401_6330.hwp.

[55]Levenstein and Suslow, *supra* note 29, at 839–841.

[56]*Id.*, at 833–834; KFTC Decision, *supra* note 54, 7.

4.4 Different Positions Where Developing Countries Are Placed

A. Positions of Developing Countries and Least-Developed Countries (LDCs) in Adopting and Enforcing Competition Law

(1) Economic Structures of Developing Markets

As regards to the level of competition in developing market economies, economists have divided opinions. An economist argues that developing countries exhibit segmented product markets, discretionary government regulations and considerable corruption; hence, they are not very competitive.[57] On the other hand, the other economist states, through various statistical proofs, that developing countries are subject to no less, if not greater competition, than advanced countries.[58]

Regarding the economic structure of developing markets, it is noteworthy that lots of DCs have dualistic structure of market economies. The dualistic structure means that a large modern sector consisting of a few big companies, occupying a big portion of total output, coexists with the other large traditional sector of small enterprises, which contribute an almost equal portion of the economy's output. In developing countries, compared to developed countries, the employment rate of the small-enterprise sector would be larger than the output portion due to the bigger differences in capital intensity of the two sectors in these countries.[59]

While the true competition level in developing market economies is up to economical discussion, from competition policy and the law's perspective, the level of regulation and enforcement in DCs needs to differ depending on the characteristics of a sector, either a small-scale sector with less than 10 employees but a higher employment rate or the modern sector with a large output ratio. In terms of a cartel regulation, concretely, if a cartel regulation indifferently applies to collusive anticompetitive behaviors of both sectors, the penalty will cause a wide range of negative results to employment and the development of national economy. When commerce in the small sectors faces external economic repression, the operation of their businesses, constituting the major foundation of national employment, needs to be protected, and, under some conditions, to be exempted from a cartel regulation.

Moreover, several structural weaknesses in developing countries need to be brought under attention as opposed to advanced market economies. Small-sized

[57]Laffont (1994), at 237–257. The position is followed by economists supporting structuralist theory solution regarding the Asian financial crisis.

[58]Singh (2002), at 4. He provided another supplementary statistics indicating that there is greater turnover as well as entry and exit of firms in the small number of emerging markets for which such studies have been carried out than for advanced countries. *See id.* at 4–6 and Table 5. The position is followed by Tibout who argues that the existing empirical literature does not support the notion that LDC manufacturers are relatively stagnant and inefficient.

[59]*See id.* at 3–4 and Tables 1 and 2.

markets with less competition have limited access to essential inputs, more limited distribution channels, and a higher dependency on imports and exports. In addition, immature liberalization policies enable a greater proportion of local markets to be insulated from national trade liberalization policies, and a greater incidence of administrative barriers to imports.[60] Although a state or private monopoly is replaced by a number of private enterprises, a former monopolist may make use of inherited advantages from knowing restrictive market conditions, such as less-developed financial markets, and make difficult the survival of new entrants.[61]

(2) Immature Social Infrastructure

1) Limited Financial Resources

Most developing countries have few resources to fund competition authorities at the initial stage. The limited resources available for other governmental expenses necessitate overwhelming financial benefits to justify further expenditure. Without promised outcomes, developing countries' governments will hesitate to expend further resources to competition authorities. With the limited financial resources, the nascent competition authorities can not attract skilled experts and professional staffs.

2) Necessity to Attract Substantive Expertise

Developing countries experience the critical shortage of specialists with academic or practical training in competition law or economics of competition policy since there has been rare vocational demand.[62] Additional effort should be devoted to raising the level of sanction. In light of the past experience of South Korea, as the sanctioning of competition authorities grew powerful, officers in competition authorities became more popular.[63] In addition, they can raise professional staffs with specialized tasks, such as a cartel or M&A team. With the special task incentive, young public officers and professionals will be attracted to the competition law practice. The problem, which developing countries face at the nascent stage, can be overcome with further training of staffs and participation in international technical assistances. International cooperation among competition authorities can expose their officers to global practices and an advanced level of enforcement skills.

3) Less Powerful Professional Associations and Consumer Groups

In developing economies, professional bodies such as bar associations, and consumer groups did not, in most cases, make an effective forum for operating a

---

[60]OECD CFC (2003), at 5.

[61]*Id*. at 6.

[62]Kovacic (2001), at 306. Kovacic cites statement of Michael Trebilcock and Laffont who examined reform efforts of transition economies.

[63]Cha, *Omnipotence of KFTC: one of three retired senior officers moved to big law firms* [무소불위 공정위: 퇴직간부 3명중 1명 대형로펌으로 옮겨], Hankyung (8 Aug. 2007), *available at* http://www.hankyung.com/news.

new legal regime. As social autonomy to develop consumers' movement is weak, consumers groups have insufficient power to become strong supporters for cartel enforcements. Rather, they would be controlled by political influences. As professional groups are less diversified enough to support competition policy, the building of the foundation of academic research and the enhancement of professional skills are too weak to play a pivotal role for rooting competition culture. The upgrade of professional groups and consumers groups requires patience in time.[64]

(3) Weak Foundation of Legal Institutions

1) Less Serious Attitude to Cartel

Most DCs have not adopted or enforced competition law until recently. Only sixteen DCs had operated formal competition law until 1990. The reason for the absence of competition law in DCs was clear: there was no need. Widely practiced governmental control over economic activities and state-operating enterprises did not allow anticompetitive business behaviors by companies or industries.[65]

However, the number of countries which adopted competition law in the 1990s increased, 10 times, to 50, starting from 5 in the 1980s. If countries under preparation to adopt competition law are included (of which there are twenty-seven), the level of expansion pertaining to the implementation of competition law is even more striking. The in-detail analysis of the reasons of the sudden increase is in 4.4.

It is noted that among the DCs which adopt competition law cartels are treated with less attention than other competition law issues.[66] Most competition authorities in DCs have focused more on monopoly control, or unfair business practice than on cartel regulation.[67] The different treatment may reflect the priority of competition policy in each country. The less priority leads to the less serious attitude as 2.3 reveals.[68] In terms of enforcement of competition law, a survey of top- and middle-management firms in each country indicate that competition authorities in advanced countries are 40 % more effective than their counterparts in DCs.[69] However, the damages from cartel activities in DCs with few serious investigations against cartels are not to be considered trivial, if less than those in the advanced countries.[70]

2) Ambiguous Distribution of Administrative Discretion

Discretion of government agencies is poorly defined by rules that supposedly need to be transparent and fair. Public officers play broad discretion spontaneously, which are seldom under public review. Conflict of interest rules came in few

---

[64]Kovacic (1997) at 403–420.

[65]Singh, *supra* note 58, at 6.

[66]*See id.*

[67]Lee (2008), at 55.

[68]Ratio for the level of enforcement in DCs compared to that in advanced countries does not reach the ratio of damages. *See* 2.3 of Chap. 2.

[69]IMD (2001); The WB Group (2002).

[70]*See* Sect. 4.2.A of this chapter.

cases.[71] The ambiguous distribution of power caused resistances from other economy-related departments, which resulted in attack on function of competition authorities.[72]

3) Procedural Hurdles for Rigorous Competition Law Enforcement

Quite a few transition economies are short of the institutions that allow expeditious review and compulsory procedure.[73] Such insufficient enforcement tools impede rigorous investigation and punishment. In addition, incorrect accounting data and widely spread window-dressing are additional hurdles for competition authorities to find correct data.[74] Auditing and screening functions remain immature.

On the other hand, some countries have restrictions on evidentiary standard. In Russia, the evidence which verifies a price-fixing agreement should be a writing which shows a concerted conduct.[75] Other countries permitting spoken conversations to prove a concerted action may not approve the expansive use of surveillance techniques such as wire-tapping.[76]

However, as the powers of competition authorities grow bigger and successful practices accumulated, it is expected to reform the insufficient institutions.[77] The Supreme Court in South Korea, along with the interpretation of cartel prohibition of Monopoly Restraint Fair Trade Act (MRFTA), lightened the evidentiary standard for proving a cartel by holding that the existence of restrictive business practice (RBP)s, e.g., the same price, and the restriction of competition in a related market, notwithstanding the absence of the proof of a collusive agreement, are sufficient elements to prove a cartel.[78]

---

[71]Kovacic, *supra* note 64, at 421.

[72]KFTC was criticized with its overarching investigation, arguably impeding in affairs of other departments. Ki-Hyun Cha, *Is an administrative guide a collusion?* [행정지도가 담합이라니], Hankyung (7 Aug. 2007), *available at* http://www.hankyung.com/news.

[73]OECD GFC, *supra* note 42, at 6.

[74]Kovacic, *supra* note 64, 426–427. He introduced an interview with the manager of a state-owned firm and the incorrect information that he submitted.

[75]*Id.*, at 426. Capelik, Vladimir, & Slay, Ben, *Antimonopoly Policy and Monopoly Regulation in Russia*, in Slay (1996), at 65–66.

[76]Kovacic, *supra* note 64, at 426; Whalley (1998), at 571.

[77]Fourteen emails with public officer, Hang-Rok Oh, at KFTC (from 18 Dec. 2006 to 19 Jan. 2007) (on file with author). According to him, companies under investigation have never rejected the administrative investigation which are not compulsory with warrant but powered with sanction of maximum US $ 200,000 in case the companies reject.

[78]S.Ct.[대법원] 2002.3.15. Decision[선고] 99 두 6514, 6521. Art. 19 Sec. 5 of MRFTA states, where two or more enterprisers are committing such acts as price fixing, market allocation, or price restriction, that practically restrict competition in a particular business area, they shall be presumed to have committed an unfair collaborative act despite the absence of an explicit agreement to engage in such act.

4) Deficient Judicial Function

Judges in developing countries' courts are inadequate umpires for enforcing competition law which requires economic analysis.[79] Unlike the U.S.'s historical development of antitrust law, some judicial bodies have not only expressed a lack of interests in economic reasonings but suspended their trials, especially in private actions, until competition authorities issued final decisions.[80] Some judicial or semi-judicial systems[81] in DCs that are tainted with corruptions are more inclined to be captured by interesting parties as competition law cases usually impose a large amount of fines on companies with substantial market shares.[82]

(4) Political Resistances from Existent Interest-Holders

Countries experiencing communist party' control had difficulty in overcoming anti-reform resistance against market-oriented economic reform including anti-monopoly and anti-cartel regulations. Although the transitional governments adopted policy measures to reduce state ownership of business enterprises with pressure from international organizations, state-owned enterprises still occupied a pretty large share of developing economies.[83] The national-leveled reforms due to less-developed democratic system are ineffective from the level of local public officers to regional governmental bodies even to national ministries.[84]

Domestic producers, to make matters worse, participate in the political opposition. The threat from competitive foreign companies incites domestic producers to

[79]*See* Kovacic (1997), pp. 420–421; Dean and Mohieldin (2001) at 13. Kovacic points out exceptions at footnote 50 by describing aspects of Zimbabwe's judicial and commercial law jurisprudence that would facilitate implementation of a competition policy system. *See also* Kovacic (2001), at 306.

[80]The District Court of Seoul, in *Daum Inc. v. Microsoft*, in South Korea, suspended the civil action by the time Korean Fair Trade Commission issued its final decision. Other developing countries have such judicial branch problems as considerable delays and a lack of independence. *See* Garcia-Rodriguez (1995), at 1177; *see also* Rowat et al. (1995); Bentley (1994).

[81]Decisions related to competition law can be issued from the administrative body in charge of competition policy, e.g. FTC, as well as the judicial body. Semi-judicial decisions are the decisions from the administrative body.

[82]A research by Transparency International demonstrates that, in more than twenty-five countries, at least one in ten households reported paying a bribe to get access to the court system, and that widespread corruption in judicial bodies impedes development of legal system. Herald Tribune Europe, *Judicial corruption undermining legal systems worldwide*, (24 May 2007), *available at* http://www.iht.com/articles/ap/2007/05/24/europe/EU-GEN-Britain-Transparency-Judicial-Corruption.php (visited on 3 Apr. 2008). Particularly, in South Korea, seven officers received cars from Hyundai Automobile company which was under investigation of KFTC. People Power 21[참여연대], *Unfair Business Practices of public officers*[공무원들의 불공정거래], 24 Nov 2006, *available at* http://www.peoplepower21.org/?s01:i:b18223-12-1-1164340490 (visited on 3 Apr 2008).

[83]The WB (1995), at 1.

[84]Kovacic, *supra* note 62, at 304.

pressure governments to use trade sanctions[85] or to postpone strong competition policy.[86] The former interest-holders' resistances against trade liberalization would involve the use of corruptive measures to pay bribes to public officers.[87] It would take time to make compromises with them.

On the other hand, new competition authorities, whether they are created within an existing ministry or are established as new entities, lack the political ties or bases which would support their active enforcements by overcoming objections from resisting enterprises. The new authorities are susceptible to criticism, thereby being much influenced by the shift of political regime.[88]

B. Difficulty of Reaching Consensus Regarding Cartel Law Among DC Groups

(1) Classification of Developing Countries Under UNCTAD

The category of DCs, distinctive from developed countries, includes a broad level of socioeconomic development from South East Europe to heavily indebted poor countries in Africa.[89] As the category includes such a diverse range of countries, it is not apparent which level of development the category of developing countries places emphasis on. The thesis examines respective categories of DCs under 2005 UNCTAD Handbook of Statistics.[90]

1) Major Petroleum Exporting Countries

This group consists of all OPEC member countries and non-OPEC countries where the share of petroleum and petroleum products was not less than 50 % of their total exports and exports of the products reached at least US$ 1.5 billion on average from '99 to '01.[91] Some countries, e.g., Azerbaijan and Tajikistan, of CIS

---

[85]Such sanctions with respect to competition law are predatory pricing or anti-dumping suits. Kovacic, *supra* note 64, at 423.

[86]Kovacic, *supra* note 62, 302–304.

[87]It is especially true of public officers in charge of tax code violations under the guise of settling tax claims. *See id.*, at 304.

[88]KFTC, although it has its twenty-seven-year-old history, are criticized for its large amount of fines and overarching investigations in South Korea. Ki-Hyun Cha, *Series of Omnipotence of KFTC: indiscrete investigatory pressure to industry* ['무소불위' 공정위] (상) 산업계 무차별 조사 압박], Hankyung (7 Aug. 2007), *available at* http://www.hankyung.com/news. A Korea's major newspaper of Hankyung wrote a series of nine articles criticizing KFTC' overarching investigation, disharmony due to leniency policy, large amount of fine, and a hybrid function of administration and judiciary without participation of entrepreneurs.

[89]According to UN's definition of developing countries, in international trade statistics, countries from the former Yugoslavia are treated as developing countries while countries of eastern Europe and the former USSR countries in Europe are not included in under either developed or developing regions. However, from the perspective of cartel regulation, this thesis includes these countries in developing countries. UN Statistics Division, Definitions, *available at* http://unstats.un.org/unsd/cdb/cdb_dict_xrxx.asp?def_code=491 (visited on 2 Apr. 2008).

[90]UNCTAD(2005), at 10–16.

[91]*See id.* at 12. Algeria, Angola, Indonesia, Iran, Iraq, Kuwait, Libya, Nigeria, Qatar, Saudi Arabia, Venezuela and United Arab Emirates are OPEC members. Bahrain, Congo, Gabon, Yemen, and Oman, among other countries, belong to non-OPEC countries within this group.

may belong to this category. With significant revenue from petroleum trade, the countries are trying to diversify their economic structure.[92] The competition policy, particularly cartel regulation under less diversified national industry, is less highlighted than other economic regulatory laws and policies as efficiency-focused market system does not grow sufficiently to consider consumers' welfare seriously. The development of democratic politics and legal system does not grow maturely to empower competition policy and cartel regulation.

2) Major Exporters of Manufacturers (MEMs)

This group[93] is made up of twelve countries with such standards that the share of manufactured goods was not less than 50 % of total exports and that exports of the products amount to at least US$ 20 billion on average during the same three-year period. Newly Industrialized Countries (NICs) belong to the group.[94] As manufacturing industry in the countries has produced significant products, their economies reveal considerable competitiveness in manufactured goods. Efficiency-based market systems play important roles in further development, and the vitality of competition policy and cartel regulation is recognized to exports. The protests from business group need to be controlled by political and legal systems. The effective cartel enforcement is in urgent need along with regulation of the other competition law areas.

3) High-Income Developing Countries

Countries with per capita GDP above US$ 4500[95] belong to the group apart from two above mentioned countries. As the level of GDP is beyond a medium level, the scale of consumers' welfare may necessitate effective enforcement of competition policy and cartel regulation similar to the NICs. Legal, economic, and political development can affect the level of development of domestic cartel regulation.

4) Middle-Income Developing Countries

Countries with per capita GDP between US$ 1000 and $ 4500 constitute the group.[96] As cooperation is still emphasized rather than competition in domestic market, strict enforcement of cartel regulation or competition law will face hard protests. Although South Africa recently enacts competition law strictly under the auspice of democratized government and legal tradition, most countries in this group do not demonstrate effective enforcement of the competition law and cartel regulation.

---

[92]Isabel Gorst, *Wealth is being deployed to cut dependence on oil*, FT Special Report of Azerbaijan, at 2 (25 Jan '08).

[93]Besides Brazil, India, China which belong to emerging markets called BRICs, Malaysia, Mexico, Philippines, Thailand, and Turkey, along with NICs, belong to the group. UNCTAD (2005), 12.

[94]Singapore, Hong Kong, Taiwan, and South Korea are called NICs.

[95]Argentina, Chile, Uruguay, and Puerto Rico belonged to the group in 2000.

[96]Bolivia, Dominica, Fiji, Peru, and Morocco belong to it. *See id.* at 12.

5) Low-Income Developing Countries

Countries with per capita GDP below US$1000 form low-income developing countries. This group includes the least-developed countries (LDCs), landlocked countries, and heavily indebted poor countries (HIPCs). Particularly, LDCs, designated and reviewed regularly by UN ECOSOC, are under special treatment of international trade law because the countries endure per capita GDP below $ 750 and weak human resources characterized by nutrition, health, education, literacy, and economic vulnerability.[97] Cartel regulation or competition policy in this group usually does not appeal to the public or public officers. As normal enforcement of cartel regulation is difficult to expect, special treatments are needed in the group.

(2) A Remote Chance for Harmonized International Cartel Law in the South

The prospects for the majority of developing countries to reach an agreement to enact international cartel law under the competition approach remain very low, due to diverse levels of situations where they are located. Although they agreed with the 1980 UN Set, including the anti-cartel provision, many of them have adopted the liberalized market approach since the late 1980s. Current diversification within the group, along with the growth emergence markets, and subsequently different attitudes to the competition law hinder the further development of international cartel law. As the disruptive negotiation in Cancun indicated, the ACP 77 group, representing mostly low-income countries, expressed strong objection against adopting competition policy as one of the Doha agendas. On the other hand, G-21, representing high-income or middle-income countries, was not seriously against the competition policy issue, although it took a hard line attitude against agriculture negotiation.

Low-income countries with a less diversified economic structure and low capital investments have different interests in cartel regulation from high-income countries where industries need to grow further in a competitive market. From the former countries' perspective, sovereign restriction accompanied with international cartel regulation might undermine cooperation necessary to develop national industries. On the contrary, most high-income countries want to raise their industrial competitiveness through the implementation of sophisticated competition law and its enforcement, including a cartel regulation. They want international standards and cooperation with advanced competition authorities to assist in their current cartel practices.

[97]Total 50 countries belonged to LDCs in 2005. Three-year average estimate of GDP per capita under $ 750 is qualified for inclusion in the list but above $ 900 means graduation. Economic vulnerability criterion consists of (i) instability of agricultural production, (ii) instability of exports of goods and services, (iii) the economic importance of nontraditional activities, (iv) merchandise export concentration, and (v) the handicap of economic smallness, and the percentage of population displaced by natural disasters. UN, What are the Least Developed Countries, *available at* http://esa.un.org/unpp/definition.html#LDC (visited on 23 Dec '07).

On the other hand, major petroleum exporters (MPEs) have different interests in cartel and competition law from major exporters of manufactures (MEMs). As a considerable portion of the national income in MPEs depend on petroleum under governmental management, legislations for efficiency-maximizing market structure do not attract much interest. They might have a negative impression on competition policy supporters who condemn state-monopolies and governmental control over petroleum production. Meanwhile, the MEMs, most of which have enacted competition law, are more inclined to be concerned with the loss of consumers' welfare that develops under the market economy and have interest in international cartel law. It is because the international law can potentially regulate international cartels which would be beyond the reach of their competition.[98]

4.5 International Competition Law Reflecting Development

A. NIEO as Evolution of Economic Co-operation Among Developing Countries

(1) Emergence of NIEO

The successful political cooperation under the Non-Aligned Movement, among countries which were not allied to either the United States or the Soviet Union, but are a part of the so-called the Third World, was joined by newly independent countries in 1960s, leading to economic cooperation among them. With the growth of their power in the international community, the Third World countries expressed their arguments in cooperative ways through the UNCTAD. The UNCTAD, established in 1963, was a forum where interests of developing countries were integrated through discussion, through which subsequent development-oriented declarations were initially adopted, and new economical and legal principles were created. The emergence of the Group of 77, Declaration on Non-Alignment and Economic Progress at the third Summit of the Non-Aligned States in Lusaka in 1970, and the adoption of 'Action Programme for Economic Co-operation among Non-Aligned Countries' at the Georgetown meeting of Foreign Ministers in 1972 are such examples.

The fourth Summit of the Non-Aligned States in Algiers, held in 1973, introduced the concept of the New International Economic Order (NIEO). Subsequently, the UN General Assembly passed the Declaration on the Establishment of NIEO in May, 1974, the most important interest of which was in correcting both unequal distribution of income among countries and the existent economic system which had maintained such inequality and had been established mostly by industrialized countries beside DCs, not independent at the time.

---

[98]The effort of extraterritorial application of competition law by developing countries, even MEMs, does not demonstrates effective investigation or strict punishment against international cartels. *See* Chap. 2.2.5.

(2) Contents of NIEO

The NIEO aimed for the prosperity of the whole international community, especially by focusing on the development of the developing countries.[99] The NIEO had a broad coverage of issues, including trade, commodities, the allocation of radio frequency spectrum (RFS)s, and MNCs.[100] The foundation of the NIEO was, among other things, upon the sovereign equality of states, their broadest cooperation, full and effective participation in the solving of world economic problems, their full permanent sovereignty over its NRs, regulation of the activities of transnational corporations, and their right to regain effective control over their NRs and economic activities under colonial domination and foreign occupation.[101] The more concrete founding principles of NEIO are preferential and non-reciprocal treatment for developing countries, just and equitable relationship between the prices of raw materials, primary commodities, and goods exported by developing countries and those imported by them, the need of developing countries to concentrate all the resources for the cause of development, and the need for all states to put an end to the waste of natural resources including food products.[102] NIEO even includes the founding principle of facilitating the role which producers' associations may play within the framework of international cooperation,[103] besides accelerating the development of developing countries as well as assisting in the promotion of a sustained growth of the world economy.

(3) Impact of NIEO on Cartel Regulation

The point which the NIEO heads toward is a more development-oriented approach rather than one centered around the freedom of market. The concrete methods allow seemingly unequal treatment which supports countries with weak economic foundation. The original cause of competition law also promoted an equal distribution of income. The principle of facilitating the producers' association under the NIEO, however, has the potential to be in conflict with the rule of competition law. The means of facilitating the producers' association, by rule of thumbs, covers the restraint of competition among producers, which has a negative impact on consumers' interests. The reason why the NIEO treated commodity cartels differently from private cartels is that developing economies relied on commodity production and that, for their economic development and their public's survival, commodity cartels needed to be separate from private cartels. The powerful impact of the OPEC on the global economy in the 70s contributed to the mentality of NIEO.

---

[99]GA Res. 3201 (S-VI), 6 (Special), UN GAOR, 6th Spec. Sess. Supp. No. 1, at 3, UN Doc. A/9559 (1974), para. 2 and 3.

[100]Sell (1998), at 72.

[101]*See* UN G.A. Res. 3201, para. 4(a)–(i).

[102]*See id.*, para. 4(j)–(s).

[103]*See id.*, para. 4(t).

The UN Set which regulates RBPs of MNCs came about from the increasing influences of the South on the international economy and politics. Developing countries aimed to restrain anticompetitive activities of the MNCs which impeded economic development, making most of their national interests by controlling the activities of the MNCs. A dozen DCs enacted domestic RBP-controlling legislations, modeled after the laws of developed countries; however, the legislations played different roles from those in the original countries. It was not a foundation to promote competition policy, but rather a part of the governmental control system of economic power. It was not a post-regulation for direct control over market powers of companies established in the market, but rather a prior restraint for settling the legal responsibility of market powers that were not regulated before.[104] A cartel regulation belongs to the RBP-control. Without supplemental conditions to enforce competition policy, the RBP regulations had the basis on national economic policy which was susceptible to political influence. Particularly, cartel regulations with such a policy basis tend to be under-enforced with insufficient support.

Meanwhile, the North, especially the U.S., accepted with willingness the negotiation for international codification restraining RBPs, as the U.S. wanted merits of antitrust and a free market economy to be widely acknowledged. The U.S. would promote the drafting of the code in a sophisticated manner, reflecting its rich experiences in pro-competitive policy.[105]

(4) Demise of the NIEO and Its Impact on the UN Set

During the 80s, the NIEO lost its significant power in the 70s. The North went away from the UN Set in light of new policies developed under domestic practices. The influence of the Chicago School of Economics strongly challenged antitrust policy in the U.S. thereby leading to more exposure to the economic analysis of efficiency with a focus on output and price.[106] While monopolistic behaviors or vertical restraints with an enhanced efficiency are approved under this approach, the horizontal cartel behaviors are to be prohibited. In addition, the emergence of Japan as a strong competitor in a technology industry affected the competition policy of the U.S. and the EU in a permissive way because Japan had pursued a lenient antitrust attitude as to corporate cooperation, e.g., joint R&D. As a result, the U.S. export cartels were immune from antitrust enforcement under the 1982 Export Trading Company Act designed for promoting export. Meanwhile, cooperation for a new R&D was encouraged with a waiver of the antitrust law under the 1984 National Cooperative Research Act, which, however, excluded commercialization efforts such as joint manufacturing and production. Similarly, the EC, in 1984, adopted blanket provisions allowing R&D arrangements, including

---

[104]Sell (1998), at 147–149.

[105]*Id.*, 143–149.

[106]*Id.* at 158–159. Only business practices that reduce output and increase price are anticompetitive; business practices that expand output are pro-competitive.

commercialization,[107] and exempted joint ventures from Art. 85(1) of the Treaty of Rome. The lenient antitrust approaches of Japan, the U.S., and the EU in the 80s undermined the spirit of the UN Set in spite of the warnings of the UNCTAD Secretariat's annual reports.[108]

The development issues starting from the RBPs of MNCs in the UN Set, which addressed the interest of the South, did not produce further concrete provisions in cartel regulations. While the North kept away from the agreement, the South threw doubt upon the power of the Set.[109] With the lessening power of commodity producers, a reduced number of direct foreign investments, and the increasing foreign debts of developing countries in the 80s, Southern solidarity grew weakened.[110] A resurgence in protectionism in the North and a drop in commodity prices made matters worse. The loss of strong negotiation powers led to the weakening of the UN Set.[111] In response to the feeble compliance of the UN Set, the South group tried to inspire further effectiveness in the UN Set. All the proposals, such as providing the set with legally binding power, shifting the status of the group reviewing compliance to a strong committee level, and convening in subsequent review conferences, were rejected due to flat disagreement from the North.[112] Moreover, as the IMF and the World Bank placed a Northern-styled competition regime as a condition to its loan program, many developing countries enacted competition laws, including cartel regulations. The other countries in the South abandoned the NIEO approach and adopted the trade liberalization policy including a competition law and a cartel regulation stubbornly insisted by the U.S.

(5) Legacy of NIEO

Although NIEO is weakened, it has had a significant impact on current international law. It has established or confirmed important international economic laws such as the acknowledgement of sovereign control over national resources, distinctive treatment of commodity cartels from private cartels, and developmental-concern in the global economic system. The rules are deserving notices as they achieved a consensus of the North and the South in comparison to current disputes. Following is an in-detail discussion of its impact on international law.

B. Emergence of International Development Law

By mid 1970s, the influence of the NIEO on international law generated new legal principles which try to reduce the current gap between the economic

---

[107]*See* Commission Regulation (EEC) No.418/85 of 19 Dec. 1984.

[108]Sell (1998), 162–163.

[109]*Id.*, at 142.

[110]*Id.*, at 34.

[111]*Id.*, at 32–33. Even OPEC's solidarity was undermined by member countries' cheating e.g. overproducing.

[112]*Id.*, at 170–171.

development level of industrialized countries and that of developing countries. Formal equality-based principles in international trade law, such as non-discrimination and national treatment, created without participation of most developing countries, did not pay attention to the agenda of 'development', the goal that developing countries desired to achieve. Facing the lack of consideration of their interests in international trade law in spite of their increase of political power, developing countries had strived for a set of new rules which would be designed to regulate economic relations between developed and developing countries. The new rules tried to be distinctive from those applied to economic relations between developed countries. From the establishment of UNCTAD through the General Agreement on Tariffs and Trade (GATT) and the Agreement Establishing the WTO (the WTO Agreement) to the Doha Ministerial Declaration, beside the free trade agenda, special considerations have been provided with regard to the economic development of developing countries (DCs) and least-developed countries (LDCs). The following rules were established under the cause of constituting international development law: non-reciprocity, differential treatment, and approval of producing countries' association.

(1) Non-reciprocal Principle

The non-reciprocity principle, in contrast to the existent reciprocity principle, is a measure to guarantee real equality of opportunities between trade partners with a wide gap of economic development. According to the so-called 'implicit reciprocity' theory, formal reciprocity can not be applied to the exchange of concessions in the North–South trade, which is operated under a structural asymmetry of demand. The asymmetry is due to such double-edged dependence of developing countries that any trade concession by a developing country leads to tendencies to increase its imports and to the exacerbation of the disequilibrium of its external trade.[113]

The non-reciprocity principle was adopted into international agreements or resolutions by international organizations. General Principle Eight of Final Act and Report at the first session of the UNCTAD states that developed countries were to grant concessions to all developing countries and not to require any concessions in return from them.[114] Subsequent resolutions of the UNCTAD affirm the non-reciprocal principle. Developed countries should extend all the concessions exchanged among themselves, e.g., reducing of tariff or other barriers, to all DCs and not expect reciprocity for their favorable measures.[115] In addition, the GATT

[113] *See id.* at 80–81.

[114] UN, Proceedings of the U.N. Conf. on Trade and Development(UNCTAD), Final Act and Report, at 10–11, Second Part, A.I., U.N.Doc., E/CONF.46/141,Vol.1, U.N.Sales No.64.II.B.11 (1964).

[115] UN, Proceedings of the united nations conference on trade and development, 3rd Sess. Report and Annexes (Vol. 1), Res. 46(III), para.1.III. at 60 and Res. 82(III), at 61-2, U.N.Doc. TD/180, Vol. I, U.N. Sales No.E.73.II.D.4 (1972). *See also id.*, 4th Sess. Res. 91 (IV), para. I.10. & II.15(d) at 15-6, U.N. Doc. TD/218 (Vol.I), U.N. Sales No.E.76.II.D.10 (1976).

addressed the concept of non-reciprocal treatment at Art. XXXVI para. 8 of Part IV of the GATT 1964,[116] and para. 5 and 6 of 1979 GATT Decision 'Differential and More Favorable Treatment, Reciprocity and Fuller Participation of Developing Countries', so-called the Enabling Clause.[117] Although para. 6 of the Enabling Clause as well as Art.XXXVI para. 8 of the GATT applied the principle to the lease developed countries (LDCs), para. 5 of the Enabling Clause expanded the application to all DCs rather than limiting it to LDCs.[118] The Enabling Clause did not mention the temporary characteristics of such special treatments, thereby implying their possibility as permanent measures in the future trading system. Recently, the UN Millennium Declaration focused on the special difficulties of the DCs, the countries with transitional economies facing globalization, and the LDCs. It urged the industrialized countries to grant duty- and quota-free access to essentially all exports from LDCs.[119]

(2) Differential Treatment

The differential treatment in favor of DCs started with demands from the DCs, particularly the LDCs, to pay special attention to their needs and situations. The first success that realized the differential treatment was Generalized System of Preferences (GSP), a work of UNCTAD in 1964 although it conflicted with the Most Favored Nation (MFN) clause based on the equality and non-discrimination principle of international trade law. It came out after the four-long years of arduous negotiations to be inserted into the existent GATT scheme as a waiver to the obligations of the Agreement under Art. XXV para. 5. The International Law Commission of the UN formally acknowledged the GSP as an exception to the MFN.[120] Although the GSP did not fully embody arguments of international development law within the traditional GATT system,[121] it was an international acknowledgement of such new legal principles as non-reciprocity and differential

[116]Developing countries claim that Part IV has been without practical value as it does not contain any obligations for developed countries. WTO, *Work on special and differential provisions*, 4, *available at* http://www.wto.org.

[117]Art. XXXVI para. 8 states, the developed contracting parties do not expect reciprocity for commitments made by them in trade negotiations to reduce or remove tariffs and other barriers to the trade of the less-developed contracting parties. Para. 5 of the 1979 GATT Decision use the same languages except using 'developing countries' instead of 'less-developed contracting parties'.

[118]GATT, Decision on Differential and More Favorable Treatment, Reciprocity and Fuller Participation of Developing Countries (1979).

[119]UN G.A., GA Res. 55 Sess. 55/2, para. 15 (A/Res/55/2) (2000).

[120]Berthoud (1984), at 71 and 80. Art. 23 among proposed articles on the MFN principle from the UN's International Law Commission (ILC) states that a beneficiary State of a MFN clause (a developed country) is not entitled to treatment extended by a developed granting State to a developing third State on a non-reciprocal basis within a scheme of generalized preferences established by the granting State.

[121]*See id.*, at 78–80. In-detailed arguments of developing countries and weakness of the GSP were explained.

treatment, reflecting international economic relations between countries with a wide gap in economic development. The resolutions of UNCTAD have explicitly affirmed preferential treatment for DCs and particularly LDCs.[122]

In response to it, there is an argument that differential treatment is not a separate legal principle but an exception with limited application.[123] As one of international competition laws, the UN Set requires, under the title of 'preferential or differential treatment for developing countries', the development, finance, and trade needs of the developing countries, particularly of the LDCs, be taken into account in the application of the UN Set in order to ensure its equitable application.[124] However, from the perspective of international trade law, the ILC of the UN hesitated to accept the treatment as a general legal principle by stating that the tendency of formulating a concept of differential treatment had not yet crystallized sufficiently to permit it to be embodied in a clear legal rule in light of the MFN clause.[125] Particularly, the ILC argued that the GSP as a temporary reliever, which continued beyond the initial period of 10 years, would not resolve the long-term problem but exacerbate the economic situations.[126] In addition, Art. XVIII of the GATT approves, with special procedures, free but temporary deviation from its provisions of members whose economies can only support low standards of living and are in the early stage of development.[127] The same article allows government assistance to a member whose economy is in the process of development as well as the former members on the condition that the special treatments do not allow any deviation from MFN, and nondiscriminatory administration of quantitative restrictions (QRs).[128]

The very passive attitude as regards to the differential treatment can be overwhelmed by many concrete and detailed laws reflecting the treatment. GATT ministers agreed to adopt so-called the Enabling Clause as GATT Decision in 1979. Para. 2 enumerated several circumstances in which to apply differential and more favorable treatment, besides GSP under (a), such as nontariff measures under (b) and special treatment on the LDC under (d). Para. 3 states that the differential treatment to DCs shall be designed to respond positively to their developmental, financial and trade need. Para. 8, succeeding the initial treatment, provides that a particular account shall be taken of the serious difficulty of the LDCs in making concessions and contributions in view of their special economic situations and

---

[122] UN G.A. Res.82(III) A.1(b)(c) and B2; Res.91(IV) I.6, 9, 13 and 14.

[123] Berthoud, *supra* note 120, at 83–85.

[124] Part IV. Sec. C (iii) of the UN Set.

[125] Berthoud, *supra* note 120, at 85. Report of the International Law Commission (ILC) on the Work of its Thirtieth Session, 1978, UN Doc. A/33/10, 173 ff; ILC, Summary record of the 1494th meeting: Most-Favoured-Nation clause, vol. 1, 100, UN Doc. A/CN.4/SR.1494 (1978), *available at* http://www.un.org/law/ilc/index.htm (last visited on 23 Sept. 2007).

[126] ILC, *supra* note 123.

[127] Para. 3, 4(a), Sec. A, B, and C of Art. XVIII.

[128] Para. 4(b), Sec. C and D. Para. 20 and 23 of art XVIII, Art. I (MFN), and Art. XIII (nondiscriminatory administration of QR).

needs.[129] Moreover, Art. XXXVII of the GATT requires developed members to consider diverse concessions to meet LDCs' necessity of economic development. Para. 1(a) of the same article orders that the developed members should accord high priority in reduction and elimination of barriers to products of particular export interest to LDCs. Furthermore, in Art. IV of the General Agreement on Trade in Services (GATS), in order to increase participation of DCs in world trade, the point of emphasis is on the negotiation of specific commitments relating to strengthening the domestic services capacity, efficiency, and competitiveness of DCs through access to technology, improving their access to information networks, and liberalizing market access in sectors of supply of export interest to them.

Recently, the WTO ministers in the Uruguay Round (UR) adopted lots of provisions in overall agreements for the differential and more favorable treatment of DCs and LDCs.[130] Among other things, the Agreement Establishing the WTO specified that there is a need for positive efforts to ensure the economic development of DCs, particularly, the LDCs.[131] They also decided that expeditious implementation of all special and differential measures in favor of the LDCs shall be ensured through regular reviews, and that MFN concessions on tariff and non-tariff measures agreed in the UR on products of export interests to the LDC may be implemented autonomously, in advance and without staging.[132] The rules and provisions in the UR should be applied in a flexible and supportive manner with sympathetic consideration to specific concerns of the LDC.[133] Additionally, the General Council issued, in June 1999, the Decision on Waiver regarding Preferential Tariff Treatment for LDCs, which allows waivers from the WTO rules in favor of them. Moreover, the Agreement on Trade-Related Aspects of Intellectual Property Rights (TRIPS) also adopts this treatment in its Preamble, Art. 66,[134] Art. 66.2,[135] and Art. 67.[136] The UN Millennium Declaration called on the industrialized countries to provide more generous development assistances to DCs, financial and technical assistance to the landlocked DCs, and to deal with debts of low- and middle-income DCs with measures which can make their debt sustainable

---

[129]GATT, Decision of 28 November 1979 (L/4903).

[130]*See* Docalavich (2007), at 75: WTO, Annex II: Summary of Provisions Contained in the UR Agreements for the Differential and More Favourable Treatment of Developing and Least Developed Countries, *available at* http://www.wto.org.

[131]GATT, Agreement Establishing the World Trade Organization, 2nd para. of chapeau.

[132]GATT/WTO, Decision on Measures in Favor of Least-Developing Countries, 2(i) and (ii).

[133]*See id.* (iii).

[134]The Art. 66 provides LDCs with a longer time-frame to implementation Delay for up to 10 years from most TRIPS obligations and the possibility of extension following duly motivated the request.

[135]The Art. 66.2 requests developed members to provide incentive to companies to encourage technology transfers to LDCs.

[136]The Art. 67 requires technical assistance for the LDCs' to be provided. Art. 12.3 and 12.7 in Agreement on Technical Barriers of Trade of the UR require very similar technical assistance for the LDCs.

in the long term, e.g., a debt relief program and the Barbados Program of Action.[137] All the provisions that allow special and preferential treatment to LDCs or developing countries approve the differential treatment as the general legal principle.

(3) Approval of an ICA

The necessity of regulation over an agreement over producing primary commodities is emphasized more than the security of consumer interests through non-regulatory competition. In international trade with food or nonrenewable natural resources, a normal market mechanism does not stabilize 'inelastic' supply and demand of the nonrenewable natural resource, which not able to manipulate, in a short time, the production which needs relatively long adjustable time and the indispensable demand which daily life activities accompany. The fact that most LDCs and quite a few DCs depend on export earnings from commodity production is noteworthy. Unless producers' economic interests are specially considered, they might face excessive price-reducing competition and end up with premature exhaustion of the limited natural resource, and volatile price of commodities. Such results harm the interest of importing countries as well as exporting countries with subsequently very low export earnings.

The argument for international arrangements is based mostly on concern about developing countries' stable external revenues and raising the stability level of international trade. Art. 57 of the draft Havana Charter provides that member recognize that intergovernmental commodity agreements are appropriate for certain achievements, among other things, to prevent the serious economic difficulties which may arise when adjustments between production and consumption cannot be effected by normal market forces alone as rapidly as the circumstances require.[138] Consumers' interests that can be protected through fierce competition in a market may be weakened in the short term by the ICAs that moderate market competitive conditions because the price-reducing competition of the product is restrained by the agreement. In the long term, however, the supply of nonrenewable natural resources may last for a longer time. The importance of securing the sustainability of commodity production has achieved international consensus through numerous resolutions, including UN Conference on New and Renewable Sources of Energy, the Havana Non-aligned Countries' Policy Guidelines on the Reinforcement of Collective Self-Reliance among Developing Countries, and the International Development Strategy for the Third United Nations Development Decade (hereinafter DD III).[139]

---

[137]G.A.Res.55/2, U.N. GAOR, 55th Sess., para. 15–18, U.N.Doc.A/Res/55/2 (2000). The Barbados Programme of Action is a plan for developing small island DCs under the formal name of 'Programme of Action for the Sustainable Development of Small Island Developing States.' *Refer to* UN (1994), Chap. I, resolution 1, annex II.

[138]UNCTAE (1948), at 39. The International Natural Rubber Agreement held, as its objectives, the stability of the export earnings from natural rubber of exporting members and the increase of their earnings at fair and remunerative prices. *See* Art. 1, para. (c), 1979.

[139]Section III. H of the DD III Strategy. *See* Adebanjo (1984), at 175.

(4) Assessment

The new legal principles to establish the NIEO had a firm basis on the general norm, such as GATT Art. 1 because the principles were embodied as exceptions or waivers to the general principle under the existent international agreement. The NIEO found its founding international agreement in the Charter of Economic Rights and Duties of States (CERDS) which recognizes sovereign power of states over their natural resources.[140] The CERDS is considered as a framework code toward generalized compliance under a binding power as Art. 31 obligate all states to contribute to the balanced expansion of the global economy by considering interests of both developing countries and developed countries. The DD III also focuses on the rational development, management, and utilization for purpose of preventing early exhaustion of finite resources and overburdening of renewable resources.[141]

International development law is in the process of making effective the NIEO, seemingly in conflict with the traditional international legal principles. To promote equitable international trade and competition among developed countries and developing countries, the new area is necessary to be put into effective practice and harmonized with the existent international law. Although special and differential treatment (SDT) is necessary in competition law as well as trade law, lengthy debates as to the effectiveness of SDT in the area of trade law argues that non-reciprocal preferences causes relatively small benefits to most recipient countries and that benefits from the SDT go to exporters in the recipient countries but negatively affects long-term development by creating inefficiency and encouraging rent-seeking activities.[142] However, a cartel regulation and the other areas in competition law require a sufficient level of capacities to analyze market data and point out illegal behaviors to have effective enforcement power. Through the international agreement, competition authorities in the developed countries need to provide technical aids, experience, and enforcement know-how. In addition, international competition laws may allow more exemptions to competition laws in the DCs that are facing urgent development issues than it does to those in advanced countries. However, the exemptions shall not be on arbitrary bases but under objective criteria.[143]

---

[140]The CERDS is adopted by UN GA, 12 Dec. 1974. GA Res. 3281, UNGAOR, 29th Sess., Supp. No. 31, at 50, UN Doc.A/9631 (1975). It is appraised as modern expression of basic principles of international public law because it is impossible that the traditional fundamental rights deriving from the existence of states have their realistic and effective projection, able to ensure an international order on the basis of justice, equity and cooperation, without recognition of these economic rights enumerated under the Charter. Berthoud, *supra* note 120, 91–94.

[141]Section II.

[142]Hoekman (2006), at 95–96. *See* ILC, *supra* note 123.

[143]*See id.* at 99.

So as to look into the difference of two regimes in terms of competition law including a cartel regulation, analysis of the fundamental approach of respective regime is beneficial in order to achieve harmonization.

C. Competition Law: Development Approach V. Market Approach

As multinational corporations (MNCs) occupy more portions of international trade, international trade regulations, focusing on removing governmental barriers to competition in markets under the GATT regime, need to address private barriers, that is, RBPs of the MNCs, such as a cartel or abuse of market dominant position.[144] The concern of the countries whose economic systems are sensitive to the RBPs of the MNCs tried to enlarge the coverage of international trade law from the traditional government-imposed barrier to MNCs' RBPs. However, since legal institutions and economic powers of developing countries with small-size markets are not in such strong positions to regulate the MNCs as those of developed countries where their headquarters are located, developing countries' negotiation with a MNC by each individual country has not produced satisfactory results.[145] A group of developing countries utilized, as an alternative solution, the regulatory power of international organizations, such as the UN and UNCTAD, where they had political influence with their weight of voting power based on the number of their members. As a result, the international competition regulations reflected the development-oriented perspective. The representative examples of the development-oriented international competition law came out as the UN Set in 1980 and Draft Code of Conduct on Transnational Corporations in 1988.[146]

On the other hand, market-oriented international competition laws, which reflect the practices of developed countries, came out in a distinct path from that of the development-approach. Originally, modern competition laws in developed countries came into existence to regulate anticompetitive business practices which imposed harm on competition in markets. The birth of conglomerates through industrialization caused concentration of market power or abuse of the dominant position of the conglomerates, which were a big threat to small-sized enterprises' survival.[147] In addition, the collusive and exclusive business practices among competitors, or cartelistic behaviors, restricted competition in price or quality of

[144]Dean and Mohieldin, *supra* note 79, at 26; Levenstein and Suslow, *supra* note 127, at 807. They cite a speech by the Former Assistant Attorney General for the Antitrust Division of the US Department of Justice.

[145]Singh analyzed the reasons as the follows: (i) inadequate development of the legal and institutional framework, and (ii) lack of information and difficulties of proving that prices were manipulated by international cartels. *See* Singh, *supra* note 58, at 12–14.

[146]Draft Code of Conduct on Transnational Corporations is adopted by the UN Economic and Social Council, 1 Feb. 1988. UN Doc. E/1988/39/Add.1 (1988).

[147]*See* Standard Oil Co. of New Jersey v. U.S., 221 U.S. 1, 47–49, 31 S.Ct. 502, 510–511 (1911).

protect, and reduced significantly the consumers' welfare that had been maximized through competition in markets.[148] The maintenance of competition was the very object of competition law practice. 'Economical efficiency' as the sum of consumers and producers' welfare grew as the main method by which cases in violation of competition law could be decided.[149] Development issue, as the developing countries' most important concern, was set aside under the realm of other economic policies.[150]

The market-oriented competition law, which had played an active role in advanced markets, took its efforts to control the MNCs' anticompetitive activities in the form of the OECD Guidelines for Multinational Enterprises in 1976.[151] Under the Guidelines, the MNCs should refrain from participating in or purposely strengthening the restrictive effects of international or domestic cartels or restrictive agreements which adversely affect competition and which are not accepted under an applicable national or international legislation.[152] In addition, the MNCs need to cooperate readily with competition authorities by providing information under applicable safeguards.[153] The covert tendencies of cartel conspiracy in countries with an under-enforcement of cartel regulation and unskilled competition authorities made difficult the effective enforcement of cartel regulations. The complexity of the MNCs and the difficulty of clearly perceiving their hidden behaviors aggravated the degree of ineffectiveness. After the Guidelines, so as to promote cooperation of competition law and minimize anticompetitive activities, developed countries made their efforts both individually and collectively by bilateral cooperation agreements, and regional agreements.[154]

In the '90s, the developed countries' group which succeeded in establishing a new international organization, the WTO, suggested four topics, representatively known as the Singapore issues[155] including competition policy, on the negotiation table for furthering global free trade policies. Through lowering governmental trade

---

[148]*See* Rail Road Trust Inc. case of the U.S. S.Ct.

[149]Dean and Mohieldin, *supra* note 79, at 4, Dean and Mohieldin explains the 'economic efficiency' as the maximization of the sum of the discounted present value of the surpluses of consumers and producers which assumes static and dynamic efficiency in the way that the current welfare losses may be tolerated if the same factors generating the losses also cause efficiency gains in the long run.

[150]For more information, *refer to* Chap. 4.

[151]The OECD Guidelines for Multinational Enterprises were adopted by the OECD Council on 21 Jun. 1976.

[152]Para. 3. *See also* para. 1 prohibiting the MNCs from abusing a dominant position of market power through anti-competitive acquisitions, predatory behaviors, unreasonable refusal to deal, abuse of industrial property rights and discriminatory pricing.

[153]Para. 4.

[154]*Refer to* Chap. 2 for the in-detailed research.

[155]The four issues are investment, competition policy, governmental procurement, and trade facilitation, which were dropped out at 2003 Cancun Ministerial Conference.

barriers in national markets, the member countries of the WTO exposed their domestic markets to foreign products. However, the DCs which lowered public trade barriers still maintained private trade barriers such as collaborative and exclusive business activities. The under-enforcement or lack of competition law against such anticompetitive business practices led to the adoption of competition policy into the multilateral trade negotiation of the WTO. The concealed desires of advanced countries to correct anticompetitive activities in emerging markets and to facilitate multinational corporations' active cross-border merger and acquisition under harmonized merger regulations might have incited them to address the competition law. The OECD Recommendation against Hard Core Cartel in 1998, the WTO Doha Declaration in 2001, and the Guiding Principles and Recommended Practices on Merger Notification and Review Procedures of International Competition Network (ICN), are examples of the market-approach to international competition law.

The 'development approach' focuses on the increase of employment and the protection of human rights in particularly developing countries rather than on promoting efficiency and lowering price.[156] Collective actions toward development among DCs or LDCs tended to be recommended or at least condoned although the actions lead to cartel activities such as price-fixing or output quantity restriction.[157] Concretely, intergovernmental arrangements for producing nonrenewable natural resources or commodities including agricultural products were permitted under the approach. On the other hand, although a cartel as one of collective restrictive business practices (RBPs) is prohibited,[158] private MNCs' collective RBPs need to be under control of governments from the viewpoint of the development-approach as well as the market approach.[159] Para. 8 and 10 of Draft Code of Conduct of TNCs, besides behaving under observance of domestic laws, regulations and established administrative practices, particularly, require conforming to development policies and cooperating with governments to contribute the development process.

Distinguished from the market approach, however, exemptions to cartel prohibition are to be under positive consideration of the competition authorities. An exemption of R&D cartel is more likely than not to be approved by the competition authorities so that long-term investment policies of the MNCs in developing countries may be promoted under governmental controls. In addition, under the

---

[156]Rossen (1984), at 287.

[157]*See id.*, at 285 and 287. Rossen states, the conclusions of a report to UNCTAD V in 1979 included recommendation concerted measures at the intergovernmental level that would promote structural changes in the world economy and a favorable environment for sustained development at the global level. *Id.* at 285.

[158]*See* para. 37 of Draft Code and para. 3 of Part IV, Sec. D of the UN Set.

[159]*See* Rossen, *supra* note 156, at 286–287. The protection-oriented government policies were tackled by the efforts of UNCTAD in the similar way to the market approach. It cites a report to UNCTAD V (1979), UNCTAD document TD/225, Policy Issues in the Field of Trade, Finance and Money and their Relationship to Structural Change at the Global Level.

development approach, so-called exemptions to crisis cartels are to be allowed so generously as to sustain the level of employment and economic development of the developing market. Efficiency, as a method to achieve development, is not an exclusive measure to decide upon the violation of competition law and cartel regulations in developing countries with mostly small or middle-size markets where developments in overall economic areas are necessary. Competition policy needs to be in the coordinating position with other economic policies toward the development of economies in developing countries' market.

From the perspective of the market-oriented approach, since the development is not a major concern of developed' countries, competition policy and cartel regulations of their countries have operated with its foundation on economical reasoning through sophisticated efficiency arguments rather than with a development purpose. As a result, the market-oriented competition law does not permit a R&D cartel which produces products with controlled prices or restricted output quantities unless the improved efficiency by far outweighs the decreased consumer welfare, because the cartel reduces current and future chances to increase economic efficiency, e.g., reduced price and increased output, through reducing competition in markets. Even in the case of a crisis cartel in economic recession, the market approached competition law has argued, as the U.S. Supreme Court has held, for a long time that any kind of horizontal price restraint violates the competition law because the restraint restricts competition of price, which, while reasonable at the time, could prove to be unreasonable later.[160]

D. The Concern of DCs About Competition Law

(1) Theoretical Disputes

Economists have discussed the relationship between competition and development. In a traditional theory, it is acknowledged that the greater the intensity of competition, the better the economic performance. Modern economic theories threw a serious question to the proposition by indicating that maximum competition is not necessarily an optimal degree of competition for promoting economic welfare in the static sense or maximizing the growth of productivity in the dynamic way.[161] The proponents of strong competition policy place emphasis on removing regulatory barriers to entry with the assumption that competition can be a return to a market, similarly to competitive equilibrium in the long run rather than a constant state of

---

[160] *The U.S. v. Socony-Vacuum Oil Co.*, 310 U.S. 150, 213 (1941). However, recently, the U.S. Supreme Court held that a vertical agreement setting minimum resale price should be decided based on its impact on competition in a market. Leegin Creative Leather Products, Inc. v. PSKS, Inc., 127 S.Ct. 2705, 2714–2718 (2007). As a result, per se illegal rule is limited to a horizontal price-fixing agreement.

[161] Singh, *supra* note 58, 7. Singh cites Amsden and Singh, *The Optimal Degree of Competition and Dynamic Efficiency in Japan and Korea*, 28 Eur. Econ. Rev, at 941–951, and Laffont, *supra* note 57, at 237–257. Singh added, at fn 11, that the concept of competition which he discussed is as regards an incentive to elicit maximum individual or organization effort while the one formulating general equilibrium leads to a Pareto-optimal allocation of resources under specific conditions.

market equilibrium.[162] Such assertions may conflict with development of developing countries where quite a few public barriers to trade have existed to promote domestic enterprises. However, the government barriers can play a role in establishing secure bases for investment and long-term efficiency gains with the exchange of reducing a static economic efficiency in the short term. In the same line, the evolutionary economics argues that a proper competition policy in developing economies should have more interest in science and technology policy as well as industrial policy toward enterprises and innovation.[163] Even a recent theory argues that interfirm coordination among horizontal competitors can cause substantial welfare benefits in relation to innovation.[164]

The economic development of East Asia, especially in Japan, South Korea, and recently China, has not strived for economic policy to maximize competition but to achieve an optimal balance of both cooperation and competition.[165] Countries in less-developed circumstances need to upgrade their technological and managerial capabilities so as to achieve a rapid and sustained growth of economy which is considered a priority of economic development. Such an upgrade is possible only when infant sectors grow under the protection of government, as countries with successful economies are currently experiencing.[166] A group of economists argue that advanced countries have forced developing countries to adopt the free trade regime, which impedes economic development in the long term, at the cost of effectively proved mixed policy options.[167] They criticize that the free trade theory has promoted specialization in sectors with low productivity in poor countries rather economic development and that free trade is suitable only for countries at the same level of development.[168] Apart from some developing countries with big internal markets, the bulk of developing countries should be allowed to pursue their own policies even in competition law areas. A combination of cooperation and competition will enhance more social welfare than competition policy alone.[169]

(2) Appropriate Competition Policy in DCs

The primary purpose of competition policy in developing countries can not be the promotion of competition in and of itself, but fostering economic development

---

[162]The proponents are Dasgupta, Stiglitz, and Bain. *See* Dean and Mohieldin, *supra* note 79, 6–7.

[163]See Rowthorn (2005).

[164]Baumol (2001), at 736.

[165]Chang and Bad (2008), at 15 and 21. While Chang illustrates the examples of South Korea and Japan, economic policy of China recently adopted free trade regime pervasive under remaining control of the state after its accession to WTO.

[166]Martin Wolf, *The Growth of Nations*, 6 Fin. Times (21 Jul. 2007). For instance, industrial districts in Italy and other European countries through the Marshall Plan in post-war period.

[167]Chang, *supra* note 165, 74–78 and 158–159. *See also* Reinert (2007), at 165–181. Reinert illustrates the retrogress of Mongolia's economy after its sudden market open in 1991 and names it as primitivization which contrasts to globalization which economic policy aimed at originally.

[168]Chang, *supra* note 165, 73.

[169]Singh, *supra* note 58, 8.

as well. The difficulty of developing countries in devoting their efforts to maximizing competition is due to its budgetary constraints, under-developed skills or institutions to enforce competition law, and small-sized enterprises with small capital. The competitive equilibrium assumes quite a few conditions,[170] most of which are lacking in the developing world. Especially, a high level of investment as necessity of economic development needs to be based on reasonable, if not high, rate of profits. With the securing of the reasonable profits in priority in developing countries, the level of competition policy may as well choose too little as too much.[171] The governments of developing countries have adopted a coordinative approach regarding investment so as to prevent the waste of insufficient resources.

Since they are facing limited resources, they want to operate the hybrid policy of balancing competition and cooperation in optimal ways for their economies. The competition laws, in light of the economic circumstances, need to make an adjustment to the original laws from developed countries.[172] Their concrete aspects may differ in each country, but three issues are to be addressed.

First, a cartel regulation shall include a research and development (R&D) exemption for the utmost necessity in increasing investment in technology. The investments that are essential for economic development in the developing world can be increased when cooperation in a market is treated as legitimate without threat of cartel penalties. However, the possibility of abuse is to be challenged under screening procedures with regular intervals.

Second, so-called a crisis cartel may be approved under reasonable conditions. Strict anti-cartel enforcement was not accepted even in the U.S. during the Great Depression when a large scale of demand contraction and excessive capacity prevailed.[173] When less diversified business structures with small enterprises are damaged beyond the normal level by the recession, autonomous collaborated behaviors in a manner less restrictive to competition system should be temporarily approved under limited conditions. The maximum time span for the exemption is to be addressed in the related provision so that the collaboration can not be maintained long enough to generate a negative result such as a chronicle cartelized market. The collaborative behaviors in the light of direct harm to consumers and to market mechanism are to be reviewed by competition authorities. Such reasonable measures as a collective production plan to escape from current difficulties are examples of approved collaboration. Consistent enforcement of competition law with the limited conditions can control abuse of the cartel exemption.

[170]Laffont, *supra* note 57, 237. The conditions are large number of participants in all markets, no public goods, no externalities, not information asymmetries, no natural monopolies, complete markets, fully rational economic agents, and a benevolent government which provide lump sum transfers to achieve any desirable redistribution.

[171]Competition goes too much when it leads to price-reducing wars with sharp falls in profits and when it diminishes the desire to investment of companies. *See* Singh, *supra* note 58, at 16.

[172]*See* Cook et al. (2004).

[173]*See* Appalachian Coals v. U.S. 288 U.S. 344, 360–363, 53 S.Ct. 471, 474–476 (1933).

Third, state-operating cartels with respect to nonrenewable natural resources are the area where developing governments derive their financial resources. Excessive competition to exploit such natural resources generates a waste of excessive capacity which leads to exhaustion of the natural resources. If the limited sources from which developing governments can have stable incomes are treated in the same way as a manufactured product under a cartel regulation, it will lead to promoting an insensible competition policy which does not distinguish public entities or nonrenewable resources from private entities or reproducible products. The nonrenewable natural resources which governments themselves operate should not be under a cartel regulation unless extreme cases occur such as the arbitrary controlling over price or production irrespective of market demand.

4.6 Roadmap Toward Binding International Cartel Agreement

A. Wide-Spreading Competition Policy to the Developing World

(1) Modeling Competition Law Reflecting Economic Development

Global economies can not avoid expanding competition policy as well as trade liberalization policies since the trade liberalization of the WTO, which has covered developing countries as well as advanced countries, become effective. The liberalization policies necessitates competition policy to restrain restrictive business practices arguably as private market barriers caused by monopolistic or collaborated local companies or as the abuse of market powers caused by foreign investors. The emerging economies, particularly, which have enjoyed the benefit of trade liberalization and strict domestic competition policy in advanced countries, face pressures to adopt a competition regime along with further trade liberalization from the advanced countries.

Market-principle-based competition laws in advanced countries, however, are not welcomed by developing countries although their advanced skills are worthy of adoption. Developing countries with a priority on economic development still want to sustain their national economic growth under protection. They have inner-concerns that the unfamiliar regime of competition law might enable competitive foreign companies to tread over, arguably, their less-competitive domestic companies. It is one of the reasons why competition law with cartel regulation has been unpopular in the developing world.

To persuade developing countries to adopt competition laws including cartel regulations, it is important to assuage their fear by introducing development-perspective competition law to them. As the first sub-theme under the left box of Fig. 4.1 points out, modeling a competition law in the light of their urgent necessity of economic development or their initial stage of practice is to be the first step. In cartel regulations, a recommendable example includes the exclusion from the regulations or the authorization of several types of cartels or state-operated cartels

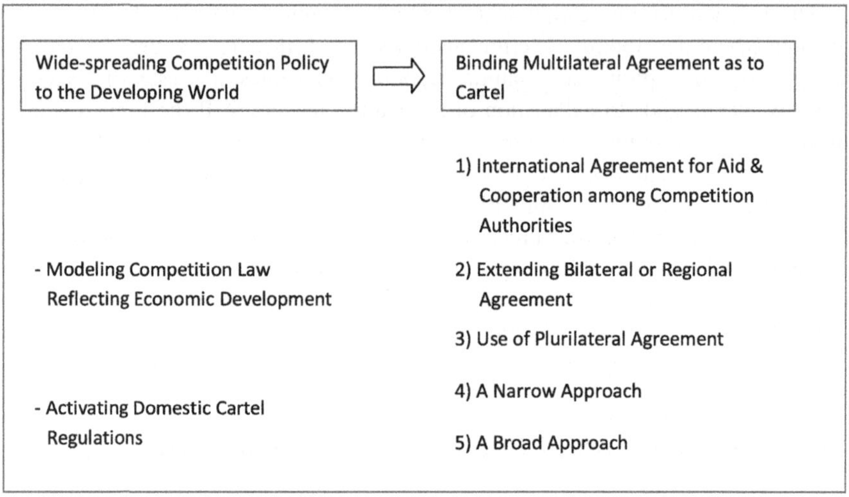

Fig. 4.1 Picture of road map

as they represent public interest that is overvalued by each respective country. The public interest may be served through R&D, rationalization, or supporting small and medium sized enterprises, international competitiveness, or technical and economic progress.[174] The possibility of abuse of the exemption is to be discussed in Chaps. 5 and 6.

(2) Activating Domestic Cartel Regulation: Assistance in DCs' Enforcement

Under-enforcement of a competition law or a cartel regulation has been a characteristic of the DCs which had adopted the regulation. It was because competition authorities do not place emphasis on anti-cartel policy, do not have experts or practical know-hows, or do not receive sufficient institutional and financial support. Among other things, it might be due to the public's low level of awareness regarding the serious damage to the DCs' interests caused by a cartel. As the second sub-theme under the left box of Fig. 4.1 indicates, the international community needs to make an effort on providing research data regarding cartels' damages and the benevolent long-term effects of active anti-cartel policy, introducing successful investigation practices, and providing update knowledge and skills as to cartel investigation to authorities.

The right-box and its concrete five steps of Fig. 4.1 will be explained in B (1)–(5).

B. A Strategy for Binding Multilateral Agreements

(1) Int'l Agreement for Aid and Cooperation Among Competition Authorities

According to Revised Recommendation of the Council of the OECD concerning Co-operation between Member Countries on Restrictive Business Practices (RBPs)

174 Immenga (1999) at 350–351.

affecting International Trade,[175] a cooperative procedure asks a requested member country to take appropriate remedial actions, including an action under its legislation on RBPs. The procedure is beyond the coverage of the positive comity principle[176] because it allows the requested country to take measures in a case where the competition law of the requested country has not been violated and does not permit any remedial action.[177] Procedure for international aid for competition authorities in their novel stage will be a good initial legal foundation for international community to go for a binding international cartel law.

(2) Extending Bilateral Agreement and Regional Agreement: Limitation of Extraterritorial Application

Domestic legislation often has difficulty in dealing with an international cartel. Currently, the extraterritorial application principle of domestic law against international cartels looks to prevail in competition law practices in major advanced countries. However, the extraterritorial application, as a temporary phenomenon, causes conflict with the sovereignty principle of international law since the enforcement against a company or activity in a foreign country is an overreaching of the territory-based jurisdiction principle and the investigation requires an examination of a personnel or collection of evidence located in the other territory. To facilitate the oversee investigation, it needs close cooperation with authorities from other related countries so as to make bilateral agreements.

The recently developed 'comity' principle under the bilateral agreement is an attempt to reduce the obstacles caused by extraterritorial applications. The comity provision, however, exposes a loophole when the substance of competition laws between requesting and requested countries differs. As the *Hart Ford* Case indicated, the law of a country where cartel activities occur, which is the UK, allowed the cartel activity while the law of a country under the effect of the cartel, which is the U.S., penalized it. The U.S. could not ask the UK to enforce its competition law against the cartel under the positive comity. The extraterritorial application was an effective way to protect the consumers in the U.S. from anticompetitive effects of the cartel. Therefore, bilateral agreements for achieving a convergence of cartel regulations are efficient tools to reduce problems out of extraterritorial application between countries with similar economic development levels.

Meanwhile, a bilateral agreement between countries with different level of development is unlikely to work well. Immature skills and development-oriented competition policy in a less-developed country can be main hurdles to achieving the bilateral agreement because an advanced country will not trust the effectiveness of cartel regulation of the developing country or overall legal system. Meanwhile, the

---

[175]Doc. C(86)44 of 21 May 1986.

[176]It requires the requested country to take a measure only when the involved activity violates its competition law.

[177]1.B.4. of Revised Recommendation of the Council of the OECD concerning Co-operation between Member Countries on Restrictive Business Practices affecting International Trade (Doc. C (86)44 of 21 May 1986).

developing country worries the impact of the efficiency-oriented competition law on its market.

As an international cooperative measure of competition policy, a bilateral agreement between countries under a similar economic level is an important foundation. Afterwards, such a bilateral agreement can be extended to cover another or more countries as the antitrust agreement between Australia and New Zealand included Canada. Moreover, a regional agreement regarding competition law can be the other foundation to build multilateral cartel regulations. The facts that the EC Treaty of Rome or APEC adopted provisions of competition law including cartel regulations are noted.

(3) Using Plurilateral Agreement

As the WTO competition policy negotiation proved, the consensus-based decision to launch international competition law or international cartel law causes so much conflict of opinion among the interests of countries with different levels of practice with the law, that the conclusion or launch of the law itself may not be expected in a short time. A plurilateral agreement can reduce the cost of negotiation and launch as only the member states which have interest in the cartel regulation may participate in the negotiation. There is no need to negotiate with countries which contest international cartel law. The law is effective to only members which adopt the agreement. As the cartel law or competition law can be effective under certain infrastructures and a level of economic development, such an optional approach with a plurilateral agreement may fit its characteristics. The burden of confined sovereignty through its binding power may be reduced by such options as allow only interested countries to accede.

(4) A Narrow Approach: Building International Cartel Law with the Narrow Coverage

Although there will be divergence among countries depending on each country's circumstance as to the substance of cartel regulation, it is important to reach an agreement of punishing egregious cartels with proper sanctions to eliminate improper profits through the cartels. A narrowly defined cartel can achieve the agreement more conveniently than the broadly defined one. It is because a certain type of cartels under hard core cartels can accommodate international consensus than other types of cartels. As many countries penalize bid-rigging, the bid-rigging can be an initial object of international cartel regulation with binding power. Price - fixing and production limitation may be the subsequent objects of the international regulation. It is noted that, in light of respective country's situation and development perspective, several exemptions with outweighing public effects should be acknowledged in the regulation.

(5) A Broad Approach: Establishing Cartel Law Under International Competition Regime

As the analysis of advanced and developing countries' competition laws demonstrate, effective cartel practices have proved to be possible with the operation of the whole competition regime. Since effective enforcement of competition law requires several conditions from a certain level of economic development to economic research, as this thesis suggests, binding international competition law with specific and concrete provisions are less likely to attract member states sufficient to take the international law into effect. To reduce the fear of DCs and the burden of advanced countries from acceding to the international competition law, principle-based competition law is recommendable. It will be good if the principles in the law are the ones which countries have widely agreed with, e.g., control over monopoly practices and prohibition of hard core cartels. Subsequently agreed concrete procedures, such as compliance, harmonization, and coordinated cost-reducing procedure, can complement the principled-based agreement. The special and differential treatment (S&D) shall be considered for a flexible commitment to international competition law including cartel regulation. The S&D treatment, which determines the level of commitment in light of the level of its competition culture as well as economic development in each country, can attract more member states as the members of the treaty.

4.7 Conclusion

International competition law cannot avoid considering the development-perspective of competition law since the majority of the constituents of international organizations which tried to adopt competition law are experiencing developing market economies or all under the category of least-developed economies. As the 2003 Cancun Ministerial Conference demonstrated, the unilateral market-oriented competition policy from the advanced countries was not welcomed in the developing countries' context even though competition law produces legal guidelines to business activities among competing companies along with providing much benefit in increasing consumers' welfare and efficiency. The failure looked to be predestined when Mark Brown, a head of the UN Development Program as one of the leading bodies in the development effort of UN, focused on the necessity of strengthening internal capacity and institutions as well as the training of people rather than trying to insert an infrastructure or an industry into a nation without taking into account its social and economic context.[178]

In light of the development-approach, there need to be flexible rules acknowledging exceptions to cartel regulations and assistance in operating cartel regulations in developing economies. Based upon the non-reciprocal principle and the SDT of

[178]Fasulo (2004), at 169–170.

NIEO, some exceptions, under temporary bases, should be acknowledged. The developing countries under the initial period of activating cartel regulations or with immature techniques need to benchmark successful punishment cases against hard core cartels. There may emerge a problem as to the confidentiality of the shared information. Such an issue needs to be addressed with multilateral agreements among countries involved in information sharing for support of competition policy in DCs.

From the developing countries' perspective, on the other hand, introducing competition law including cartel regulation, with which they are unfamiliar, is to enact the operation of free market mechanism based on competition and not to condone traditional collusive behaviors among competitors in normal commerce activities. Active enforcement of the competition law in the process of economic development sometimes may result in the loss of less-competitive domestic companies. Effective enforcement of competition law, including cartel regulations, in developing countries requires substantial time, legal institutions, and investigation techniques.[179] The developed world needs to demonstrate the point that competition policy benefits their economic development and to provide technical support and know-how to enforce cartel regulations and competition law.[180]

Major aspects of international development law, e.g. differential treatment, non-reciprocity, and convention of commodity-producing and consuming countries in markets, need to be adopted by international competition law since the international competition law is currently in the initial stage and the wide gap of experience in practice between advanced countries and developing countries can not be regulated under a single standard. Concretely, state-operating cartels in nonrenewable natural resources, although they affect international economy, are to be approved under the state-sovereignty principle unless it severely restricts rights of the other countries. Commodity cartels under state-operation need to be consoled in the light of economic structural dependence on the trade of the commodities in LDCs. Private cartels, on the other hand, are to be regulated by international competition law, regardless of the market approach or the development-approach. Exemptions to cartel regulations, however, may be provided particularly in the context of economic development. With the economic situation in mind, research and development, overcoming crises, recovery of small and mid-sized enterprises, technical standards and rationalization of production or distribution are exemplary cases where cartel activities are to be allowed.

However, the main rules of WTO law, such as MFN, national treatment, and the opening of service markets to greater competition, may not be damaged by the international competition law. The S&D treatment shall operate as an exceptional basis of mechanism that reviews information submitted by a benefit-recipient

---

[179] Singh, *supra* note 58, 6–7 and 13–15. Singh cites Scherer, Competition policies for an integrated world economy (Brookings Inst. 1994) and argues that it takes about 10 years for countries to acquire the necessary expertise and experience to implement such laws effectively.

[180] For argument for an appropriate framework for international cooperation, *see* Singh, *supra* note 58, 14–15.

country in the light of an original objective and the effectiveness of the measure.[181] Such considerations can reduce the fear and objection from developing countries where cartel regulation and competition law are enacted in their nascent stage or under political consideration for adoption. The roadmap, which this thesis introduced, reflects situations and concerns of the developing world.

As binding international cartel law can help foster competition policy in less-competitive markets, it will support MNEs or companies from advanced countries which want to expand their market. On the other hand, it can also proffer benefits to developing countries where the level of economic development outgrows its low level and international trade occupies a growing portion of Gross Domestic Product (GDP). It is because further economic development needs competition policy to overcome inefficiency in markets and public policies. International competition law, including cartel regulation, will encourage and support the settlement of competition policy in their markets.

References

Books

Chang H-J, Bad S (2008) The myth of free trade and the secret history of capitalism. Bloomsbury Press/Random House, London

Docalavich H (2007) The UN and the global marketplace. Mason Crest Publishers, Broomall

Fasulo L (2004) An insider's guide to the UN. Yale University Press, London

Laffont J-J (1998) Competition, information, and development, annual World Bank conference on development economics. The World Bank, Washington

IMD (2001) World competitiveness yearbook 2000. IMD, Lausanne

Sell S (1998) Power & ideas: north-south politics of intellectual property and antitrust. State Univ. of N.Y. Press, Albany

Slay B (ed) (1996) De-monopolization and competition policy in post-communist economies. Westview Press, Boulder

Reinert E (2007) How rich countries got rich and why poor countries stay poor. Constable & Robinson Ltd, London

UNCTAD (2005) UNCTAD handbook of statistics 2005. UN, Geneva

The World Bank (1995) Bureaucrats in business: the economics and politics of government ownership. The World Bank, Washington

Articles, Papers

Adebanjo MT (1984) Economic cooperation among developing countries: a component of international development strategy. In: Cutajar MZ (ed) UNCTAD and the south-north dialogue: the first twenty years, 175

[181] *See* Hoekman et al., *supra* note 142, pp.100–101.

Baldwin RE (2008) Failure of the WTO ministerial conference at Cancun: reason and remedies, 10 Jul 2008. http://www.fordschool.umich.edu/rsie/Conferences/CGP/May2004Papers/Baldwin.pdf

Baumol W (2001) When is inter-firm coordination beneficial? The case of innovation. Int J Ind Org 19:727

Bentley J (1994) Egyptian legal and judicial sector assessment. Report prepared for the U.S. agency for International Development, Washington

Berthoud P (1984) UNCTAD and the emergence of. In: Cutajar MZ (ed) UNCTAD and the south-north dialogue: the first twenty years

Consumer Unity and Trust Society (CUTS) (2003) Pulling up our socks: a study of competition regimes of seven developing countries of Africa and Asia: the 7-up project. http://cuts.org/pulling.pdf

Cook P, Kirkpatrick C, Minogue M, Parker D (2004) Competition, regulation, and regulatory governance in developing countries: an overview of the research issues. In: Edward Elgar (ed) Leading issues in competition, regulation, and development. http://www.competition-regulation.org.uk/publications/crc_books/Leading%20issues.pdf

Dean BAE, Mohieldin M (2001) On the formulation and enforcement of competition law in emerging economies: the case of Egypt. Egyptian Center for Economic Studies

Evenett S, Levenstein M, Suslow V (2001) International cartel enforcement: lessons from 1990s. World Bank Policy Research Working Paper No. 2680

Garcia-Rodriguez S (1995) Mexico's new institutional framework for antitrust enforcement, 44 DePaul L.Rev. 1149

Hoekman M (2006) Improving: some proposals. In: van Dijck P, Fabered G (eds) Developing countries and the Doha development agenda of the WTO. Routledge, London

Immenga U (1999) Conflicts between competition policy and industrial policy: a comparative view on potential responses. In: Zaech R (ed) Towards WTO competition rules: key issues and comments on the WTO report (1998) on trade and competition, pp 350–351

Khor M (2003) An analysis of the WTO's fifth ministerial conferenc., Inter-governmental group of 24, Cancun, 10–14 Sept 2003. http://www.g24.org/khorgva.pdf. Visited on 16 Jul 2008

Kovacic W (1997) Getting started: creating new competition policy institutions in transition economies. Brook J Int'l 23:403–424

Kovacic W (2001) Institutional foundations for economic legal reform in transition economies: the case of competition policy and antitrust enforcement. Chi.-Kent L. Rev. 77:265–310

Lee S (2008) Using action in damages against cartels in developing countries. Curr Int'l Trade L J 55, 16–2

Levenstein M, Suslow V (2003–2004) Contemporary international cartels and developing countries: economic effects and implications for competition policy. Antitrust L J 71:801–818

Mehta PS (2003) Competition policy in developing countries: an Asia-Pacific perspective. Consumer Unity and Trust Society, Bulletin on Asian Pacific Perspective 2002–2003. http://www.unescap.org/drpad/publication/bulletin%202002/ch7.pdf. Visited on 16 Jul 2008

OECD (2002) Report on the nature and impact of hard core cartels and sanctions against cartels under national competition laws. http://www.oecd.org/dataoecd/16/20/2081831.pdf

OECD Global Forum on Competition (GFC) (2003) How enforcement against private anticompetitive conduct has contributed to economic development. CCNM/GF/COMP(2003) 7, 27 Oct 2003. http://www.oecd.org

OECD GFC (2004) How enforcement against private anticompetitive conduct has contributed to economic development. CCNM/GF/COMP(2004)4 Sess. IV. 3 Feb 2004

Rossen S (1984) Global management of processes of change and adjustment. In: Cutajar MZ (ed) UNCTAD and the south-north dialogue: the first twenty years, 260

Rowat M et al (eds) Judicial reform in Latin America and the Caribbean. World Bank Technical Paper No. 280 (1995)

Rowthorn B (2005) Reviews: evolutionary economics, 111 prospect (Jun 2005) (reviewing Paul O (2005) Why most things fail. http://www.prospect-magazine.co.uk/article_details.php?id=6906 . Visited on 18 Apr 2008)

Singh A (2002) Competition and competition policy in emerging markets: international and developmental dimension. G-24 Discussion Paper No. 18, Sep. 2002. http://www.unctad.org/en/docs/gdsmdpbg2418_en.pdf

The World Bank Group (2002) Annual report 2002. http://www.worldbank.org/html/extpb/2002/index.htm. Visited on 16 Jul 2008

UN Conference on Trade and Employment (UNTAE) (1948) Final act and related documents. UN document E/CONF. 2/78

UN (1994) Report of the global conference on the sustainable development of small island developing states, Bridgetown, Barbados, 25 April–6 May 1994. U.N. publication, Sales No. E.94.I.18 and corrigenda

UNCTAD (2003) Can developing economies benefit from WTO negotiations on binding disciplines for hard core cartels? UNCTAD/DITC/CLP/2003/3. http://www.unctad.org

UNCTAD (2004) Competition, competitiveness, development: lessons from developing countries. UNCTAD/DITC/CLP/2004/1. http://www.unctad.org

U.S. General Accounting Office [GAO] (2004) Congressional report analyzes WTO negotiations collapse at Cancun, 16 Jan 2004. http://usinfo.state.gov

Whalley J (1988) Priorities and practices- the antitrust division's criminal enforcement program. Antitrust LJ 57:569

White and Case LLP (2003) WTO talks collapse in Cancun: a splash of cold water, or dead in the water? Vol. IX WTO REPORT: Special Report on the WTO Cancun Ministerial No. 6, 16 Sept 2003

Chapter 5
The Regulation of Cartels in Developing Countries

Abstract Developmental aspects of competition regimes are analyzed, respectively, in four advanced countries, such as the U.S., UK, France, and Germany, and four DCs including Mexico, South Africa, China, and South Korea. Based upon the analyses, it is highlighted consensus-building process for cartel enforcement with respect to economic development, and proposed institutional supports for adopting cartel regulations, particularly sanctions, leniency program, and bounty system. It is argued that DCs should have international collaboration in order to develop and cooperate each other toward better and effective cartel regulation.

Keywords Regulatory development · Consensus-building · Cartel enforcement · International cooperation · Competition authorities · Leniency program · Bounty system

5.1 Introduction

Mark M. Brown, while serving as the head of UN Development Program, had stated that, with focus on importance of the independent capacity-building of DCs, development is not a linear thing, whereby we could solve human suffering with throwing money. According to him, developing countries and those who assist them should invest in people through education, health, and make space for a strong private sector with suitable rewards along the way to development in the shape of aid from the World Bank and other donors.[1] Compared to other issues in competition policy, an effective cartel regulation causes the reform of business environment into a competitive one by directly raising efficiency and consumers' welfare. Therefore, the effective cartel regulation contributes to building a strong private sector under a competition culture because a cartel causes inefficiencies through the malfunction of market mechanism and direct damage to consumers' welfare.

[1]Fasulo (2004), at 170.

J.S. Lee, *Strategies to Achieve a Binding International Agreement on Regulating Cartels*, DOI 10.1007/978-981-10-2756-7_5

Transitional economies' concern about keeping long-standing state-monopoly is not an issue for cartel regulations. Protecting domestic companies from foreign investors' mergers and acquisitions is only a collateral problem in cartel regulation. Activating effective cartel regulation in DCs, therefore, looks to generate net benefit to DCs, and even LDCs.

The practices of cartel law in DCs, however, do not reveal a strong attitude in implementing the law. The reality of their cartel policies demonstrates that they face poor resources, e.g., insufficient personnel and funds, ineffective institutions, immature skills, unstable support for anti-cartel policy, and a lack of understanding of competition norms. DCs are not equipped with the type of environments for the rigorous enforcement of cartel regulation in comparison with advanced countries that have developed cartel regulation and its enforcement with a long duration of time and much investment of financial and human sources. It is almost impossible that DCs strongly support or approve international competition law or cartel regulation with the coarse circumstances left intact in the countries.

As the front part of strategy for founding international cartel law, this chapter addresses the development of cartel regulatory regimes by studying four examples of development of competition laws, respectively, in advanced and developing countries. It moves its focus on the issue of consensus-building for cartel regulation in developing countries by demonstrating the low awareness of the advantages of cartel regulation, the relationship between competition and development, and methods to activate domestic enforcement against cartels. This chapter further provides research on legal institutions of cartel regulation through studying political economic theories and investigating how to place both a social foundation for its effective enforcement and economic sources for the legal regime. At last, it addresses the issue of raising capacities to create an effective regulation and, particularly, the ways to cooperate with developed countries.

5.2 Development of Cartel Regulation in the North and the South

A. The Standard of Cartel Regulation in Advanced Countries

(1) The U.S.

The Sherman Act, a principal competition legislation in the U.S., was adopted by the U.S. Congress during the economic situations in 1890 when the complaints from small and middle size companies and consumers were raised because of the high prices imposed by cartel members. Although there were some derivative decisions, the U.S. courts have developed a judicial rule of per se illegal separately from the rule of reason standard under common law tradition, thereby dividing cartel cases according to each category. Up until the end of WW II in 1945, the U.S. looked to be the only country to enforce cartel regulation and competition law seriously.

The Sherman Act, adopted as a result of hot discussions regarding a competition issue, penalized a 'commerce-restraining' agreement under section one instead of a 'competition-restraining' one, without enumerating its in-detail category.[2]

Section 1 Every contract, combination, in the form of trust or otherwise, or conspiracy, in *restraint of trade or commerce* among the several States, or with foreign nations, is declared to be illegal. Every person who shall make any contract or engage in any combination or conspiracy hereby declared to be illegal shall be deemed guilty of a felony, and shall be punished by fine not exceeding $100 million if a corporation, or $1 million if any other person, or by imprisonment not exceeding 10 years, or by both said punishments, in the discretion of the court.

The language of Sec. 1 of the Act implies that consensus as to competition-restraining activities was not successful. As a trust or a cartel practice restricted competition, causing a threat to sustaining the whole economy and the survival of non-member small or middle-sized enterprises (SMEs), the new Act targeted a trust or a cartel under its original plan. However, it was in 7 years after the U.S. adopted the Sherman Act when the Supreme Court announced that a horizontal price-fixing agreement was illegal under the Sec. 1 of the Act, whether it is valid or otherwise under common law.[3] Subsequent cases enabled the U.S. courts to develop sophisticated case laws constructing the Sec. 1 of the Sherman Act, which prohibits every trade-restraining agreement including a cartel.[4] Regarding such cartels as price-fixing, market allocation, output restriction, and group boycott, the judicial body has developed a strict per se *illegal* rule that does not allow any defense except ones explicitly allowed by legislations.[5] The rule is the result of judicial experiences that, in light of economic analysis of such hard core cartel, any positive effect that the hard core cartel might generate is outweighed by enormous damages that the cartel brings about. Therefore, the rule proclaims that the judicial body will not be involved in economical reasonings in the types of cartels.

In the other areas, besides the hard core cartel, cartel law practices are subject to rule of reason analysis of the judicial body. As to the other types of cartels, such as a collective refusal to deal, American courts have considered the defense of benevolent effects to economies and have issued decisions out on the balancing of negative effects against positive effects of the cartels. U.S. courts expressed their intention that the judicial body will consider economic reasoning only in the other type of cartel cases.

---

[2]The Sherman Act § 1, 15 U.S.C. § 1 (1890).

[3]Trans-Missouri Freight Ass'n, 166 U.S. 290, 341–342 (1897). The decision (5-4) had five supporting justices and four dissenting justices.

[4]U.S. v. Addyston Pipe and Steel Co., 85 F. 271 (6th Cir. 1898), *modified and aff'd*, 175 U.S. 211 (1899); U.S. v. Joint Traffic Association, 171 U.S. 505, 19 S.Ct. 25, 43 L.Ed. 259 (1898); Northern Securities Co. v. U.S., 193 U.S. 197 (1904).

[5]U.S. v. Trenton Potteries Co., 273 U.S. 392, 47 S.Ct. 377, 71 L.Ed. 700, 50 A.L.R. 989 (1927); U.S. v. Socony-Vacuum Oil Co., 310 U.S. 150 (1940); Fashion originators' Guild of America (FOGA) v. FTC, 312 U/S. 457 (1941).

Despite the jargon of Sec. 1 of the Act, the main standard for the judicial body to decide violation of the Section is the probability of the restraint of competition or whether there existed net harm to the public, recently defined as consumers' welfare in economical term. In *Addyston Pipe & Steel Co.* (1899), the Supreme Court held that a market division agreement fell on the common law's restraint of commerce, causing harm to public interest.[6] *The Trenton Potteries* case, on the price-fixing of toilet bowls, confirmed the importance of public interest by stating that the Sherman Law and judicial decisions are based upon the assumption that the public interest is best protected from the evils of monopolies and price control through the maintenance of competition and proclaiming that price-fixing is per se illegal without consideration of its economic effect and rival economic theories.[7] The *Socony-vacuum oil* case dismissed reasonableness argument and followed the per se illegal rule by stating that the reasonableness of prices has no constancy due to the dynamic quality of business facts underlying price structures.[8] It implies that consumers are able to enjoy the best result from a market when price is determined by market system reflecting business facts, e.g., demand, supply, and prices of alternative products in the market.

On the other hand, the U.S. has maintained narrower concrete exemptions of cartel regulation than other countries. Export cartels are exempted from the Webb–Pomerene Act, which are analyzed to cause harm to importing countries by raising prices or restraining consumers' welfare. Agricultural cooperatives, cooperative research and development arrangements, insurance companies' rate-setting, baseball player assignments, and labor union collective bargaining practices are exempted from the Sherman Act.[9]

(2) The United Kingdom (The UK)

After the WWII, the UK, which had loosened a strict attitude regarding a cartel through common law, has developed sophisticated legislations and enforcement system of competition law throughout more than half a century period. It took a long time to adopt legislations regarding competition, particularly cartels, and enact them effectively.

The White Paper on Employment published during the WWII suggested that a competitive economy would make a policy of full employment most likely possible, which contributed to enacting the Monopolies and Restrictive Practices Act (MRPA) 1948 as the first modern competition law.[10] The Monopolies and Restrictive Practices Commission, established by the MRPA 1948, issued its Report on Collective Discrimination. In respect of the minority opinion of the Report, which urged effective sanctions on restrictive business practices including cartel

---

[6]*Addyston Pipe and Steel Co. v. U.S.*, 175 U.S. 211, 237–238 (1899).

[7]U.S. v. Trenton Potteries Co., 273 U.S. 392, 395–396 and 399 (1927).

[8]U.S. v. Socony-Vacuum Oil Co., 310 U.S. 150, 221 (1940).

[9]Scherer (1994), at 52–53.

[10]Whish (2000), at 2. Whish cites Cm6527 (1944). *See id.* Footnote(fn) 4.

activities, stricter regulations regarding restrictive practices, separately from monopolies, started under the Restrictive Trade Practices Act (RTPA) 1956.[11] In 1968, the RTPA was reformed to strengthen its control over cartels, which extended the provision of powers to catch information agreements, and made unregistered but registrable agreements void in terms of any relevant restrictions.[12] However, the trial produced unsatisfactory results because the legislation lacked the investigatory power and its sanction sufficient to attack serious cartels. Meanwhile, innocuous agreements were registered so as to avoid the uncertainty of complex provisions of restrictions and the risk of voidness.[13]

Through the Fair Trading Act in 1973, at last, the UK expressed its serious attitude of enacting competition policy. The enactment of the 1973 FTA had its background that the UK joined the European Economic Community in the same year and that Art. 85 and 86 of the Treaty of EC, related to competition policy, were directly applicable. The 1973 FTA established the Office of Fair Trading (OFT), created the role of its Director General, and included service industries, formerly regulated under the RTPA. Subsequent legislations made changes to the UK system of competition law: the Competition and Markets Authority (CMA) replaced the roles of OFT and Competition Commission pursuant to the Enterprise and Regulatory Reform Act of 2013. Before and during the OFT, investigations and law enforcements against hidden cartels were inactive, while many sources were spent on registrations of innocuous cartels. Several Restrictive Trade Practices Orders[14] tried to reduce the duty for registering innocuous agreements. Green and White Papers issued from the UK government proposed that the RTP legislation should be reformed toward an effective one and modeled on Art. 81 of the Treaty of EC.[15] As one of the trials to overcome weak powers to punish unlawful cartels, substantial fines were imposed on participating firms in a ready mixed concrete cartel in 1995.[16]

Reform for strong competition policy was not possible due to political disputes related to the adoption of the EC-typed cartel regulation until 1998 when the Labor Party took a helm over British Government.[17] Section 2 of the Competition Act 1998 adopted languages very similar to the Art. 81(1) of Maastricht Treaty. The

---

[11]*See id.* fn 5. Whish cites Cmd 9504 (1955).

[12]*See id.* at 3.

[13]*See id.*

[14]The Restrictive Trade Practices Order in 1989 (SI 1989/1081), in 1996 (SI 1996/348), in 1996 (SI 1996/349), in 1997 (SI 1997/2945), and the Anti-Competitive Practices Order in 1980 (SI 1980/979).

[15]Review of RTP Policy (Cmnd7512) (Mar. 1979), Review of RTP Policy: a Consultative Document (Cm 331) (Mar. 1988), and Opening Markets: New Policy on RTP (Cm 727) (Jul. 1989).

[16]The Restrictive Practices Court imposed £8.4 million. Fair Trading (Autumn 1995 issue). *Re* Supply of Ready Mixed Concrete (No. 2); DGFT v. Pioneer Concrete (UK) Ltd and Another [1995] 1 AC 456; [1995] 1 All ER 135.

[17]Rodger and Macculloch (2000), at 171–72.

provision prohibits agreements, decisions of association, and concerted practices (hereinafter agreement, etc.), which have as their object or effect the prevention, restriction, or distortion of competition. Section 2(4) reflecting the article of the Treaty, currently Art. 101 of Lisbon Treaty, proclaims any agreement, etc., prohibited by subsection (1) as void. Financial penalty against a cartel was raised up to 10 % of turnover for every year of the infringement up to maximum 3 years. The Act has several exemptions, such as individual, block exemption, or parallel exemption, for example, R&D and specialization agreements.[18] Section 2(3) adopts the implementation approach of the Treaty. Meanwhile, the UK government and a legislator disagreed with the adoption of the pure effect doctrine even in case when the EC interprets the implementation in a broad way enough to include effect.[19] After the Brexit vote and operation of CMA, UK cartel regulation needs to be carefully watched.

(3) France

While France has a culture in favor of individual liberty, it has a negative attitude against a free market system. Such irony is due to the contribution of an industrial policy to a successful transformation of France's economic structures in the era of post World War II. French government policy to promote high-tech industries was successful in raising their international competitiveness, although attempts to promote some inefficient industries, such as textile or steel industry, resulted in the loss of government budget. The anti-cartel provision of the Napoleonic Penal Code, which generated the tolerance of cartels during the pre-war times was applied to only a few cases due to the strict requirements of the criminal statute, e.g., the difficult proof of artificiality and abnormality of the desired price.[20] The lenient attitude against cartels shifted when a decree issued in 1953 (modified in 1958) prohibited agreements that impose minimum prices or trading margins, agreements which allow an individual trader to discriminate habitually in terms of sale or through refusal to sale, and concerted actions which aimed at interfering with competition. These prohibitive behaviors are allowed under certain exemptions, such as market improvement and economic progress by rationalization and specialization.[21] However, the 1953 decree was not effectively enforced because industrial policy prevailed over competition policy.[22] Such prevalence of industrial policy precluded the growth of public awareness of competition culture and norms.

---

[18]Provisions for individual and block exemptions are Sects. 4–9 while parallel exemption system is based on Sect. 10. *See id.* at 170 and 177. Section 4 under a strict authorization system provides the power to grant an exemption to Director General.

[19]*Id.* at 176. In Gencor Ltd v. Commission [1999] 4CMLR 971, a merger case, the Court of First Instance opened the potential for a wide interpretation.

[20]*Refer to* Chap. 3, Sect. 3.3 2(2) of this book.

[21]Rodger and Macculloch, *supra* note 17, at 34.

[22]The governmental policy strategically focused on several high-tech industries e.g. the aero or railroad industry. State-operating companies led investment in the high-tech industries. Such policy succeeded in raising France's economic level.

One example of such government intervention still remaining in industries is the newly elected central-right winged president's promise to pressure big retailers to reduce their prices as an initiative to boost households' purchasing power.[23]

When France was integrated to the EU system, adopting competition rules under Art. 81 and 82 of the Treaty of Rome, its competition law enforcement including cartel regulation grew stricter. The remodeled competition law of France, or the Law on Liberalization of Prices and Competition of 1986, had Art. 7, Decree No. 86 (1 Dec. 1986), similar to Art. 81 of the Treaty of Rome. The article adopted a general prohibition to all kinds of concerted restrictive practices, including price-fixing, market division, and output restraints. Article 10, No. 2, Dec. No. 89, exempted economically desirable cartels on the legislative basis. Its economic policy was influenced by new liberalism from the Anglo-Saxon countries, the UK and the U.S. Although not preferring a radical deregulation over almost all areas, France privatized quite a few public service industries and public monopolies under the 1992 *grand marche interieur* (big internal market).[24]

(4) Germany

After the WWII, on the contrary to the former approach condoning cartels, West Germany started to develop strong competition laws by the adoption of democracy and a free market system under the influence of the new Freiburg School, economists who were firm believers in a competitive-free market system and pointed out the distortions, which cartelization brought about in the German economy after the WWI.[25] The Act against the Restraint of Competition of 1958, as a stringent competition law, adopted the prohibition principle that prevented collaboration itself among horizontal competitors under Sec. 1 with such special exceptions as structural crisis, rationalization, export, import, and condition (discount and payment terms) cartels.[26] The Cartel Office took a cautious position at first, but gradually held strong actions against the cartels. Administrative correction and surcharges (administrative fines) have been main sanctions dealing with concerted practices. German-policy was to induce potential cartel members to seek exemptions under the ARC. Currently, two kinds of exemptions function under the ARC. Once notified to Cartel Office, the following cartels under 'unopposed' exemption are permitted unless the Office objects: agreements about standards and terms of doing business (sec. 2), specialization cartels (sec. 3), and agreements among SMEs (sec. 4). However, Germany did not accept EU-typed exemption for

[23]Ben Hall, *Sarkozy unveils measures to curb prices*, FT 10 (Nov. 30, 2007).

[24]Christian Stoffaes, Chairman of the Board, Centre d'Etudes Prospectives et d'Informations Internationales, Speech at 2007 Fordham Conference, in Hawk, B. ed. (2007), Annual Proceedings of the Fordham Corporate Law Institute: International Antitrust Law and Policy (hereinafter IALP), Fordham Law Institute (FLI), at 256.

[25]*See id.* at 29–30. Ludwig Erhard, the first economic minister who pursued a strict competition policy, later became the chancellor of the Federal Republic of Germany. Walter Eucken and Franz Boehm, economists, were major adherents to the School.

[26]*Id.* at 30.

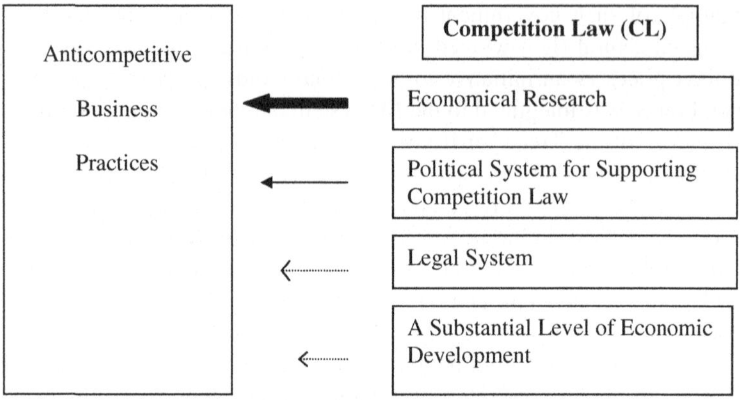

Fig. 5.1 Level and strength of competition law enforcement depending on its several bases

'promoting technical or economic progress'.[27] Meanwhile, those under 'authorized' exemption, such as rationalization cartels (sec. 5) and crisis cartels (sec. 6), require prior approval from the Office. Since 1970s, informal collusion or clandestine agreements to restrict competition has been illegalized in spite of several exemptions.

(5) Analysis

In the course of economic development, advanced countries faced competition-restricting business activities among enterprises including cartels, and treated such activities with different attitudes. For instance, Germany, with a focus on waste of resources from excessive competition, adopted a general approval policy subsequently with control over abusive activities. On the other hand, the UK and the U.S., although different in degree, have kept stringent cartel-prohibiting policies under the common law tradition that free competition generates public good. The analyses of development of competition law in advanced countries indicate that several bases of competition law enforcement decide its coverage and strength. Figure 5.1 demonstrates the level and strength of competition law enforcement depending on several external conditions in a country.

Since a competition-restricting activity, particularly a cartel, contributes to the accumulation of corporate wealth, the companies with a substantial proportion of existent market shares, face the temptation to avoid severe competition and exclude new competitors by collusion. Meanwhile, consumers have endured negative effects from such competition-restriction through increased prices, reduced output, and stagnated quality. Since public policy makers find more interest in economic growth, which consists mostly of corporate production, they find more favor in pro-corporation policy including competition-restricting measures. However,

[27] Wise (2005), at pp. 18–20.

economic growth through such wealth-expanding policies does not provide efficiency-based competition in a market. As entrepreneurship, nurtured under a competitive market structure, is an important element to economic development, competition policy plays an important role in further economic development.

Competition-facilitating rules as well as free trade rules function when a market economy outgrows an initial level and expands for further growth. The first box on the right-sided bottom in the figure illustrates this. The achievement of cross-border free trade is diluted by anticompetitive activities in domestic markets, such as exclusive business practices, and inefficient or unfair activities of existent companies. International laws regulating international trade have developed to reduce or eliminate competition-restrictive activities of the existent companies as private trade barriers. Although cartel-facilitating academic researchers in Germany were regarded as prominent economists in the past era, they did not foresee the integration of the domestic economy toward the regional market, such as the EU, and the global market. An individual country cannot win merit-based competition in other markets, while looking over anticompetitive inefficiencies, e.g., a cartel in a domestic market. France's example illustrates the increasing awareness of the importance of anti-cartel law when it faced the integrated market of the EU and the global market. Although France used to keep a national-champion policy in strategic industries, it is now a serious anti-cartel law enforcer.

The legal system needs to be developed to support accumulation of competition law jurisprudence. The second box from the right-sided bottom indicates this. The independent institutional system in charge of competition law is necessary to enforce a high level of competition policy; the objective of competition-facilitation is depreciated or not considered when the pro-corporate political pressure affects competition law enforcement or decision. For instance, in the UK, the OFT, established for investigating malfunction of markets against consumers, was succeeded by a single organ, the CMA, merging the OFT and the Competition Commission. Investigation under legal procedure, transparent decision-making through publication, exposure to public discussion, and the authorities with review power over initial decisions contribute to competition law development. In Germany, the Federal Cartel Office in charge of the anti-cartel policy has developed competition norms under its independent policy goal. In the U.S., the Antitrust Division of the Department of Justice has worked against hard-core cartel activities through Sec. 1 of the Sherman Act to achieve judicial decisions on penalizing their activities as a felony under criminal law. Other cartel activities go to the FTC, for balancing their anticompetitive effect against pro-competitive effect. The FTC has issued its decision for which judicial review is available.

It is not easy, however, to activate competition law under undemocratized political institutions or societies because it needs political support from less powerful social members, such as consumers and small- and middle-sized companies. The third box from the bottom illustrates it. In the U.S. when Congress adopted the Sherman Act, angry local railroad companies excluded by national trusts and users facing high fees were strong advocates on passing the Sherman Act. Although the Supreme Court hesitated to follow a strict application of Sec. 1 of the Act under the

UK common law tradition,[28] Congress continued to pursue its initial goal of strong competition policy by adding supplementary legislations, such as the Clayton Act and the Federal Trade Committee (FTC) Act.

Furthermore, competition law enforcement needs academic research for aiding competition policy,[29] as the fourth box from the bottom shows. Particularly, economists who strongly advocate competition law place hypothetical foundations for pursuing a competition policy. Germany could not have developed a modern competition policy without positive participation from the Freiburg school. The UK also activated modern anti-cartel law because of government papers warning of the negative effect of anticompetitive practices on the future British economy. The U.S. antitrust law has been under strong influences of powerful economical analyses, such as Chicago school and Harvard School.

At least a medium level of economic development involved in international trade, legal system, political democracy, and academic background decide the level of competition law enforcement as the figure above shows. When more conditions are satisfied, the level of competition law enforcement goes stronger. The bigger arrows, as higher from the bottom, demonstrate such stronger enforcement. The analysis of development of competition law in advanced countries supports the hypothesis.

B. Cartel Regulation in Developing Countries

(1) South Africa

1) The Era under Apartheid Policy

South Africa adopted the Regulation of Monopolistic Conditions Act (RMCA) of 1955 as its first general competition law. The RMCA regulated a number of monopolistic conditions with an administrative examination of rule of reason on the standard of public interest. The Board of Trade and Industries in charge of investigations, recommendations of remedies, negotiation, and supervision of compliance, had no independent powers while the Minister of Trade and Industry had decision power. The overall structure of the investigation and decision-making is susceptible to political pressure. In addition, the law did not have active enforcements during its 24 year history.[30] A review of the RMCA in two decades evaluated

---

[28]Some justices opposed literal interpretation of ‘every restraint of commerce’ by adding a restriction to the language of the provision such as undue or unreasonable. Finally, the rule of reason standard was adopted in the Standard Oil of New Jersey case in 1911. In hard core cartel cases, the Supreme Court has excluded the rule of reason rule from the U.K. common law tradition since the Trenton Potteries case.

[29]Dabbah (2003) at 57.

[30]Among a total of eighteen investigation cases ordered by the Ministry, It looks that there were the eight cartel cases which were found to be contrary to the public interest. Almost all cases turned out to be in negotiated settlements without penalty. Sanction was imposed on one case by the Ministry. OECD (2003a, b), at 12.

that the RMCA was unsuccessful in light of its poor regulatory records and a dramatic increase in oligopolies.[31]

In response to critics against deficient enforcements and political influences, the Maintenance and Promotion of Competition Act (MPCA) in 1979 was created. Although the Competition Board, newly established for enforcing the MPCA, had its own independent power of investigation into competition complaints, the Minister of Trade and Industry still had the power to appoint members to the Board and make a final decision whether he accept or refuse a recommendation from the Board, which makes a room for political influence.[32] Although a regulation issued by the Minister stipulated that such cartel practices are per se unlawful as horizontal collusion on price, terms, or market share and bid-rigging, and that violation of the regulations are crimes, there was no history of criminal sentence beside one guilty plea case. Overall, there was not much improvement even through the 1979 MPCA.[33]

The economic development of South Africa was centered on the extraction industry of diamonds and gold for export purposes. The economic policies of South Africa protected investors in the industry and tried to widen the economic growth to local manufacturing and farming. Monopoly concessions were conferred on state-owned enterprises around the turn of the nineteenth century. On the other hand, racial discrimination was reflected in public policies and protected white-owned businesses from black enterprises' competitions, thereby maintaining low labor costs from a large black-labor supply. When the international community imposed economic sanctions against racial discrimination policies, policies of autarky and import substitution under governmental intervention were strengthened.[34] In the era of apartheid repression, however, the enforcement of competition law under the industrial policy, which had been designed to promote South Africa's economy, was not active. Among other reasons, the political climate of South Africa contributed to the under-enforcement of competition law. South Africa has adopted a socialistic economy since the African National Congress passed the Freedom Charter in 1955, which made a weak foundation of implementation of competition policy with focus on free market mechanism.[35] The South African government under the control by the white minority had limitations to pursue a

[31]The Competition Commission of South Africa, *About Us: the Introduction*, *at* http://www.compcom.co.za.

[32]Fox and Davis (2007), at 163.

[33]According to Department of Trade and Industry, the 1979 Act did not address the extent of concentration of ownership or vertical or conglomerate relations, and had little leverage to prevent mergers expanding concentration. In addition, it did not have an explicit provision for strongly prohibiting anticompetitive activity. *See id.* On the other hand, OECD criticized that public interest as its substantive standard was undefined. *See* OECD (2003a, b), at 13.

[34]*Id.*, at 9–10.

[35]Fox and Davis (2007), at 164. Prior to 1955, South Africa's economic system was capitalism with the most highly concentration in conglomerate forms.

competitive and free market system as it discriminated the black in economic activities under the apartheid.

2) Establishment of Competition Act under Democratic Government: Competition Act of 1998 and 2009

However, after the democratic government assumed power in 1994, it developed a reconstruction and development program, which included strict antitrust legislation to create a more competitive business environment and to remove anticompetitive practices. The 1994 Constitution tried to rebuild the state and its laws on a democratic foundation.[36] The National Economic Development and Labor Council (NEDLAC) launched consensus-building among government, business and labor, and community NGOs, and organized debates over the proposed competition law with their broadly inclusive participation.[37] With the 5-year debates and political support, the 1998 Competition Act took effect with a priority on the national economic reform plan. The new Act aimed at overcoming the shortcomings of the old 1979 MPCA, promoting competition jurisprudence, and improving the chronic imbalances of the South African economy inherited from the apartheid. Three major objectives of competition policy, such as efficiency promotion, competitiveness-strengthening, and equity-enhancing, were reflected under Sec. 2 of the Competition Act of 1998.[38] The Competition Act of 1998 established the Competition Commission of South Africa (CCSA) in charge of investigation and control over restrictive business practices including cartels, and two adjudicative organizations, such as the Competition Tribunal (CT) and the Competition Appeal Court (CAC). Under the Act, the CA had power to impose administrative fine or surcharge through civil proceedings as an independent adjudicative organization, while the CAC had the authority to review appeals from CT decisions.[39] The efficiency-driven competition policy of South Africa was reveled through a decision of the CT, holding that if the equity objective conflicted with efficiency as a main concern of competition policy, equity could prevail over efficiency only when the loss of public interests related to equity is considerable and certain.[40]

[36] OECD (2003a, b), 11.

[37] *Id.* at 16.

[38] The purpose of the Act is, according to Sec. 2, (a) to promote the efficiency, adaptability, and development of the economy, (b) to provide consumers with competitive prices and product choices, (c) to promote employment and advance the social and economic welfare of South Africans, (d) to expand opportunities for South African participation in the world market, (e) to ensure SME's equitable opportunity to participate in the economy and (f) to promote a greater spread of ownership, particularly of the black people. The purposes from (a) to (c) can be categorized under efficiency and the (d) under competitiveness while (e) to (f) are under equity.

[39] Sections 26–28 stipulates constitution and operation of the CT while Sects. 36–37 states establishment, functions and constituents of the CAC.

[40] Schumann Sasol Ltd v. Prices Daelite Ltd, 2001–2002 CPLR 281 (CT), *available at* http://www.comptrib.co.za/decidedcases/html/23LMMAY01M.htm. Fox and Davis, *supra* note 31, 167–168.

Competition-restrictive horizontal agreements or concerted practices of competitors, either under an association or through covert gatherings, are prohibited under a 'rule of reason' if they substantially lessen or prevent competition in a market. The prohibition can be overcome when pro-competitive gains outweigh the anticompetitive effects; however, the pro-competitive gains are limited to technology, productive efficiency, or other factors related to the competitive effect of restraint.[41] On the other hand, in practice, a per se rule applies to the most serious anticompetitive horizontal agreements, e.g., price fixing, market division, and collusive tendering, without requiring a showing of actual harmful effects or permitting a showing of net efficiency.[42] The per se rule is limitedly extended to a competition-restrictive agreement regarding any other trading condition closely connected to price, quantity, and quality.[43] The exemption from the Act, reflecting other social or economic policies, such as promotion of small-business competitiveness, applies to both standards, rule of reason and per se illegal.[44]

The Act shifted the burden of proof regarding an anticompetitive agreement to a defendant. If firms engaged in a common practice have a common director or substantial shareholder, or reciprocal significant ownership interests, they are presumed to have made the agreement. The presumption can be rebutted when defendant proves that the practice was a normal response to prevailing market conditions.[45] The intent of this policy is to encourage firms related through complex and loosely connected investment structures to dismantle the structures or to make their control relationships more transparent. Agreements entirely among the members of a corporate group of wholly owned subsidiaries or similar structures are not prohibited under either the rule or reason or the per se rule.[46] However, in spite of reforms of the 1998 Competition Act, there had been a rare enforcement action against horizontal restraints.[47] With the 1998 Act, eleven cases were reported to be settled after cartel investigation, and few were reported to be in either the CT or the CAC.[48]

The reason for the under-enforcement of South Africa's anti-cartel policy was analyzed as follows: (i) less focus on cartel enforcement than monopoly enforcement, (ii) low public awareness of cartel-causing damages, and (iii) the difficulty in locating horizontal agreements. First, solving the chronic monopoly and subsequent economic concentration issues in the context of South Africa's economy and

---

[41]Section 4(1)(a) of 1997 Competition Act. *See* OECD (May, 2003), at 22–23.

[42]Section 4(1)(b).

[43]OECD (2003a, b), at 23.

[44]Section 10.

[45]Section 4(1)(b) and Sec. 4(2).

[46]Section 4(5). OECD (2003a, b), at 23.

[47]OECD (2003a, b), at 13 and 23–24. The paper reported two cases, one on an export cartel resulting in the Competition Commission's decline to accept a proposed consent order and fine, and the other on fee and other restrictive practices in the legal profession service sector, resulting in a failure of imposing conditions on an exemption of the sector in a trial.

[48]OECD (2007), at pp. 2–3.

politics takes priority over competition policy. A competition commissioner from South Africa who participated as a panel to the American Bar Association (ABA) Annual Session of Antitrust Law acknowledged that the anti-cartel practice had not taken a priority position in practice.[49] In considering the huge amount of damage to consumers and to the market caused by a cartel, the acknowledgement of the commissioner implied that even experts did not consider seriously the severe damage that a cartel generates in markets let alone the public. Moreover, while a monopoly was externally revealed by market share investigation, a cartel with covert agreements was not easily uncovered by price investigation because it requires additional proof demonstrating collusive behaviors. The inherent difficulty in locating a cartel contributed to under-enforcement of cartel regulation.

In light of such criticism, the 1998 Competition Act was revised with Competition Act of 2009. Among other new characteristics of the new Act, particularly regarding horizontal competition-restricting agreements, Competition Act of 2009 formally enacted leniency program along with serious penalty against individual members of a cartel. According to the new Act, an individual who willfully commit or implicitly acknowledges a cartel activity may be subject to criminal punishment, either a fine not exceeding South African Rand 500,000.00 or imprisonment of not more than 10 years, or both, unless he/she reports to the CCSA the activity with concrete evidence and the CCSA evaluates the report worthy of leniency proceeding. In case the CCSA certified the reporter under leniency program, CCSA should make submission to National Prosecutor's Office in support of leniency.[50]

(2) People's Republic of China (PRC)

1) Shift from Planned Economy to Market Economy which Led to Growing Awareness of Competition Law

The central-planned economy under the reins of the Chinese Communist Party (CCP) has pursued its fundamental reform toward a market-based economy since 1978 when Deng Xiaoping initiated it. Before 1978, the state-owned most enterprises, set prices for almost all goods and services, and assigned workers to enterprises. However, the planned economy brought about enormous inefficiencies such as low production and low quality due to the low incentive for hard-work, or the waste of resources based on inaccurate forecasts.[51] State-owned enterprises (SOEs) with convoluted social objectives tended to bring about inefficient management and a waste of resources. In response to the challenges, reform to provide autonomy and property right to enterprises and farmers greatly expedited the increase of local productivity and activated the emergence of private enterprises. In 1992, when the CCP officially pronounced a socialist market economy as a goal of

[49]Interview with a commissioner, South Africa's Competition Commission (Mar. 31, 2006). The author of the thesis interviewed, on the topic of cartel enforcement, with South Africa's commissioner who participated as a panel in the 2006 ABA Annual Session of Antitrust Law.

[50]Section 76 of Competition Act of 2009.

[51]Owen et al. (2004), pp. 126–127.

the economic reform, price control under the Chinese government was abolished in majority of products in the following sectors: raw materials, food, transportation and light industry goods. 648 out of 737 prices formerly under the governmental control were under a free market mechanism. By 2006, price determination in 90 % of industry was entrusted to the free market mechanism.[52] Private enterprises and foreign investment inflow grew at a tremendous speed. By 2004, the private enterprises, which had occupied only 0.2 % of China's national industrial output,[53] accounted for 55.6 % of GDP, 58.9 % of retail sales, and 62.3 % of exports.[54]

Through economic reform, political leadership became more aware of the anticompetitive harms of undue state control over the economy, and felt a threat from rapidly increasing foreign capital flow, which led to an interest in competition law. Under a strategic plan, the government substantially reduced control over nonessential industries, e.g., electronics and textiles, while retaining control over key industries. Still, industrial associations, consisting of SOEs subject to the control of the government, sanctioned anticompetitive practices of their members and even adopted self-disciplinary prices with function similar to price-cartels. There was no institution in place to correct the inefficiencies in the administrative practices.

As an initial form of competition law, the Countering Unfair Competition Law (CUCL) had worked since 1993 by 2007. The CUCL expressed the intents of Chinese legislators to safeguard the transitional economy with the following goals: wholesome development of the socialist market economy, encouragement of fair competition, curbing unfair competition, and protecting the rights of businesses as well as consumers. The substance of CUCL had the characteristic of a nascent stage in competition law. Article 15 of the CUCL prohibited a broad coverage of anti-competitive business practices, including the banning of price-fixing or bid-rigging, along with traditional unfair trade practices, e.g., business bribes, infringement of business secrets, and misleading advertisements.[55] Since Chinese legislators adopted additional laws regulating price and competition, e.g., Price Law of 1997 and Telecommunications Regulation of 2000 after CUCL, the broad coverage resulted in overlaps with the other laws.[56] However, insufficient subsequent legal

---

[52]Eichner (2012), pp. 590–591.

[53]Report of China's State Statistics Bureau. *See id.* at 127.

[54]*Id.* at 128.

[55]Owen et al. (2004), at 138–139. They argue that a society where legitimacy of competition law is skeptical usually incorporates into its competition law consumer protection, or the issues of unfair practices that promote economic efficiency, which even dominates its competition law practices. On the other hand, in China, the unfair trade practices were supervised by a local agency under the leadership of a local government which had to reflect other local interests, e.g. local development.

[56]For an example in overlaps of bidding-rigging responsibilities, Art. 27 of CUCL states that when bidders collusively act to force up or down the bidding price, or a bidder colludes with a tender-inviter for the purpose of pushing out their competitors, the successful bid shall be invalid, and the supervision and inspection department may impose a fine of not less than RMB 10,000 but not more than RMB 200,000. Meanwhile, Art. 53 of the Law on Tender Invitation and Bidding added, with invalidity of the bidding, that a fine should be not less than 5 % and not more than

process did not coordinate the overlaps.[57] The CUCL, as the initial law, did not have regulations regarding the M&A, market allocation, boycott, and resale price maintenance.[58] The regulation of abuses of administrative monopolies by governmental agencies was seldom enforced due to other public objectives of the law, such as regional development.[59] Meanwhile, the Provisional Rules for Prevention of Monopoly Pricing (effective Nov. 11, 2003) included the prohibition of price coordination, supply restriction, and bid-rigging. The similar treatment of monopoly and cartel practices, however, could confuse business people under the Rules and weakened the warning against collusive behaviors among companies, the market share of which did not reach a monopoly position but still restricted competition significantly. From the competition policy's perspective, while monopolies may sometimes unavoidable, hard core cartels are almost always harmful to consumers under a per se illegal principle and need to be avoided.[60] If the law did not provide a clear division of legitimate and illegitimate business practices, competition law could deter enterprises' pro-competitive behaviors.[61] The scattered rules and regulations of competition regime during the pre-AML era led to overlaps, inconsistency of laws, and impractical usage of the laws.

Chinese legal system has not demonstrated sufficient capabilities to support consistent enforcement of competition law. The National People's Congress (NPC), the legislative body, has a simplistic approval procedure while the Commissions for Legislative Affairs (CLA), under the NPC, researches and proposes a draft with comments from experts. The State Council in the executive branch, mostly in charge of law enactment and enforcement, can act without a legislative grant of authority. The law enforcements are subject to a narrow scope of judicial review, complicated procedure for the review and bias in favor of the government. The judiciary body with much discretion, although supposed to be independent under the Constitution, is exposed to the influence of the leadership in the Communist Party and government at all levels. In addition, due to a lack of *stare decisis*, interpretations of the Supreme People's Court cannot be cited by other courts. As a result, predictability based on precedents is weak.

2) Anti-Monopoly Law

The 2007 Anti-Monopoly Law (AML), consisting of 57 articles, was adopted after more than a decade of discussion from 1994. Three central-governmental

---

(Footnote 56 continued)

10 % of the amount of successful bid, illegal gains be confiscated, and qualification of bidding may be revoked one or two years, along with subsequent public announcement. Criminal responsibilities should be investigated.

[57]OECD GFC (2001), at 5. The paper illustrates the overlap of liabilities of bid-rigging both under Art. 27 of CUCL and Art. 53 of the Law on Tender Invitation and Bidding.

[58]OECD (2007), at 4.

[59]Article 7. *See also* OECD GFC (2003), at 3.

[60]Owen et al. (2004), at 143.

[61]*Id.* at 144.

authorities designated by the State Council, named National Development and Reform Commission (NDRC), State Administration for Industry and Commerce (SAIC), and Ministry of Commerce (MOFCOM), have played divided roles with respect to the AML enforcement. NDRC enforces price-related rules, and SAIC implements non-price-related rules of the AML while MOFCOM is in charge of activating merger control under the AML. The allocation of enforcement powers is characteristics of the 2007 AML subject to criticism that some rules were overlapped between NDRC and SAIC due to hybrid nature of cartelistic practices.

Although the AML is considered as targeting foreign mergers, it also included the banning of horizontal monopoly agreements as cartelistic behaviors under Art. 13. The prohibited cartel activities are (i) price-fixing, (ii) output-limiting, (iii) market allocation, (iv) limiting of the purchase of new technologies or new facilities, (v) joint boycott, and (vi) other agreement determined by the Anti-monopoly Law Enforcement Agency.[62] However, the prohibitions may not be applicable if the parties' aim is (i) to improve technologies, or develop new products, (ii) improve efficiency or unify standards, (iii) improve competitiveness of small to medium enterprises (SMEs), (iv) serve public interest causes, e.g., protection of environment or energy, (v) overcome economic downturn, (vi) secure legitimate interests in foreign trade, e.g., export or import cartel, or economic cooperation, and (vii) other reasons stated by the State Council.[63] The justification will be acknowledged if the agreement does not restrict competition substantially in the relevant market, and if consumers share the benefits of the agreement.[64] The AML, moreover, did not apply to alliances or concerted actions of agricultural producers and rural economic organizations with respect to production, processing, sales, transportation, and storage of agricultural products.[65]

The passed AML, as response to recent cartelistic behaviors of trade associations, prohibits trade associations from organizing companies in their industries to take monopolistic actions.[66] Its penalty for cartel members, an administrative fine amounting to 1–10 % of the sales revenue in the previous year under Art. 46 without criminal penalty, is considered much lower than the level of advanced countries'.[67] In case of a green mung bean cartel, its leader received RMB 1 million (US$ 146,700), almost the highest in the enforcement history of AML. In spite of

[62]Susan Ning, Overview of the Anti-Monopoly Law of China, at 3 (Mar. 2008) (unpublished manuscript, on file with ABA Section of Antitrust).

[63]Article 15. *See* Sharon Mann, Enforcement of China's Antimonopoly Law, at 8 (Mar. 2008) (unpublished manuscript, on file with ABA Section of Antitrust).

[64]Article 15. See Ning (2008), at 4.

[65]Article 56. *See id.*

[66]Xinhua, *China adopts anti-monopoly law*, Aug. 30, 2007, *available at* http://www.chinadaily.com. As a recent case of cartelistic behaviors, instant noodles trade association in China increased price of instant noodles by 10 % in July 2007, thereby causing social antipathy.

[67]Eichner (2012), pp. 602–603.

the conspicuous institutional reforms,[68] China's hesitant stance to adopt the whole competition culture and to focus on consumers' interests under its unique political and legal system might function as impediment to effective cartel regulation. In 2006, when China's vitamin C trade association raised price, U.S. consumers brought class action suit to the Supreme Court of Eastern District New York.[69] Although the AML includes private parties' rights to compensate damages,[70] and to receive relief, such rigorous usage of action in damages, as the U.S. case illustrates, cannot be easily achieved without a rich pool of competition law experts, transparent judicial system, supplemental financial support for competition authorities, and legal institutions to facilitate private actions like class action. However, with growing economic power and global cooperation with U.S. DOJ and JFTC, competition authorities appear to gain weight: the NDRC fined total RMB 407 million yuan (US$ 60.6 million) on eight multinational shipping companies based upon their bid-rigging and market division in 2015.

(3) Mexico

Mexico adopted active industrial policies with the basic idea of protecting so-called the 'infant industry' during the 1960s. Under these policies, the government had taken control over market price and launched state-owned enterprises to reduce the evils of private monopolies under the monopoly prohibition of the 1917 Mexican Constitution.[71] As a result of such policies, Mexico succeeded in promoting some important industries but caused huge inefficiencies and market distortion, particularly collusive practices, due to excessive government control until the mid 1980s.

Around 1984, however, came out negative results from the protection-oriented economic policy, such as the inefficiencies of resource allocations due to few options, high price and low quality, reduced entrepreneurial creativity, and highly concentrated market. The negative points were evaluated to outweigh some successful outcomes of the policy. Such analysis led to a policy shift toward open trade without targeting a specific sector distinguished from the pick-and-choose type policy. The unstable market situations under the closed national market, such as high and variable prices, exploding interest rates, and unpredictable exchange rates, urged an open economic structure. The wide coverage of an open market policy brought about the adoption of free trade agreements (FTAs), free investment, and deregulation policies. Partners of overall FTAs under the open market policy were 43 countries, among which the North American Free Trade Agreement (NAFTA) in

---

[68]In terms of authority, rather than diversity, China tried to bring competition issues to the central authority because the CUCL revealed the lenient practices of local agencies in favor of local interests.

[69]*In re* Vitamin C Antitrust Litigation, 237 F.R.D. 35 (June 7, 2006).

[70]Article 50. Actual loss, defendant's profit, and plaintiff's legal expenses belong to damages. Owen et al. (2004), 147.

[71]OECD (2004a, b), at 12.

1994, and the subsequent FTA with the European Union are famous.[72] The opening of the market expanded the trade in imports and exports, respectively by 1000 % and by 555 % during the 1984–2002 period when economic policies had been shifting.[73] Import liberalization stimulated domestic competition in tradable goods industries. The adoption of the Federal Law of Economic Competition (LFCE) and the creation of the Federal Competition Commission (CFC) were necessary due to Mexico's commitment to the proscription of anticompetitive business conduct under NAFTA.

On the other hand, economic crises, such as the peso crisis of the mid 1990s and subsequent disorders, accompanied the policy shift to open trade.[74] The difficulties led to governmental reacquisition of formerly privatized firms. Although Mexico's economy recovered through strong exports, ex-president Salinas who was in charge of open trade policy and his political successor president Zedillo faced severe criticisms. Competition law and the CFC were considered as involuntary institutions imposed by NAFTA. With the 2002 economic development program of President Fox who was elected democratically, competition policy sustained its position as a prominent tool within the program in spite of insufficient public support. The subsequent practices of the CFC to pursue strong competition policy, the judicial acknowledgement of its authority, and legislators' support of the law, notwithstanding the lobbies of powerful interests, enabled the successful operation of the CFC throughout its development.[75]

The WTO Mexican Telecommunication case occurred in the context where the open trade policy still conflicted with remaining anticompetitive government practices. The General Agreement on Trade in Services (GATS) has a Telecommunications Annex and a Reference Paper, which requires signatory nations to maintain reasonable measures to prevent major suppliers from engaging in or continuing anticompetitive practices.[76] When the other Mexican competition-regulatory agency in the telecommunication and broadcasting sectors, the Federal Telecommunications Commission (COFETEL), authorized multiple Mexican firms to terminate calls in Mexico, it adopted rules that provided the largest Mexican carrier, Telmex, the sole right to set the termination fee and required that all other carriers elevate their prices to the set level. Additionally, the rules required market sharing among the firms that would be available at the Telmex-set price. The U.S. brought a complaint to the WTO by arguing that Mexico arranged a cartel for price-raising and market sharing as an anticompetitive practice not pursuant to the GATS. In this case, mixing public with private restraint,

[72]Hawk B (ed), IALP (2007), at 248; OECD, *id*, at 10.

[73]OECD (2004a, b), at 10. Trade with the U.S. and Canada tripled after the implementation of NAFTA.

[74]*Id*. at 12.

[75]*Id*. at 14.

[76]Article 1(1) of Reference Paper to the Telecommunications Annex to the GATS, reproduced at 36 I.L.M. 367 (1997) and Art. 5(a) of Annex on Telecommunications to the GATS.

the penal held that such rules were against commitments that Mexico made to accede to GATS and Annex on Communication.[77]

Cartels are regulated as either absolute or relative monopolistic practices. The absolute monopolistic practices are prohibited per se and agreements are legally void without allowing any efficiency defense. Meanwhile the relative monopolistic practices may not be found illegal unless the respondent has substantial power in a defined market and fails to prove an efficiency defense.[78] The latter standard represents the rule of reason standard applied to collective boycotts, and other competition-restrictive practices under Art. 10. Section VII as a catch-all provision. The per se prohibition applies to four types of hard-core cartels: price fixing, output restriction, market division, and bid-rigging under Art. 9. Such absolute prohibition has played an important role of eliminating the remaining price constraints. Mexico's law regulated the prices of most goods and services until the mid-1980s and the Ministry of Economics encouraged industry members to discuss and set price levels in business chambers. Still, there remained legal provisions which authorized the federal government to set a maximum price.[79] By reforming price control and business chamber provisions, the market-setting price mechanism was instituted but still there were traditional price setting customs among companies. To overcome this challenge, the 1998 LFCE Regulations specified that certain circumstances would constitute circumstantial evidence of price fixing such as two or more competitors adhering to a price announced by a business chamber.[80]

While the 1998 LFCE had administrative sanctions, such as corrective orders and administrative fines for monopolistic practices, subsequent revisions, in 2006 and 2011, empowered the CFC with measures, such as increasing the maximum level of the fine increasing, 10 % of the annual revenue in Mexico.[81] The 2011 revision of the LFCE granted the CFC power to conduct dawn raids. The CFC under the LFCE had power to refer to prosecutors criminal charges under Mexican Criminal Code against individuals involved at such monopolistic cases as severely affected the necessities market. However, criminal charges appeared to be ineffective in light of the comment of the chairman of the CFC that Mexico had no criminal sanctions.[82]

---

[77]Fox (2006), at 279 and 281–290; Panel Report, Mexico: Measures Affecting Telecommunication Services, WT/DS204/R (2004) and WT/DS204/9/Add.8 (2005).

[78]Article 9 regulates absolute monopolistic practices while Art. 8 does relative monopolistic practices.

[79]Mexico's Const. Art. 28 allows the federal government to set maximum prices for articles or services deemed necessary for the national economy or popular consumption. Article 7 of the LFCE implements the provision by stating that an agreement between the Ministry of Economics and producers to discuss an action necessary to minimize its effect on competition is not a violation of the LFCE.

[80]OECD (2004a, b), 19.

[81]LFCE was revised in 2006, 2011, 2013 and 2014. 2006 revision included leniency program and improved procedures for investigations.

[82]Eduardo Perez Motta, Chairman of Mexico's Federal Competition Commission, Speech at 2007 FLI's IALP Conference. *See id.*

By 2007, the only instance of criminal referral of a price-fixing case, involving an association of tortilla manufactures in 2000, resulted in a public prosecutor's decline to pursue a criminal trial due to the insufficient proof of a charge.[83] As to extraterritorial application, the CFC proclaimed that the LFCE applies to all agents whose actions impact markets in the Mexican territory.[84] However, the CFC has avoided investigating a controversial case by obtaining jurisdiction over foreign entities through voluntary submissions and by focusing on cooperation agreements with foreign experienced competition authorities. Vitamins and citric acid cartels were the two international cartel cases investigated and sanctioned by CFC, after U.S. successful investigation, during the first decade of twenty first century.[85] After experiencing hardship of investigating foreign companies related to the international cartels, the 2006 LFCE adopted leniency provisions so that the first cartelist fully cooperating during the investigation (and a future trial) after report and present sufficient evidence to CFC or COFETEL can receive full immunity from administrative fine while the second and third cartelists can have fines reduced in light of their evidence and chronological order of the filed leniency applications.[86]

Although the LFCE acknowledged no small-firm defenses, small firms were permitted to coordinate business activities under a program administered by the Ministry of Economy for facilitating the creation of one entity or partnerships among small and medium-sized firms and exposes them to scale economies and increased efficiency.[87] As to other exemptions, Art. 28 of Mexican Constitution stated that the state function in 'strategic areas' was not deemed to constitute monopolistic practices, such as the postal service, telegraph and radio telegraphy, petroleum, nuclear energy, electric power, radioactive minerals, the functions of the central bank in producing coins and paper currency. Moreover, export associations, operating as export cartels, are exempted with some requirements.[88] However, the LFCE provides no exception on the ground that a state or local agency undertakes to restrict interstate or foreign commerce. Mexico's Constitution approves the power of federal government to regulate anticompetitive acts of state authorities, e.g., establishing an interstate trade barrier.[89]

[83]The sub-group of the association agreed on different prices and there was no agreement among the association's members to fix a single price. OECD (2004a, b), 19–20.

[84]*Id.* 17. *See also* CFC, Annual Report, 28 (1994).

[85]OECD (2004a, b), 17: UNCTAD, Cross-border anticompetitive practices: The challenges for developing countries and economies in transition, p. 12 (2012).

[86]*Refer to* LFCE.

[87]*See id.* at 20.

[88]Article 6 states five requirements: (i) region's main income source, (ii) the goods not sold or distributed in Mexico, (iii) voluntary membership, (iv) no grant or permit issued, and (v) compliance with the law of the domiciliary state. The English-version of 1998 LFCE is *available at* http://www.apeccp.org.tw.

[89]Mexico's const. Art. 117 s.V and Art. 14 and 15 of LFCE.

After Enrique Peña Nieto took the presidency in 2012, competition law and policy was improved under the Pact for Mexico, a political agreement with other major parties on reform agenda, including competition policy and legal system. Through 2013 constitutional amendment, CFC started to function as a legally independent organ with more commissioners under more democratic and transparent selection process. The Federal Institute of Telecommunications (IFETEL) as the other independent organ replaced the function of the COFETEL. Mexican congress enacted a new LFCE, which repelled the former LFCE. The 2014 LFCE is considered to strengthening and supporting powers of the CFC. Among other things, it made an investigation unit within the CFC separated from its decision-making function, and its resolutions no longer subject to a judicial stay pending the outcome of litigation.[90] Although the legislative reform needs effective enforcement and subsequent regulations, the competition regime should be noted for its advancement in competition policy.

(4) South Korea

South Korea adopted its competition law, the Monopoly Restraint Fair Trade Act (MRFTA) in 1980 after several trials starting from the late 1960s. The enactment of the MRFTA was due to the acknowledgement of politicians that Korea's economy, where conglomerates had maintained oligopoly market structures, could not be strengthened without establishing competitive markets. The MRFTA previously operated under a sub-group of the Ministry of Economic Planning (MEP) until 1994, so the Act did not make an impressive achievement. As the Yong-Sam Kim (YS) administration adopted globalization and competition as a political motto since 1993, the Korea Fair Trade Commission (KFTC), an independent institution from MEP, took the role of implementing competition policy. However, the economic reform of the YS administration was appraised as producing less fruit than expected in 5 years when the Korean economy faced a lack of foreign exchange under the influence of the Asian financial crisis. The YS administration requested rescue funds from the IMF. South Korea had to endure being subject to the conditionality of the IMF loan. The subsequent Dae-Jung Kim (DJ) administration, taking regime during the economic crisis, proclaimed both restoring the economy and establishing a democracy as their main goal. With the pressure on conglomerates to dispose inefficient companies, the DJ administration focused on the restructuring of industries and the restoring of confidence on Korea's credibility. The KFTC, the institution in charge of competition policy, went forward to regulate inefficient conglomerates and improved its reputation among the public.

Since 1994, when a KFTC was launched as an independent commission from other ministries, the number of cartel cases amounted to more than 20 annually as the Table 5.1 demonstrates. The serious attitude of KFTC against cartel regulation went along with the independent operation of competition authorities since the surcharge was contributed to the yearly budget of the KFTC and cartel surcharges

[90] Aydin (2015), pp. 13–16.

Table 5.1 Total cartel cases at KFTC with imposed sanction

Year	'81–'92	'93	'94	'95	'96	'97	'98	'99
Cases	91	16	19	26	36	22	37	34
Year	'00	'01	'02	'03	'04	'05	'06	'07
Cases	47	43	47	23	35	46	45	44
Year	'08	'09	'10	'11	'12	'13	'14	'15
Cases	65	61	62	71	41	45	76	88

occupied more than half of the total surcharges of the KFTC. KFTC, however, brought a few criminal referrals with all of them ending up with a fine on the culprits.

It was with a more democratized bureaucracy and political turmoil due to the conditionality of IMF rescue fund that significant improvement of investigations and criminal referrals was made. As Korea's economy was under pressure to root open and create competitive structure as a condition of the IMF rescue loan, competition law enforcements grew strict. The level of cartel enforcement went seriously increasing. Although the concentration of economic power in conglomerates and mergers were the major issues to which the competition authority of the KFTC devoted itself to satisfy the structural adjustment program of the IMF, surcharges against cartels and criminal referral cases of the KFTC have increased since 2000, as illustrated below.[91] The KFTC announced that the proportion of cartel surcharges out of the total of surcharges was on average 61.2 % during 20 years and 96.2 % in 2005.[92] The KFTC, with its utmost interest, even proclaimed 2004 as the year for sweeping cartels and 2006 as the year of regulatory improvement (Table 5.2).

Further adoption of incentive systems, such as the leniency program in 1997 and rewards to whistle blowers in 2002, contributed recent increase of cartel cases. An initial cooperator, which submits a paper report to the KFTC, prior to launching of an initial investigation, can be exempted from the KFTC's sanction under the leniency program. The qualification for exemption can be extended to cover a second reporter before investigation and an initial cooperator after its investigation even through verbal reports. The discretionary exemption is changed to mandatory exemption.[93] As the table below reveals, the leniency program has brought about tremendous effect particularly since 2005. Meanwhile, a reward system has been operating since 2002 to provide a monetary award to a person who reported to the KFTC an illegal cartel with submission of evidence. The maximum of the reward

[91]KFTC (2004a), at 127–128 (2004b); KFTC (2014), at 171 (in 2001, there was no cartel case with surcharge imposed).

[92]The average proportion is calculated from 1986 to 2005. KFTC, *Proportion of Surcharge against Cartel* [카르텔 과징금 비율], *available at* http://www.ftc.go.kr.

[93]The mandatory exemption consists of no sanction to the first reporter or cooperator and 30 % reduced sanction to the second reporter.

Table 5.2 Surcharge against collusive behavior (cartel) of KFTC

Year	‘81–‘97	‘98	‘99	‘00	‘01	‘02	‘03	‘04	‘05
Cases with surcharge (S)	30	19	15	12	7	14	9	12	21
Total S (US$ mil = KW 1.1 bil)	18.2	29.1	32.87	180.7	25.2	48.3	99.85	26.5	226.7
Average S	0.61	1.53	2.19	15.06	3.60	3.45	11.1	2.21	10.8
Criminal referral	4	0	0	3	4	0	5	3	4
Year	‘06	‘07	‘08	‘09	‘10	‘11	‘12	‘13	‘14
Cases with surcharge (S)	27	24	45	21	26	35	24	28	56
Total S (US$ mil = KW 1.1 bil)	100.5	279.1	179.5	48.1	532.6	525.4	362.6	331.6	699.5
Average S	3.72	11.6	3.99	2.29	20.5	15.0	15.1	11.84	12.49
Criminal referral	3	7	5	5	1	8	2	13	36

KFTC (2014), at 36 and 61

Table 5.3 The application of leniency program at KFTC

Year	99	00–01	02	03	04	05	06
Case (surcharge-imposed case)	1(1)	1(1)	2(1)	1(1)	2(0)	7(6)	7(6)
Year	07	08	09	10	11	12	13
Case	10(10)	21(20)	17(13)	18(18)	32(29)	13(12)	23(23)

See id. at 182; KFTC (2012), at 204–205

has increased from US$ 1–3 million. During the 11-year-long operation, the system had exposed 39 illicit cartels with total award reaching no more than US$ 632,500 on overall reporters.[94] A more generous level of award will expectedly contribute more to activating the reward system (Table 5.3).

The KFTC had initial cases to practice the extraterritorial application of the MRFTA through investigating international cartel cases, in the vitamin and graphite electrode industry, in 2004. The investigations ended up with issuing surcharges to multinational companies without a branch in Korea. In May 2010, The KFTC successfully revealed an international cartel of air-cargo carriers' fixing freight rate and imposed total US$ 113 million surcharge on twenty-one airlines through formal procedure for the first time in the world.[95] KFTC, after having a leniency report from a member airline of the cartel, cooperated in the investigation through raid on

[94]KFTC (2014), at 171–172.

[95]KFTC (2011), at 171 (2011) (the U.S. and Canada used plea bargaining, resulting in no trial, and EU's decision was issued later than KFTC).

members' offices and continuous communication with US DOJ and EU Competition Commission.

The KFTC has promoted consumer awareness through actively investigating cases related to a large scope of consumers. In a school uniform bid-rigging and price-fixing case, major uniform manufacturers and distributors made price ranges in each locality and interrupted official bids at schools. The KFTC issued a large surcharge against the manufacturers and placed a criminal referral against major implementers under the violation of Art. 19(1) of the MRFTA.[96] Subsequently, 3525 consumers who purchased the uniforms with a high price brought a private suit to a court to redress monetary damages caused by the fixed price and received around a total US$ 217,000.[97] After crushing the cartel, the uniform price went down.

(5) Analysis

First, complex institutions of competition law are to be adopted when a national economy, after experiencing a limitation in inner growth, opens its market to foreign companies. The DCs face the necessity of having a competition policy and effective implementation when they raise the level of development of a market economy beyond an autarky economic structure and facilitate companies' business activities.[98] Although they might have a basic level of regulatory legislation on unfair business practices when they do not fully open their market, the legislation is likely to be under-enforced with insufficient support for and less emphasis on competition. In the PRC, for example, the CACU included basic regulations on anticompetitive activities, such as hard core cartels, with other business torts. It was after China acceded to the WTO when it adopted its complex competition-regulating legislation including anti-cartel provisions. Without competition pressure from global markets, companies do not devote their energies to improving their strength, thereby leading to collusion among competitors or abuse of monopoly power to maintain their existent positions. Cartel regulation is under

[96]Article 19(1) of MRFTA, under the title of prohibition of unfair collaborative acts, states that no enterpriser shall agree with other enterprisers by contract, agreement, resolution, or any other means to jointly engage in an act, or let others do an activity, for example, (i) an act fixing, maintaining, or changing prices, (ii) an act determining terms and conditions for transactions of goods or services, or payment of prices thereof, and (viii) any practice that substantially lessens competition in a particular business area by means of interfering with or restricting the activities or contents of business. In addition, Art. 315 of Korea's Criminal Code impose maximum 2-year imprisonment or seven thousand dollars on bid-riggers.

[97]Jin-Hee Lee, *Did you remember school uniform suit 4 years ago: court decided that the manufacturer redress damages to parents* [4년 전, 교복소송 기억하십니까? 법원, "교복제조사, 학부모에게 배상하라" 판결], Chungnam Sisa, Jun. 28, 2005, *available at* http://www.bjynews.com/news/read.php?idxno=9348.

[98]*See* Taylor (2006), at 74. Taylor mentions Papua New Guinea's historic stance as the foundation of his argument that an important precondition for competition law is an effective institutional setting and threshold level of economic development but did not further explains the meaning of the effective institutional setting.

more attentions when the market mechanism to secure free and fair competition becomes more pronounced and when the awareness that cartels cause tremendous damages and inefficiency is widely spread to market systems. Governments with a plan of economic development propose competition laws, the result of which depends on the political structure of each country. In the PRC, the National Congress usually passes drafts from local governments while, in South Korea, the Congress vetoed governmental drafts several times in the 60s and early 70s.

Second, the serious enforcement of competition law depends to a significant degree on politics where institutional, financial, and public support derives from. The rigorous enforcement of competition law, particularly cartel regulation, needs political support. For instance, South Africa put serious effort into the enforcement of competition law since the democratic government representing the majority of the black people oriented economic reforms toward open market and competition in 1994. In Mexico, an open market and competition policy were adopted in 1984, which succeeded through the democratized government of the Fox administration in 2002. In South Korea, strengthened competition law, initiated in the 1993 Yong-Sam Kim administration, was rigorously enforced in the 1998 Dae-Jung Kim administration and the subsequent 2002 Moo-Hyun Roh administration. Sometimes strengthened competition policy was one of the conditions or requirements in negotiations with oversee counterparties, such as Mexico's commitment in NAFTA, or the conditionality of a rescue loan from the IMF. People representing the weak part of a national economy opposed a competition policy as well as an open market policy, but governments with a democratic foundation and with benefits from strong export increases could sustain their original positions.

Third, development of a legal system contributes to the foundation and progress of competition law including cartel regulations. Administrative decisions with respectable legal and economical reasonings, judicial holdings under consistent and reasonable interpretations, and legislative support for a specialized governmental agency in charge of competition policy are vital elements for furthering competition law since transparent decision-making and a review process with predictable results come from the formerly illustrated legal facilities. The 2013 legislative reform of LFCE in Mexico under the Pact for Mexico was a good example. Based upon legislative history of LFCE and judicial precedents that affirmed the former statutory scheme of its competition authorities, the 2013 LFCE strengthened the function of the CFC and IFETEL. Currently, Mexican competition authorities are not considered any more as weak or ineffective to collect fine.[99]

Moreover, the World Bank (WB) recommended that developing countries should put an emphasis on institutional strengthening rather than enacting competition laws that may be misunderstood or improperly enforced.[100] Although it does not further analyze the meaning of institutional strengthening, it is constructed

[99]Aydin (2015), pp. 6–13; OECD (2004a, b), at 13–14. Mexican Supreme Court had held that a large part of LFCE including the statutory scheme of the CFC was constitutional.

[100]Taylor (2006), 74.

as capacity-building of the institution in charge of enforcing competition laws. Next to open market economy and democratic political system, the legal system including administrative and judicial function is the most important institution to develop competition laws in light of the experiences of the advanced countries, e.g., the U.S., the UK, and Germany. The recommendation of the WB confirms the argument of this thesis.

Fourth, cartel regulations in the DCs have presumption provisions with a background policy. In South Korea, Art. 19(5) states that, where two or more enterprisers are committing any categorized act which practically restricts competition in a particular business area, the enterprises shall be presumed to have committed an unfair collaborative act despite the absence of an explicit agreement to engage in such an act. Such presumption provision has its intent of relieving the less experienced competition agency, the KFTC, from finding the proof of a secret cartel agreement itself. The Supreme Court in South Korea held, with regard to the provision, that the KFTC does not need direct proof of an agreement for the unfair collaboration, or a cartel, as long as it can prove that competitors engage in a cartelistic activity which restricts competition in a market.[101] In Mexico, the 1998 LFCE regulations include the provisions specifying that the CFC will deem that certain circumstances, such as when two or more competitors adhere to a price announcement from a business chamber, will constitute circumstantial evidence of price fixing. The regulation implies that the CFC has a policy to get rid of traditional price control from business chambers consisting of industry members.[102] In South Africa, when firms engaged in a common practice have a common director, shareholder, or reciprocal ownership, they are presumed to have agreed, which can be rebutted by a showing that the practice was a normal response to prevailing market conditions.[103] The presumption in the policy is to encourage companies related through complex and loosely connected investment structures to dismantle the structure or at least to make the control relationship transparent.[104]

However, the wide application of the presumption provisions needs caution because pro-competitive business activities may satisfy the elements of the provisions. To secure sufficient counter-proof, a proof of the absence of the agreement, to overcome such presumption is an almost impossible burden to related parties. The role of the presumption provisions is confined to supplementing the lack of circumstantial evidences for a cartel and cartel enforcement of less-skilled competition authorities. The presumption provision of South Korea has not been used often since the judicial body approved the interpretation.[105]

Fifth, since economic research is not pervasive in the context of DCs to back up pure efficiency or consumer welfare-based competition enforcement, the objectives

[101] 대법원 [The Supreme Court of Republic of Korea], 99두 6514, 6521 (Mar. 15, 2002).

[102] OECD (2004a, b), 19.

[103] Section 4(1)(b) and 4(2) of 1999 Competition Act.

[104] OECD (2003a, b), 23.

[105] Email interview with Hang-Rok Oh, public officer, KFTC (Jan. 2007).

that the competition laws pursue take into consideration a development-perspective as well as a competition-perspective. The 2007 AML of PRC has, besides the original objectives of competition law, e.g., protection of fair competition and enhancing economic efficiency, the unique objectives in China's context, which are maintenance of 'public interests' and promotion of the healthy development of socialist market economy. The public interest cause works as a concrete exception to a monopoly agreement including a cartel agreement.[106] Although the exception illustrates saving energy, protecting the environment, and providing disaster relief, the public interests can include the stabilization of an economic situation, development of the whole economy, or the increase of employment.[107] Foreign investors worry about the patriotic application of the 'public interest' through protecting of a domestic market from foreign companies. China's concerns about both the acquisition of domestic companies by multinational corporations (MNCs) and additional competition for small and middle-sized enterprises (SMEs) make the worry severe.[108] Although the ambiguity of public interest dilutes the cause of competition law, however, such worry is not likely to bring about general partial enforcement. As the practices of competition in advanced countries reveal, only an insignificant portion of regulation cases apply the exception.

Every country, either developed or developing, needs an exception to cartel regulation enforcement as well as in other competition law issues. In consideration of the level of economy in more developed economies, the DCs cannot avoid allowing more exemptions to cartel regulations than advanced market economies. Among other things, the cartel for enhancing competitiveness of SMEs is approved in all four DCs above,[109] and other countries, e.g., the de minis rule of Hungary.[110] Advanced competition law with a focus on efficiency does not currently approve such an exemption but treat SME issues with monopoly restraint. However, in the

---

[106]Article 15(iv) states monopoly agreements may be exempt to service public interests such as saving energy, protecting the environment, providing disaster relief.

[107]OECD interprets, similar to the cases of Germany or other EU nations, that public interest refers to economic situation and employment, etc. *See* OECD GFC, China Sess. I, at 4. Concretely, Art. 15(v), exemption for crisis cartel, is for stabilization of an economic situation. Para. (vi), exemption for international trade, is related to economic development. Para. (vii) is the general exemption provision which allows the power to specify to the State Council.

[108]Owen et al. (2004), 131–133.

[109]Section 10 of the '98 Competition Act in South Africa. In Mexico, the LFCE does not provide any SME exception, but, so as to encourage scale of economies, the Economics Ministry' program for integrating companies with small and middle size, allows the establishment of a single price by the joint venture or activities and small firms' participation in the venture. In South Korea, Art. 19 (2).VI. enumerates the enhancement of competitiveness of SMEs as an exemption of the unfair collusive acts. PRC still has the perspective that repetitive investment at low levels by small businesses generates suicidal competition. In 1999, the Bureau of Civil Aviation prohibited airlines from offering air ticket discounts, citing the adverse effect of price competition on the healthy development of the airline industry. *See* Owen et al. (2004), 132.

[110]Hungarian competition law in 1996 has a de minis rule stating that agreements of minor importance, regardless of their content, are not prohibited if the combined market share of the parties is below 10 %. Vissi (1999) at 558–559.

past, even the U.S. had antitrust law served to protect small firms from competition.[111] Relatively insufficient resources compared to industrialized countries, the urgent necessity to increase competitiveness of small companies in open markets, and the large number of small companies and their importance in domestic markets support the SMEs exemptions from cartel regulation in the DCs. Similar to the SMEs exemptions, the other exemptions in the DCs need to demonstrate policy bases so that the exemptions may not extend to unreasonable cases, in the DCs. Placing the policy bases with respect to competition-promotion within proper time plan under regular governmental screening can avoid the possibility of the abuse of the exemption.

5.3 Building Consensus to Enforce Cartel Regulation

A. Cartel Regulations Within Competition Policies

Competition laws in DCs, where a competition culture is not developed to a sophisticated level, have simple but overbroad types of cartel regulations, thereby omitting regulation over some cartels and making the uniqueness of cartel regulation vague. On the other hand, the competition laws in DCs often have the regulations of other business torts as the CUCL of PRC demonstrated. The less delicate divisions of cartel regulations from other business torts, however, are inappropriate tools to cope with the competition-restricting activities of cartels, which require sophisticated investigation skills with expertise knowledge, an understanding of the importance of competition toward economic development, and political support. Cartels are treated similarly to a misdemeanor or as an act with a low penalty in spite of large damages. Such under-enforcement causes repetitive commissions of cartels because their large profits outweigh penalties. The large profit may lead to bribery for maintaining their existent positions. The under-enforcements of cartel regulations are usual phenomena of DCs where the primitive level of cartel regulation is established or competition laws including cartel regulation are implemented with a lack of experience and insufficient resources.

Some cartels give a positive effect to the development of a market economy in the DCs although the effect is temporary. Export cartels do not generate harm to domestic market mechanisms and domestic consumers unless a product returns to the exporting country. Cartels among SMEs can form a foundation for further economic development by promoting economic cooperation in the weak part of economies. Similar to the 'infant industry' defense in international trade law, SMEs cartels need special treatment as bases of future economic growth. However, the inefficiencies from the restriction of competition, when accumulated enough to

[111]Owen et al. (2004), 124.

function as impediments to a market mechanism, will drag down the impetus of corporate entrepreneurship and further growth of an economy.

The initial institution of cartel regulation, although needed to be adopted by LDCs, is to be transformed into a complex competition law which has cartel regulations as a part. The appropriate time for this transformation is no later than when economic development in DCs reaches the high-income level under categories of DCs, e.g., Mexico.[112] Alternatively, in the case where a political motive drives competition policy, e.g., South Africa and China, the time to transform is when the economic development of a country reaches the middle-income level.[113] The cartel regulation is not effective without fully understanding competition in relationship to economic development. The high degree of economic development necessitates a competition policy including a cartel regulation because inefficiency in national market is a main obstacle to high economic growth, which can be effectively overcome with a competition law regime.

On the other hand, cartel rules may have the plural objectives or the exemptions of competition law reflecting diverse economic situations, political backgrounds, legal traditions and cultures of commerce of each country. The fair distribution of economic development or the protection of SMEs or rural sectors is an example. However, the acknowledgement of such objectives should not deter the effective enforcement of cartel regulation because active cartel enforcement does benefit both the sound growth of domestic economy and fair distribution of wealth to consumers.

B. Economic Development and Competition Law

(1) Development Without Competition?

This chapter tries to answer the question whether economic development is possible without a competition policy including a cartel regulation.[114] Although economic development needs the private entities' strenuous efforts to raise their wealth, a type of public policy, so-called industrial policy, can accelerate value-creation in the private sectors toward economic development. An industrial policy has been found in many countries in many different forms, although some countries with a strong competition policy are reluctant to use the term. In order to figure out clearly the relationship between competition policy and economic

---

[112]According to the UNCTAD Handbook of statistics, having a current GDP per capita above US$ 4.500 is considered a part of the high-income level group of DCs. UNCTAD (2005), at 12.

[113]DCs with a per capita GDP between US$ 1000 and 4500, e.g. South Africa, is in the middle-income level group. *See id.* While China belonged to the low income level group in 2005, China's per capita GDP approached US$2458 in 2007. China's overall GDP in 2007 reached $3.249 trillion, the fourth largest in the world. *See* US Department of State, Bureau of East Asian and Pacific Affairs (Apr. 2008), *available at* http://www.state.gov/r/pa/ei/bgn/18902.htm (last visited on Apr. 21, 2008).

[114]In this chapter, competition policy includes cartel regulation and its active enforcement as the inevitable area.

development, the question of whether industrial policy can achieve economic development without competition policy is to be answered.

1) Defining Industrial Policy and its Effect in relation to Competition Policy

Industrial policy is described as state activities involving the economy, including all policies, which aim at an increased industrial performance in general.[115] In the broadly defined meaning, it looks to include competition policy as competition policy belongs to a state economic policy. However, the distinction between the two polices is on the goal. While an industrial policy targets at increasing national industrial performance, the competition policy aims at increasing competition in a market, thereby facilitating efficient allocation of economic resources.[116] An increase in national wealth through industrial performance can be made in a short term without increasing competition. Meanwhile, increasing competition in a market might cause to decrease national wealth in a situation when competitive foreign companies take their profit out of the domestic market. In light of the situations above mentioned, both policies look to have different effects on national wealth.

Arguably, industrial policy has three types of patterns to pursue economic development: firm-size oriented policy, sector-oriented policy, and framework condition improving policy. To analyze the relationship of industrial policy with competition policy, it would be more accurate to examine each policy type from a competition policy perspective.

First, a firm-size-oriented policy is created to facilitate large and powerful corporations, so-called national champions. As to the policy, research and empirical data indicated that in the long term the policy could produce such negative result that large corporations were not successful in further developing economies while the policy would cause positive effects in the short term.[117] For instance, the South Korean government's unbalanced industrial policy in favor of conglomerates in the 1960s and 1970s led to a market concentration, corruptive relationships with bureaucrats, a shortage of medium-sized firms, and high market barriers for innovative small enterprises with new technology in the 1980s and 1990s.[118]

Second, a sector-oriented policy makes an economy grow through focused investments and governmental support on several industries with a strategic economic development plan. The two main examples are the French government's emphasis on the defense industry after WWII through public procurements of large projects, and Mexico's regulatory policy on the transport, telecommunication, and financial sector.

---

[115]Immenga (1999), at 346.

[116]Scherer (1994), 2.

[117]Baumol (1990) and Fikentscher (1995), at 116–117. The main positive outcomes are economies of sale, learning-by-doing, economies of scope (spin-off) and lower transaction costs while negative outcomes are inefficiencies from monopoly and rent-seeking.

[118]Park (2006), 2–5.

However, the sector-oriented policy has the high risk of being misled by insufficient information and asymmetrical information. Economists point out the possibility of government failure through a state not possessing enough information to correct future planning.[119] In addition, a state may have less of an ability to obtain valuable information involving markets than firms, subject to industrial policy, with a wide social network.[120] The contributions of the three strategic industries in Mexico are outweighed by inefficiencies, high prices, and government failures.[121] The anticompetitive price-fixing in Mexico's telecommunication industry was acknowledged by the WTO panel.[122] In the Mexican Telecommunication termination fee[123]-fixing rule case, after Mexico acceded to the WTO agreement to liberalize and open its telecommunication market, a major issue was the rule of the Mexican regulatory agency which endowed the right to set the termination fee on the largest Mexican carrier, Telmex, and required the other authorized carriers to share the market at the price set by Telmex. The U.S., which argued that the rule which allows Mexico to operate a cartel facilitates anticompetitive practices, won the dispute. The WTO panel decision held that the cartel activities were not relieved from anticompetitive behaviors on the bases that they operated as state acts in the name of public interest and industrial policy.[124] On the contrary, to its former focus on industrial policy, the French government pursued a competition policy under the Treaty of Rome during the process of its integration into EU.[125] The past experiences of government failure in the 1970s and 1980s, e.g., unfruitful public assistance to the steel, textile, and machine tool industry, were reasons for such policy shift.[126]

Third, there is a framework condition improving policy, which indirectly affects national industrial performance and competitiveness. Infrastructures to stabilize economic conditions, e.g., transportation, level of education of workers, and tax burdens on business as whole, are important industrial frame work conditions that need to be focused on by public officers and legislators. Article 157 of the Treaty of Rome includes more concrete policies, such as the adjustment of industries to structural changes, the development of favorable conditions to inter-company

[119]Chang (2003), at 136–137. Chang cites Burton and Grossman.

[120]*Id.*

[121]Motta (2007), at 216–220 and 245–247.

[122]Panel Report, Mexico: Measures Affecting Telecommunications Services, WT/DS204/R (June 1 2004). Mexico did not appeal. *See* WT/DS204/9/Add.8 (Aug. 19, 2005).

[123]The 'termination fee' is the price which Mexican carriers charge foreigners to receive in Mexico calls originating abroad, a considerable portion of which the U.S. carriers were obliged to pay. Fox and Davis (2007), at 170.

[124]*Id.* at 169–72.

[125]Stoffaes, Speech at 2007 Fordham Conference, in *supra* note 24, at 256. *See id.* at 260. Politically, France recently experienced a resurgence of industrial nationalism in front of a series of international mergers, but to a much less degree than the degree of former industrialization in the 1960s and 70s.

[126]*Id.* at 259–260.

cooperation, and the improved usage of innovation and technology. Such policies contribute to promoting the competitive advantage of industrial locations in international business. Although the development of inter-company cooperation may conflict with the promotion of competition, the article states that it should not provide a basis for the EC to introduce measures, which might lead to a distortion of competition.

2) Limitations of Industrial Policy: the Importance of Competition Policy

Industrial policy without the consideration of its impact on competition produces negative results on economy, which impede further economic development. In an economy under the strong control of governmental policies, competition within a market is less severe than expected. It is because the focus of companies on competition in a market is affected by their incentives to obtain benefits from governmental policies. In addition to the less focus on competition of private companies, collaborative behaviors led by governmental policies diluted the importance of cartel regulation under competition law. As a result, restrictive business behaviors of existent companies, including cartel activities, tend to be condoned or treated less severely than other economic regulations. As restrictive business practices prevail, economic inefficiency increases and functions as hurdles to further economic growth and competitiveness between industries. In the long term, economic benefits through focus merely on industrial policies, which neglect competition policy, may be outweighed by subsequent diseconomies.

In addition, industrial policy itself is not a panacea to cure national poverty but is susceptibly exposed to the exclusive activities of existent market participants in order to maintain their inefficiencies, thereby tending to be corrupted. Moreover, as a government has less incentive than market participants and less of a chance to be accessible to up-dated information than private parties, the governmental-forming policy generates un-intended inefficiencies, obsolete policy decisions, and avoidance of responsibility, thereby causing a failure of public policy.[127]

The popularity of a privatization and liberalization policy under neo-liberalism before 2008 economic turmoil reflected governments' efforts to follow the success of shifting governmental control to private control under a market system. As the former example of Mexico demonstrated, protection-oriented industrial policies caused a lower level of competitiveness in the Mexican economies. Rooting a competition culture into industries has been progressing under the sincere efforts of the Mexican government. Some advanced countries which focused on improving competitiveness and revenue in the domestic industry, e.g., the U.S. and West Germany, have developed strong competition policies including strict anti-cartel enforcement. The Treaty of Rome that adopted market liberalism and competition policy originally from the Anglo-Saxon countries, such as the UK and U.S., has invoked a competition culture into other countries with less liberalized economic systems as shown by the former example of France. Still, in France, some

[127]Immenga, *supra* note 117, 348.

industries, e.g., electricity, are under state regulation. Providing such a public service is, however, not an automatic exemption from competition rules. Public service offering companies, either state-owned or private-owned, may not be engaged in monopolistic practices unless they are in an inevitable situation.

3) Temporary Protection of so-called 'Infant Industry'

Public policy to protect the so-called infant industry[128] for a temporary period is needed. If not, competitive foreign companies may dominate entire industries. Highly competitive industries in industrialized countries demonstrate the effectiveness of protective policies, e.g., Toyota of Japan in 1930s, and manufacturing industries of the U.S. in 1830s.[129] However, it is noticeable that developing countries with fear that foreign companies take control over domestic markets have kept a negative attitude in opening up their markets, even in the mature industries. Such protective policies generated uncompetitive infrastructures, thereby causing harm to consumers who had no choice but to select low-quality and high-priced products or services in less efficient markets. With existing cartel practices accumulating, the protective industrial policies cause a lot of damages and inefficiency in the market. In the long run, the policies can impede the development of competitive industries, contrary to the original goal of the industrial policy. For example, South Korea's legal service market had banned the operation of any branch of foreign law firms into the country until 2009 when the National Assembly passed the Foreign Legal Consultant Act which allowed a branch of a foreign law firm to have consultation regarding laws of a country where the firm was licensed or to represent a client in international arbitration where applicable law is foreign law or/and international law.[130] The result of long-lasting strong protection policy was high-priced legal services and the stagnancy of market growth. Although Korea has almost 120 year-long history of modern legal services and the scope of Korea had grown around the tenth largest in the global trade, the scope of the legal service market had remained much less than those of other countries. In 2007 when Korean legal service market has around US$ 1.4 billion in sales, only 0.2 % of GDP,[131] the

[128]'Infant industry' came from infant industry argument for protectionism. Infant industry means an industry which does not have economies of scale as other competitors from industrialized countries but high potential to contribute to economic development in developing countries. The industry needs to be protected until it attains similar economies of scale.

[129]In the 1830s, the average tariff of the U.S. was 40 %, the highest in the world, allowing the development of manufacturing industries until World War II when the country achieved the manufacturing supremacy. More recently in 1939 Japan kicked out General Motors to protect Toyota which at the time was uncompetitive in the global market. Wikipedia, Infant Industry, *available at* http://en.wikipedia.org/wiki/Infant_industry (visited on Apr. 29, 2008).

[130]The backdrop for opening up traditionally closed legal market was the Free Trade Agreement with the U.S. and the negotiation of the Doha Development Agenda (DDA) which required the government to open its legal service market.

[131]2006 GDP of South Korea is around US$ 888 billion. Jung-Won Ryu, *South Korea's scope of legal service market and its opening* (Nov. 24, 2004), *at* http://www.lawtimes.co.kr (visited on Nov. 16, 2007).

proportion of the U.S., UK, Canada, and Japan's legal service market to their GDP has remained around 2 % of GDP.

(2) Economic Development Through Competition

When industries grow out of their nascent period, they need to be exposed to a certain level of competition for further development. As companies grow larger, they shall face higher level of competition both in domestic and international market. Competition in itself has proved as an incentive in making economic development possible by focusing companies' attentions to consumers' concerns, thereby leading to innovation and better service. High-level business culture with focus on consumers' interests can be developed through cartel regulation.

A trade liberalization policy pursuing a free market system needs competition policy as its complimentary measure. Although trade policy for welfare-maximization needs governmental intervention into a market, the intervention that drives the focus of companies toward a governmental measure can cause inefficiencies in markets and, in a case of policy failure, welfare losses.[132] Meanwhile, competition policy focuses on raising efficiency and drives the attention of companies toward consumers through the establishment of a competition-facilitating scheme. Under the open economies, which have been involved in the competitive international trade, domestic competition law can expose domestic companies to the discipline of market mechanisms in advance. In order to correct derivative negative effects of trade policy, governments need to use advantages of competition policy.

Particularly, when cartel regulations are not effective in domestic competition law, enterprises tend to collude with strong foreign competitors and cause price increases and market allocations. As cartel members want to maintain their existent market share and revenue, they reveal exclusive behaviors to new market participants, thereby treading down the potential chance of developing new products or increasing market share. As a result, new enterprises face many blocks in order to participate in the market with existent participants without having the chance to compete with each other based on merit.

Effective enforcement of cartel regulation brings about many benefits. The reduction of cartels transfers wealth from companies to consumers. Price decrease and market share shift due to new participants are usual market phenomenon after cartels were crushed. Consumers with more product selections may be educated to find a better product, thereby facilitating the possibility of competitive enterprises gaining higher market share and revenue.

[132]Akbar (2003), at 5. Akbar distinguishes trade policy from competition policy. Trade policy focuses on government activity with basis on multilateral negotiations to be applied ex-ante. Meanwhile, competition policy emphasizes on private entities under a cases-by-case approach to be applied on ex-post basis.

(3) Synthesis: Harmonizing Cartel Regulation and Economic Development

A free market system is a vital connecting tool between cartel regulation and economic development. Under the state-regulatory economic system, market participants pay more attention to obtaining public assistance by winning public contests rather than focusing on attracting consumers in markets. The historical experience of the collapse of the former Soviet Union demonstrates that a state-planning economy or dirigisme does not bring about growth in economic wealth and welfare. Unless in an extreme depression period when a free market system did not operate effectively enough to distribute products and resources to people, competition law including cartel regulation can promote economic development through invoking competition mechanism into free market economy.

Competing private entities' cartel behaviors in normal free markets deceitfully transfers welfare from consumers to sellers through high-priced and low-quality products or boycotting new competitors from entry. The inefficiency caused by the cartel and investment into the maintenance of status quo rather than innovation are the outcomes of a cartel. While some monopoly practices cause net pro-competitive effects outweighing anticompetitive effect, cartel behaviors directly exploit consumers' welfare and causes inefficiency. Figure 5.2 illustrates comparison between competition policy and industrial policy in the pursuit of economic development.

Governmental intervention leads to regulated competition, and goes with market protection. The growth of corporations under state-intervening and protective market may function well in a temporary period, but does not constitute a strong incentive to innovate themselves. If economic development is not limited to the temporary growth of corporation but includes growth of wealth of the total population and the rooting of an economic structure and legal institution for furthering autonomous economic growth, deprival of consumers' welfare as well as a

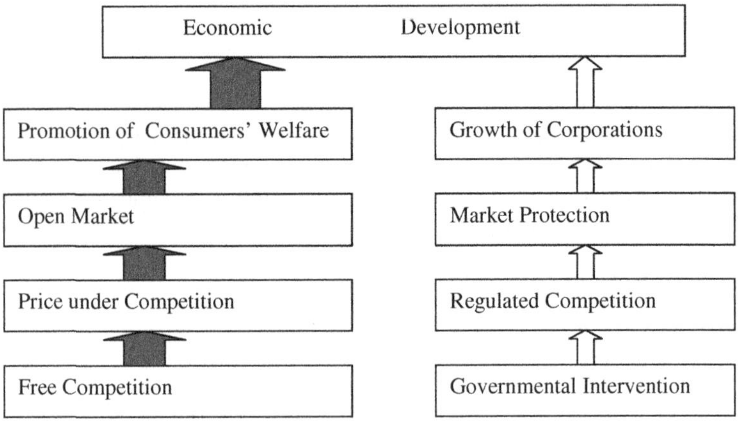

Fig. 5.2 Competition policy and industrial policy

split-over of cartel activities remaining in the market will operate as hurdles to further economic development.

Market economy has proved that a free and competitive market itself can be a strong incentive to further investment and development. Free market established under competition policy produces low priced high quality products. Corporations invest into technologies for efficient production. Such a free competitive market does not wither but enhance its size when the corporations face an open market. The structure of open, free, and competitive market contributes to promoting consumers' welfare. In the long run, it provides great institutional support to economic development.

Industrial policy toward economic development in this sense needs to adopt competition policy. Mexico's chairman of CFC confirmed the importance of competition policy by stating that industrial policy should be carefully tailored to consumers' interests by counteracting the lobbying efforts from existing firms.[133] In addition, the EU's Commissioner of Competition, Neelie Kroes, stated that industrial policy should not seek to shield domestic industry but to place conditions for market participants to flourish with increasing competition.[134] The WTO members with a high level of market economy are equipped with an effective competitive environment, which is evaluated as a comparative advantage which trains their companies under a global-level competitive pressure.[135] Anti-cartel law enforcement is as an important policy measure the very condition for market participants with good quality products to flourish.

It is understandable that the EU placed a priority on competition policy over industrial policy under title XVI of the industrial policy of the Treaty of Maastricht founding EU. The Treaty announced that it should offer no basis to bring any action that might produce distortions of competition. When the EU's position of prioritizing competition policy including cartel regulations is agreed with by other countries in the international community, a consensus of international cartel regulation would be sufficiently reached. The German Monopolies Commission's conclusion stated, to this cause, that the debate about how a national trade policy can develop measures to protect domestic industries and business sectors only reveals the lack of an internationally orchestrated and functioning competition policy.[136]

C. Modeling Cartel Law in the Context of Politics and Economic Development

(1) Necessity and Advantage of Adopting Competition Law

When a country take the open trade approach, it is necessary to adopt a proper level of competition law depending on its economy's circumstances. Private monopoly practices or collusive behaviors of formerly competing companies can

[133] Motta, FLI's IALP (2007), at 212.

[134] Neelie Kroes, speech at FLI's IALP Conference (2007), at 204.

[135] Zaech (1999), at 400-01.

[136] Fikentscher, in Cheng (1995), at 117.

make private trade barriers to new foreign competitors. As foreign direct investment, after trade liberalization, facilitates mergers and acquisitions with existent domestic companies, the government needs a policy measure to prevent a severe concentration of market power or mergers with severe anticompetitive effects. The public measure, if enforced without sophisticated guidelines or founding data, might threaten the market participants' active business practices due to the unpredictability of the measure, which could deprive benefits of trade liberalization from the market. The well-structured and consistently enforced competition law including cartel regulation is a benevolent framework for business practices, which can attract more investments and other important production factors, e.g., know-how, labor, and energy.[137]

(2) Treating Political Interests with Limited Criteria

When a country enacts and pursues competition law, each country considers one's own public interests. The public interests usually reflect political interests since political supports are necessary to initiate and strengthen the enforcement of competition policy. Such public interests are expressed as the objectives and in exemption provisions of each competition law.[138] The provisions involving public interests may justify political interests to affect competition law decisions.

However, influences on competition law from politics shall not be arbitrary. The statutory limitations need to be supplemented with the enumeration of concrete categories of public interest and with a proof requirement of outweighing values. The consistency of administrative practices and judicial reviews is to be secured with administrative guidelines. The institutionalization of political independence of competition authority can reduce the abuse of political influences.[139] Establishing a fair competition norm in a domestic market system under nondiscrimination principles is deeply related to ensuring an adequate level of independence of a competition authority. With limited political influence, impartial cartel regulations will cause no prejudice, if any, to foreign companies working in domestic markets.

(3) Reflection of the Development-Perspective on Cartel Regulation

As a measure to foster a competition policy in the South, the singular goal of efficiency or consumer welfare in cartel regulation from a pure economical perspective is not welcomed by the DCs, although it contributes to the economic development. Unless DCs reach to an advanced economic level, economic development will be the most important concern of the South. The DCs shall find value in competition policy through contribution of the policy to economic development. In light of the situations, competition laws in the DCs need to adopt the economic

[137] Zaech (1999), at 401–402.

[138] Dabbah (2003), 61–62. Dabbah cites Doern and Wulks (1996), Comparative Competition Policy, Oxford University Press, at 15.

[139] *Id.* at 62.

development as one of its objectives.[140] Concrete applications of the objective come out as exemptions of cartel regulations or other regulations in competition law.

If the incorporation of economic development into competition law cannot be acknowledged, the majority of developing countries will not be likely to devote their resources to enact a competition law. They will hesitate or refuse to adopt the law because they fear that competition regime may work against economic development.

Unlike the ambiguous public interest reflecting political interests, economic development is unlikely to be abused in a way that it stems the sincere enforcement of cartel regulation. Economic development is a less ambiguous term because it has the measuring tools to find out how much economic development has been achieved, e.g., GDP or GNP. It is relatively not difficult to determine whether there is economic development outweighing inefficiency from cartelization.

D. Raising Public Awareness of Competition and Cartel Norms

Arguably, there are two ways to raise public awareness of cartel regulation along with competition policy: the effective enforcement of the regulation or legislation and the placement of a foundation of competition advocacy.

Successful domestic cartel investigations increase the public awareness of the damages caused by cartels, and deter potential conspirators. In Mexico, the CFC was criticized for its weak enforcement by politicians from the opposition and the public. Criticism grew severe when the public endured economic crises after the initial adoption of competition and market liberalization policy. With the continuous supports from the Fox administration in power and a series of decisions from judicial branch, the CFC continued to enforce cartel regulations and competition law, thereby gaining enforcement power and getting rid of the former weak image. In South Korea, the KFTC focused more on cartel regulations by punishing both domestic and international cartels, effectively operating leniency programs, and announcing 2007 as the year of treading over cartels. Although the business community expressed opposition against the seemingly uncontrolled power of the KFTC, discussion on the proper institution of a competition agency or appropriate level of fines brought the issue of the cartel-causing damage into the public sphere.

Competition advocacy encourages the competition authority's participation in economic policy decision-making, and proposition of the economic policies, which causes less detriment to consumer welfare or builds competition-facilitating foundation. As adoption and application of such an economic policy can determine the level of competition in an economy, participation is a good way to invoke a competitive spirit in economic policy.

---

[140]Article 1 of the Anti-Monopoly Law of 2007 in PRC has 'the promotion of the healthy development of social market economy' as one of its objectives. Article 1 of MRFTA of South Korea also states 'balanced development of the national economy' as one of its objectives.

On the other hand, the public needs an education on the benefits of competition because the public sometimes resist newly adopted competition policy out of the concern of severe competition and, in extreme situations, cartel regulations that causes direct harm to consumers welfare. Discussion regarding competition policy, seminars with scholars and practitioners, review of major successful cases, and research of advanced competition practices and the role of competition in economic development are good ways to stimulate experts and mass media to spread the information on the necessity of cartel regulation and cartel damages to the public.[141]

The publicly available data on competition regime, e.g., decisions, summaries of investigation, and press releases, help the private sector to learn competition law enforcements and thereby promote discussion in the public. The guidelines on cartel regulation, leniency policies, or exemption processes, similar to merger guidelines in advanced countries, let business communities' practices comply with the law.[142] The public's ability to bring specific questions in a situation is helpful to reduce confusion on cartel enforcement.

5.4 Securing Institutional Supports for Cartel Regulation

A. Adoption of Sanctions: Step-by-Step Frame

(1) Civil Enforcements

Civil sanctions include corporate fines and injunctive relief. First, corporate fines, categorized as administrative fines in civil law countries, are popular sanctions necessary to deter cartel activities, which generate huge economic benefits to companies that collude. Most of the advanced countries, e.g., Germany, France, and Japan, and DCs, e.g., South Korea, Mexico, and China, adopt the administrative corporate fine as their main anti-cartel sanction. Although the ideal level of deterrence needs the fine to be around 150 % of turnover in the light of undetected cases,[143] current statutes in jurisdictions with strict anti-cartel sanctions confine its maximum fine to 10 % of turnover.[144] The suggested level of fine may work as an utmost deterrent but places an excessively un-proportionate burden on the company, similar to corporate capital punishment. The reasons are because the penalty provides financial harm to innocent peoples related to the companies, e.g., stockholders, employees, and because the negative spill over of possible bankruptcy may affect the whole national market, particularly the small markets of developing countries. The payment ability of the convicted corporation, additionally, shall be taken into consideration to decide the amount of the fine.

[141]Dabbah (2003), 66–68.

[142]*See id.*

[143]Fingleton et al. (2007), at 16.

[144]Examples are the EU, and Japan. *See id.*, at 15; Aubert (2007), at 128.

On the other hand, the corporate fine may reveal another negative effect. Business managers or executives, although aware of such financial sanctions, might participate in a cartel under discretion and leave the company in advance before the company pays the fine. So-called the agency problem, under different incentive designs, comes out in the circumstances where business managers may take the risk of being charged with a cartel because they can receive a reward of high profits deriving from a cartel conspiracy and they do not pay any corporate fine, unless they are charged with a rare personal penalty. This situation necessitates an individual penalty against managers or executives, either financially or physically. As individual financial penalties can be paid by the companies under a hidden employment contract, nonfinancial personal penalties need to be attached to individual financial penalties.

Second, injunctive relief needs to be adopted in domestic cartel law as it reduces the extension of damages on the market by on-going cartels. The probable basis for such an injunction are: (i) evidence on the collaboration among competitors or intent to restrict competition and (ii) the probability of huge damages caused by the cartel. Injunctive relief can work not only as an administrative sanction but also as a private action. In most cases, as public enforcers have more capabilities to recognize cartel activities and the power to collect evidence, the relief, e.g., injunctive order, can be issued by competition authorities.[145]

(2) Criminal Enforcement

The lack of probability of optimal fines and the impact on innocent corporate personnel highlights the necessity of individual criminal penalties.[146] Strong individual sanctions are appropriate in criminal justice system where penalties against individuals have worked and protections of their rights have been developed through criminal procedure.[147] Individual fines and imprisonment are the traditional penalties in criminal law under a procedure for defending individual rights. They can work as effective deterring sanctions against cartel participants.[148] As individuals are more averse to risk than corporations, the same level of deterrence can be reached through punishment against culpable individuals without corporate penalties which affect innocent people.[149]

Such an opinion, in light of Ireland, UK, and Canada experiences in criminal enforcement, is noteworthy that criminalization is not an area that can quickly

---

[145]For instance, the MRFTA in South Korea enabled the KFTC to issue cease and desist orders when companies commit undue collaborative behaviors or cartels.

[146]Scott (2007), at 67–68. Scott cites Richard Posner's economical justification and Werden and Simon's practical justification of incarceration, thereby applying the analysis to all criminal sanctions possibly including disqualification.

[147]Protective procedures for an indicted person are 'beyond reasonable doubt' standard of conviction, strict evidential hurdles, and so on.

[148]Fingleton et al. (2007), 17. They state that cartel members are careful not to commit the offence in countries where cartels are criminalized.

[149]Scott (2007), 76.

achieve expected results but requires a sufficient base of experienced staff and institutional supports from active civil enforcements and other regulatory works, e.g., market studies, under a long-term plan.[150] South Korea's under-enforcement of criminal penalty against cartels during the last 25 years confirms the difficulties in entrenching rigorous criminal enforcements in a young competition authority.[151] As the enactment of criminal penalties against cartels requires a substantial investment of resources in institutions and procedures, the best time for active criminal enforcements would be in a decade after civil sanctions have been successfully entrenched into a country. In order to pursue effective criminal enforcement, both public awareness and social culpability of cartel-caused damages as necessary elements of criminality should sufficiently increase with entrenched civil enforcements.

In addition, 'director disqualification' is the other type of punishment against a culpable corporate officer. Under the 1986 Company Director Disqualification Act in the UK, English courts have the power to disqualify individuals from acting as a director of a company or being involved in the management, promotion, or formation of the company. As the basis of the disqualification, the 2002 Enterprise Act (2002 EA) added, besides criminal penalties for people engaged in a cartel, particularly, Ch. I of the Competition Act 1988 and Art. 81 of the former EU Treaty (currently Art. 101 of the Lisbon Treaty).[152] The 2002 EA enabled the OFT to apply for a Competition Disqualification Order (CDO) specifically. Although the disqualification is not a criminal penalty under criminal procedures, it causes direct damage to the director's reputation, earnings, and future career, thereby a severer penalty than an individual fine. In exchange for adopting the alternative honor-based penalty, trade-offs are to be considered such as the loss of business expertise and the subsequent impact of disqualification of able businessmen on economic development. The object of disqualification is limited to the director level and does not include middle management.[153]

(3) Private Action

Victims, such as consumers or new competitors, still endure damages from cartel behaviors after the collusion is revealed and administrative or criminal sanctions are

---

[150]Fingleton et al. (2007), at 20–22; Scott, *id.*, 70–73. The crown has experienced difficulty in securing convictions in contested price-fixing cases and attaining the maximum fine level due to Canadian criminal courts' reluctance to convict. For in-detail cases, *see* Scott. at 70–71. *Refer to* Chap. 5, 5.1 A and Chap. 6, 6.5 B(3) and C(2).

[151]Lee (2008), at 58.

[152]Chap. I of the Competition Act 1998 functioned as the domestic equivalent of Art. 81 of the Maastricht Treaty, currently Art. 101 of the Lisbon Treaty. Section 2 under Ch. I prohibits coordinated practices of two or more competing enterprises from attempt to restrict or restricting competition within the UK. It illustrates price-fixing, production control, market allocation, and discriminatory treatment to other competitors (McDermott 2003).

[153]*Id.* at 18–19.

imposed on participators. The necessity of redressing the damage requires the adoption of a private action in damages.

The trial procedure of a private action depends on public enforcement in some points. As private parties have less power and ability to bring initial cases to courts than competition authorities, preparation of private suits starts with the public release of competition authorities' investigation.[154] In addition, a private action is usually suspended until a decision from a competition authority is issued. This delay comes from the necessity of a judicial body to review technical decisions and supporting evidences adopted by a competition authority.

Moreover, the incentive of bringing a suit by private parties, particularly consumers as the main victims of a hard core cartel, is limited as an individual consumer endures a small-amount of loss for damages. The tiny portions of individual welfare loss can reach a sum large enough for an action in damages only under the system of a mass consumers' joint suit. Class action and treble damages unique in the U.S. are for overcoming the limited private incentive to bring private actions to court. The adoption of class action system as an incentive for consumers to bring a suit, however, needs to consider its trade-offs, e.g., the shrinkage in business cooperation and the increase of legal counsel costs under the threat of mass litigation, and the reform of civil procedures for its efficient operation. The trade-off can be reduced if class action treats a hard core cartel with relatively clear border line with legitimate business practices, and has a measure to manage large costs, e.g., imposing the costs on a losing party.[155] With respect to the system of treble damages, the damages need a jurisprudential basis to justify the excessive amount of damages under the proportionality as a constitutional principle. Similar to a corporate fine, its subsequent financial burden to innocent corporate employees and shareholders impedes the adoption of such severe financial compensatory systems.

On the other hand, the activation of private actions can contribute to spreading public awareness of the damages that a cartel causes, as shown by the U.S. legal history.[156] Plaintiffs who bring private actions may be either consumers or competitors who endured the harm of horizontal collusion. As they bear monetary loss due to an anticompetitive behavior, they have incentive to bring a suit under proper legal institution. In the countries where the level of criminal enforcements is less than expected due to low public awareness and subsequent low investment, institutional supports for activating private actions can be an effective strategy to strengthen criminal enforcement. As public awareness regarding cartel regulation increases through active private actions, competition authorities can have a growing number of advocates for their enforcements.[157] Because more public support leads to the highlighting of cartels in politics, more governmental budget can be allocated to activating criminal enforcement. In order to firmly entrench cartel regulations,

---

[154]Lee (2008), 64–65.

[155]*Id.*, at 66.

[156]*Id.*, at 65.

[157]Scott (2007), at 76.

the facilitation of private actions for compensation with support from appropriate legal institutions for mass-consumer litigation is a better strategy than placing inefficient focus on criminal enforcement as advanced countries have proved.[158]

B. Leniency Program and Bounty System

(1) Benevolent Institutions to DCs

Competition-screening authorities in DCs do not have much experience or expert practice skills. Meanwhile, cartel members do not expose covert evidences of their collusive behavior to investigators, although there are some naïve cartel members in DCs who do not know anti-cartel regulation and let public officers have all the internal related data. The more penalties against cartel members, the more covert the conspiracy becomes. Particularly, when an international cartel were reveled by an advanced country, and when the cartel is doubted to affect markets in DCs, competition authorities in DCs face hurdles to investigate related multinational or foreign companies with domestic competition laws. Related companies usually do not launch independent companies or open even branches in DCs and are less likely to keep or deliver to competition authorities in DCs the information of competition-restricting practices in the region.[159]

The leniency program, which exempts or reduces sanctions for a cartel member who cooperated before or during a cartel investigation through submitting important evidence of collusion, can help young competition authorities successfully pursue penalties against a cartel. Researchers argue that the extension of the leniency program to a second informer or a first informer after the investigation is launched may be efficient because, in light of a budget constraint of the investigatory agency and the difficulty in locating proof, the extension can save the cost and time of finding decisive evidence.[160] In young competition authorities in the DCs, under the pressure to show off their effectiveness, a speedy investigation and locating key evidence are the important factors to bring awareness to the public of cartel damages to consumers and the necessity of cartel regulation and competition policy in their countries' economies.

The program, in spite of critics, proved effective not only in the U.S., which introduced the program originally, but also in other countries that subsequently adopted it.[161] Aubert argues that two major reasons of its success in the U.S. are due to the fear of imprisonment for corporate officials and the increase in fines.[162] In South Korea, the continuous efforts to reform the program toward a more transparent and expanding system, which lures a cartel member, have successfully

[158]Lee (2008), 61–63. For more explanation, refer to Chap. 6, 6.5 C(2).

[159]KFTC (2004a, b), at 7–8.

[160]Aubert, in Ghosal (2007), 126.

[161]The U.S. adopted the program in 1993, the EU in 1996, and South Korea in 1997, which achieved notable successes in prosecuting cartels. Aubert, in Ghosal (2007), 125. Refer to South Korea's increase of cartel penalty which applied the leniency program in this Chap. 5, 5.2 B(4).

[162]*See id.*

upgraded the system. The eligibility, procedures, and benefits of the leniency became concrete.[163]

(2) Bounty System

While the leniency program, applied to a cartel-participating member, reduces or exempts the penalty depending on the timing and type of cooperation, a bounty system gives a large monetary benefit to everyone who informs a competition authority of a conspiracy or submits evidence of a cartel to the authority. Private actions for redressing the damages due to a cartel do not belong to the bounty system because they usually follow public investigations and a competition authority does not give monetary rewards to private plaintiffs. Some examples are the U.S. Civil False Claims Act (CFCA) that rewards the reporter of fraud in procurement contracts with a substantial share of the collected fines and South Korea's Reward for Cartel Reporter (RCR), which endows a monetary prize of up to US$ 1 million on a cartel informant who submits related evidence.

The bounty system itself, with similar characteristics of a whistle-blowing program, makes pay-off because it makes more revenue increase than the cost of paying a reward. More discovered cases under the bounty system can contribute to the increase of fines which outweighs the total payment of the bounty. According to the KFTC's analysis, total payments of all RCR cases are less than 16 % of an average fine per case, and less than 2 % of total fines out of the cases supported by the reports with evidence.[164] Similarly, in the U.S., total rewards under the CFCA are around 16–20 % of total fines of cases reveled by bounty system.[165] Meanwhile, over 80 % of the fines went to redress governmental revenue loss due to bid-rigging.

Moreover, the bounty system is effective to deter a cartel as it provides a reward to any person involved in a cartel who reports the conspiracy. The system garners huge potential threats, if not calculable, to potential conspirators. As cartel participants need to secure at least more profit than the bounty for the maintenance of secrecy, the reward system makes cartel formation and operation costly.

(3) Problems

Despite the advantages of a leniency program and bounty system, critics argue that they cause problems in the economy and society. First, the coverage of a

---

[163]The beneficiaries not only include the first informant before investigation, but also the second informant. The benefit is mandatory exemption for the first informant and 30 % reduced penalty for the second informant, which is confirmed through providing the informant conditional amnesty position during the subsequent investigation. Oral application is valid, subsequently within 15 days, with supplemental documents. *See* KFTC (2004a, b), 180–82.

[164]Since the RCR was adopted in 2002, total payment of reward in South Korea is US$ 104,930 while the total fine of eight cases supported by the report with evidence is US$ 5,357,200. The average fine per case is around $ 670,000. KFTC (2004a, b), 182–183.

[165]The total reward is much higher than Korea in consideration of compensation for foregone future wages. Until Sep. 2003, U.S. Dep. Of Defense and the Dep. Of Health and Human Services recovered $1,592,513,253 with reward of $ 291,031,106, and $ 5,117,682,597 with $ 851,646,391 to informants. Aubert, in Ghosal (2007), 125. fn. 3.

cooperator under a leniency program is so wide as to cause an unfair result. For example, the company that creates and operates a cartel as a leader with substantial market share through soliciting other cartel members with threats or fraudulent promises may exclusively benefit from leniency by reporting the cartel. The other participants who hesitantly followed the leader can face a large fine.

Second, commercial atmospheres in domestic markets may change from cooperation to mistrust. Trust takes a long time to build but just a few occasions can break the trust. The result of mistrust can lead to a decrease in joint venture-like common investment or R&D, lack of cooperation among SMEs, which are pivotal elements for developing a national economy. The bounty system brings about a closed corporate human relationship by limiting cooperation-related information that flows to only a few individuals.

Third, the bounty system creates adverse incentives for high-level executives who can decide corporate behaviors. They might temporarily collude in the hopes that they can obtain bounties in the future although shareholders wanted competition.[166]

Fourth, amnesty to corporate managers who participated in a cartel might cause a political reluctance in that influential corporate figures were beyond the coverage of law. Even advanced countries as well as the developing countries that have economic dependency on corporate growth expressed their hesitation in punishing the CEOs of major corporations in the country.[167] Such loose enforcements can invoke corporate managers' recognition that they will not face severe punishments in any cartel activity as long as they cooperate immediately after they find out the investigation into their conspiracy.

(4) Proposals for Improving Both Institutions

Solicitation of a largest company in a market for cartel participation can brings about other small-sized competitors involuntarily joining in a market where the solicitation is difficult for small companies to reject. The leniency program needs to exclude such solicitor from its benefits. The program needs to exclude a cartel member using a coercive or fraudulent measure because other members were involuntarily led by the member. This type of requirement is found in the Antitrust Division of the U.S. DOJ where leniency beneficiaries are limited to corporations which are not leaders or originators of the illegal activity and do not coerce others to participate.[168] However, current criticism in the U.S. as to the requirement opines that the firm or person with the highest level of culpability has the greatest

[166] *See id.* at 126.

[167] Christopher Caldwell, *Financial crime and punishment*, Fin. Times (Mar. 24, 2007); Song Jung-a, *Hyundai chairman avoids jail*, FT, at 17 (Sep. 7, 2007). A presiding judge in charge of the chairman's embezzlement trial mentioned much contribution of Hyundai Motor to Korea's economic growth as one of the major reasons for the lenient penalty. He added, after stating that the chairman, its hands-on leader, was the symbol of the company, "I am also a citizen of the Republic of Korea. I was unwilling to engage in a gamble that would put the nation's economy at risk."

[168] Jacobs (2006), at 38.

motivation to be subject to the government's amnesty inducement.[169] The exact balance between the necessity of limiting beneficiaries and of designing an incentive for efficient practices shall be made depending on each country's culture and legal system.

Regarding the mistrust issue, while a competition culture is an important virtue for sound market economy growth, the securing of sound business cooperation needs to be highly evaluated. If cooperative measures, such as exemptions for R&D, SMEs' competitiveness, and the overcoming of depression, are to be allowed in cartel regulations and other commerce laws, worries over mistrust can be lessened. Publishing explicit guidelines from competition authorities on cartel law violations will help reduce the concerns.

Incentive-design for managers comes from conflict of interests between shareholders and managers. Managers receive a salary in relation to companies' profits under a temporary contract period, whatever business practices they are employed in. They are exposed to temptations to collude with competitors. Shareholders, who do not decide on concrete business practices, have a more negative attitude toward competition-restricting activities. Stock-related compensation for managers can reduce such a gap in interests. As the example of stock-option illustrates, since managers receive company stock as a part of their salary, they will at least share similar interests with shareholders and have a risk-averse attitude toward violations of competition law.[170] In addition, the bounty system should exclude, from the coverage of beneficiaries, people who created the illegal conspiracy, in other words, managers who made up the conspiracy in order to prevent conflicts of interest because they could receive the benefits of individual amnesty and corporate immunity under a leniency program. Otherwise, they may gain from dual benefits.

Regarding the injustice issue, in the developing world where public awareness of the anti-cartel norm is less widespread, public resistances to the leniency program will not create problems, as current practices in advanced countries reveal. So to prevent abuse of such programs by cartel members with trivial or irrelevant evidences, the leniency program needs some restrictions. The scope of cooperation shall require decisive evidence to prove a cartel conspiracy, e.g., a document pointing to a conspiracy. Germany's leniency program adopted this requirement to prevent cartel members from submitting ambiguous or incredible evidence out of the intent to be discharged. In addition, the benefit of full immunity shall require cooperation at the pre-investigation stage. The first cooperator after the investigation or the second cooperator shall not be immune from penalty but receive a reduced penalty. The level of reduction shall take into consideration the time of cooperation, e.g., 20 % of the original penalty before the investigation (80 % reduction), or 50 % of the original penalty after investigation (50 % reduction). Meanwhile, the bounty shall reach a large amount to compensate for the loss of a job for an informant.

---

[169] *Id.* at 38–39.

[170] Aubert, in Ghosal (2007), at 127.

5.5 Capacities Building Through International Cooperation

A. Practical Aid from the Advanced Competition Authorities

Young competition authorities in DCs require aid and advice from advanced countries to develop their practice skills. The modern design of competition policy in South Africa, for instance, owed in a large part to expertise counsel from the advanced competition policy experts. Although South Korea adopted a modern competition law with its own initiative in the context of economic and political development, its enforcement was modeled after successful institutions of advanced competition authorities, e.g., the U.S., Germany, and Japan. The KFTC's investigations of international cartels, e.g., electric graphite or vitamin cartels, similar to other competition authorities' practices, were initiated by a public announcement from the U.S. DOJ that discovered an international cartel conspiracy. Although the KFTC did not fully enjoy sharing information with other competition authorities due to the lack of any bilateral agreement and confidentiality issues, the public officers of the KFTC were able to obtain publicly available information from the competition authorities of the U.S. and the EU.[171] The KFTC acknowledges that its future investigation against an international cartel will, to a large extent, depend on preceding investigations from such advanced competition authorities.[172]

International organizations as well as individual industrialized countries have assisted to further improve competition law and cartel regulation through practical experiences and wisdom. The International Competition Network (ICN), Organization of Economic Cooperation and Development (OECD), and the United Nations Conference on Trade and Development (UNCTAD) have operated conferences and meetings to provide practical tips from advanced competition authorities.[173] The UNCTAD focused on supporting the entrenchment of competition law in DCs pursuant to the UN Set, and thereby provided technical assistance, for instance, to Jamaica and Kenya, and other regional cooperation, e.g., CARICOM, UEMOA, and SACU.[174] In addition, OECD along with its Competition Committee has endeavored to promote cooperation in competition law

---

[171]KFTC (2004a, b), 5–7.

[172]*Id.* at 5 and 8.

[173]Each organization has different characteristics, e.g. practical support of competition law enforcement for the ICN, contribution of competition policy to economic development centering the North for the OECD, and promotion of competition policy centering the South for the UNCTAD.

[174]UNCTAD, UNCTAD'S Contribution, Within its Mandate, to the Implementation of, and to the Review of Progress Made in the Implementation of, the Outcomes of the Major UN Conferences and Summits, at 16, TD/B/53/6 (2006), *at* http://www.unctad.org/en/docs/tdb53d6_en.pdf (visited on Mar. 18, 2008).

enforcement through issuing a series of Council Recommendations. However, as OECD does not include LDCs or many DCs with its strict membership standard, its efforts to encourage the cooperation of competition law have demonstrated limited, although successful, effect on immature competition authorities. Although DDA negotiations are struggling, the WTO received the EC's multilateral framework agreement including, as one of three elements, specific support for competition institutions in developing countries.[175]

B. Settling a Firm Foundation of Competition Policy

(1) Unilateral Aid

For capacity-building in the initial stage, young competition authorities require unilateral aid, although temporary, from the previously experienced competition authorities. The special and differential treatment principle of international trade law is to be applied in a similar way. At the early stage, young authorities need to concentrate on both entrenching a competition policy under whole national economic policies and obtaining political support to further develop the competition policy. Direct harms to consumers and inefficiencies by cartels in markets will be publicly acknowledged through subsequent effective enforcements along with the aid of economical research.

(2) International Agreements Among Similarly Leveled Competition Authorities

Just after the nascent stage, externally, a bilateral agreement with other competition authorities with a similar enforcement-level under a close economic relationship supports further development.[176] A bilateral agreement, for effective cooperation through the positive comity principle during this stage, does not seem to attract countries with different levels of economic development or competition policies. Advanced competition authorities are not induced, because they do not consider young competition authorities trustful in sincerely keeping confidentiality and pursuing enforcement. OECD's Best Practices for the Formal Exchange of Information between Competition Authorities in HCC Investigation of 2005 (2005 OECD Best Practices), although a multilateral agreement, and U.S. International Antitrust Enforcement Assistance Act of 1994 (1994 IAEAA) as the legal basis of bilateral agreements confirm the concern of advanced competition authorities.[177]

---

[175]First (2003), at 39.

[176]*See* Gunzman (1998), at 1546. Through illustrating economic models, he argues that the greater the similarity in trade, the smaller the compensatory transfer payment that must be paid from countries that benefit from the antitrust law agreement to countries that do not.

[177]OECD (2005), at 4, II.A.3. It states that a competition authority under request of exchange of information from the other competition authority should have discretion to provide or not to provide the requested information. One of the enumerated reasons justifying refusal to the exchange is that the requested jurisdiction believes that confidential information under request may not be sufficiently safeguarded in the requesting jurisdiction. Meanwhile, Sec. 12 of 1994 IAEAA enumerates concrete ways to secure confidentiality in an international antitrust assistance agreement, including requirement of remedial actions.

On the other hand, young competition authorities hesitate because the threat of stronger sanctions from advanced authorities may undermine voluntary cooperative attitudes from defendants in front of young competition authorities. As a result, advanced authorities with strict laws are inclined to adopt extraterritorial applications of domestic laws.[178] By the time a competition law is to be firmly established as an effective law through assistances and the efforts of a young competition authority, the competition authority would find more cooperation with a similar level of or closely related competition authorities.

Competition authorities under a regional market-integration agreement or those with the similar level of economic development or domestic market size would have a greater possibility of benefits from regional or bilateral agreements.[179] The exchange of confidential information between Canada and the U.S. in the Citric Acid case[180] is an example of successful cooperation. The success was possible since both continued to sincerely pursue criminal penalties against cartels and to maintain effective cooperation. Canada's investigation caused a serious concern for the legal counsel of a Japanese defendant regarding a future charge in the U.S., which will be facilitated by MLAT between two countries. Pursuant to the recommendation of the counsel, the defendant applied for a leniency program in the U.S.

Achieving a multilateral agreement for exchange of information is also more successful when members are in the similar level of economic development. Appendix of OECD's Recommendation Concerning Cooperation on Anticompetitive Practices Affecting International Trade[181] is an example, which includes procedural measures for cooperation through supplying information to a requesting member, and seeking oversea information by means of a request. However, as OECD consists of countries, which enjoy a high standard of economic development, the procedural measures do not apply to a majority of developing countries.

(3) Cooperative Investigatory Techniques

Cooperative investigation, currently active, is able to help other competition authorities develop investigation skills. The Guiding Principles of OECD

---

[178]Even the prosecutorial ability of the UK Office of Fair Trading in its maiden international price-fixing criminal case is doubted by the US DOJ Antitrust Division, thereby causing the defendants to be convicted twice for the same conspiracy. Peel, M., UK group attacks price-fixing court deal with U.S., FT (Dec. 13, 2007). Gunzman (1998), 1507 and 1532–1533.

[179]*Id.* at 1546.

[180]Zanettin (2002), at 154. In the Citric Acid carte case, a counsel for one of the Japanese defendants out of fear that the US proceedings would result in Canada proceedings immediately cooperated with the Canadian Bureau in order to obtain the best settlement for its client under the Canadian leniency program.

[181]OECD Council, Guiding Principles for Notification, Exchange of Information Co-operation in Investigation and Proceedings, Consultations and Conciliation of Anticompetitive Practices Affecting International Trade, Appendix, C(95) 130 final (Jul. 27 and 28, 1995).

acknowledge such coordinative investigation by suggesting concrete steps.[182] The five steps are: (i) providing notice of time period and schedule for decision-making, (ii) sharing information subject to domestic laws governing confidentiality, (iii) pursuant to the domestic laws, requesting that the subjects of investigation voluntarily permit the cooperating countries to share some or all of the information in their possession, (iv) coordinating discussion regarding remedies that require cross-border actions, and (v) in countries where advance notification of mergers is required, requesting that the notification include a statement identifying notifications made to other countries.

The cooperation in investigation works even between a young competition authority and the advanced one, which may lack tools to investigate a cartel organized in the developing world.[183] Some examples of the cooperation are joint drafting or simultaneous issuance of dawn raids, subpoenas, civil investigative demands, document requests, which can reduce the risk of the destruction of far-located evidence by a conspirator with an oversee office.[184] A recent simultaneous investigation into a freight delivery fee fixing conspiracy among international airlines by competition authorities with a related airline company's major branch in their respective jurisdiction, including a DC, demonstrates the effective usage of some of the new techniques.[185]

C. Challenges from the Exchange of Confidential Information

Overall international cooperation in competition law, particularly, in cartel regulation, is not so popular as in other laws, such as criminal law, tax law or securities law where close cooperation approaches have been implemented.[186] Although investigatory cooperation is one area that helps DC and advanced countries assist each other, it does not necessarily lead to the level of exchanging information. It is no wonder that International Antitrust Enforcement Assistance Act (1994 IAEAA), which adopts the exchange of information including confidential data under strict standards, has produced only one agreement between the U.S. and Australia for more than a decade.[187] A research analyzes several reasons for the unpopularity, among other things, as (i) little incentive for the waiver of a

[182]OECD (1995), at 1, I.A.2. and at 8, para. 5.

[183]van Miert (1997), at 13.

[184]van Miert, *id*, 17. Waller (2000), at 98, 113–114.

[185]KFTC participated into DOJ and EU Commission's simultaneously raiding major airlines for investigating a global cargo price-fixing case by interviewing cargo business executives and removing documents from Korean Air. *Officials raid firms in air cargo price-fixing inquiry takes in Asian lines*, INT'L HERALD TRIBUNE (Feb. 15, 2006), *at* http://www.iht.com/articles/2006/02/15/business/cargo.php (visited on Dec. 11, 2007).

[186]Zanettin (2002), 128–131. *See* OECD (Aug. 2004).

[187]Its formal title is 'Agreement between the Gov. of the U.S.A. and the Gov. of Australia on Mutual Antitrust Enforcement Assistance (1999)'. The agreement is the only one which has been successfully negotiated and met strict standards under Art. 12(2) of 1994 IAEAA that allows exchanges of even confidential information. *See* Taylor (2006), 113–115.

confidentiality rule, (ii) imbalance in the power of competition authorities, (iii) worry over the dilution of privilege and leniency programs, and (iv) national interests in maintaining confidentiality rules.[188] This thesis suggests several strategic ways to overcome the problem.

(1) An Incentive System for a Leniency Applicant Who Waives Confidentiality

First, although the exchange of information occurs, cartel cases have obtained little benefit from it. The information that has been exchanged is limited to publicly released information. Although, through a bilateral cooperation agreement, exchange of information operates more conveniently, confidential information obtained through leniency program, which is pivotal evidence in many cartel cases, is not to be shared unless a cooperating party agrees.[189] Unlike merger cases, where companies have incentives to waives confidentiality to negotiate speedy decisions or joint resolutions in cross-border transaction, the waiver of confidentiality in international cartel cases is considered to be little incentive with much at stake.[190] It is because it can bring about subsequent litigations including public sanctions and private actions in other affected jurisdictions. As an incentive-promoting system, there should be linkage among leniency programs or a system, which links a leniency applicant to reduction in penalties or damages in other countries.[191] Under the system, a leniency applicant that waived confidentiality in a country can have benefits from the leniency program, or of reduction in damages (in a private action) or penalties (in public enforcement) of the other country that enjoys the exchange of information through the waiver. For example, once a person who is investigated waives confidentiality rule in the U.S. under a Mutual Legal Assistance Treaty (MLAT) with Canada, he/she shall enjoy a reduction or immunity of the penalty under Canada's leniency program. However, even under the incentive system, confidentiality waiver might not work well with respect to a country where its competition authority does not demonstrate an effective investigation capacity. A person under investigation would expect neither a severe penalty from the country nor a serious attitude to conserve confidential data of the country. Still incentive for the waiver is low, but expected loss subsequent to the information sharing, e.g., exposure of information to private sector through a corrupt official or unsecured data preservation system, is large.

---

[188] Zanettin (2002), at 131–145; Waller (2000), 108–109.

[189] Telephone Interview with Hye-Rim Chang, Public Officer, The Department of International Cooperation at KFTC (May 13, 2008).

[190] Taylor (2006), at 113.

[191] Telephone Interview with Hee-Eun Chung, Public Officer in charge of leniency program, KFTC (May 13, 2008). Ms.Chung acknowledged that there was a trial of OECD to exchange confidential information obtained through leniency program, which failed due to lack of member countries' consents. van Miert, *supra* note 182, 24. Van Miert states that in cases of serious infringements like cartels, the necessary good will is not there, unless the companies are willing to cooperate in order to get more lenient treatment.

In light of the situations, the countries which need the exchange of information and expect many waivers should develop a domestic legal system to build trust from cartel members in other countries and other competition authorities. Institutions for building trust are a system that secures the limited usage of the information and one which enables the serious maintenance of confidentiality. Concrete measures are to be mentioned later.[192] In addition, in order to induce a person who is investigated to waive confidentiality rule, the countries that want exchange should indicate effective cartel enforcements and the transparent linkage to their leniency programs of a waiver.

(2) A Multilateral Information-Exchange Agreement with Preferential Treatment

Second, the issue of power imbalance is currently unavoidable. As Chap. 1 illustrates, the U.S. and EU have the most serious anti-cartel enforcement and some advanced countries impose comparably large fines while other countries endure under-enforcement of cartel penalties. International cooperation between countries with different level of competition law enforcement does not work well. A cartel investigation in one country with strong competition policy does not induce a cartel participant to reveal their conspiracy to a 'young competition authority', which subsequently launched investigation. It is because the cartel participant does not expect the young authority to be so competent or to have so willingness to penalize them as the former country with strict competition policy. For instance, vitamin cartel members did neither reveal their conspiracy to nor cooperate with Brazilian competition agency although they revealed their conspiracy to U.S. DOJ.[193] The cartel members must have considered that Brazil had no leniency program or competence to successfully convict them.[194]

Although the gap of competition law enforcement can be mitigated through practical aid or assistance from advanced competition authorities and international organizations, in terms of the exchange of information, a multilateral cooperation agreement reflecting preferential treatment for less experienced competition authorities is worth trying. The multilateral cooperation agreement should facilitate the exchange of information, which covers a wide range, including confidential information. Such a wide range of information exchange can contribute to active enforcement of competition laws against an international cartel through promoting competition authorities' abilities to gather overseas evidence.[195] However, the same level of information exchange under reciprocity principle does not help young competition authorities to develop their enforcements as explained below.

---

[192] *Refer to* the following (3) for the concrete measures of the systems.

[193] De Araujo (2002), at 7.

[194] *Id.* at 4.

[195] Taylor (2006), 114. Since Canada and the U.S. reached an agreement for sharing confidential information on competition law enforcement in 1990, Canadian prosecutions against international cartels uncovered by the U.S. DOJ resulted in around US$ 100 million-amount fines of Canadian competition authority during the next decade.

In light of the special circumstance of immature competition authorities, a preferential treatment for young competition authorities will work better for achieving the facilitation of information exchange and the development of competition laws in their nascent stages. The preferential treatment is that young competition authorities may exchange a current level of general information while experienced authorities should allow even the exchange of confidential information. A party who is considering applying for leniency program of a mature competition authority does not need to be concerned about the differential treatment. One reason is that he can enjoy the benefit of linked leniency program among mature competition authorities. Another reason is that several hurdles for young competition authorities to pursue their anti-cartel enforcements regarding an international cartel will prevent the effect of sharing confidential information of the party from being expanded to an extent that overall young authorities impose severe fines. As the international vitamin cartel case illustrates at Chap. 1,[196] most competition authorities of developing countries did not succeed in imposing heavy fine on the cartel members although some of the authorities had exchange of information from the U.S.

Lastly, limitation in the exchange of information voluntarily provided to competition authorities under leniency program is necessary in less experienced competition authorities of which competition law enforcements need to be increased. As a former vice-president of KFTC agreed, KFTC cannot exchange information obtained through leniency program as public officials are under duty to preserve confidentiality of secret of an enterprise.[197] When the coverage of information-exchange extends to those obtained through leniency program, enterprises would continue their uncooperative attitudes against young competition authorities because business information, once voluntarily submitted under domestic competition law, can flow abroad thereby exposing the enterprises to subsequent penalties. Although there is a system that links a leniency applicant to the reduction of penalty in other countries, fines from advanced competition authorities will lead to passive attitudes of cartel members in front of less developed competition authorities. From the perspective of promoting cartel enforcement, the evidence obtained from leniency program in DCs should be limitedly or not shared with other competition authorities unless the investigated party agrees.

(3) A System Which Secures Limited Usage of Shared Information

Third, in order for an information-offering country to have trust in the recipient's usage, shared information shall strictly be limitedly used only for the original purpose by a competition authority. When the information is exposed to other

[196] *Refer to* Chap. 2, 2.5 D.

[197] Interview with Byung Bae Kim, former Vice President, KFTC (Mar. 27, 2008). The author had an interview with Byung-Bae Kim, former vice president of KFTC, at 2008 ABA Session of Antitrust. He stated that, due to KFTC's legal obligation to keep the confidentiality of information under leniency under Art. 62 of MRFTA, the information would be difficult to share even though there is an international agreement regarding information-exchange.

authorities or for other purposes, it may result in the collapse of international cooperation system due to mistrust.[198] 1994 IAEAA stipulates that antitrust mutual assistance agreement will be terminated if the confidentiality under such agreement is violated with respect to antitrust evidence, and if adequate action is not taken both to minimize harm from the violation and to ensure that the confidentiality is not violated again.[199] Imposing a serious penalty on the people who abuse the information can strengthen the security of the information. Procedural controls, e.g., the screening of a high-level executive officer, a limited time frame, and prior agreement for compensating damages from the breach of confidentiality, may be complimentary measures.

Moreover, when the confidentiality rule provides to a competition official a lot of discretion on whether evidence may be shared, the possibility of abuse may increase due to domestic interests. The abuse undermines precious public supports for young competition authorities. The partly adoption of mandatory information exchange into international cooperation practice will contribute to reducing the abuse. Mandatory exchange with respect to evidence obtained through compulsory investigation, in distinction with information through cooperation, is one example. This measure can be an incentive system for cartel members to cooperate with competition authorities.

5.6 Conclusion

The analysis of the histories of advanced competition laws indicates that development of cartel law is facilitated by four conditions: (i) progressing a market economy along with an open international trade policy, (ii) political support on the basis of a democratic power system, (iii) developed legal institutions that can produce competition jurisprudences, and (iv) economic research which figure out economic damages from a cartel. Particularly, cartel regulations in the U.S., Germany, and UK are the typical models which demonstrate that cartel regulation has been developed with the foundation of the conditions while France's cartel regulation has been stimulated by the EU competition policy. Moreover, study of advanced cartel regulations, particularly, France and Germany, demonstrates that cartel regulations had been infrequently enforced by themselves until the whole competition regime supported cartel regulations.

The comparative research of cartel regulations in the four major DCs shows that a competition policy need to be seriously implemented around the time when they open their domestic markets to foreign competitors. Political support is a key ally

[198]Taylor (2006), 115.

[199]Article 12 (2)(G).

that can reduce objections against the launching of competition law and can provide institutional, financial, and public assistance. In addition, a substantial part of competition law development depends on the level of development of the legal system. The progress of rules and reasonings through the accumulation of both administrative and judicial decisions can contribute to a sophisticated system of competition laws and cartel regulations. A cartel regulation with a presumption provision may be beneficial to alleviate the burden of proof that a young competition authority must present to penalize a covert cartel. The foundation of economic research for a competition policy is relatively weak in the DCs, which leads to more room for political influence. The coverage of exemptions from cartel regulations needs to be much broader in DCs than in advanced market economies. Otherwise, DCs will not acknowledge competition law or cartel regulation at all. The wider exceptions reflect politicians' concerns that the poor economic environments in the DCs might be undermined by a competition culture.

Although an industrial policy, in a strict meaning, may look to conflict with a competition policy, inefficiencies inherent in governmental policy, as an obstacle to further economic development, necessitate the encouragement of competition in a private sector through privatization and liberalization. However, the immediate adoption of a competition policy to the general scope in DCs should be approached cautiously because there are quite a few industries where indigenous poor economic situations lead to the collapse of weak domestic companies when they compete with foreign companies. However, the protective policy that shields weak industries from international competition shall be limited, under regular renewals, to a period temporary enough to stimulate autonomous efforts to raise efficiency. Since continuous economic development requires a competition policy and the cartel regulation is the maxim of the competition policy, an industrial policy should be harmonized with the competition policy and, particularly with the cartel regulation to lift economic development.

The model cartel regulation in competition law may adopt other objectives reflecting public policies as well as competition-facilitation. Particularly, as political support is necessary to a successful enforcement of competition laws, the allowance of political influence as objectives in the DCs competition law is inevitable. However, the competition authorities should be equipped with preventive tools to control arbitrariness. Economic development, among other political influences, is the appropriate objective to be introduced because it can be measured with economic analysis, thereby removing abuse of political influences. In order to raise the level of pubic awareness about the damages that cartels cause, the effective enforcement of the regulation and the creation of a foundation for competition advocacy are important ways to achieve effective cartel enforcements.

As a method to assist cartel practices in DCs, an exemption provision should be allowed to approve some kinds of cartels, which can promote long-term competitiveness. To control its arbitrary usage by a political body, however, several institution or systems are needed, such as an independent panel with competition experts, transparent decision-making system, and a regular review system of exemption.

In addition, a leniency program and a bounty system do a lot of good to help cartel investigations. Several concerns on these reward institutions have been expressed, which can be minimized with the reform measures that can limit the possibility of abuse of the institutions, e.g., the exclusion of a leader who used a coercive or fraudulent method, the approval of efficient cooperation, incentive-design systems to prevent managers' abuse, the requirement of decisive evidence, etc.

To build the capacity of competition authorities, young competition authorities need practical aid from advanced competition authorities and international organizations. Internally, policy priority is to position a competition policy firmly under the whole economic policy and to widen the foundation of political support. Externally, bilateral or regional agreements between countries with similar levels of competition authorities under a close economic relationship will help to achieve more.

International cooperation agreement in competition law has been less popular than those in other law areas because there is a threat of subsequent litigations and penalties after offering information, the imbalance in power of competition law between advanced and young competition authorities is large, business information related to competition law is linked to national interests, and reciprocal mistrust in securing confidentiality impedes the exchange of business information. The creation and operation of systems, which promote incentives for private parties to cooperate or secure confidentiality is necessary to solve problems. A linkage system that leads a leniency applicant in a country who waives confidentiality rule to benefits of leniency programs or reduction in penalties or damages (in private actions) in other countries which obtain the information through the waiver is a good model. On the other hand, a multilateral cooperation agreement that adopts preferential treatment with respect to a range of information under information-exchange provision is another desirable system. The preferential treatment will lead cartel members to cooperate with competition authorities in DCs. Since less experienced countries still face many hurdles to imposing fines on an information provider, the provider will face similar penalty compared to the situation that he cooperates with a competition authority in an advanced country. Reducing discretion of public officers in decision of exchanging information is one way to promote cooperation from the cartel members. The strict limitation of the usage of shared information on the case concerned and to the competition authority that requested the data needs concrete measures to secure the limitation, e.g., remedies, penalty, and termination of cooperation agreement. Successful enforcement of domestic cartel laws with limited usage of shared information can contribute to building up trust among competition authorities. Leveling the playing field for competition authorities in the North and the South can, in the long term, make international cooperation strengthened by reducing current mistrusts.

References

Book

Akbar YH (2003) Global antitrust: trade and competition linkages. Ashgate Pub., Surrey

Chang H-J (2003) Globalisation, economic development & the role of the state, third world network. Zed Books Ltd, London

Dabbah M (2003) The Internationalization of antitrust policy. Cambridge University, Cambridge

Fasulo L (2004) An insider's guide to the UN. Yale University Press, New Haven

Korea Fair Trade Commission (KFTC) (2004a) Whitepaper [공정거래백서]. KFTC, Seoul

KFTC (2011) Whitepaper [공정거래백서]. KFTC, Seoul

KFTC (2012) Whitepaper [공정거래백서]. KFTC, Seoul

KFTC (2014) Whitepaper [공정거래백서]. KFTC, Seoul

Scherer FM (1994) Competition policies for an integrated world economy. Brookings Inst., Washington

Taylor M (2006) International competition law: a new dimension for the WTO?. Cambridge University Press, Cambridge

UNCTAD (2005) Handbook of statistics. UN Doc. TD/STAT.30, UN

Zanettin B (2002) Cooperation between antitrust agencies at the international level. Hart Pub., The Rocks

Articles, Papers

Aubert C (2007) Instruments for cartel deterrence, and conflict of interests. In: Ghosal V, Stennek J (eds) The political economy of antitrust (Contributions to Economic Analysis 282:123–148), Emerald Group Publishing, UK

Aydin U (2015) Competition law and policy in Mexico: successes and challenges. Presentation paper at "Competition law and policy in developing countries" workshop. Kenan Institute for Ethics, Duke University

Baumol W (1990) Entrepreneurship: productivity, unproductive, and destructive. J Polit Econ 98 (5):893–921

De Araujo MT (2002) The Brazilian experience on international cooperation in cartel investigation. www.seae.fazenda.gov.br/central_documentos/documento_trabalho/2002-1/doctrab21.pdf

Eichner AW (2012) Battling cartels in the new era of Chinese antitrust enforcement. Tex Int Law J 47(3):587–618

Fikentscher W (1995) Collaborative activities among industrial competitors—in German, European, and U.S. Antitrust Law, and in the Draft International Antitrust Code in the GATT/WTO System. In: Cheng C-J et al. (eds) Int'l harmonization of competition laws, vol 109, pp 116–117

Fingleton J, Girard M-B, Williams S (2007) The fight against cartels. In: Hawk ed., IALP, FLI, NY

First H (2003) Evolving toward what? The development of international antitrust. In Drexl J (ed) The future of transnational antitrust—from comparative to common competition law, vol 23. Staempfli Pub., Bern

Fox E (2006) The WTO's first antitrust case-Mexican telecom: a sleeping victory for trade and competition. J Int Econ Law 9:271

Fox E, Davis D (2007) industrial policy and competition-developing countries as victims and users. In: Hawk B (ed) annual proceedings of the fordham corporate law institute: international antitrust law and policy (hereinafter IALP), Fordham Law Institute (FLI), NY

Gunzman A (1998) Is international antitrust possible? NyUL Rev 73:1501
Immenga U (1999) Conflicts between competition policy and industrial policy: a comparative view on potential responses. In: Zaech R (ed) Towards WTO competition rules: key issues and comments on the WTO report on trade and competition. Kluwer Law Int
Jacobs LW (2006) Criminal enforcement of antitrust laws—problems with the U.S. Model. In: Hawk ed., IALP, FLI
KFTC (2004b) KFTC's experience in dealing with international cartels. http://www.jftc.go.jp/eacpf/05/APECTrainingProgramMarch2004/KE.experience.Jand.pdf
Lee S (2008) Activating action in damages to improve criminal penalties against cartels: comparative analysis of competition law of the U.S. and South Korea. Curr Int Trade Law J 58:55–69
McDermott (2003) Bird & Bird UK: competition provisions of the EA 2002 enter into force. http://www.twobirds.com/english/publications/articles/UKCompetitionprovisionsoftheEnterpriseAct2002enterintoforce.cfm. Visited on 1 May 2008
OECD (1995) Revised recommendation of the council concerning co-operation between member countries on anti-competitive practices affecting international trade, C(95)130/FINAL
OECD (2003a) Competition law and policy in South Africa: an OECD peer review. http://www.oecd.org/dataoecd/52/13/2958714.pdf. Visited on 28 Apr 2008
OECD (2003b) Country studies: South Africa—peer review of competition law and policy. http://www.oecd.org/dataoecd/43/58/34823812.pdf. Visited on 13 Nov 2007
OECD (2004a) Competition law and policy in Mexico: an OECD peer review. http://www.oecd.org/dataoecd/11/15/31969311.pdf. Visited on 18 Jul 2008
OECD (2004b) OECD and non-OECD economies agree to continue work on tax information exchange. http://www.oecd.org
OECD (2005) Best practices for the formal exchange of information between competition authorities in hard core cartel investigations. http://www.oecd.org/dataoecd/1/33/35590548.pdf
OECD (2007) Plea bargaining/settlement of cartel cases: South Africa. DAF/COMP/WP3/WD (2006)61
OECD Global Forum on Competition (GFC) (2001) Contribution from China, CCNM/GF/COMP/WD(2001)10
OECD GFC (2003) The objectives of competition law and policy the optimal design of a competition agency—China (session I), CCNM/GF/COMP/WD(2003)1. http://www.oecd.org/dataoecd/17/62/23720833.pdf. Visited on 18 Jul 2008
Owen B, Sun S, Zheng W (2004) Antitrust in China: the problem of incentive compatibility J Compet Law Econ 1(1):123
Park H-J (2006) The perspective of small business in South Korea. KDI School Working Paper Series 06-13
Rodger, BJ, Macculloch A (2000) Prohibition: prohibiting cartels, or permitting verticals? Or both? In: Rodger BJ, MacCulloch A (eds) The U.K. competition act: a new era for U.K. Hart Pub., The Rocks, pp 171–180
Scott S (2007) Criminal enforcement of antitrust laws: the U.S. model—a Canadian perspective. In: Hawk ed., IALP, FLI
van Miert K (1997) international cooperation in the field of competition: a view from the EC. In: Hawk ed., FLI, IALP
Vissi F (1999) Antitrust in transition economies: the Hungarian experience. In: IALP, FLI
Waller SW (2000) Antitrust cooperation. In: Evenett L, Steil (eds) Antitrust goes global: what future for transatlantic cooperation? Brookings Inst. Press., Washington
Whish R (2000) The competition act 1998 and the prior debate on reform. In: Rodger BJ, MacCulloch A (eds) The U.K. competition act: a new era for U.K., vol 2. Hart Pub., The Rocks
Wise M (2005) competition law and policy in Germany. OECD J Compet Law Policy 7/2:7–66
Zaech R (1999) Competition law as comparative advantage. In: Zaech R (ed) Towards WTO competition rules. Kluwer Law Int

Chapter 6
The Need for the Development of International Law on Cartels

Abstract International communities have strived for achieving a binding multilateral cartel regulation in distinct from commodity agreement since the late 1940s, which turn out to fail except a nonbinding multilateral agreement centering on industrialized countries, or 1998 OECD Recommendation on Hard Core Cartel. Various trials, such as spreading bilateral agreement, adopting a multilateral agreement, revealed its ineffectiveness or inherent limitation when they faced hurdles such as immature domestic competition law practice, less awareness of cartel-causing damages, and fear in a domestic against severe competition. The current widespread of free trade rule under WTO and the rapid development of emerging economies and transitional markets tempt companies to collude tacitly, so the necessity for a binding international cartel law continue to grow. A more proper strategy to fulfill its necessity is to expand a plurilateral agreement, either through the expansion of either a regional/bilateral agreement or an internal agreement within one international organization under short-term and long-term approaches. Roughly speaking, the short-term approach is that the coverage of international cartel agreement needs to be narrowed down to bid-rigging, sufficiently to achieve member countries' consensus while the long-term approach is to adopt an international agreement on competition with exemptions offering out weighing public interests, such as special and differential treatment to LDCs and low- or mid-income DCs. Distinctive features of commodity under the agenda of sustainable development led to international commodity agreements, formerly defunct, requiring, for adjusting to current trade law system, the following reforms ①productivity-focused model and ②multilateral cooperation model to reflect multistake holders' interests.

Keywords Binding multilateral cartel regulation · Short-term approach · Long-term approach · Bid-rigging · International commodity agreement · International cartel law

---

Sections 6.1, 6.3, 6.4, and 6.5 were edited versions of a law journal article by the author. *Refer to* Lee (2009), p. 149–185. Prof. Lee as a copyright holder received approval for publishing this book from the journal.

J.S. Lee, *Strategies to Achieve a Binding International Agreement on Regulating Cartels*, DOI 10.1007/978-981-10-2756-7_6

6.1 Current Stage of International Cartel Regulation

Although many cases of bilateral cooperation have worked successfully, negotiation for a binding multilateral agreement for competition law under the World Trade Organization, e.g., the Doha Development Agenda (DDA), faced strong resistance from a majority of developing countries (DCs), e.g., the African Caribbean and Pacific (ACP) group comprising 77 DCs. Meanwhile, assistances and cooperation from the International Competition Network (ICN) attracted both DCs and developed countries. The Organization for Economic Co-operation and Development (OECD), since 1998 when it produced recommendation on hard core cartel (HCC), has produced regular reports on the progress of cartel enforcement of its member countries. The OECD, through granting observer status to a nonmember country has encouraged a developing country, which has recently adopted competition law or which is preparing the adoption, to reveal its status to obtain opinions and advice from advanced countries. The United Nations Conference on Trade and Development (UNCTAD) has continued to have regular conferences on development issues, including the relationship of development with competition, since it produced the UN Set in 1980. The support for competition regimes from the UNCTAD has been offered by assisting in launching new competition laws in emerging or transitional economies. However, an insufficient political power for competition policy within the UNCTAD may stem a further commitment to regulate private cartels.

Regulating cartels still sounds threatening to the economic development of quite a few DCs, the economy of which depends on the production of primary commodities and do not have enough local markets to raise competitive companies. Developing economies (DEs) need to foster small or mid-sized domestic enterprises until they grow large international companies which can compete with foreign global companies, whereby increasing national production and employment. Cartel regulations which restrict cooperation in markets looks like an obstacle to their economic policy. Meanwhile, a commodity agreement in DEs brings important monetary resources to boost the economies. Although a commodity agreement was excluded from the definition of a cartel in many advanced countries' competition law, many DCs still worry that an international cartel regulation may extend to control an important economic tool, the commodity agreement. Their concern is reasonable because the broad definition of a cartel may cover intergovernmental producers' associations (IPA).

This chapter, based on the analyses of the former Chaps. 2, 3, and 4, is divided into two parts, respectively, addressing strategies for a binding international cartel law and reforms for effective intergovernmental commodity agreements (ICAs). This chapter examines current popular methods. First, this chapter discusses the limitation of bilateral agreements in the framework of international cartel regulations. Second, it examines hurdles to achieve a binding multilateral agreement regulating cartels. After figuring out certain weaknesses, the chapter then demonstrates several strategies for achieving the multilateral agreement in the long term.

A front part argues that a plurilateral agreement approach supplemented by many bilateral agreements is a realistic intermediate way to the binding international cartel regulation, and suggests two approaches to a binding multilateral cartel law: a narrow and a broad approach. The narrow approach concentrates on specific aspect (s) of cartel, e.g., bid-rigging, while the broad approach is a principle-based multilateral agreement toward the competition regime including cartel regulations.

The second part consists of policy-focused discussion for appropriate models for effective ICAs. It argues that, rather than former market-interrupting measures, e.g., buffet stock and supply control, market-adjusting measures and structural policy will be effective and long-lasting functions of an ICA in commodity markets. In light of close relationship of commodity production to sustainable development, this thesis proposes two ICA models as multilateral systems, (i) a model focusing on the productivity increase and (ii) the other model inducing multistakeholders to participate in and use their expertise for the operations of an ICA. At last, it suggests the roles of ICAs dealing with food commodities in the current high food price era.

6.2 Hurdles to a Binding Multilateral Agreement

A. Reasons for Failure to Reach a Binding Multilateral Agreement

Even though over 90 countries have adopted domestic competition laws including cartel regulations under the auspices of international organizations, e.g., WTO, UNCTAD, and OECD, most of their enforcements are in the initial stage of development or do not have sufficient capabilities to pursue international cartels and even tacit domestic cartels. In response to immature practices, international organizations, such as ICN and OECD, have highlighted the facilitation of domestic enforcement, e.g., through reducing barriers for information located overseas.[1] However, trials for major international organizations to achieve a multilateral agreement have not reached the level of a binding competition law or cartel regulation in spite of their continuous efforts.

(1) The Lack of International Consensus

Reasons for such failures or standstills of the trials can be analyzed with persuasive arguments.[2] Obstacles to a binding agreement are analyzed to come from such diverse national interests as the level of dependency of national economic structure on state enterprises or major products,[3] the level of economic

[1]First (2003), at 42–43.

[2]*Refer* to Chap. 4, Sect. 4.2.

[3]It is deeply related to nationalism which protects national champions from open competition; Kennedy (2001), at 620. Kennedy mentions this national pride as a strong hurdle to a successful multilateral agreement.

development, political perspective on competition, the foundation of the legal system, and the level of economic research. Among these reasons, the most important obstacle is an insufficient consensus on international cartel regulation.[4] Still, the majority of DCs and least developing countries (LDCs) do not believe that international competition laws, including cartel regulations, will support their economic development because economic efficiency promotion through competition policies do not always increase domestic wealth. They want, at best, a domestic competition policy, modified by development concerns and uninterrupted by international law. Still, a substantial number of countries among WTO members have not adopted competition laws, including cartel regulations at all.[5] Some of the countries argue that market failures in open international trade are not serious enough to enact generic competition law including cartel regulations.[6]

(2) Insufficient Preparation: Insufficient Development of Institutions

Another group of countries have internal oppositions severe enough to delay enacting cartel regulations because they have to spend many financial sources to competition-facilitating institutions.[7] These countries do not place much value on competition in economic development process. Often, they usually have less diversified economic structures with a focus on commodity productions. Equitable distribution of profits and production is more emphasized than an increase in efficiency through competition. In addition, political support from small- and medium-size enterprises (SMEs) for adopting a competition regime is not strong enough to overcome structural weaknesses. Less democratized communication of political opinions and weak foundations for SMEs are the reasons for the feeble support.

Similarly, due to the lack of institutions and resources, the other group of countries does not want sophisticated competition law including cartel regulations.[8] The group of LDCs, where financial resources and institutional bases are limited, is an example. Besides a low level of economic and political development, the untransparent legal system and arbitrary discretion in the group of countries are not proper to competition law enforcement. As predictable rules in competition policy and cartel regulations contribute to promoting competitive entrepreneurship, a certain level of capacity in the legal system and economical analysis of market data is required to operate the competition law regime.

---

[4]*Id.*, at 603–605 and 608. Some countries favor price-fixing.

[5]As of 1999, among 144 member states, only 70 states adopted competition law. A Business Roundtable WTO Policy Paper: The WTO's Role in Maintaining Competitive Markets (May 2003), *available at* http://www.businessroundtable.org.

[6]Brunei belongs to this group of countries. *See id.*

[7]Malaysia belongs to this group. *See id.* at 74.

[8]*Id.* Papua New Guinea formerly belonged to the group but enacted competition legislation in 2002. As to the group, The World Bank recommended that such nations should concentrate on institutional strengthening rather than enacting competition laws that may be misunderstood or improperly enforced.

(3) Diversification of Interests Within the Developing World

The conflicting viewpoints on anticompetitive business practices between the North and the South, although once converged for the UN Set in 1980, did not produce conspicuous compromising results in the DDA, thereby ending up with removing the competition issue from the agenda. The economic powers of the North, although having acknowledged the development concerns of the South in principle under its growing power,[9] did not permit to accommodate the concerns to concrete provisions in the UN Set. While the cartel regulation in the UN Set prevented enterprises from agreeing to fix prices, it did not have exemptions for R&D, crisis, or small-size enterprises, beneficial for sustaining or developing markets in less developed economies. The WTO regime, in favor of free trade, tried to reflect efficiency-oriented objectives of competition but did not produce any adjustment or exemption which reflects unique economic circumstances in the South.

Diverse voices within the South, different from the 1970s, were the result of independent policies that developing countries pursued to solve their economic crises since the mid-1980s. After the collapse of the Soviet Union, most of the communist regimes shifted their economic systems toward a market economy, thereby devoting their efforts to entrenching free and competitive markets. Some of them, for example, China and Vietnam, developed their economies much more than 20 years ago. Along with China and Vietnam, markets in India, and Brazil, so-called emerging markets, are expected to grow fast. The emerging markets enacted competition law regime although the level of enforcement is not so rigorous as advanced countries.[10] Other countries have struggled to develop a market economy in spite of financial depressions from the U.S. and the EU. Their salient achievements need adjustment and time. For example, many African countries are attracting foreign investment, but still do not appear ready for serious competition law enforcement.[11] Although there has been a power revival in the South, the same allied opinion within the South from the 1970s appears not to be possible due to many of the transitional and emerging markets, effectively developing free and competitive markets and adopting competition regime. Quite a few transitional and emerging markets are pursuing the path which the advanced countries took.[12]

[9]Sell (1998), at 21 and 27–32. The South' power in international community came from OPEC's demonstrated strength and commodity power.

[10]In 2007, China adopted the AML. Vietnam enacted competition law in 2004. Meanwhile, Brazil and India has longer history of competition law. Brazil and India have run its competition laws, respectively, a competition law no. 4137 since 1962, and the Monopolies and Restrictive Trade Practices Act since 1969.

[11]Andrew Bounds and Laura Dixon, *EU to dilute trade deals to avert crisis*, FT (Nov. 19, 2007).

[12]Vietnam, Hungary, and Russia are representative examples of transitional economy. Mexico, India, and China belong to major emerging markets.

B. Inherent Limitations of Multilateral Agreements

Although a multilateral agreement is a very effective method in promising uniform international cartel regulatory agreement to all nations, any multilateral negotiation takes long to achieve unanimous consent. The expensive and uncertain process often results in the lowest denominator.[13] The international legal principle, *pacta tertiisnec nocent nec prosunt*, under Art. 11 of the Vienna Convention on the Law of Treaties, states the rule of unanimous consent to make multilateral negotiations effective. Since all participating countries have national interests in conflict with the utilitarian good, the unanimous consent rule is susceptible to minority members' selfish vetoes, or large nations' political power. Multilateral agreements tend to have minimal contents which can attract unanimous consents in order to avoid dissent from even a minority. As the standstill of DDA negotiation demonstrates, strenuous efforts among supporters are, in many cases, less successful than expected. The uncertainty of becoming a success lessens the incentive for supporter groups to devote further endeavors.

C. Fear of Restraining Sovereignty

Providing binding power to a multilateral agreement brings about more or less the restriction of sovereignty of an individual country.[14] As an independent state, a member country will not limit its domestic power unless there is benefit outweighing such restriction. In a circumstance where it is not easy to find a common denominator among member countries, a binding multilateral agreement cannot avoid big challenges. However, the procedural cooperation and substantial harmony from a multilateral cartel agreement can have much wider coverage than from a bilateral agreement. The careful selection of common denominators and the acknowledgement of different national interests in each country will be the main issue for achieving a binding multilateral agreement.

D. DDA not Working as a Bumper to the North and South Conflict

Although the slow-paced multilateral agreement susceptible to an external minor dispute, once achieved, can control international cartels effectively, international consensus sufficient for a multilateral cartel-regulatory regime lacked among the South. Strong support from the DCs for the UN Set in 1980 turned out to be strong rejection from the same group against the WTO Doha Round with similar competition-regulating provisions in 2003, around two decades later. Although acknowledgement by the South of the objective of the DDA and WTO, which is the realization of free trade in overall sectors, enabled initial negotiations, the opposition by a majority of DCs against the inclusion of competition provisions into the DDA made the competition issue dropped off from the negotiation table. The point that the UN Set and draft competition provisions under the DDA use very similar language implies that the shift of position held by a majority of DCs regardless of

[13] *See id.* 138–139.

[14] Dabbah (2003), at 151–153.

similar provisions is due to change of political position with little concern about wordings of the draft. Several trials and errors for a multilateral agreement demonstrate that the consensus for a binding international competition regime is very feeble.

It is necessary to redress the fear of or real loss from adopting a binding international competition regime. However, the DDA regime with a broad coverage of delicate trade topics seriously affecting national markets cannot place sufficient focus on the balance of interests in negotiating a competition regime between the North and the South. The exclusion of a competition policy was an inevitable result, which reflected the perceptive gap between the North and the South with respect to competition law. Such difference of positions comes from the level of economic development because perspectives regarding competition law are modified in accordance with the level of economic development.

E. Addressing Doubts Regarding Multilateral Agreement Regulating Cartels

In spite of the formerly mentioned reasons of failures, international agreements regulating cartels need to be developed to deal with challenges from growing cross-border competition-restrictive business practices. Particularly, a researcher demonstrated that international cartels caused as huge amount of damages to the developing world as one-third level of development assistance from international organization during the late 1990s. As corporate business and anticompetitive practices went beyond national territories, domestic competition laws had faced their limitation for investigating such practices. Extraterritorial application of domestic competition pushed up by advanced competition authorities exposed high possibility of conflicting with national sovereignty when it was widely accepted. These are the backgrounds of adopting the UN Set in 1980, and OECD Hard Core Cartel Recommendation in 1998. Although trials for a binding multilateral cartel-regulatory agreement has faced frequent failures, the agreement, if wisely planned and succeeded in overcoming the hurdles, can bring about much benefit to consumer protection and operation of free and fair trade regime. Still the aim of multilateral agreement is worthy of trying to make come true.

6.3 Functions of a Bilateral Agreement Toward a Multilateral Agreement Regulating Cartels

Currently, bilateral agreements are favorable measures in facilitating cooperation between competition authorities. Particularly, free trade agreements (FTAs) have played important roles to overcome the deadlocks of DDA negotiations. In spite of very positive function of bilateral agreements and FTAs,[15] their effects on

[15]*Refer to* Chap. 3, Sect. 2.2.

international convergence competition law are more limited than that of multilateral agreement because bilateral agreements cause large transaction costs, and conflict out of dissimilar legal schemes. Other reasons of the limitation are due to the lack of reciprocal confidence, and practices susceptible to national interests under political influences. For instance, it took around 7 years for FTA between Korea and U.S., including competition law, to be effective in both countries since the two countries shared their interests in 2005. The negotiation managed to progress through political struggles. A bilateral agreement with such hurdles, difficult to become a major tool, will work the basic but supplementary function on the way to the creation of a binding international agreement regulating cartels.

A. Bilateral Agreement as a Popular Tool

(1) The Effect of Bilateral Agreement Under Regional Economic Integration on Competition

As regional economic integration grows expended and effective, agreements of regional integrating organization with other countries have much wider effect than that of ordinary bilateral agreements. The agreements include competition chapter in many cases. For example, the EU had made 19 bilateral agreements including cooperation of competition policy by 2009. The U.S., with a long history of strict law enforcement against cartels, has reached bilateral agreements, particularly on the issue of antitrust, since 1976 when 'Antitrust Accord' between the U.S. and West Germany was made. The contents of the bilateral agreements with respect to antitrust tend to deal with reciprocal assistance and cooperation in competition law practices as well as confidentiality of shared information. Although they do not focus on cartel issues, the cooperation, if settled down with good precedents, can work to support and to promote cooperative cartel investigation.

(2) FTAs Including Competition Chapter

As anticompetitive business practices may impede free trade supposed to be secured by a FTA, FTAs usually include competition chapter. The U.S., with special bilateral agreement on competition law, has already included competition chapter in FTAs with the following countries which have enacted or are considering the enactment of competition law: Singapore, Chile, Peru, and Australia. Competition chapters in the FTAs with the countries have similar structures though their contents and wordings reflect the unique characteristics of each FTA. Although South Korea have not reached a bilateral agreement regarding competition law, Korea which has pursued FTAs with more than 11 entities, has gradually included competition chapter inside the agreements.[16]

[16]FTAs with Chile (2003), with Association of Southeast Asian Nations (ASEAN) (ratification in 2007), and with the U.S. (2011) have competition chapter.

B. Inherent Limitations of Bilateral Agreement

As a source of international law-regulating cartels, a bilateral agreement or a FTA has the following weakness: large transaction costs, dissimilarity, lack of reciprocal confidence, and favor for inherent national interests.

(1) Large Transaction Costs in the Light of a Wide Coverage of Network

Let us assume that 90 countries at this moment have cartel-regulatory laws. In order to cooperate effectively under a bilateral agreement regime, each country needs to have 89 bilateral agreements to cover all the other competition authorities. According to a mathematical calculation, this network which links all the countries with cartel law with each other requires a total of 4005 bilateral agreements.[17] Even with a conservative estimate, under the assumption that an individual country wants a cooperation agreement with 30 countries with a similar level of cartel policy or economic development, the network needs around 1335 agreements. As the number of countries with cartel regulation continues to grow, the number of required bilateral agreements shall increase geometrically. The cost of making so many commitments can outweigh the benefit of it. The large cost leads to a negative attitude on a bilateral agreement.

(2) Dissimilarity in Cartel Regulation

Cooperation through the use of bilateral agreements becomes effective when the substance and procedure of cartel-regulatory regime work similarly under similar legal systems. For example, a memorandum of understanding (MOU) between Australia and New Zealand in 1988, covering cartel regulation, has been appraised as a representative case on close cooperation because the innovative procedures of the MOU allowed the 2 countries to extend their jurisdictions into reciprocal territory. The MOU between the two common law countries was made in the context, where the integration between the Australian Trade Practices Act 1974 and the New Zealand Commerce Act 1986 had been increasing.[18] The highly harmonized competition laws, common law system, and extensive bilateral trade in both countries contributed to the achievement.[19]

On the contrary, differences in procedures and substances of cartel regulation can make international cooperation difficult.[20] A positive comity principle does not work well when the substantive or procedural cartel law of a requested country is

---

[17]The applicable mathematical formula is $N = (n*(n-1))/2$. 'N' is the number of bilateral agreements required while 'n' represents the number of countries with competition laws including cartel regulations at a given time. *See* Taylor (2006), at 120–121.

[18]Simpson Grierson, Bridging the Great Divide, FYI Competition Law (Jul. 2004), *available at* http://www.simpsongrierson.com. On June 29th, 2004, the Australian and New Zealand government announced a joint study on the harmonization of two competition laws.

[19]*See* Taylor (2006), at 119–120; Kennedy (2001), *at* 621.

[20]European Commission Group of Experts on Competition Law stated in 1995 that it is difficult to imagine the emergence of a level playing field if this were to be founded only on a group of inevitably heterogeneous bilateral agreement. Taylor (2006), at 139.

different from that of a requesting country. Particularly, cartel laws in the developing world tend to reflect their national interests more than those in advanced countries, which lead to diverse cartel regulations. It is no surprise that bilateral agreements have been made by centering on the most advanced competition authorities, where economic efficiency has been acknowledged as the major objective.

(3) Lack of Reciprocal Confidence Between Old and Young Competition Authorities

Cooperation will not work well without trust in the capabilities of reciprocal competition authorities, e.g., investigation, evidence-gathering, and security for exchanged information. The possibility of abuse of power or corruption by officials with discretion under an untransparent administrative system in competition authorities of developing countries may make advanced competition authorities less trustful. The mistrust of the advanced competition authorities on the authorities with less experience and skills may cause disruption in the creation of widespread bilateral agreements.

In a recent oil-transferring marine hose price-fixing case, three British executives, who pleaded guilty in the U.S. courts, had to promise to plead guilty for a UK case with similar charges in front of the U.S. Department of Justice (DOJ). The practice pursuant to an international agreement between the U.S. DOJ and UK Office of Fair Trading (OFT) is that a competition authority which has investigated an international cartel may obtain promises of guilty pleas for a case under investigation by another competition authority. Although in-detail contents of the agreement between the UK OFT and the U.S. DOJ are not revealed, the practice raises important issues regarding the infringement on the human right for a fair trial and intervention into sovereignty principle. In terms of human rights, it matters whether it violates the double jeopardy principle for the three defendants. As a governmental authority in the U.S. requested defendants' promises of guilty pleas in a case of the UK, it can violate the defendants' right to have fair trial in the UK, unless the agreement has the same effect as legislation which can intervene on individual rights under constitutional law.

The agreement contributed to the progress of the first price-fixing prosecution of the OFT. However, the practice revealed the mistrust of the U.S. DOJ on the UK authority's capability to perform a proper prosecution itself,[21] and the dependence of the OFT on the US DOJ's prosecution. Although the positive comity principle, which enables one party to ask the other party to enforce its competition law in its jurisdiction, promotes reciprocal respect for the sovereign function of cartel enforcement in each territory, practical cooperation between countries with different levels of cartel enforcements, as the marine hose price-fixing case indicates, may impede the performance of the positive comity principle. The UK may argue that the intervention into sovereign function is acknowledged for its progress of cartel

[21]Michael Peel, *UK group attacks price-fixing court deal with US*, FT (Dec. 21, 2007).

practices under the agreement, but the practice conflicts with normal cooperative activities under a bilateral agreement, e.g., simultaneous raid and information-sharing.

(4) Practices in Favor of Inherent National Interests

Most bilateral agreements are feeble to resistance on the basis of national interest. Administrative officers in charge of investigation and issuance of civil penalty under competition law are unlikely to enforce competition laws strictly if such enforcement causes hindrances to their national interests.[22] Moreover, under the voluntary cooperation approach, which most bilateral agreements use, 'patriotic' regulations and enforcements in favor of domestic welfare rather than global welfare are inevitable.[23] Courts issued, from time to time, decisions preferring national interests to international comity on antitrust cases. For an example, U.S. Courts have held that the Act of State doctrine is not a defense to an antitrust complaint when a foreign sovereign only approves or condones, not compels, a certain conduct.[24] Particularly, requests for confidential business information by governments have been very difficult to be approved as the documents relate to important national trade interests.[25] A high-level officer of the OFT in the UK agreed that the reason for the lack of bilateral agreements between the U.S. and member countries of the EU even after the 1994 International Antitrust

[22]Taylor (2006), at 121–122.

[23]Drexl (2003), at 57; Guzman (Guzman 1998), at 1524–1531 and 1540–1541; Rosenthal (1998), at 568. Guzman illustrates the economic models for proving the biased competition law and its application.

[24]*Refer to* Chap. 2 III.1.(2).1) and VI.3. Among other cases, Hartford Fire Insurance v. CA, 509 U.S. 764, 795–796 and 798–799, 113 S.Ct. 2891, 2909 and 2910–2911 (1993). However, there is a case which resulted in forcing incompatible duties. Westinghouse, which had breached contract to supply uranium to electric utility companies due to an international uranium cartel's refusal to supply and been suited *in re* Westinghouse Elec. Corp. Uranium Contracts Litigation, 405 F.Supp 316, 319 (J.P.M.D.L.1975), sought to produce documents located in Canada, Australia, Britain, and South Africa through the letters rogatory procedure. However, both the Canadian and Australian courts refused to respect letters of request to produce documents in their countries. While the High Court of England accepted the letters rogatory under the Hague Convention on the Taking of Evidence Abroad in Civil and Commercial Matters, to which the U.S. and Britain are signatories, the House of Lords denied effect to the letters in response to British producers' appeal. Subsequently, in a separate antitrust action lodged by Westinghouse against uranium producers of the international cartel in 1976, a district judge acknowledged its jurisdiction and ordered the disclosure of these documents despite the foreign statutes which impose criminal penalties against the information disclosure. The following interlocutory appeal regarding the jurisdiction of the District Court with amici curiae from appellants' governments was rejected. Westinghouse Elec. Corp. v. Rio Algom Ltd, 617 F.2d 1248, 1253–1256 (7th Cir. 1980); Kahn (1980), at 476.

[25]The Westinghouse litigation brought modification or enactment of five foreign statutes. The most important was the British Protection of Trading Interests Act (1980). *See* Kahn, *id.*

Enforcement Assistance Act (IAEAA) is due to the member countries' fear that sharing certain information will lead to the loss of competitive advantage in their business entities.[26]

C. Prospect that FTAs or Bilateral Agreement Work as a Major Tool to International Agreement Regulating Cartels

In light of the situations of repetitive failures of multilateral negotiations and rigorous pursuit of FTAs as an alternative way to promote international trade, an argument that FTAs should be major forces to make international law regulating cartels grows persuasive. The expansion of bilateral or regional agreements joined by the other nations[27] can be a founding bloc to a plurilateral agreement. While South Korea had FTA with Association of Southeast Asian Nations (ASEAN) take effect in 2007, the ASEAN also made FTA with Australia and New Zealand (ANZ) effective in 2010. The expansion of some regional agreements consisting of many members can have the potentiality to work as an alternative to a multilateral approach. Examples of the expanding regional agreements can be recognized in the evolution of competition policy within the APEC and in the expansion of EU competition law into Central and Eastern Europe.[28] The APEC, established to facilitate regional cooperation including competition law and policy, has developed international competition policy with several detailed plans since 1995.[29] The accumulation of the plans succeeded in producing a framework of common principles for an APEC-wide competition policy (APEC Competition Principles).

Competition chapter in FTAs has not been actively used to the level of regulating cartels substantively and seriously, but remained as recommending not only cooperative procedure, but also equal enactment of competition law to both domestic and state enterprises. In order to function as a main tool to leverage competition chapter to an international agreement regulating cartels, the competition chapter in respective FTA needs to address cartel issues more specifically by illustrating hard core cartel activities and to harmonize provisions under the chapter reflecting development of competition law of each trading partner.[30]

[26]Interview with Stephen Blake, Deputy Director on Cartels, UK OFT (Mar. 26, 2008). The author attended 56th Antitrust Law Spring Meeting of American Bar Association in Washington DC in 2008, and had an interview with Blake.

[27]Taylor (2006), at pp. 138–139; Rosenthal (1998), p. 568.

[28]Taylor, id. at pp. 139–140.

[29]The Osaka Action Agenda as the APEC Leaders' Declaration in 1995 initiated a competition law and program. In 1996, Manila Action Plan included member nations' action plans on competition policy. In 1999, the nations agreed on the APEC Competition Principles.

[30]Special and differential treatment between advanced competition authorities and nascent authorities is to be considered in competition chapter with due respect to a different level of competition policies. *See* Article 45.2 and 45.3 of the Cotonou agreement.

6.4 Strategies for Achieving a Binding Multilateral Agreement

A. Preliminary Measure, Short-Term and Long-Term Strategies

(1) A Plurilateral Agreement as a Preliminary Measure

A plurilateral agreement toward competition law may be a good preliminary path to a binding multilateral agreement. At the current stage, when many bilateral agreements have been made out of the necessity of cooperation among competition authorities and when the ICN assists competition authorities in immature competition cultures, the failure of competition policy discussion in the DDA cannot be a permanent obstacle to the creation of a binding multilateral agreement. A plurilateral approach to a multilateral competition regime may overcome strong objections from a majority of DCs because the approach only needs to attract countries that have an interest in cooperation with respect to competition policy, and does not need to persuade countries in immature stage for or with strong objections against competition policy.[31]

(2) Narrowly Focused International Cartel Law: A Short-Term Approach

Separating cartel issues from other competition law issues can contribute to averting divergent dissents from different national perspectives on competition policy. Unlike other competition law issues, cartels impose direct harm on consumers' welfare and cause inefficiencies in market mechanisms except in some cases where exemptions are allowed due to outweighing public welfare. Hard core cartels are seen as causing a lot of direct inefficiencies and harms on consumers by a majority of economists. The prohibition against cartels has obtained an increased level of international consensus centering on advanced markets, as demonstrated through the OECD Hard Core Cartel Recommendation. The Doha Declaration explicitly proclaimed a hard core cartel provision as one of the issues to be further discussed. There is more of a possibility that a binding agreement on only cartels under the definition of this book is to be reached.[32]

As much as possible, the object of international cartel regulation should be narrowed enough to achieve international consensus. A narrowly focused topic, e.g., bid-rigging regulation, can break the current standstill. The first reason is that, as proved by the success of the OECD HCC Recommendation, such a focused topic can achieve an international consensus in an efficient way without discussing

[31]Rosenthal (1998), at 569; Taylor (2006), at 298–300. A 'Group of Experts in Competition Law', appointed by EC Competition Commissioner Karel Van Miert (EC group) proposed a WTO plurilateral competition agreement in 1995.

[32]Rosenthal (1998), at 560. Rosenthal introduces prof. Petermann's paper which urged a competition agreement to focus on hard core cartel with international dimension.

complicated issues of divergent competition law.[33] Bid-rigging is an area of cartel-regulatory realm which has achieved wide consensus in prohibition with criminal penalty due to fraudulently causing huge loss to governmental budget among countries.[34] Regardless of the adoption of cartel regulation, not only advanced countries, e.g., the U.S., but also many DCs and LDCs have penalty provisions against bid-rigging.[35] Second, the bid-rigging has occupied a high portion of cartels cases. According to a research which analyzed 845 cartels in 234 markets, almost one-third of the markets were affected by bid-rigging cartels.[36] Particularly, DCs have discovered and punished bid-rigging, which occupies significant portions of cartel law enforcement under the less developed competition regime.[37] On the other hand, bid-rigging regulation could be underenforced due to corruption or protests from existent interest holders.[38] Not only plurilateral agreement on Government Procurement of WTO but also most FTAs include provisions for securing competitive procurement process.[39] Developing a binding multilateral agreement with focus on bid-rigging, international law can become a precious foundation of a binding multilateral regulating cartels.

(3) International Agreement Reflecting Competition Principles: A Long-Term Approach

The adoption of a whole competition regime with cartel regulation, under a long-term approach, is necessary for enacting active cartel regulation. Effective enforcement of cartel regulations has been possible within the whole competition regime according to the analysis of Chap. 5 of this book regarding competition policy in industrialized and DCs.[40] The analysis demonstrated that general administrative or criminal sanctions regulating cartels only are insufficient measures

[33]Kennedy (2001), at 604. According to a table showing consensus level, hard core cartels (HHCs) on price-fixing, bid-rigging, output restriction, and market allocation have the highest degree of consensus to regulate through multilateral agreement. Export cartel, vertical restrains, abuse of a dominant position and mergers are following HHCs in order of the level of the consensus.

[34]South Korea and Republic of China have bid-rigging penalties in other laws, separate from competition law. *Refer to* Chap. 5, 5.2, B(2) and (4).

[35]The U.S. government has made bid-rigging conspiracies with a higher priority. *See* Connor and Lande (2005), at 543. For DCs and LDCs, *refer to* Chap. 4, 4.3, B(2).

[36]Connor and Lande (2005), at 536–537. Connor and Lande mention that bid-rigging might be about one-fifth less injurious than other forms of collusion as it raises price less than other collusions and occurs locally or nationally rather than international scale. However, as they acknowledge that big-rigging has been treated in the harshest way in the U.S. Sentencing Guidelines, it is true that bid-rigging has achieved the most consensus in punishment among other cartels.

[37]OECD (2001), at 8–10. All the cases introduced by China were bid-rigging.

[38]Taylor (2006), at 205–207. It mentions the underenforcement of bid-rigging in Japan, so-called 'dango'.

[39]*Id.* at 207. *See* Art.VI.4(Technical Specifications), X.1(Non-discriminatory Selection Procedure) and XV.1(a)(a Condition of Limited Tendering) of WTO Agreement on Government Procurement.

[40]*Refer to* Chap. 5, 5.3, A(5) and B(5).

to cultivate the capacity of examining market data and the screening of exemptions. For example, cartel regulation in South Africa had been underenforced for four decades since 1955 when the first law regulating cartels was adopted until 1998 when a modified complete competition regime was enacted.[41] France had shown scarce cartel enforcements for three-quarter century since 1923 when a criminal penalty against cartels was legislated in 1923 until the late 1990s when a whole competition law regime in relation to its integration into the EU market was respectfully acknowledged with sincere efforts for working it on.

However, it takes time to fully enact whole competition law since its serious enforcement was possible on several requirements: a (democratic) political process which enables a reflection of public opinion, the development of a free and open market economy, the improvement of a reasonable legal system, and the support of economic research.[42] The requirements are burdensome for DCs and LDCs. They are major conditions for DCs and international organization to cowork for in order to operate effective cartel regulations. Meanwhile, the concentration on cartels under the short-term approach is possible in the first stage where the former requirements are not met.[43] Although the requirements constrain the possibility of the success of cartel regulation in DCs, the short-term approach suggests a practical tip for enacting effective cartel regulation.

On the other hand, since competition policy has a deep relationship with domestic economic development, concrete provisions in competition law might conflict with domestic economic policy, thereby making countries hesitate to accede to the agreement. In order to overcome the limitation, the long-term approach needs to enact principle-oriented provisions.[44] While competition law agreement in APEC with respect to competition policy is a plurilateral agreement, its provisions centering on principles demonstrate one of the models worthwhile to consider as a long-term approach.

B. Plurilateral Cartel Regulation

Various obstacles has impeded active enforcement of cartel regulations in most DCs. One of the main hurdles is insufficient or lack of international cooperation among competition authorities. Although business practices tend to cross national borders, it is still not easy for a competition authority to find evidences located in foreign jurisdictions due to the lack of institutional cooperation between two countries. During the investigations into international cartels, international cooperation is necessary, so securing institutional cooperation among competition authorities through an international agreement is an important step toward a binding multilateral agreement on regulating cartels.

---

[41]Around 18 actual cartel cases were brought during around the 50 years. *See* Chap. 5, 5.2, B(1).

[42]*See* Chap. 5, 5.2, A(5).

[43]Rosenthal (1998), at 561.

[44]*Id.* at 557–567. Rosenthal introduces principle-based proposals of the EC group, prof. Jenny, Petersmann, Fox, and Shyam Khemani of the World Bank.

(1) Directions for the Plurilateral Agreement

Noticeably, the goal of a plurilateral agreement on competition law, or an agreement among more than 2 countries, is to share the benefit of converged competition law regime through a widened network. The plurilateral agreement is expected to be formulated among countries where the level of enforcement of cartel law has left much to be desired. As a cartel regulation without a complete competition law regime tends to be underenforced, the effective enforcement of cartel regulation needs a total competition regime. However, facing the whole competition law regime which addresses all the issues in competition policy, potential members might hesitate to participate in the plurilateral agreement with no mandatory accession, thereby placing little impact on further multilateral agreements. In light of the fear on the restriction of sovereignty over domestic economic policy, it would be better to start from a procedural convergence through the plurilateral agreement with less of a burden on members. The harmonization of procedures in the plurilateral agreement has much more benefits than cost. The procedural convergence can attract more foreign investment since it reduces the cost of legal searches into foreign legal procedures. Increasing trend of foreign investment in Mexico after the Pact for Mexico in 2013 is a good example.[45] A conference, formal or informal, through the agreement can be a forum to learn advanced skills and experiences of cartel investigations as well as to place the foundation of cooperative workings. Acquiring up-to-date information regarding a cartel can reduce the loss to consumers and efficiencies in each member country's economy. International Competition Network (ICN) is a model if it operates on the formal basis of international agreement.

Harmonizing the substances of the competition law might as well be the next step after widening the purilateral agreement covering procedural aspects. However, as there exist some areas where a negotiation for substantive convergence is not ready, the agreement would be achieved first in the issues where convergence is possible.[46] The APEC is a successful model that subsequent plurilateral agreements pay attention to.[47] Concrete provisions may be added with further amendments. In light of such a country which accedes to the agreement but needs an adjustment period, a greater length of time with a minimum commitment should be permitted.[48]

[45]UNCTAD FDI-TNC-GVC Information System, FDI/TNC database. (www.unctad.org/fdistatistics) (Mexico was ranked as a country with the tenth largest investment in the world in 2012–2013)

[46]*See* Taylor (2006), at 419. Taylor calls such strategy as the 'selective convergence'.

[47]*Id.*, 419–420. He calls APEC competition law as 'soft law principle'. He suggest the concept of co-regulation in which certain provisions in converging areas would be expressed with binding legal obligations while other elements in still diverging areas would be expressed in ambiguous and nonbinding terms under so-called soft law.

[48]*Id.*, 416.

(2) Internal Agreement Within International

Since the plurilateral approach does not require all of the members within an international organization to participate, an international organization treating issues of multinational corporations can propose an international competition agreement including cartel regulations as the part of their laws. Similar to constituent agreements in the Annex IV of the WTO Agreement, an international cartel-regulatory agreement can be adopted by the member countries willing to strengthen their abilities to regulate international cartel activities under the benefit from the agreement. Besides the WTO, the UNCTAD or UN may have a plurilateral cartel-regulatory agreement since not all members need to harmonize their views on cartel regulations in light of their diverse national interests and levels of economic development.

Since a large number of countries has adopted or been preparing for the adoption of a competition regime including cartel regulation after analyzing its cost and benefit, they need assistance from experienced advanced countries. When the benefit of sharing information or technical assistance is granted to new members, international competition agreement will be palatable to the members. With strict protection of confidential information and severe penalty on revelation of the confidential information, potential members' concern about abusing the shared information will lessen.

(3) The Rationales

In international relationships, two theories derived from interpretivist neoliberalism can apply to explain the difficulty of consensus between the North and the South and increase the possibility of reaching the consensus among states with similar interests. The first theory focuses on the 'consensual knowledge' which enables interested actors to command sufficient agreement which serves as a guide to public policy.'[49] In order to be consensual, the knowledge must transcend adhesion to a group and be trans-ideological, thereby providing the basis for the construction of a new international regime.[50] However, cartel regulation in itself does not reach the level of consensus because the cartel regulation as a part of competition policy meets negative responses in DCs and LDCs and because the countries fears that the regulation may interfere with cooperative atmosphere, thereby impeding domestic economic development. Moreover, quite a few states still want to hold control over the free market that has competition in private sectors, although a growing number of countries have adopted competition law. From the perspective of the countries which wants to control markets, the cartel regulation might interfere with profits-earning from international commodity trade. Still supporters of an international cartel agreement have not transcended the group centering on advanced economies to reach the majority of DCs and LDCs.

---

[49]Sell (1998), at 24.

[50]*See id.*

The second theory argues, through a lenient approach that learning and knowledge can play important roles in cooperation even when the consensus limitedly exists within a particular group. Rothstein who argued the second theory agreed with the first theory in the point that intergroup consensual knowledge is a relatively rare + phenomenon.[51] Further Rothstein insists that it is easier to build consensus within each group than between groups because conflicts in values and interests at the intergroup level are likely to be sharpest and the need of each group to maintain unity may mean that the resulting group position is impervious to knowledge and learning and genuine bargaining.[52] As the consensus within each group can impede the building of consensus across groups,[53] the consensus in the advanced countries that efficiency-based competition is important for further economic development has hindered another consensus-building between the North and the South in competition law. Although many developing countries, or transitional economies have adopted competition law regime as a result of developing countries' struggle to survive external economic environment, still the DCs emphasize on economic development rather than on competition because a majority of them have less competitive domestic industries and need to promote cooperation rather than competition. In other words, although efficiency-oriented competition ideology appeared to prevail over economic development agenda due to the weakened unity in the Third World since the mid-1980s, DCs have demonstrated that they prefer the importance of economic development to efficiency-oriented competition through the first exclusion of competition policy among several agendas and the subsequent failure of the DDA negotiation. Rather the efficiency-oriented competition ideology has stemmed the growth of trans-group consensus that a competition regime reflecting both efficiency and development can be created.

In spite of sharp disputes between efficiency and development, cartel regulation needs to be promoted to international law to challenge against globalized practices of multinational firms. In light of the difficulty in harmonizing the contents, a plurilateral agreement as to cartel regulation is recommendable as a convenient method to reach that harmonization. A fragmentary consensus, especially rooted in a discrete ideological position and economic situation, cannot easily reach a mutual compromise.[54] Although there is no mandatory requirement to accede to an agreement, countries will opt for accession when they are aware of the necessity of international law because many countries have voluntarily introduced competition law regime in order to become competitive in a global economy.[55] The countries currently widening a bilateral agreement or assisting in a multilateral agreement can

[51] *See id.*

[52] *See id.*

[53] *Id.*

[54] *Id.* at 31–32.

[55] Dabbah (2003), at 48.

save their time, efforts, and money by becoming a member of a plurilateral agreement and suggesting that their partners also become members.

C. Short-Term Approach: A Binding Multilateral Agreement on Cartels

(1) Members and Target of the Agreement

A multilateral agreement under a narrowed approach tends to be made more conveniently in an organization consisting of countries with similar economic situations, e.g., the OECD, than an organization of countries with diverse levels of economic development, e.g., the UN.[56] Even if full harmonization efforts toward an ideal law succeed in achieving a multilateral agreement consisting of a large number of countries, cost incurred and time spent by the time of such achievement are expected to be significantly high. In addition, its negotiating procedure reflects political struggles, thereby representing the opinions of powerful countries rather than those of less powerful ones.[57] A result of strenuous negotiation tends to be in favor of powerful countries, thereby failing to make real consensus. As membership of the WTO covered more than 150 countries, of which DCs comprise three-quarters,[58] and as the Doha Agenda under the auspice of WTO included whole competition regime unfriendly to most DCs, the failure of the DDA was somewhat expected. So, a binding multilateral agreement on cartels should start among countries with a similar economic level.

As to the coverage of the agreement, a narrow-focused HCC is appropriate as the initial target of the agreement. A narrowly focused object is very convenient to achieve a binding multilateral regulatory agreement. Bid-rigging can be an initial target for such binding multilateral agreement as fraud against public procurement which causes a huge waste in a governmental budget.[59] For example, the second largest cartel in Western Europe was a Dutch construction-industry bidding conspiracy with around US$ 80 billion in sales.[60] The economic development concern among the DCs will not impede the reaching of a consensus on prohibiting bid-rigging as trust in state function and integrity of governmental contracts are necessary components to economic development. Protecting governmental budget from cheating through bid-rigging does good to the public as the budget consists of a tax on the public. The social condemnation against such an extortion of a public

---

[56]Sell (1998), at 75; Taylor (2006), at 342. Taylor wrote that, as a rule of thumb, the greater the differences between nations and the greater the number of nations involved in multilateral negotiations, the greater the range of issues upon which agreement will be required, the more ambitious the harmonization effort (including associated time and costs) required, and the less likelihood there would be of ever reaching multilateral agreement. Even the experience of the EC consisting of a dozen countries indicates that the harmonization of competition laws was difficult to achieve.

[57]Taylor (2006), at 343.

[58]*Id.*, 420.

[59]In the UK, over hundred firms were accused for rigging their bids for multimillion pound contracts. The conspiracy allegedly cost taxpayers hundreds of millions of pounds. *Building Firms Accused of Rigging Bids*, SKYNEWS (Apr. 17, 2008), *at* http://news.sky.com.

[60]Connor and Helmers (2007), at 15–16.

bid has been acknowledged as most countries, either industrialized or developing, have severe sanctions on bid-rigging.[61] Even the countries that do not adopt competition law have legislation against collusive tendering.[62] Practically, penalties imposed against bid-rigging tend to be severer than other cartel activities. The KFTC imposed a US$ 110 million surcharge on bid-riggers, one of the highest surcharges issued by the KFTC, for a three-year military fuel conspiracy.[63]

Subsequently, price-fixing which clearly brings enormous harm to consumers, needs to be addressed as it is a convenient issue to reach a consensus on among members. Price-fixing, the most well-known form of cartel activities, has been considered per se violation of competition law in many countries.[64] Although price-fixing in international trade, e.g., export cartels, has been treated with exemption from competition law in quite a few countries due to sensitive national interests, regular reviews over the exemption are required so that such exemptions may not be abused in a way to hide other cartel activities. Output restriction which reduces the level of production causes the price increase, similar to the outcome of price-fixing. Except for some cartels where approval is necessary for sustaining overall economic structure or public interests outweighing inefficiency, the output restriction falls on the violation of cartel law as a restrictive behavior of competition. Market allocation as the artificial division of markets among competitors impedes market integration and restricts competition in the divided markets. The acquisition of a semi-monopoly position through the allocation agreement takes away consumer benefits which would have been otherwise possible, and attributes them to colluders. While the former four behaviors under the category of hard core cartels do not invoke a debate on subsequent pro-competitive effects, other collusive cartel activities need in-depth study on the balance of pro- and anticompetitive

[61]In the U.S., Sec. 1 of the Sherman Act penalizes a bid-rigger with a fine up to US$ 10 million for a corporation, or fine up to $ 350,000 and/or imprisonment up to 3 years for an individual. In addition, such collusion among competitors may constitute other federal felonies e.g., wire or mail fraud statute, or the false statement statute. Besides criminal penalties, there remains a civil action provision, Sec. 4 of the Clayton Act, which enables victims to recover treble damages. In the UK, under a cartel penalty provision, a bid-rigging participant faces a fine up to 10 % of its annual turnover for the duration of the infringement and imprisonment of up to 3 years. The UK also allows civil liability. In Canada, a fine for both an individual and a corporation involved in bid-rigging is decided by a court and does not have a maximum confinement term. Individual can face imprisonment of up to 5 years. Canada adopts civil damages. In Korea, the KFTC can impose a surcharge of up to 5 % of the turnover. As for criminal penalties, an imprisonment of up to 3 years or a fine up to US$ 200,000 can be imposed. There remains civil liability. *See* OECD (2002), at 24–25.

[62]U.N. (2007), at 25. It illustrates the People's Republic of China (prior to adopting the 2007 AML), and Kenya.

[63]In a subsequent civil action where a subsidiary under the military department filed an action in damages, a district of court in Korea held that a total of 81 million in damages should be redressed. Press Release of KFTC, Civil action on the basis of military fuel bid-rigging received US$ 81 million recover [군납유류 입찰담합 관련 민사소송에서 810억 배상판결] (Jan. 2007), *at* http://ftc.go.kr/data/hwp/20070123_101790.hwp.

[64]U.N. (2007), at 24.

effects. Regulations of the collusive activities will be more appropriate under a long-term approach.

(2) Contents of the Agreement

A multilateral agreement under the short-term approach requires all members to be bound by contents of the agreement. However, international trials for a multilateral agreement with sophisticated provisions covering all the competition issues have failed and are not likely to succeed in the near future due to strong domestic interests. One of the interests is for a country to maintain sovereign power over economic policy as a multilateral agreement with broad competition issues causes the inevitable restriction of sovereign power in choosing domestic policy and legislation. To reduce the country's concern, it is important to examine the respective aspect of cartel behaviors with a narrow focus. Only the anticompetitive behavior(s) that most countries agree to regulate need to be included as concrete object(s) of the agreement under the short-term approach. With efforts to cover other horizontal agreements which do not clearly show clear intents or results to restrict competition from the first stage, it will be almost impossible for the approach to obtain international consensus for the creation of a binding international cartel agreement. Reaching the consensus will need serious discussions regarding each country's different standard of evaluating the competitiveness of each categorical behavior under a collusive horizontal agreement.[65] As past trials illustrated, the discussion may make completion of the multilateral agreement almost impossible. Once a binding multilateral cartel agreement is created, the clear enumeration of narrowed illegal cartel behaviors will support the compliance of companies working globally without confusion and will persuade countries to accede to the agreement. Although the adoption of rule of reason may arguably be proper regarding the other aspects of horizontal agreements, the narrowed anticompetitive act(s) under the agreement matches the per se rule better. Properness of the per se rule against narrowly defined cartels is confirmed by the APEC countries' experiences.[66] A case with a pro-competitive effect outweighing an anticompetitive one needs to be addressed with categorized exemptions under the per se rule.

The exemption provisions that approve certain cartels with proof of outweighing efficiency or public interest reflecting situations in DCs should accompany the strict prohibition of cartels with the per se rule. The World Bank stated that it prefers limited competition law to no competition law at all.[67] Besides the one-entity exemption where two competing companies merges or establishes a joint venture, a crisis cartel, a small-and-middle-enterprise (SME) cartel, a R&D cartel, and an efficiency cartel are the examples of permissive cartels. Such exempted cartels, however, need to be screened by a transparent standard in order to prevent

[65]Taylor (2006), at 94 and 95.

[66]*Id.*, at 95.

[67]*Id.*, at 100. fn 45.

loopholes of the main rule.[68] If the coverage of the exemptions is too wide and allows arbitrary approval of an anticompetitive cartel, it undermines trust in the international cartel-regulatory agreement. When an exemption is granted, a principle where any exemption should be no greater in scope than necessary for the public interest should be clearly stipulated.[69] It is noted that quite a few countries within APEC hesitates to broaden or even abolish the exemptions since the exemptions turned out to bring about more harm than good, e.g., Japan and Korea's repeal of extensive cartel exemption.[70]

(3) Exemptions from Cartel Regulations
1) Positive Roles of Cartel Exemption

Exemption from cartel regulation is an area in competition law where other policy considerations may intervene along with the promotion of competition as the primary objective of the law. A large number of developing countries, where competitiveness in domestic industries does not develop sufficiently, can hardly promote economic development without using industrial policies for their economic development. An exemption provision which allows to use industrial policy with competition policy may take away from the DCs the fear that competition may obstruct economic development, thereby working as an incentive to adopt a competition law including cartel regulation. As one of special and differential treatment (SDT) to DCs, the cartel exemption for industry promotion will solicit the support of DCs for international cartel law.

Besides the exemption for industrial policy, diverse cartels, e.g., a depression cartel, a research and development (R&D) cartel, and a cartel for professional organizations, are allowed to be exempted in many jurisdictions for reasonable grounds.[71] The cartels, respectively, work to overcome depression in overall the economy, to promote R&D, and to secure professional ethical standards.

In addition, a cartel for producing primary commodities is inevitable to the survival of producers, as the cartel promises fair reward to producers in LDCs under less diversified economic structure and smallholders in advanced countries.[72] A commodity cartel, which produces primary commodities, stabilizes the volatile prices of farm, forest, fishery or any mineral product, the production of which needs to be planned beforehand with an expected demand. As the production of primary

[68]Kennedy (2001), at 624–625. Kennedy emphasizes on the competition advocacy through the promotion of transparency as an effective competition policy.

[69]*See* Taylor (2006), at 100.

[70]*Id.*, 99; Huh (2002), at 109–112. Korea's Omnibus Cartel Repeal Act in 1999 repealed 20 cartel exemptions under 18 legislations. The Act included repeal of fee settlements in nine professional services by each association, repeal of the management of price and production in export of agricultural products, and limitation of objects of collective optional contracts for small and medium enterprises among other things.

[71]*See* Chap. 2, Sec 2.3, C.

[72]Scherer (1994), at 52. For instance, the U.S. exempts agricultural cooperatives from the Sherman Act.

commodities can hardly, if ever, meet the shift of demand as fast as artificial product due to its inflexible supply condition, prices will increase rapidly when supply quantity is outnumbered by demand in a market. Meanwhile prices will decrease in case of overproduction when the supply exceeds the demand. The inflexibility of commodity prices threatens the survival of producers and consumers as their living depends on earning and procuring from the commodity trade. The management of production with forecasted demand contributes to sustaining the price stability of commodities.

2) Rationales to Justify Exemptions in the Developing World

A majority of competition policy researchers have objected to the exemptions mainly because the approval of certain cartels causes a loss in consumer welfare through a higher price than one without a cartel. Another reason is that an incentive to increase a firm's efficiency lessens by maintaining inefficient firms in exchange of sacrificing either efficient firms' growth or consumers' welfare, thereby diminishing market efficiency.[73] However, due to the insufficient information about DCs and LDCs, critics tend to overlook the scarce sources and existent obstacles in raising the level of investment. If any exemption category is not allowed, the most efficient global companies with mass intra-company capital will occupy a large part of domestic industries in the DCs. The result means the permanent collapse of domestic industries in these countries as the examples of Mongolia and Peru illustrate.[74] Providing temporary protection to cartels with long-term benefit outweighing temporary damage to consumer welfare contributes much to the economic development of LDCs and to the majority of DCs.

The experiences of advanced cartel regulations demonstrate that the exemptions have been used in light of economic and political situations. Even industrial policies with political support prevailed over competition policy in advanced competition law practices. In France, cartel laws had been underenforced up to a few decades after the WWII. High courts in the U.S.[75] and the UK approved exceptional cases during great economic depressions. The U.S. governmental cartelization plan to rescue a severely depressed economy was effective under the National Industrial Recovery Act.[76] While the U.S. had adopted general exemptions for entire industries in the first half of the twentieth century, it enacted transactional or

[73]*Id.* 636–637 for crisis cartel. *See also* Taylor (2006), 233; Waller (1997), 397; Rosenthal (1998), at 559–563. Rosenthal introduces opinions of prof. Immenga, prof. Fox, and Shyam Kemani of the World Bank regarding elimination of export cartel exemption.

[74]Reinert (2007), at 173–179. Since Mongolia opened up its market to the world in 1991, almost overnight, most industrial sectors and production were down by more than 90 % in physical volume. In Peru, at the end of 1970s, abrupt free trade caused industrial death. *See id.* at 183 and Fig. 15 for deteriorating terms of trade.

[75]Appalachian Coals Inc. et al. v. U.S. 288 U.S. 344 (1933).

[76]Due to its vague standard and unbridled discretion to President or private associations, the NIRA turned out to be unconstitutional in the Supreme Court decision, *ALA Schechter Poultry Corp. v. U.S.* (1935). Peritz (1996), at 130–131.

event-specific exemptions in the last half of the century. One of the latter examples is the 1982 Export Trading Company Act which authorizes the creation and operation of joint selling agreement relating to foreign sales.[77]

However, the exemption provisions have worked only as exceptions to principal anticartel rule. According to the experiences of other countries with cartel regulation, cartels approved by competition authorities had occupied a tiny portion of the total of cartel cases.[78] In Germany, the Minister of Economics has the authority to override decisions by the Federal Cartel Office (FCO) to prohibit a cartel under (i) outweighed general economic advantages, (ii) justified predominant public interests, or (iii) consideration of international competitiveness of the firms. The division of power, which allows the exemption of cartel regulation, has caused little, if any, noticeable trouble in cartel regulation practices.[79] In the EU, only two crisis cartel cases were approved for exemption under Art. 80(3) of the EC Treaty in the EU Commission during the last two decades.[80]

3) Screening Exemption Abuse

Although cartel exemptions are approved, a broad coverage of exempted cartels or the usage of ambiguous terms, e.g., public interest, still brings about concern on the abuse of exemptions. Insufficient legal barriers to political influences or lenient treatments against bribery in DCs increase the possibility of abusing the exemptions. The exclusive business practices of cartel members, although the cartel was previously approved, impede the progress of efficient companies in the markets.[81]

In order to prevent the abuse of an exemption procedure, any exemption should be no greater in scope than necessary for the particular national concern to be addressed.[82] For this purpose, recommendable is a review system with the

[77]15 U.S.C. Sec. 4001–4003. *See* ABA (2007).

[78]South Korea also demonstrates only a few cases for cartel approval among competitors under six exemption categories. Only four competition-restriction cases among competitors had been approved for 24 years (1981–2004) while 138 cases by the association of entrepreneurs had been approved during the same period. KFTC, *Statistics regarding Approval of Cartels* [공정거래위원회통계연보: 부당한 공동행위 및 사업자단체의 금지행위시정], *at* db.kosbi.re.kr/include/download.asp?fl_nm=200511000.xls&seq=200511000. visited on May 5, 2008. Meanwhile, Japan had six approval cases from 1947 up to 1957. Other cartels were exempted from the coverage of Japan's Antimonopoly Law by other laws with exemption provisions. Kwon (1999), p. 132.

[79]Immenga (1999), at 351–352. Until 1998, out of 121 prohibition of mergers and 16 demands of ministerial authorizations, 4 % (six cases) had been approved under specific conditions. In addition, the Monopoly Commission expressed positive opinion as to the separation of power. Immenga states that the lesson applies to cartels in the same way.

[80]Fiebig (1999), at 622. Two cases are Commission Decision 84/380, 1984 O.J. (L 207) 17, 18 (so-called Synthetic Fibres cartel) and 94/296, 1994 O.J. (L 131) 15, 17 (Stichting Baksteen cartel).

[81]Taylor (2006), at 205. It illustrates a case where an oil import cartel in the U.S., once authorized by the US DOJ, later performed anticompetitive conducts in the domestic market, thereby resulting in a deprival of the authorization.

[82]*Id.*, 100.

following three concrete conditions: (1) an independent panel with the participation of competition experts, (2) transparent and nondiscriminatory decision-making, and (3) a regular review of reasonability of the exemption. The authority in charge of cartel regulation usually has the initial function of reviewing exemption applications. As political influence is strong enough to override a competition authority, a decision-making quasi-judicial panel needs to function independently. In addition, concrete analyses from competition experts of the inefficiency of a proposed cartel as well as their benefits should be included in the decision. The decisions are to be published for public review. Subsequent petitions, trials, or legal debates can develop competition law jurisprudence and reduce unreasonable political influence and the possibility of corruption. Standards for decision-making should be so nondiscriminatory that an exemption process should be equal to associations with similar economic impacts regardless of members' nationalities. Since an economic situation, one of the bases of decisions, may change, the authority should screen the exempted cases in a regular time interval. In other words, it should be under a regular review to evaluate whether the objectives, behaviors, and negative effect of the cartels avert the standard of an original approval.

As competitive market structure grows entrenched, many cartel exemptions will be withdrawn by a nation's own screening procedure. International law needs to address the building of a transparent and clear exemption-screening system.[83] Among 27 countries which adopted explicit export cartel exemption in their competition laws, at least 37 % removed the exemption from 1995 to 2005.[84] Particularly, South Korea, through so-called Cartel Repeal Act in 1999, repealed cartel exemptions of nineteen legislations according to the analysis which indicated that the exemptions had been abused or obsolete.[85] Japan also repealed its extensive cartel exemptions as such exemptions caused more harm than good.[86]

(4) Voluntary Export Restraint Under the Category of Export Cartel Exemption

Voluntary export restraint (VER) or voluntary restraint agreement (VRA) is an aspect of export cartels as well as a measure of trade policy that has been utilized when an importing nation requests an exporting nation to restrain its exports voluntarily. VER or VRA requests were usually made when an exporting country arguably trades with unfair terms e.g., through dumping, export subsidies, or causing significant injury to an importing country's industry.[87] When the exporting country does not accept the request, an import quota or antidumping/counter-veiling duty will be placed. The VER provides benefits to both an importing nation and an

[83]Taylor (2006), at 99.

[84]Levenstein and Suslow (2005), at 815. They surveyed 55 countries, and at least ten countries rewrote their competition laws by removing explicit export cartel exemptions. Currently, 17 countries offer statutory exemptions.

[85]Kwon (1999), at 156. Korea is currently making its efforts to prepare its second Cartel Repeal Act of 2008.

[86]Taylor (2006), at 99.

[87]Scherer (1994), at 49.

exporting nation in the following ways. First, a part of the increased high price under quantity restriction, which would accrue on the importing nation's tariff budget, will go to the exporting nation's producer. Second, the importing nation can avoid the exporting nation's potential complaint about a reprisal move that would be taken by the importing nation without the VER.[88]

On the other hand, consumers in the importing country endure loss due to high prices and reduced import quantity through either the VER or import quota. Since the importing nation is an initial actor in asking for such a measure, a court facing a private action subsequently brought by consumers will find it difficult to apply laws to the situation that a decision may conflict with the trade policy of its government. In the U.S. a private action against members participating in the VER was not successful.[89]

(5) Regulation of Export Cartel: Positive Comity Versus. Extraterritorial Application

An export cartel, which operates within a home country but supply its product beyond the country, tends not to be regulated by the home country as they provide great profits to the country despite damaging consumers in a foreign market. A research model illustrates that international cartel law cannot include export cartel regulation as a part and that the extraterritorial application of domestic cartel law in advanced countries will play the regulatory role.[90] According to Gunzman's theory, a net exporting country (A) is not willing to provide its consent to a binding anticartel multilateral agreement because the agreement, trying to eliminate export cartel exemption and to include positive comity provision, can demolish its export cartels (EC) and cause a loss in its national wealth (Fig. 6.1).[91]

Let us assume that the anticartel multilateral agreement is binding both nations. Even if a net importing country (B) and a net exporting country (A) enforce each domestic competition law against respective EC, the positive economic impact of the domestic enforcement against its domestic EC will be smaller in A than that in B. It is because A's economic profits from the EC A are larger than B's from the EC B as size of arrows and circle of EC A indicate.[92] Considering its larger benefit, A will neither want the assumption to come true nor accede to the anticartel

[88]For in-detail explanation, refer to Scherer, *id.* at 50–51 and Fig. 4.2.

[89]The Consumer Union brought a lawsuit against the VERs in 1969 adopted by Japanese and European steel producers under the pressure from the U.S. government. On the contrary to a district court decision that the VER violated the Art. 1 of Sherman Act, an appellate court held that negotiating the VER belong to the U.S. president's foreign policy power. Consumers Union of U.S., Inc., v. William Rogers et al., 352 F. Supp. 1319 (1973); *vacated on appeal in* CU of the U.S., Inc. v. Henry Kissinger et al., 506 F. 2d 136 (1974), *cert. den.* 421 U.S. 1004 (1975).

[90]Guzman (1998), at 1503–1505 and 1508.

[91]*Id.*, 1528–1529. Positive comity provision requires a net exporting country to enforce its cartel law against its export cartels.

[92]A net exporting country is the nation where exports of imperfectly competitive goods (artificial product on the contrary to agricultural product) outweigh its imports while a net importing country is the nation where its imports outweigh its exports.

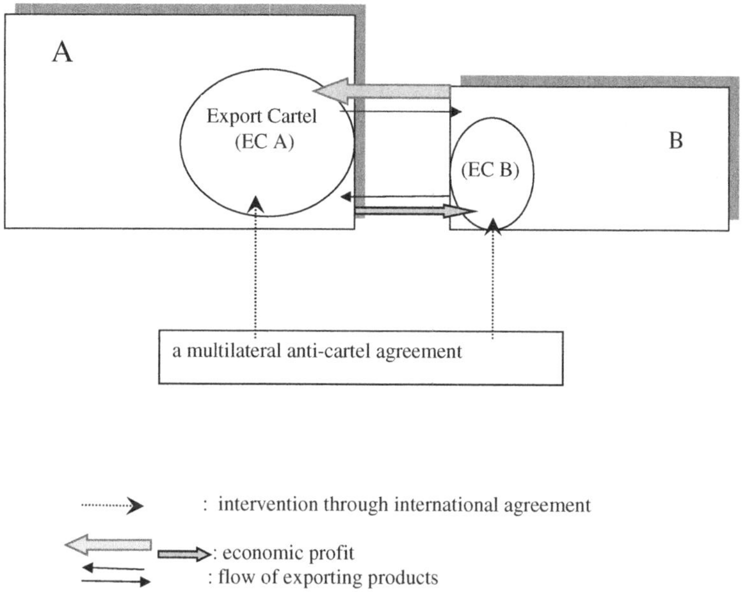

Fig. 6.1 Export cartels of net exporting nation and net importing nation under international agreement

multilateral agreement. A will stick to EC exemptions and extraterritorial applications of domestic cartel law against EC B in B. On the other hand, B tries to propose international cartel-regulatory agreement including positive comity with no exemptions for an EC.[93] A represents advanced countries while B represents DCs.

Current multilateral negotiations against cartels reflect Gunzman's argument. For instance, while the Model Law of the UNCTAD representing net importing countries does not address the export cartel exemption,[94] the 1998 HHC Recommendation of the OECD representing net exporting countries approves export cartel exemption along with other national exemptions.[95] Meanwhile, both the Model Law and the Recommendation did not address the extraterritorial application issue, which most bilateral agreements address. It is thought to be that the U.S., with a strong extraterritorial application policy, did not want to bring the issue to multilateral international negotiations but brought the issue to a negotiation table with neighboring trade partners, where extraterritorial applications established an actual dispute. A bilateral agreement or a unilateral restraint which respect

[93]Guzman (1998), at 1535–1538.

[94]Chapter III, Sec. II enumerates several conditions for exemption, (1) advanced proper notification, (2) who is engaged by companies subject to effective competition, and (3) competition officials conclude that the agreement as a whole will produce a net public benefit.

[95]I. A. 2. b) (ii) of the OECD Recommendation take away from the coverage of recommendation the arrangements excluded from national competition laws.

comity and self-restraint principle, as a realistic alternative to a multilateral agreement, can be appropriate measures, which control the problems coming from extraterritorial application.[96]

As the narrowed approach for a binding multilateral rule requires a consensus from advanced economies in the nascent stage, an export cartel needs to be treated as one of the exemptions allowed for public interest.[97] However, profits earned from export cartels result from the sacrifice of the same amount of foreign consumers' welfare, and export cartel practices are incompatible with nondiscrimination principle.[98] Therefore, the multilateral cartel agreement should negotiate to eliminate export cartel exemption as a long-term goal. Moreover, each export cartel exemption is to be screened by each competition regulator under an international agreement for the possibility of abuse.[99] A study on the application of the U.S. Export Trading Company Act designed to provide small companies with cost savings through a common sales organization, reveals a harsh reality where the law fosters hard core cartel activities rather than operating under its original intent.[100] As a result, pursuant to similar standards of other public interest exemptions, regular reports on export cartel practices are to be submitted, screened, and reviewed for further approval on the basis of the reports. When the export cartel practices conflict with the original intent, they should lose their exemption status.

D. A Long-Term Approach: Multilateral Agreement on the Whole Competition Regime

(1) Obstacles in Reaching International Competition Law

Activating an effective cartel regulation needs to correlate with promoting a national competition regime as the practice of cartel regulation requires the advanced skills and the institutional power of a market analysis which can be facilitated under the whole competition law. According to the former experiences of DCs and advanced economies, the incorporation of a HCC regulation into an administrative regime or criminal law system without an overall competition policy will result in under enforcement without sufficient support. Therefore, an effective international cartel regulation needs to address the activation of a competition regime.

96 Kennedy (2001), 626.

97 Waller (1997), 398. He mentions that export cartels are facts of economic life, the attitude of which need to be adopted.

98 *Id.*, 398–399; Taylor (2006), 233.

99 Scherer (1994), 46. Scherer illustrated two concrete measures, e.g., the registration of an association seeking export cartel exemption, and the disclosure of its functions.

100 Among 94 export trading companies (ETCs), around 25 % of the total ETCs worked closely to the intent of the Act, e.g., four for foreign government liaison, nine for joint promotion activities, four for the promotion of a U.S. region, four for warranty service, and seven for project coordination. The remaining 75 % of the ETCs were engaged in fixed prices (37 cases), coordinated bids (36), and customers allocation (14). *Id.* at 45.

An international agreement which includes a whole competition law regime, however, has more hurdles in securing sufficient accession than the narrow approach. Consensus as to the level of state involvement in economic development, the level of competition in light of the necessity of cooperation among small- or middle-sized enterprises (SMEs), the prioritization of the efficiency over employment or national wealth, will not likely be achieved as each country considers their unique economic situations, such as the promotion of a less competitive industry, and the point that competition itself does not always grow national economic wealth. The failures of competition policy discussion under the WTO, e.g., the Cancun failure and the abandoning of the Draft International Antitrust Code by the WTO, reveal the lack of consensus regarding the adoption of a whole competition regime due to differing interests among nations.

(2) Principle-Based International Competition Law

1) Rationales

In order to succeed in achieving a multilateral international agreement regarding competition law, core principles approaching a level of international consensus, for example, that private competitors shall not collude to restrict competition, should be explicitly settled to guide the content and application of domestic competition laws.[101] The reason why a principle-based international competition law is prioritized is that spending too many sources to achieve a level of nearly full harmonization of concrete substantive and procedural provisions is a wasteful strategy in light of past failures. Taylor argued that, through an attempt to quantify the benefits and costs of international harmonization of competition laws, marginal benefit decreases and marginal cost increases as national competition laws converge from status quo to full harmonization under a total divergence-harmonization continuum.[102] In light of high costs required for full harmonization of a competition regime, a better strategy toward international harmonization is to concentrate more efforts to achieve international consensus on several topics where consensus-making is less costly where greater benefits can derive.[103] According to Taylor, laws prohibiting price-fixing, anticartel laws, and laws regulating horizontal restraints other than cartels are three major issues of competition law where

---

[101]Taylor (2006), 76 and 95.

[102]*See id.* at 338.

[103]Taylor explains that the optimal point should be where marginal cost equals marginal benefit, which falls somewhere between convergence and partial harmonization in the continuum. *Id.* at 340–345.

Table 6.1 Convergence-harmonization continuum

Status quo	Convergence	Partial harmonization	Full harmonization
Current level of convergence	A state less than partial harmonization within which two or more nations achieve a reasonable degree of similarity in domestic competition laws but continue to hold different standards	Uniformity of their substantive competition obligations and procedures between 60 % & 80 % of their competition laws	Near uniformity of their substantive competition obligations and procedures for more than 80 % of their competition laws

convergence can expectedly bring about the most benefit.[104] The past failures in the creation of concrete provisions in international competition law demonstrated that in-detail stipulations regarding controversial areas, where diverse domestic regulations exist, could not make sufficient accessions or ratifications (Table 6.1).[105]

2) Objectives of International Competition Law

A principle-based agreement covering a whole competition regime may include objectives, such as fair distribution, nondiscrimination, and differential treatment in light of national interests, which have been disputed among countries with advanced competition law and those with less advanced ones. The principle-based international competition law will not lose its focus on strengthening efficiency due to the harmonization with other national interests, such as employment, investment for research and development, and protection of national security, because competition regime and effective cartel regulation necessarily lead to the improvement of efficiency. The countries which accede to the principle-based agreement shall at least be urged to put effort to enact such competition laws.[106] As a result, principles in international competition law will work toward fostering international convergence for domestic competition laws.[107]

The concrete contents of a domestic competition law will depend on each country's policies, economic situations, and institutional developments. Although

[104] *Id.* at 347. Taylor cites the Global Competition Policy (ed. Graham and Richardson) (Institute for International Economics, IIE) and requests attention to the IIE Survey stating the four major elements which creates great benefits.

[105] *Id.* at 308.

[106] *Id.* at 358. Taylor state to the same cause that the agreement can pressure its members to increase the level of competition in their domestic markets, and let the competition regime established and work in a transparent way.

[107] *Id.* at 354.

the principle-based approach is adopted, however, the cartel regulation is unlikely to be so divergent. In a case of the APEC, the similarity in the general content and structure of competition laws of member countries owes much to commonly accepted microeconomic theories, precedents established by the earliest statutory formation of competition law, e.g., the Sherman Act of the U.S. and the Treaty of Rome which established the European Community, and common economic influences among the member countries.[108]

3) Positive Functions of Principle-based International Competition Agreement

Countries with advanced competition law practices do not need to criticize the approach for ineffective rules or low level of convergence in DCs' competition laws, but to stick to maintain the level of their current enforcements.[109] As long as extraterritorial applications of competition laws are allowed, the acceptance of the low level of convergence by advanced competition regimes causes few, if any, damages to domestic laws in advanced countries. Rather, an international competition agreement can work as a stick to pressure DCs to enact competition law seriously. Particularly, cartel regulation will be under serious pressure to improve its enforcement as the regulation has obtained the broadest consensus among other areas of competition law. The acknowledgement of diverse regulatory regimes can diminish the DCs' blind protests against a competitive market system, thereby leading them to more competitive market systems.

4) An Example: GATS Annex on Telecommunications

The General Agreement on Trade in Services (GATS) Annex on Telecommunications is an example of a good model of a principle-based international competition law.[110] Different from detailed provisions of the GATS, the Annex has provisions which ensure several important principles for the telecommunication service trade. Art. 4 of the Annex requires member countries to provide information on their conditions of access to public telecommunication transport networks and services in order to remove arbitrary restrictions through a transparent standard of information submission. Art. 5(a), (b), (c) and (e) require member countries to provide access to public telecommunication transport networks and services through reasonable, nondiscriminatory, and necessary conditions. The WTO Panel acknowledged, in the decision of Mexico-Measures Affecting

[108]*Id.* at 75.

[109]*Id.* 352. Joel Klein, assistant attorney-general of the U.S. Department of Justice, stated that efforts to achieve a minimum set of competition principles could end up legitimating weak and ineffective rules, which would not serve the goals of trade liberalization. However, he neglected the benefit of enacting competition law in DCs.

[110]Taylor (2006), 360.

Telecommunications Services, that the use of an ambiguous word in the GATS Annex was intended for WTO members to reserve a degree of flexibility in meeting WTO members' commitments.[111]

(3) Special and Differential Treatment (SDT)

SDT, as a precious principle of international development law, can be applied to an international competition agreement.[112] SDT has been adopted widely as an exception to nondiscriminatory principle including most-favored nation (MFN) and national treatment (NT) in international trade law since the New International Economic Order emerged. As international competition law and trade law have some areas in common and negotiations for an international competition agreement frequently took place with regard to international trade regimes, e.g., ITO, GATT/WTO and UNCTAD, nondiscrimination principle has been argued as one of the objectives which an international competition agreement should adopt.[113] In light of the close relationship between nondiscrimination and SDT, that is, principle and exception, there is no reason why SDT should be excluded in an international competition agreement, separately from nondiscriminatory principle. Particularly, in light of a wide range of countries from LDCs to DCs to advanced countries, which have adopted a competition regime, and several conditions for effective operation of competition law, formal equal treatment may result in the collapse of overall industries in LDCs and less competitive industries in DCs which will work as fundamental forces for future economic development in the countries. With the formal NT principle which does not allow adjusting measures, current less diversified economic structure in LDCs and low income DCs will have few chances of cultivating domestic companies necessary for economic development because global competitive companies request nondiscrimination under domestic competition law, thereby prevailing over domestic companies with a nascent level of investment. With the formal MFN principle which does not allow special treatment, immature companies from LDCs need to compete with global companies which have accumulated capital, skills, and experiences. Such formally equal positions actually result in the maintenance of status quo of unequality. On the contrary, SDT helps less skilled competition authorities in LDCs and DCs to obtain technical assistances from advanced competition authorities. Moreover, DCs may have flexibility in complying with the obligations of the agreement under respective time schedules for adjustment.[114] The SDT principle may even permit a LDC to be excluded from some provisions in light of its economic situation.

---

[111]*See* Report of the WTO Panel, Mexico-Measures Affecting Telecommunications Service, WT/DS204/R (2 Apr. 2004); Taylor (2006), 359.

[112]Taylor (2006), fn 88 at 325. He proposed SDT as one of general exceptions of a nondiscrimination principle.

[113]*Id.* at 321–325; Dabbah (2003), at 241–242; Rosenthal (1998), 563. Rosenthal cites prof. Eleanor Fox's proposal.

[114]Taylor (2006), 415.

In order to persuade DCs and LDCs, which enact competition law or are considering its enactment, to accede to a binding international competition agreement, the SDT is indispensable to establish international competition law.[115] Through the SDT of GATS Annex on Communications, DCs are allowed to help strengthen their domestic infrastructure and capacity through technical cooperation with advanced countries,[116] and to increase their participation in international telecommunication service trades and development programs of international organizations.[117] Article 6(d) of GATS mentions that special consideration shall be made for development of the telecommunication infrastructure and the expansion of service trade in LDCs.

Advanced countries can enjoy, in exchange of the SDT concessions, the enhancement of market access to markets in DCs. As the relationship of SDT to NT and MFN is not a permanent exception but temporary one, the establishment and operation of an international competition law will provide level playing field even in DCs' markets for global companies. In order to prevent willful abuse by existent interest holders, transparent review mechanism shall be secured with regular submission of information by a council consisting of representatives from both advanced countries and DCs shall be secured.

(4) The Establishment of International Competition Law Procedure

As most procedural differences are not so directly related to public interest as substantive differences, procedural negotiation has more of a chance to reach a consensus. An international competition agreement needs, largely, three types of procedures: compliance-securing procedures, harmonized procedures, and coordinated procedures.

First, compliance-securing procedure discourages members from condoning restrictive business practices within their territories. Dispute settlement procedure, which solves conflicts regarding domestic competition law among member countries, falls under this category. The dispute settlement procedure is necessary for the successful operation of a binding competition agreement as it can ensure member countries' efforts to apply agreed principle-based provisions to domestic laws.[118]

With respect to the institution in charge of dispute settlement, quite a few scholars argue that a WTO-centered dispute settlement, which has operated successfully, is a wise institution for dispute settlement system of a competition agreement with a relatively weak-consensus basis.[119] Supplementary relationship between trade law and competition law and past failures to achieve an independent institution suggest that a new international competition agreement will work better when it makes the most use of the relationship with WTO.

---

[115] *Id.*, at 142.

[116] Article 5(g) and 6(b).

[117] Article 6(a), Art. 7(a) and (b).

[118] Rosenthal (1998), 570.

[119] *Id.*; Waller (1997), 399; Taylor (2006), 184; Kennedy (2001), at 606.

A proposal for establishing a register of certain anticompetitive practices, including current regimes, e.g., block exemption of cartel regulation of the EC treaty, is noteworthy.[120] Through the international registration requirement and regular information submission, potential anticompetitive business practices shall be tackled through regular screening based upon registered data.

Second, harmonized procedures substantially reduce inconveniences from divergent procedures. The harmonized procedures will lower the large transaction costs, which have impeded companies' active operation in international business, of searching and following different procedures for the same international transaction.[121] Some researchers argue that harmonized international merger procedures should be prioritized among other procedural issues as divergent merger procedures have made companies spend much legal cost and time.[122] Different premerger notification processes in countries as well as multiple merger guidelines under the impact of a cross-border merger have placed burdens on related companies. Concern regarding the revelation of confidential business information under the different procedures might stem robust business practices.[123] An international system designed to protect confidential information is needed to reduce the concern as mentioned by the previous Chap. 5.[124] For example, an international merger report system can lessen the concern accompanied to international M&A, thereby facilitating pro-competitive M&As to progress.

Third, coordinated procedures maximize international cooperation among domestic competition law enforcers. The most effective cooperation until now has been performed under bilateral or regional agreements. Such international cooperation has exposed its limitation to competition authorities in DCs, because advanced competition authorities do not want to have bilateral agreements with less developed authorities.[125] Advanced authorities have hesitated to cooperate with less developed authorities due to mistrust in their capacities of enforcement and preservation of confidential information. Practical assistance and cooperation without a formal agreement have provided insufficient benefits for less developed authorities to fully enforce their competition laws. A binding multinational

---

[120]Rosenthal (1998), 558–559. Through experts' report to the EC, prof. Jenny and prof. Scherer urged the necessity of an international register.

[121]Waller (1997), 400; Dabbah (2003), 271.

[122]Rosenthal (1998), 557–567. A group of experts who submit reports to the EC, prof. Scherer, prof.. Fox, Khemani from the World Bank, and Schone from Neue Zuricher Zeitung suggested proposals for a competition law model for the Central European countries. Those of prof. Fingleton, Fox, Neven, and Seabright included international merger procedures.

[123]Waller (1997), 400; Dabbah (2003), 271–272.

[124]*Refer to* Chap. 5, 5.5, C. for challenges and suggestions of sharing confidential information in international cartel procedure.

[125]Rosenthal (1998), 568. He mentions the over-breadth and excessive penalties of U.S. antitrust law as the reasons why bilateral agreements involving the U.S. have limited potential.

competition agreement should facilitate reciprocal practical assistance in domestic competition law enforcement and build a system to prevent confidential information from being abused.

6.5 Applicability of International Criminal Law as to Cartels

A. Economic Crimes in International Criminal Law

(1) International Criminal Law

The international community developed 25 categories of international crimes through historic accidents and related treaties. Currently, international law has placed a priority over criminalizing the most serious interventions against human life and safety rather than against social, economic, cultural, and other interests. States are obligated to make the most serious interventions crimes pursuant to the international compelling law, jus cogens.[126] Some examples of the most serious interventions are aggression, war crimes, unlawful possession, use or placement of weapons under the category of the peacekeeping, and genocide and crimes against humanity under the protection of fundamental human rights.

As crimes in the level of *jus cogens* impose obligations on states to prosecute, extradite, and cooperate in prosecution without granting immunity, they are under the universal jurisdiction so that any state may prosecute and punish culprits. The criminalization of the most serious interventions against human life and safety, e.g., genocide and war crimes, is based on custom, or a part of general principles of law as well as treaty provisions. Regarding an intervention which does not reach the level of *jus cogens*, states are not obligated but merely allowed to punish perpetrators unless the states accede to a specific treaty for punishing the crime.[127] Such interventions protect social, economic, and other interests. For example, crimes, such as 'unlawful traffic in drugs and related drug offenses,' 'international traffic in obscene publications,' and the 'destruction and/or theft of national treasures,' protect important social and cultural interests. Such crimes, as 'unlawful use of mails' and 'unlawful interference with international submarine cables,' protect communication. Meanwhile, the crime of 'unlawful acts against certain internationally protected elements of the environment' protects the environment. 'Piracy' and 'falsification' have protected economic interests. However, economic interests have been treated less importantly than other interests as discussed subsequently.

[126] *Jus cogens* rules are those viewed as the most important of all, from which no derogation is possible and are binding on all states and persons regardless of their consent. The rules also give rise to obligation for a state to either punish or extradite a violator. Bassiouni (1998–1999), at 9–10.

[127] *See id.*

This category of international crimes does not impose obligations on states unless a specific treaty which the states accede to imposes duties on them.[128]

(2) Economic Crimes

Economic interests have been treated as the least important interest which international criminal laws seek to protect let alone a part of *jus cogens*. There are some international economic crimes. 'Falsification and counterfeiting' and 'bribery of foreign public officials' fall under this category.[129] 'Piracy,' traditionally acknowledged, is regulated to protect tangible economic interests and human right.[130]

Moreover, international economic crimes have been very slow to expand. It is because the protection of economic interests has been applied less seriously through international criminal law than the other interests related to human safety and lives. Conflicting views from countries with diverse economic backgrounds impede reaching a consensus on coordinating provisions dealing with economic crimes. Although quite a few international laws produce resolutions, their legal enforceability has been weak. Development of international criminalization against bribery of foreign officer, e.g., 1997 OECD Convention on Combating Bribery of Foreign Public Officials in International Business Transactions,[131] was possible mostly by supports from advanced market economies because some companies from advanced countries were treated unfairly by foreign government officers who had requested unlawful money in vain.

It has been argued that four elements need to be met to constitute an international crime: (i) intervention into a significant international interest, (ii) an egregious conduct deemed offensive to commonly shared values of the international community, (iii) transnational implications, either through the diversity of nationality of its perpetrators or means which transcend national boundaries, and (iv) the necessity of international criminalization in cases, where a conduct does not meet (i) or (ii).[132] Economic crimes, however, are difficult to satisfy the (i), (ii) and (iv) conditions.

First, economic interest is not evaluated so significant to human survival as other interests. According to Bassiouni, who divided normal international crimes into three categories, an international crime, an international delict, and an international infraction, the meaning of an international crime is confined to normative proscription, the violation of which has possible negative impacts on the peace and

---

[128]*See id.* at 62.

[129]*See id.* at 100. It quotes Bassiouni (1987) at 62.

[130]*See id.* at 59–60.

[131]For background on the OECD anti-bribery convention, *see* an interview with Eleanor Roberts Lewis, *at* http://www.fsa.ulaval.ca/personnel/vernag/EH/F/ethique/lectures/Lewis.html.

[132]Bassiouni (1998–1999), at 96.

security of humankind, fundamental humanitarian values, state action, or a state-favoring policy.[133] Meanwhile, a delict is defined as the normative proscription that affects an internationally protected interest, and whose commission involves more than one state or harms victims from more than one state while an infraction is a violation not in the former two categories.[134] For example, counterfeiting, which interrupts the integrity of a national financial system, falls under the category of the international infraction. The categorization indicates that the integrity of a financial system is not treated as seriously as other internationally protected interests. Meanwhile, under this analysis, piracy is attributed to the international delict because it threats the security of human beings on the one hand, but it infringes economic interest as tangible right on the other hand.[135]

In addition, (ii) 'egregious conduct deemed to offend a commonly shared value' element is disputed in cases where an international conduct infringes an internationally acknowledged interest. The element matters, particularly, in a case when a conduct provides net economic benefits to quite a few countries. The bribery of foreign public officials, although it interrupts pure public function and the sincerity of a government, is not considered an 'egregious conduct' in some countries where economic development concern and attraction of foreign investments outweigh the values that a punishment for bribery seeks to secure. As a foreign-friendly public policy for effective economic development is necessary in certain countries, the illegality of the means for economic development does not invoke significant public resent or constitute serious culpability among the public. Quite a few countries among LDCs and DCs have been experiencing formerly mentioned situations. As a result, the necessity of a punishment against the act of bribery is not acknowledged at least by the group of countries. For example, the OECD Anti-Bribery Convention did not impose on member states the duty to criminalize 'officers for receiving bribes' from foreign companies under a 'demand' approach, but held them to a duty to penalize 'companies for supplying bribes' to foreign officers under a 'supply' control.[136] In light of the point that the members of the OECD consist of advanced market economies, the international consensus on criminalizing bribe-offering under a supply side is still on the way toward universal criminalization. This example demonstrates the difficulty in reaching an international consensus under the category of economic crimes.

---

[133] *Id.* at 98.

[134] *Id.*, at 98–99.

[135] *Id.*, at 99.

[136] OECD, Art. 1, Sect. 1 and 2 of the Convention on Combating Bribery of Foreign Public Officials in International Business Transactions (hereinafter Anti-Bribery Convention), *at* http://www.usdoj.gov/criminal/fraud/fcpa/intlagree/related/combatbribe.html. OECD website states that a total of thirty seven states acceded to the Convention, *at* http://www.oecd.org/department/0,3355,en_2649_34859_1_1_1_1_1,00.html.

B. Cartel Law

(1) The Infringement of Significant Economic Interests

Damages caused by cartels are significant in both the developing world and industrialized countries. Inefficiencies in an economy, such as a deceitful transfer of wealth from consumers' welfare to producers' surplus, and the blocking of the access of new competitive companies to markets, are measured to the level so considerable as to offset foreign aid to LDCs.[137] Additionally, cartels bring about its negative side effects on merit-based competition and consumers' and potential competitors' confidence in the functionality of a market. Moreover, they obstruct the equitable distribution of economic power.[138]

Cartel members do not respect consumers' interests under a competitive market but exploits consumers' welfare as an indispensable value in human life. However, the loss in consumers' welfare as direct damage of a cartel is not recognized as an international human right issue worthy of protection through criminal penalties. Neither the Universal Declaration on Human Rights in the UN nor the International Covenant on Socio, Cultural, and Economic Rights (ICSCE) enumerate consumers' rights to have a product or a service in a competitive market. The absence of consumers' welfare or rights implies that, although international consumer organizations are struggling to build competition advocacy, influence the works of competition authorities, and reflect consumers' complaints in governmental policies and judicial decisions,[139] the significance of the consumers' interests does not reach the level sufficient to protect through criminalization.

Competition itself, although accepted as a precious virtue in a market economy among industrialized countries, has not achieved widespread consensus among the international community. A cartel as a private entry barrier enables existent companies to sustain current market shares and profits without further efforts to innovate the quality of their products or services. The cartel undermines existent and potential market participants' trust in market mechanisms functioning as an important factor in creative investment and entrepreneurship. However, in the countries where the function of a market is not developed to such a level, the public's trust in a competitive market remains low. As a result, the functionality of a competitive market is considered to be less significant in protecting with criminal penalties. In the countries where investment resources are limited but economic development is urgent, coordinated and planned investment through the promotion of existent companies can be a more effective policy for economic development than the facilitation of competition because fostering competition may lead to duplicate investments, which are thought to be merely 'waste' in the countries. As competition or trust in market mechanism is not recognized as a universally important value, restriction on the competition or intervention into the trust is not considered damages to an internationally acknowledged significant interest.

[137]*Refer to* Chap. 2, 2.3, B(5) and Chap. 4 for 'Damages of Cartels'.

[138]Fingleton et al. (2007), at 10.

[139]Consumer International (CI) (2007), at 30.

(2) Ethical Condemnation

A cartel, although it brings about significant economic damages to a market, is not considered egregious conduct among quite a few DCs and LDCs since an intervening act into the values that anticartel regulations seek to keep intact, such as competition and consumers' welfare, has been not universally acknowledged as heinous or odious crimes deserving criminal penalties. For instance, the African Caribbean Pacific 77 group which vehemently objected to the adoption of competition policy at the DDA negotiation did not share social awareness on the value of or at least place an emphasis on competition in order to maximize consumers' welfare or efficiency as advanced countries did.

Intervention into a price-setting market mechanism through public policy is still accepted as a normal measure of economic policy in many countries. Sometimes, when the price increase of various products creates a serious burden of inflation on an economy, governments in quite a few countries, e.g., France and Russia, are eager to intervene, thereby fixing price.[140] The practice implies such a limited social value in price-setting through competition. However, the price surge of food commodities belongs to the area of commodity policy, separately from the area of a competition policy. Commodity law under international law has acknowledged governmental coordination of commodity price throughout production and distribution of a commodity.

The blocking of new enterprises from entering advanced markets through existent companies' unfair methods causes infringement of commercial ethics. On the other hand, multinational enterprises (MNEs), mostly from industrialized countries, tried to monopolize markets in the DCs. The original aim of the UN Set was to regulate such anticompetitive activities of the MNEs. However, society's blame for the anticompetitive practices, including a cartel, is not raised to an international consensus for criminalization. Support from economic research does not persuade DCs to enact or enforce actively criminal penalties against a cartel although development economics, withering nowadays, was popular in the 1970s. Scholarly works were too weak or insufficient to invoke opinion leaders' interests or to raise low public awareness, to a level of social ethics, on the harms of anticompetitive acts.

(3) The Necessity of Criminal Penalty

The necessity of criminal punishment against a cartel has not been widely acknowledged in the international community. Under international law, the type and the severity of sanctions against cartels are up to domestic legislative systems to create unless an international tribunal in charge of RBPs or international cartels is established and impose a criminal penalty on participants or unless an international treaty explicitly requires member states to adopt a criminal sanction. Moreover, as the experiences of South Korea revealed, in spite of adopting criminal penalties in

---

[140]Ben Hall, *Sarkozy unveils measures to curb prices*, FT, 2 (Nov. 30, 2007); *Taming Russian Inflation,* FT (May 2, 2008); Neil Buckley, *Russia to control food prices*, FT (Oct. 23, 2007).

Monopoly Restraint and Fair Trade Act (MRFTA), their actual enforcement has remained very low.[141] Even the U.S. practice demonstrates that defendants have prevailed in around 63 % of criminal antitrust trials. The acquittal rate is three times higher than an average acquittal rate in typical criminal trials, which is less than 20 %.[142] The high acquittal rate in antitrust crimes implies that criminal punishment is not an effective sanction even in the U.S. where cartels members are held under the most serious penalty in the world. Furthermore, the investigation and prosecution against a cartel need highly skilled personnel with practical experiences.

Therefore, focus on civil or administrative sanctions against cartels should be an important threshold to entrench cartel regulation. Activating criminal enforcement should be a following step after the threshold institution is settled.[143] A theory of the step-by-step frame with respect to anticartel enforcement measures, as introduced by the previous Chap. 5,[144] is positively appreciated by high-level officers from competition authorities in diverse countries, such as, Ireland, the UK, and India.[145] According to this theory, in jurisdictions where criminal enforcements have passed an initial stage of entrenchment, private actions against companies need to cooperate with criminal penalties against individuals because private action address private damages, which criminal prosecution does not deal with, and, thereby, can effectively improve public awareness on the damages that a cartel causes.[146] The improved public awareness of cartel-causing damages can form civil advocacy as important political support for effective criminal enforcements.

C. Assessment

(1) The Prospect of International Cartel Crime

The pursuit for international criminalization of cartel is by far less probable than that for a binding international cartel law. Even the former seeking itself is not appropriate at this moment when no binding international law on cartels has come into effect. International law to impose criminal penalties against cartel members is unlikely to be adopted, although it may be proper after settling down an

[141]Fingleton, Girard & Williams (hereinafter Fingleton et al.) (2007), at 17. Absent broad political and popular consensus that cartel activity is theft, judges may simply impose fines on guilty executives or, if a custodial sentence, suspend it or apply probation because, as Posner states, imprisonment is imposed so rarely in antitrust cases that its deterrent effect may be slight.

[142]Hawk (2007), at 117 and 131. Fingleton uses an analogy that criminal cartel enforcement is the highest risk/ highest-return stock that a competition agency can invest in.

[143]*See* Hawk, *id*, at 135; Lee (2008–2009), at 61–63.

[144]*Refer to* Chap. 5, Sec. 5.4. A.

[145]The author attended the 2008 annual meeting of the Antitrust Section of the American Bar Association, and heard that an officer, John Fingleton, who has worked in both Ireland and the UK competition authority, in light of his experience placed less priority on criminal enforcement than administrative and civil actions. The other officer, Vinodd Dhall, from India's competition authority focused on reputation- and credibility-building through civil advocacy in the initial stage. Fingleton and Dhall, Speeches at Annual Meeting of Section of Antitrust of the ABA (Breakfast with International Enforcers) (Mar. 28, 2008).

[146]Lee (2008–2009), at 64.

international cartel rule. Practical skills, financial resources, and experts sufficient to operate investigation and prosecution successfully are very limited as a majority of countries with cartel law have experienced very little enforcement or have recently adopted a competition regime itself. In light of the former three elements for international criminal law, an international criminal penalty against a cartel is analyzed to be improper at this moment.

First, the value of competition or consumers' welfare is short of the level of significant interest worthy of protection by punishment of an international crime. The determination of the significant interest should be made in light of overall countries' evaluations. Concern of public policy about protecting competition or consumers' welfare has usually remained more limited than that about economic development. Although countries with a diversified economic structure and competitive industries recognize competition as a precious principle, countries with a less diversified economic structure, depending on raw material production, consider competition as a threat to the survival of their weak industries. With a heavy weight on commodity production and trade, the less diversified economies prefer stability under price and output control compared to price decreases under rigorous competition because their earnings for living, which are relatively small in most cases compared to manufacturing or service-focused countries, depend on commodity prices. Their request for separating commodity agreements from the competition issue has faced objections since the agreements were acknowledged in a separate part of international law a few decades ago.[147]

In a simple economic structure, a domestic market operates under uncompetitive circumstances with poor financial resources. Governmental interventions into the market are considered as necessary to manage limited materials and financial resource. Competition under an autonomous market system is a mirage far from its reality. The public's consciousness regarding the principle of competition is very difficult to grow in the less developed economies.

Moreover, the value of consumers' welfare is not sufficiently recognized in the LDCs where a democratic political system, reflecting the voices of the unorganized mass of consumers, is unstable or not working effectively. As consumers are not such doctrinaire as economists, they do not have an interest in cartel unless they witness the price decrease after the destruction of the cartel or receive compensation from the damages of the cartel. Furthermore, insufficient foundation of academic research on economic effects of a cartel will place constraints on persuasiveness of complaints on the cartel activities by mass consumers or opinion leaders. If academic research discovered cartel-caused damages in markets, it would help opinion leaders spread public awareness of the damages and build competition advocacy. Even the legal system or legislation that lets consumers receive compensation for cartel damages does not operate effectively in the countries due to less developed competition law and inefficient legal institutions.

[147]*Refer to* Chap. 3.

Second, the limited experiences of free and competitive markets do not support forming economic or commercial ethics on restrictive business practices including a cartel. Rather, the managing of price level and commodity trade output with forecast are more emphasized than preserving competition because a large number of the population live by working on commodity production. As previously mentioned, the lacks of ① academic research, ② a democratic system which can form competition advocacy among the general public, and ③ legal systems promoting private actions can work as additional hurdles in forming commerce ethics regarding cartels.

Third, the acknowledgement of the necessity of international criminalization against a cartel is not ripe enough to replace two elements, 'significant international interest' and 'ethical condemnation.' Cost of criminalizing cartels and enforcing the criminal penalty is burdensome for countries with less experience in competition law. Even the advanced economies have gone a long way to achieve an effective criminal penalty regime with many resources and invested personnel. For example, the U.S., which boasts of the most effective criminal penalties, had spent not less than 17 years to convict the first defendant in a criminal case since it adopted the Sherman Act in 1890. As a criminal prosecution necessitates evidence from a market analysis, subsequent investments are required to establish a new division with trained investigators e.g., the Antitrust-Division of the U.S. DOJ, close cooperation between a market-screening institution and a criminal prosecutors' office, and to educate and train more experts. The DCs hesitate to invest further resources in criminal penalty as other less costly sanctions are expected to enjoy a similar level of benefits.

(2) Suggestion

In consideration of the former analyses, some practical measures for a long-term agenda of international criminalization of cartels can be proposed. Basically, international criminalization should be the next step after furthering the former narrow approach of a binding international cartel law. A limitation on the categories of business activities under cartel crime and the cooperation of private actions to enact effective criminal enforcement are concrete ways to pursue international criminalization.

First, the coverage of cartel activities as the object of the criminalization should be narrowed down enough to minimize dissenting opinions against the adoption of criminal penalties. For example, bid-rigging, which has already achieved a broad consensus for criminalization, will be more appropriate to be categorized as an international crime. Price-fixing and output restriction should be other types of hard core cartels that can achieve a broad international consensus as the aspects of frequently occurring cartels. Market allocation will be the following candidate for international criminalization.

Second, to gather evidence and to prosecute a cartel case effectively in a criminal trial needs high-leveled capacities. Such abilities cannot be acquired in a short time but can be cultivated through continuous investments under the auspice of political leadership. However, political support is temporarily vulnerable to the change of economic situations and the possibility of corruption or capture by interest groups. Although administrative penalty is more convenient sanction for cartel regulation than criminal penalty, administrative sanction under the control of a government is more susceptible to political concerns as the administrative regulation operates completely under the control of a governmental policy. When political situations shift toward an atmosphere benevolent to entrepreneurs, regulatory powers of a competition authority will inevitably follow such a trend.

As a result, more emphasis for operating a long-standing cartel regulation should be on a private action as a recovery system as the previous chapter argued.[148] Continuous efforts to raise cartel-enforcement capacities need assistance from nonpublic sectors which consist of academic researchers, practicing lawyers, and the general public. The facilitation of private action as a damage-recovery system is an important measure to stimulate the level of public actions.[149] Through rigorous private actions, the general public will be exposed more to cartel-causing large damages.[150] The widespread public awareness and subsequent ethical blame against cartel members will constitute civil advocacy for raising the level of public enforcement to criminal penalty.

Private action will place public enforcers under more pressure to pursue reasonable outcomes in light of pending or subsequent private actions.[151] Private action also can speed up administrative procedure because a civil court in charge of the private action waits in practice for a competition authority' final decision and its supporting evidence.

In addition, rigorous private actions can threaten potential cartel members with a huge amount of cost. Competitors who are attracted by a cartel conspiracy will hesitate to participate in the conspiracy in light of the very high cost of private and public redresses. At the annual meeting of the Section of Antitrust of the American Bar Association (ABA) in 2008, Stephen Blake, Deputy Director of the OFT of the UK, acknowledged the importance of cooperative functions between private actions and public actions and the enhancement of effective deterrence through that cooperation.[152]

---

[148]Lee (2008–2009), at 61. *Refer to* Chap. 5, 5.4, A(3).

[149]*Refer to* the step-by-step frame at Chap. 6, 6.5, B(3).

[150]Lee (2008–2009), at 65.

[151]*See id.*, at 65. Civil courts reflect technical decisions issued from competition authorities which usually provide important evidence for pending private actions.

[152]Deputy Director of Cartels at Office of Fair Trading in England, Stephen Blake, Address at ABA Annual Meeting of Section of Antitrust (Mar. 26, 2008).

6.6 Proposing a New Approach for International Commodity Agreements (ICAs)

A. Introduction

As rapid surge of oil price and food price from 2007 to 2008 threatened global economies, particularly fuel-importing countries and industrialized countries, out of their keen desires to suppress inflation led by high primary commodity prices, argued that international commodity agreements (ICAs) or international producers' association (IPAs) should be regulated similarly with private cartel regulations.[153] Fuel-importing countries severely affected by such fuel price surges were the countries where alternative energy sources had been limited and where higher levels of energy intensity in their industries had required much quantity of oil. On the other hand, the analysis of the price increase of major agricultural products demonstrated that the inflation were due to, mostly, structural factors, e.g., increasing demand for meat or wheat from emerging markets, low investment and low productivity in agriculture, and increasing biofuel production, than temporary cyclical factors, e.g., freak weather.[154] Similarly, the oil price surge was arguably attributed to increasing demand from emerging economies, e.g., China, weak dollars due to less competitive U.S. economy, the limitation of OPEC production, the slow growth of non-OPEC oil countries' production, and price manipulation by international hedge funds.[155]

In spite of such economic situations reflecting increasing commodity prices, a proper legal approach to international commodity trade cannot neglect the importance of commodity trade on less diversified economies, and the accumulated international law regarding commodity trade. In light of past researches on development of international commodity law and economic situations, a legal approach to international commodity trade will be discussed in distinction with the international cartel law.

B. Directions for Institutional Development

(1) Reasons for the Collapses of International Commodity Agreements (ICAs)

Although ICAs had been flourishing under the auspice of the NIEO, there were several structural weaknesses in ICAs. Such weak points led to the standstill or the collapse of many ICAs which used to function effectively.

---

[153] Minder and Leahy, *Asia battles with surging food costs*, 9 FT (Jan. 10, 2008); U.N. GA, Report of the Secretary-General, International trade and development, para. 4 A/62/266 (62nd sess.) (Aug. 16, 2007). An IPA means the association of producing countries rather than that private companies.

[154] Minder and Leahy, *id*; Javier Blas, *The End of Abundance: Food Panic Brings Calls for a Second Green Revolution,* Fin. Times, at 9 (June 2, 2008).

[155] Common Fund for Commodities (CFC) (2006), at 6; Clifford Krauss, *Chinese and U.S. Demand Drives Commodities Surge*, N.Y. Times (Jan. 15, 2008).

First of all, individual ICAs maintained global commodity prices to inflexible levels under the fair price principle regardless of fluctuating market. The inflexible maintenance of price led to the waste of much money because maintenance of prices similar to the former levels cost lots of money in a situation where production increased but demand gradually decreased. The growing inefficiencies under ICAs generated much indirect cost. Trade quotas and other restrictions of ICAs prevented resources from being efficiently distributed in markets. They impeded the growth of low-cost innovative productions which could have prospered in competitive cultures.

The collapse of the International Tin Council (ITC), for example, was mainly attributed to the large cost spent to sustain the price level which had neglected market conditions.[156] A buffer stock system, used to regulate price fluctuations by buying commodities in times of excess and selling in times of scarcity, required the continuous supply of sufficient capital in order to maintain the buffer pool even under the preposition that wise management and sufficient facilities for storing the stocks are provided.[157] The long-term maintenance of high commodity prices reached the exhaustive point of buffer pool capital reserves in many cases, one of which resulted in the fall of ITC in 1985.

Second, the majority of ICAs were ineffective in practice. Increasing production of food commodities with static demand in the 1980s and the early 1990s led to reduction in commodity prices. Industrialized countries opposed against active functions of ICAs which tried to maintain the former prices. Some of them quit their membership. In light of the circumstances, the ICAs could not place direct influences on respective markets although they offered important agoras for discussing and sharing crucial market information and for providing market surveillance.[158]

Third, conflicts between producing and consuming countries directly led to the withdrawal of member states with significant portions in the global market, which made ICAs defunct. For example, the International Sugar Agreement (ISA) of 1977 was weakened, after the world production boom in early 1970s, by the European Economic Community (EEC)'s political refusal to join the pact. The withdrawal of EEC, along with the introduction of the innovative product of alternative sweeteners and subsequent sugar price fall, led to the collapse of the ISA. A similar situation had occurred in 1962 when the ISA collapsed due to Cuba's withdrawal from the world market on the basis of its political conflict with the U.S. and alignment with Sino-Soviet Bloc.[159]

---

[156] McFadden (1986), at 823. McFadden analyzes the inflexibility of official price range as its main culprit of collapse of International Tin Council.

[157] Quill (1994), at 507.

[158] *Id.*, 504–505.

[159] *Id.*, 524–525.

(2) Market-Related Policies
1) Price Risk Managements (PRMs)

The price stability of commodity trade does benefit exporting and importing countries which include LDCs, DCs, and industrialized countries.[160] After the influence of ICAs grew weak, price risk management (PRM) has been used as an alternative way to reduce risk of volatile prices. While direct market interventions, e.g., directly managing supply quantity, have been rare, new measure of PRMs using financial measures, e.g., options and futures, has contributed to sustaining stable markets. The new measures, however, are arguably under the following criticisms: a little benefit compared to their large cost, consequential inaccessibility of smallholders, and the effect of speculative activities of hedge funds on markets.[161]

First, the instruments of PRMs cost more than traditional forward contracts, so the methods match the interests of large-scale traders treating a broad range of commodities with a variety of currency. The instruments increased exchanges in commodity markets to a tremendous speed so that trade volumes in Shanghai Futures Exchange went up more than four times during 2001–2002.[162] Meanwhile, to smallholders in commodity-dependent developing countries (CDDCs), such measures were not popular because fixed price forward contracting arrangements cost much and required specialized knowledge. Meanwhile, in light of the interests of the small holders, different instruments of PRM were developed in favor of the smallholders, the outcome of which is still unclear.[163] If they succeed, they can work as supplements to costly future trading in the commodity exchange market.

On the other hand, an increasing amount of money operated by hedge funds or other speculators in a financial market deviate prices of PRM instruments in a financial market from prices in a commodity market. Researchers argued that oil price hike in 2008 was mainly due to speculative activities of hedge funds in financial market.[164] According to the UN Food and Agriculture Organization (FAO), such high oil prices have exacerbated a current trend of food price surges

---

[160] *Id.*, 536; Brown (1994), at 364.

[161] CFC (2006), at 21.

[162] UNCTAD and CFC (2004), at 35.

[163] CFC (2006), at 21. *See* Department of Commerce, Ministry of Commerce and Industry of Government of India (MCI of Gov. of India) (Nov. 2002), Chap. 4 para. 4.12. The Committee recommends futures trading as the most efficient model in the long-term to achieve stable commodity market.

[164] Tony Jackson, *Speculators accumulate as risks rise for world's poor*, Fin. Times (May 12, 2008). Barbara Whelehan, *Rising food and fuel prices*, Brankrate.com (May 7, 2008), *available at* http://biz.yahoo.com. Whelehan cites the statement of Loretta Napoleoni in her book, 'Rogue Economics,' contending that a hedge fund is one of the major rogue forces which rule the world, particularly in oil price increase.

due to costlier fertilizer and diesel.[165] A researcher argued, at a recent IMF conference, that speculators and hedge funds drove up food prices.[166]

In spite of the above-mentioned problems, the trading of futures and options has a benevolent impact as a system reducing the risk of price fluctuation. Unlike the settling of prices to an inflexible level which distorts market mechanism and causes huge inefficiencies, futures trading uses anticipated demand and supply, thereby interacting through an autonomous market mechanism. The loss of efficiency does not occur. In India where a ban on agricultural commodities futures trading is under consideration as a political gesture to reduce public blame for hedge funds, a research insisted that it could not produce any firm evidence of the negative influence of the futures trading.[167] Operating a robust futures market in DCs can help so greatly assure farmers that they can reap rewards for their investment at the early stage.[168]

Moreover, a spreading trend that poor farmers use deposit into saving accounts, in African countries,[169] is noteworthy. The microfinancial service has produced successful results and permitted small-size farmers leeway for waiting until market prices of their crops increase.[170] Mobile phone services in African countries have proffered the farmers access to market prices for their crops, thereby enabling them to negotiate in an advantageous position. As long as the international community tries to have transparent regulations against the dangers of hedge funds, and to make financial services available for farmers' interests, several measures for the PRMs are expected to work effectively to stabilize commodity prices. The 2008 Rome Declaration on World Food Summit also urged governments to create opportunities for the world smallholder farmers and fishers, particularly in vulnerable areas, to participate and benefit from financial mechanisms.[171]

2) Market-Intervention Policies

Diverse levels of market interventions to prevent fluctuation of commodity prices, from direct supply control to buffer stock operation to compensation for declining prices, have been used, although generally the measures are difficult to sustain in the long term.

---

[165]Javier Blas, *UN says oil rise hits food prices harder*, Fin. Times, at 2 (Apr. 26/27, '08).

[166]*IMF Works With Vulnerable States on Food Price Policies*, IMF Survey Magazine: In the News (April 28, 2008). It cites the statement of Prof. Takatoshi Ito of the University of Tokyo in Apr. 2008.

[167]Blas, J. and Leahy, J., *India Futures ban mere posturing*, FT, at 6 (May 7 2008).

[168]Strauss-Kahn, D., *A global approach is required to tackle high food prices*, FT, at 13 (May 15, 2008).

[169]Burgis, T., *African farmers sow more profitable seeds*, FT (June 13, '08).

[170]According to the Microfinance Information Exchange, in 2006, African microfinance institution served 5.7 million savers and managed US $ 1.2-billion amount deposits. *See id.*

[171]*Refer* to para. 7.(b). of 2008 Rome Declaration on WFS.

(A) Supply Control

Supply controls among major producing countries, sometimes joined by consuming countries, have been used in many cases. For example, OPEC and ITRO, as international producers' associations (IPAs), have used supply controls effected by producing countries alone while the International Coffee Agreement (ICoA) and the International Sugar Agreement (ISA) used a quota system which allows supply control by both producers' and consumers' group.[172]

(B) Buffer Stock System

Price management through buffer stocks has been used by a few ICAs, e.g., the former International Natural Rubber Organization (INRO) and the International Tin Agreement (ITA) as bipartisan organization, and producers' association, e.g., ITRO. As the maintenance of a buffer stock requires much money to be sufficient to constitute a pool for preventing price fluctuation and as countries with large domestic markets and large capital, e.g., the U.S., operated their own pools and objected to the price maintenance through a buffer stock, the buffer stock measure would lead to frequent collapses.

(C) Compensatory Assistance

Compensatory measures can work to supplement the efforts to prevent price fluctuation under the market mechanism. The compensatory measures provide financial assistance in relation to commodity price policy under the name of domestic and international aid. As an example of international compensatory measures, the IMF has enacted Compensatory and Contingency Financing Facility (CCFF). DCs may draw necessary funds by showing the impact of the international commodity price fluctuation on their economy, e.g., extreme food price surges, or cereal import excesses beyond their control, by expressing a willingness to accept the IMF's conditions.[173] Since the original Compensatory Financing Facility was introduced in 1963, by 1999, 106 countries had drawn a total of US$ 33 billion amount over the span of 36 years.[174]

Meanwhile, the Buffer Stock Financing Facility (BSFF), established in 1969, provided assistance to members in response to their contributions to international buffer stocks of commodities. An ICA operating the buffer stocks must have met

---

[172]OPEC decides total output level of members' crude oil and allocates quota to each member. Carola Hoyos, *OPEC set to defend $ 60 global minimum*, Fin. Times (Oct. 20, 2006). Current ITRO consisting of major natural rubber producing countries also announced unilateral output reduction. International Coffee Agreement (ICoA) made up of both producing and consuming countries used import and export quotas. The International Sugar Agreement (ISA) of both exporters and importers also chose the quota system. *See* Quill (1994), 523 and 524.

[173]Krishna Guha, *IMF bid to help Africans on food prices*, Fin. Times, Apr. 25, 2008, at 6.

[174]IMF, *Review of the CCFF and Buffer Stock Financing Facility (BSFF)—Preliminary Considerations*, Chap. II.B.11.fn 11 (Dec. 9, 1999), *available at* http://www.imf.org. On average, in each year, 2.9 countries made 9.5 drawings for Special Drawing Right (SDR) 0.7 billion (around US$ 1 billion) under the CFF.

such requirements as: its main objective is the stabilization of international prices, that its membership consists of both consuming and producing countries, and that they do not maintain artificially high prices during the long-term restriction of supply. During its initial 15 years, the BSFF had 39 purchasing cases for a total of US$ 0.81 billion. However, as an ICA which matches all the requirements has not existed since 1983, with one exception of the 1995 International Rubber Agreement, none of the purchasing cases have come out since then.[175] As its operating cost is evaluated to outweigh its benefit,[176] the BSFF grew ineffective and finally is currently terminated from IMF.[177]

On the other hand, India's Price Stabilization Fund (PSF) showed an example of a domestic compensatory measure.[178] Mission of the PSF was to offer financial relief of purchasing and storing commodities from small-size growers in situations where prices of commodities fell below a threshold level.[179] Target commodities were export-oriented plantation crops, such as coffee, natural rubber, tea, and tobacco. The measure had contributed their resources to relieve smallholders of damages from extreme price volatility of the commodities.[180] The PSFs with pilot nature did not work anymore after their 10 year planned operation.[181] Recently, the PSF scheme was reestablished for perishable agricultural commodity of vegetables and cereals, e.g., oilseeds and pulses, in India.[182]

(D) Analysis

Market-intervention policies of ICAs, in many cases, caused disputes among member countries. Although the policies were effective and necessary for price stabilization in localized markets, they proved not to work well in globalized markets in the long term. It is because they have in nature characteristics against the market force and because, in most cases, discretion inherent in the policies generated conflicts between internal political powers, e.g., between large producers and small producers, or between producers and consumers.

---

[175] *Id.*, para. 29 and box 5.

[176] *Id.*, para. 33.

[177] The Legal Department of IMF, Selected Decisions and Selected Documents of the IMF: Thirtieth Issue: Termination of the Buffer Stock Financing Facility, June 30, 2006, *available at* http://www.imf.org/external/pubs/ft/sd/index.asp?decision=12142-(00/16). Art. V, Sec. 3(a), (b), and (c) decided the termination of the BSFF.

[178] S. Radhakrishnan, *The Price Stabilization Fund Scheme*, 67–69 Indian Coffee 6–7 (2003).

[179] MCI of Gov. of India, *supra* note 1145, Chap. 1 para. 1.6–1.7 and Chap. 3 para. 3.1.

[180] Rubber growers with lands up to 4 ha occupies 99 % of total rubber holdings in India and in tobacco, the small farm grower takes 93 % of the whole growers. Meanwhile, in case of coffee and tea, respectively, 92 and 74 % of holdings are the small farmers.

[181] Ch. 3, para. 3.12–27. The PSF under a state government's supervision had operated in India from 2003 to 2013.

[182] Dillip Kumar Jha and Sanjeeb Mukherjee, Price Stabilization Fund in agriculture to be used for cereals and vegetables, Business Standard, July 17th, 2014.

As a quota system or buffer stock system works differently from autonomous price-setting mechanisms reflecting supply and demand in a market, a decision regarding the appropriate level of production or price usually represents political considerations of member states. Decision-making through the political process can invoke a member(s)'s dissatisfaction with the compromise. It results in the subsequent withdrawal of the objecting member(s), and thereby the demise of an organization. Particularly, a buffer stock system, popular decades ago, is not operating well in ICAs. One remaining case of a buffer stock system is found in the International Tripartite Rubber Corporation (ITRC) as IPA with restricted membership. Indonesia, Malaysia, and Thailand with around 85 % of the world's rubber production accused the former INRO of its lack of focus on producers' interests.[183] The countries, instead, established the ITRC to manage buffer stock for further market growth and to reduce rubber output of the three countries for securing minimum prices to domestic producers.[184] It is questionable that the quantity control system with restricted membership will work well in the long run in spite of competition from nonmember producing countries.[185] The other example of internal disputes in ICAs relating to price management is American withdrawal from the ITA in 1982. The U.S. as a large consuming member with extensive stock, opposed remunerative tin price support of the ITA. While producing members disagreed with its policy to maintain the ceiling price of tin at a low level, the U.S. declined to sign the ITA. Large costs for sustaining the tin price, insufficient funds, and increasing tin exports from nonmembers brought the ITA to an end with massive losses.[186]

Output control and discriminatory pricing in favor of nonmembers reveal the same story. The collapse of the international coffee market in 1989 has something to do with the U.S. dissatisfaction with the policies of the ICoA such as artificial maintenance of high coffee price, low price sales to nonmembers, and continuous limitation of export by producers.[187] *The U.S. refused to accede to a new ICoA, and it is improbable that a new agreement could be reached. The reason is analyzed as along with the refusal* of major consuming countries to accession and the difficulty in the allocation of the global coffee market among the 52 producing countries.[188]

Price management through buffer stock and supply control has revealed the high risk of failure in ICAs. However, price management in primary commodities under international cooperation is acknowledged by international law as an important measure for the sustained economic development in the world, particularly in

---

[183]The insufficient focus on producers' interests led to the collapse of the INRO in 2001. *Curtains down for INRO at its 42nd meeting,* Bus. Times, Jul. 30, 2001.

[184]Phusadee Arunmas, *Rubber: Top Three Exporters Agree to Co-operate*, Bangkok Post, Jul. 6, 2001.

[185]UNCTAD and CFC (2004), 35.

[186]Quill (1994), at 516–518.

[187]*Id.* at 521.

[188]*Id.*

DCs,[189] in light of the states' right to natural resources and right of international cooperation. For example, the maintenance of buffer stock for poor countries under aids from IMF may be considered as a material PRM. Moreover, the trading of staple food, e.g., rice, in relation to food security shall be under special treatment as suggested later. From the long-term perspective, the ineffective measures shall be modified by new measures cooperating with market conditions better. The spreading of PRM and step-by-step reflection of the free trade system can be one direction. Elimination of export restriction and gradual reduction of export subsidy or import tariffs will be issues to be discussed further.

(3) Structural Policy for Economic Development
1) Diversification of Production

The above-mentioned market-management measures cannot replace the role of structural commodity policy as a majority of researchers would agree.[190] The diversification of production in CDDCs illustrates a good model of an ICA's work that supports less competitive producers. The diversification policy suggests that the differentiation of origin, production style under family-farming system, and quality in CDDCs' commodity production have an advantage in labor-monitoring, so that CDDCs should search labor-intensive quality products matching their environments, and commercialize them. Some regions in CDDCs have a competitive advantage in fresh vegetables and cut flowers which require much water and labor.[191] In case of Malawi, a southern Africa country, 9000 farm families succeeded in commercializing paprika peppers and birdseye chillies under the auspice of a British investment fund.[192] A more concrete example is the approach of the 'Fair Trade Certification (FTC).' The FTC labeled products have attracted quality-product purchasers and provoked their ethical sympathies because the purchasing of the products which fulfilled strict economic, social, and environmental standards reminded consumers of an image that they support poor producers' 'good' efforts.[193]

Although the initial cost for such quality-focused production and trade-increasing infrastructures, if necessary, should be taken by countries themselves, assistances from international agencies in charge of development and commodities, as CFC, UNCTAD, FAO, are beneficial to encourage the countries to further endeavor. To some countries without sufficient resources, international

---

[189]UNGA, GA Res. 3201 (S–VI), 4.(j),(m),(s), and (t), UN Doc. A/9559 (1974).

[190]Araim (1991), at 213–215; Quill (1994), 534. Quill cites Lincoln Gordon's article, *Natural Resources and the International Economic Order*, in The Future of International Economic Organizations 45, 55 (Don Wallace, Jr. and Helga Escobar eds., 1977).

[191]CFC (2006), 20.

[192]Alan Beattie, *FT Series: Part 2, The Need to Feed (Seeds of changes: Africa seeks to engineer an agricultural revolution)*, FT, June 3, 2008, at 9.

[193]Agritrade (2007), at para 3.1.

assistances are necessary.[194] As a response to food price surge in 2008, UN FAO and heads of UN agencies in Bern urged that fund amounting to US$ 1.7 billion should be provided for seeds, fertilizers, and other production-busting items in poor food-importing countries.[195] Middle-east countries with much profit from high oil prices, as well as France and Spain, expressed their willingness to join such assistance efforts.[196]

Although a series of small-scale pilot diversification projects under EU diversification assistance to ACP banana suppliers during 2000–2005 revealed difficulties due to environmental and geographical circumstances, e.g., periodic hurricanes,[197] the diversification project for promoting agricultural products toward quality products should not be ignored as several cases turned out to be successful.[198] The Plantation Reserve, the ultra-premium sugar brand of Barbados, marched successfully in British markets under combination of Barbados government's effort to commerce a superior product and foreign investment, thereby pumping up Barbados' economy.[199] In addition, the decision by a lot of UK supermarket chains to move to 'Fair Trade Certified'[200] bananas under the pressure of EU reform offered relief to Caribbean island suppliers.[201] If more strategic methods are developed under the auspices of international organizations and governments, the diversification project will be a crucial way to support the survival of less competitive countries.

---

[194]Amy Kazmin, *Burma needs aid for year*, Fin. Times, June 5, 2008.

[195]Harvey Morris, *UN taskforce to tackle global food crisis,* Fin. Times, Apr. 14, 2008, at 2.

[196]Morris, *UN to tap Gulf donors for aid*, Fin. Times, Apr. 30, 2008, at 3; Javier Blas, *Food summit to sidestep biofuels impasse,* Fin. Times, June 5, 2008.

[197]Agritrade (2007), para. 3.3. It cites the 2006 biennial report on EU's Special Framework of Assistance (SFA) which addresses less benefit from the diversification approach than competition approach.

[198]It matches the conclusion of the Feb. 2000 evaluation of EU's SFA and suggestion of the 2006 report. *See id.*

[199]Ricky Jordan, *Sweet Taste of Success*, Nation News, Oct. 3, 2007, *available at* http://www.nationnews.com/295689502108902.php.

[200]The Fair Trade Certified™ guarantees consumers that the agricultural product with the label met strict economic, social, and environmental criteria in the production and trade of the product. Fairtrade Labeling Organizations (FLO), an international organization, operates the Fair Trade Register by screening the compliance with the criteria of each producers under the Register and extends, through regional agencies, its auditing function to local importers, manufactures, and distributors. In the U.S., TransFair USA verifies the compliances of local traders and manufacturers and endows the Fair Trade Certified label on such products, as coffee, cocoa and chocolate, fresh fruit, flowers, sugar, rice, vanilla, and tea and herbs. TransFair USA, Fair Trade Certification Overview, *available at* http://www.transfairusa.org/content/certification/overview.php.

[201]*See* Agritrade (2007), para. 3.3 and 3.1. It is confirmed by the prime minister of the Commonwealth of Dominica's statement before a House of Commons Select Committee that, as critical to Dominca's development, the fair trade banana had reversed a catastrophic recession in his country.

2) Productivity Promotion

On the contrary, the diversification policy has been criticized from the productivity viewpoint by agronomists who researched the past green revolution in the 1970s. Small holders in very poor countries need to secure, argued one agronomist, their own food by improving food production before taking the diversification policy.[202] As arable land for food production decreases due to the increase of biofuel production, productivity-increase policy is highlighted in international organizations with interest in food commodities.

Productivity promotion through research and technological innovation has worked effectively in many cases. For example, under competitiveness-enhancing support, in Surinam, a banana sector increased production tonnage per hectare by 122 % from 2001 to 2005 while, in Cote d'Ivoire, production was raised by 321 % from 1991 to 2004.[203] Costa Rica, Belize, Cameroon, and Jamaica also demonstrate similar level of production improvement under the technical assistance policy.[204]

As private companies have cooperated with international organizations for productivity increase of food commodity,[205] they are expected to cowork with ICAs.[206] According to Agricultural Outlook 2008–2017 of the OECD and FAO, public and private investments in innovation and increasing farm productivity would greatly improve supply prospects by broadening the production base and reducing the chance of commodity price spikes.[207]

As genetically modified (GM) crops have high productivity, research on their usage need to be furthered.[208] However, as many people may still have concerns about their negative impacts on human health, the usage of GM crops should be under strict and transparent scientific scrutiny from the public safety perspective. As such scrutiny needs a period long enough to cover their long-term effects on human body, the research is more likely to be affected by lobbies from interests group and shifts in political situations. To eliminate such external pressure and the public's doubt, the research should operate at least under the screening of qualified representatives from each interest group.

---

[202]Beattie, FT, June 3, 2008. Beattie cites the statement of Glenn Denning, director of the Millennium Development Goals Center in Kenya.

[203]Agritrade (2007), para. 3.3. Cote d'Ivoire's yield rate increased from 9.9 tonnes per hectare in 1991 to 41.7 tones per hectare in 2004. Its exports rose from 118,400 tones out of 12,000 ha in 1991 to 229,000 out of 5120 ha in 2004.

[204]*Id.* at para. 3.1 and 3.3. Cameroon raised the average yield rate by 13.9 % between the period of 1994–1998 and that of 2002–2004 and exports by 20 % from 1998 to 2003. Belize' production increased by 61 % from 472 boxes per acre in 2001 to 760 boxes per acre in 2004.

[205]*Refer to* the following (4) 3.

[206]2008 Rome Declaration on WFS urged international organization and private sectors to increase cooperation in researching, developing, transferring, and disseminating technologies and policy approaches. *See* para. 7.d).

[207]Blas, *The End of Abundance* (*FT Series: Part 1, Need to Feed*), FT, June 2, 2008, at 9.

[208]Corrado Pirzio-Biroli, *Chief Executive of Rise Foundation, How the DCs can help in ensuring food security*, FT, May 8, 2008, at 10; Beattie, FT, June 3, 2008.

However, the increase of food production should go with both sustainable management of natural resources and elimination of unsustainable patterns of consumption and production as the Rome Declaration on World Food Security announced.[209] As 'sustainable development' has been acknowledged as an important topic of international law, production increases of food commodities of ICAs or IPAs shall be discussed within the frame of 'sustainable development.'

(4) Sustainable Development

1) Its Definition and Foundation under International Law

While the regulation of economic activity in favor of environmental protection provoked dissent from DCs arguing that the regulation would be an intervention into sovereign rights to exploit their natural resources, a compromise between economic development and environmental protection had been searched. The solution was the creation of the 'sustainable development.' Pursuant to the request of the Secretary-General of the UN that long-term environmental strategies for achieving sustainable development by 2000 or beyond should be created, the World Commission on Environment and Development (WCED), in the 1987 report,[210] suggested 'sustainable development' defined as 'development that meets the needs of the present without compromising the ability of future generations to meet their own needs.'[211] It is a concept focusing on the responsibility of our generation to future generations by reflecting respect for equitable rights of the future generations.

As the Declaration of Rio on Environment and Development in 1992 and the 2002 Johannesburg Declaration proclaimed, sustainable development needs the balance of three dimensions, e.g., economic growth, environmental protection, and social development. The sovereign right to exploit their own resources under states' own developmental policies, acknowledged throughout the NIEO, is confined by the responsibility to ensure that activities do not cause damage to the environment of other states or areas beyond national jurisdiction.[212] In addition, the right to development should be implemented so as to equitably meet developmental and environmental needs of present and future generations.[213] States should reduce and eliminate unsustainable patterns of production and consumption, and natural resource management is an overarching objective as well as essential requirement

---

[209]FAO/SAD, Rome Declaration on World Food Security and World Food Summit Plan of Action, W3613/E, fifth para. (1998).

[210]The chairman of the WCED was prime minister Gro Harlem Bruntland of Norway. Under the impact of the leadership of Mr. Bruntland, the WCED is referred to as the Bruntland Commission and the 1987 report is called as the Bruntland Report. Brown (1994), at 377–378.

[211]Our Common Future: Report of the World Commission on Environment and Development, Chap. 2 para. 1, *available at* http://ringofpeace.org/environment/brundtland.html.

[212]UN G.A., Report of The UN Conference on Environment and Development, Principle 2 and 4 (A/CONF.151/26 (Vol. I) (Rio de Janeiro, 13 June 1992).

[213]*Id.* principle 3.

for the sustainable development.[214] For social development, states should be committed not only to increasing access to basic living requirements, such as energy, food security, and the protection of biodiversity,[215] but also to cooperate for a supportive and open international economic system to achieve the sustainable development.[216]

2) International Commodity Law Reflecting Sustainable Development

In spite of urges of several declarations & resolutions of the UN General Assembly, the approach of DDA to adopt a free trade and competition regime to agricultural products and food commodities did not fully reflect the sustainable development.[217] The competitive exploitation of primary commodities is not only vulnerable to environmental degradation, but also able to make a negative impact on protecting diverse natural resources and securing equitable food distribution, thereby threatening food security. While international competition law has not adopted an explicit provision reflecting sustainable development in distinction with many domestic competition laws approving exemptions for agricultural industries,[218] Art. XX (b) and (g) under 1994 GATT may be construed as adopting a concept similar to the sustainable development.[219] On top of the foundation and the article of GATT, international commodity law should put more emphasis on the sustainable development.

Inequitable profit distribution from food productions in spite of high food prices highlighted the lack of a system which distributed fair remuneration under social sustainability.[220] In addition, the excessive exploitation, usually, of energy resources caused a problem of unsustainable environment. The increasing usage of biofuel as an alternative to nonrenewable energy sources reduced lands arable for

---

[214] *Id.* principle 8 and Johannesburg Declaration on Sustainable Development (Johannesburg Declaration), para. 11, *at* http://www.un.orgesa/sustdev/documents/WSSD_POI_PD/English/POI_PD.htm.

[215] Johannesburg Declaration, para. 18.

[216] Rio Declaration, principle 12.

[217] Rome Declaration, World Food Summit Plan of Action, Commitment Four, Objective 4.1(g) and (h); Declaration of World Food Security: Five Years Later, preamble and para. 21; UN, GA Resolution on the Right to Food, para. 13, GA Res. 56/155 (2002).

[218] Many domestic competition laws have exemptions for agricultural, fishery, and energy industries. In a case of the U.S., Sec. 6 of the Clayton Act approves agricultural organization which pursues the purpose of mutual help. The U.S. also adopted the Capper-Volstead Act to enhance the bargaining power of farmers.

[219] Article XX, a general exception clause, allows a measure necessary to protect human, animal or plant life or health under para. (b) and one to conserve exhaustible natural resources under para. (g).

[220] Kazmin,Amy, *Rocketing rice prices fail to benefit Asia's small farmers*, Fin.Times (FT), Apr. 29, 2008, at 2.

other food crops and aggravates the food crisis.[221] As a solution to the problems, international law can make member countries subject to obligations of conserving and managing resources, and doing sustainable uses under effective international cooperation. For example, Art. 6 of International Treaty on Plant Genetic Resources for Food and Agriculture (ITPGRFA) illustrate concrete measures for their sustainable use. As genetically modified plants are more productive than traditional crops, the measures under Art. 6 are mostly regarding promoting biological diversity under policy consultation.[222]

Especially, with respect to primary commodity production, international commodity law should highlight cooperation among producers for further production and environmental protection in distinction with competition law. However, the abuse of such cooperation in a way to restrict competition should be screened so that the negative outcomes of anticompetitive practices may not outweigh the benefit of sustainable development.

3) ICAs as Multilateral System for Sustainable Development

As former ICAs demised or collapsed due to expensive market intervention measures, ineffectiveness, and internal disputes, new strategies need to be considered for building effective ICAs. Two models of this thesis suggest concrete forms of ICAs toward sustainable development.

(A) A Model for Productivity Increase and Benefit-Sharing

This model represents an international cooperative regime for raising productivity and sharing benefits from the increased productivity. The facilitation of access under the model promotes research for increasing productivity and diversification, which enables to secure long-term commodity supply. Noticeably, a multilateral system for (i) facilitating access to plant genetic resources (PGRs) and (ii) sharing benefits from the utilization of the resources in a fair and equitable way was proposed by ITPGRFA.[223] Although former ICAs did not ignore the perspective, the ICAs focusing on market-intervening measures did not spare much for such research. The emphasis on the research of ICAs enables the expansion of the genetic base of crops and the wider use of varieties and species in on-farm agriculture. Agricultural scientists affiliated to International Institute of Tropical Agriculture (IITA) has researched improved varieties of crops, thereby contributing

---

[221]Blas, *UN food chief urges rethink on biofuels*, FT, Aug. 15, 2007, at 3; Bounds, Andrew, *EU boosts biofuels despite concerns,* FT, Jan. 15, 2008, at 2; Blas, *UN says oil rise hits food prices harder*, FT, Apr. 26, 2008, at 2. Int' organizations estimates the contribution of biofuels to the current food price rise from 10 to 30 %.

[222]Ward, Andrew and Dombey, Daniel, *Bush boosts food aid and modified crops*, FT, May 2, 2008; Harvey, Fiona, *Case grows for modified plants as biofuels feedstock*, FT, May 18, 2008. For such promotion policies, *see* International Treaty on PGRFA, Art. 6.2 (a) – (g), *at* http://www.fao.org.

[223]*See* Art. 10.2. For facilitated access to PGR, refer to Art. 12.3 (a) and 12.4 while, benefit-sharing, *refer to* Art. 13.1 and 13.2.

to their productivity increase. For example, they developed disease- and pest-resistant varieties of cassava, a major staple food in tropical region, which led to yielding 50 % more than local varieties.[224] Other measures can improve productivity, such as exchange of information, investment in agriculture and agribusiness, facility development, and capacity-building through education in DCs.[225] In respect of a request of international cooperation,[226] benefits from the enhanced use of PGRs should be shared fairly and equitably with DCs and transitional economies in order to support their sustainable usages of PGRs.

As productivity increase model can share some aspects of international cooperation with multistakeholder strategy stated below, ICAs may take both models for their operation. For example, agricultural companies can sell supplies, e.g., seeds, or make purchase contracts with smallholder farmers for the cultivation of crop varieties with higher quality and higher yielding under the auspice of ICAs consisting of, although partly, smallholders' representatives or private companies.

(B) A Model for Multistakeholders' Participation

The other proposal is to respond to the needs of market participants and market conditions through multilateral cooperation.[227] This proposal suggests that an ICA should promote participation from multistakeholders, particularly, private sector players, and smallholder producer organizations (SPOs).[228] The Sustainable Committee Initiative (SCI), as a forum for multistakeholders under the auspices of the UNCTAD and the International Institute for Sustainable Development (IISD),[229] belongs to this model. The SCI aims at maximizing existent multilateral approaches for sustainable development in the international commodity market through encouraging complementary private and public sector contributions. The exemplary contributions are sharing best practices, discussing better policies for improved social and environmental standards in commodity production and trade, and performing scientific research and analysis on the impact of the policies and responses.[230]

By reflecting the participation of smallholders and private sectors, ICAs can have several important benefits. First, the governance structures of ICAs can be open to small-scale producers' interests. The former structure of ICAs with power

[224]IITA, IITA supports Gabon with improved cassava varieties, The Bulletin, No. 1770, Sept. 20, 2004, *available at* http://www.iita.org.

[225]Article 13.2 (a) – (d); Para. 3 of 2008 Rome Declaration on WFS.

[226]Article 7.2 (a) – (d).

[227]IISD & UNCTAD (2003), at 14; Potts (2004), at 10; ICoO (2006), at 7.

[228]Para. 7 (b) and (d), 2008 Rome Declaration on WFS.

[229]IISD is a Canadian-based nongovernmental organization (NGO) devoted to the development and implementation of policies toward sustainable development. IISD has promoted open and effective international negotiation processes and coworked with other NGOs since 1990. For in-detailed information, *refer to* http://www.iisd.org.

[230]SCI (2007), at 1 and 11. AIDEnvironment and the International Institute for Environment and Development are the other participating NGOs.

centered on large-scale producing or consuming countries may be reformed to reflect interests of smallholders. For example, the SCI tried to learn from policies and practices of diverse Voluntary Sustainability Initiative (VSIs)[231] with small producers as their major policy objects, thereby offering forums for the smallholders' communication and sharing information. Regrettably, the International Coffee Agreement (ICoA) for operating the International Coffee Organization (ICoO) has not fully reflected IISD's policy recommendation that the Private Sector Consultative Board (PSCB) under the ICoO for global cooperation with private sector players should reserve, especially, representatives for smallholder producer organizations (SPOs) out of exporting countries' portion.[232]

Second, the reform of ICAs is expected to provide diverse supports to the small producers who have suffered from the lack of accessibility to technical assistances, financial facilities, and market data. The ICoA of 2007 proposed a Consultative Forum on Coffee Sector Finance (CFCSF) to facilitate creative dialogues toward such benevolent policies as finance and risk management for small- and medium-scale producers and local communities in coffee producing areas.[233] In addition, pursuant to Art. 16 of the ICoA allowing collaboration with NGOs, ICoO could play the role of a clearing house through supports from the SCI, e.g., the collection and publication of economic and technical information.[234]

Third, the participation of private sectors into ICAs' works will improve commodity production and supply chains[235] through either diversification or productivity promotion policy. Kofi Anan, former Chairman of the Board of Alliance for Green Revolution in Africa (AGRA),[236] which achieved a partnership agreement with major global agencies to improve productivity and rural incomes for smallholder farmers, explicitly stated that AGRA's strategic vision was to build partnerships pooling the strengths and resources of the public and private sectors, civil

---

[231]VSIs refer to strategic programs which require participating companies in the supply chain to improve the social and ecological performance of their operations beyond legal requirements with collaboration with multistakeholders and supply chain partners. Universitat St. Gallen, *Inter-organizational design of VSIs*, *available at* http://www.logistik.unisg.ch (visited on June 14, 2008).

[232]ICoO (2006), 9–10.

[233]*See* Art. 31(1) of the ICoA of 2007.

[234]Pursuant to Art. 32 (1) of the ICoA which provides access to finances for small producers, to technical information regarding productivity, and to market data from differentiated coffee markets e.g., certified-sustainable coffees. *See* ICoO (2006), at 10; SCI (2007), at 15.

[235]A commodity-production chain means the way where agricultural supplies, such as seeds, fertilizer, and tools, circulate to a farmer. Meanwhile a supply chain means the way where agricultural products circulate from a producer to a consumer. So-called an 'agricultural value chain' comprises both production and supply chains.

[236]AGRA is an association of farmers, agricultural businesses, scientists, and research institutions with the form of a African-led partnership which works across the African continent in order to rescue millions of small-scale farmers and their families in getting out of poverty and hunger. AGRA, established in 2006, has supported policies which improve all key aspects of the African value chain from seeds, soil health, and water to markets.

society, farmers organizations, donors, scientists, and entrepreneurs across the agricultural value chain.[237]

Formation of the partnership of an ICA with private sectors or international organizations with expertise in reforming commodity supply chains, e.g., the SCI, will provide the ICA with an efficient production or supply chain network. The International Maize and Wheat Improvement Center in Mexico, a nonprofit research and training center with global network of overall organizations from both public and private sectors, and people who share similar development goals in around a hundred DCs, has implemented a plan in cooperation with other international organizations and private companies, to plant high-yielding maize varieties strong in tropical environments.[238] An agreement for 'market-smart' subsidies designed to complement and stimulate private sectors is worthwhile to be considered as a part of ICAs because former state subsidies replacing the private sectors were dismantled in African countries in 1970s pursuant to the advice of the World Bank but the private sectors have not grown sufficiently to form effective production and supply chains since then.[239] As a successful model, Malawi's subsidy scheme, offering smallholders vouchers to buy seed and fertilizers, doubled the harvest between 2004–2005, and 2005–2006.[240]

(C) Eco-Labeling Systems as Cooperation between Private and Public Sectors

A labeling system for agricultural commodities may be a successful result of cooperative efforts between private and public entities. The labeling system is a concrete model which some international organizations launch to markets in industrialized countries in light of sustainable development. Such labels as Organic,[241] Fair Trade Certification (FTC),[242] Rainforest Alliance Certified

[237]AGRA, *Boosting Food Production in Africa's "Breadbasket Areas": New Collaboration among Rome-based UN Agencies and AGRA* (June 4, 2008), at http://www.agra-alliance.org/news/pr060408.html (visited on June 14, 2008).

[238]The International Maize and Wheat Improvement Center is more known as its Spanish synonym, CIMMYT (Centro Internacional de Mejoramiento de Maíz y Trigo). CIMMYT works with African Agricultural Technology Foundation (AATF), a public–private research partnership in Nairobi, the private agricultural company Monsanto, and the agricultural research systems in eastern and southern Africa for this project. The plan include for distribution of the developed varieties to African seed companies without royalties For in-detailed information, *refer to* http://www.aatf-africa.org/aatf_projects.php?sublevelone=30&subcat=5.

[239]*Id.*

[240]Beattie, *Malawi cultivates cash gains for its farmers*, FT, June 10, 2008, at 3.

[241]Distinctive feature of Organic from FTC is on its keen interest in cultivation or raising free from using most conventional pesticides, synthetic fertilizers, sewage sludge, genetically modified organisms (GMOs), or ionizing radiation, or antibiotics or growth hormones. The related information is *available at* http://www.organic.org/education/faqs.

[242]Meanwhile, FTC's interest is more on condition of farmers and laborers e.g., fair prices, fair labor conditions, and democratic organizations for producers' profits. FTC is also concerned about environmental sustainability by prohibiting agrochemicals, GMOs in favor of farmers' health as well as preserving ecosystems for future generation. In-detailed information is *available at* http://www.transfairusa.org/content/certification/overview.php.

(RAC),[243] SA8000 of Social Accountability International (SAI),[244] have grown through invoking consumers' interests in sustainable goods. Through continuous research and campaign on eco-labeled agricultural products, consumers' awareness and their sales scope have grown.[245] For example, total UK sale of fair trade products reached £1.78bn in 2013 and consumer awareness of the 'FAIRTRADE' mark amounted to 78 % recognition among UK consumers.[246] Their positive impacts on smallholder producers are never insignificant.[247] Governments have already noticed the benefits of such products to weak sectors in their economies and taken the role of a supervisor. After private sectors' efforts to commercialize the Organic foods, more and more governments have been operating Organic label-sealing through public audit under national laws.[248]

When an ICA tries to launch an eco-label as a concrete way of adapting sustainability into the market system, more studies should be taken to improve commercial traits of the label, such as quality improvement or market expansion

---

[243]Rainforest Alliance (RA) is a nonprofit organization established in 1987 to preserve biodiversity and ensure sustainable livelihoods with focus on environment of Central America. As one of its major works, RA set standards that conserve sustainability of wildlife, lands, and well-being of workers and provide certification seal to those who meet the criteria. Certification for agricultural products, former ECO-OK label, for particularly coffee and banana, works as market incentives encouraging farmers to comply with environmental and social standards. RA helps smallholders' accesses to information of certified farm products and market trend by operating information center. *Refer to* http://www.rainforest-alliance.org/programs/agricuture.

[244]Social Accountability International (SAI) is an international nongovernmental organization (NGO) of multistakeholders focusing on implementing socially responsible standards. SA8000 is an international standard for improving working conditions based on International Labor Organization and 13 international human right conventions. To obtain the certification, companies need to pass on-site audit and assessment of corporate practices by SAI-accredited auditing firms. The SA8000 may generate such benefits as improved morale, reliable business partnerships, enhanced competitiveness of products, and better worker–manger relationship. *Refer to* http://www.sa-intl.org.

[245]Baranski et al. (2014), at 1 (Higher antioxidant, lower toxic metal cadmium concentrations and four times lower incidence of pesticide residues were found in organically grown crops).

[246]*Businesses back Fairtrade Foundation's autumn campaign*, Aug. 7, 2014, *available at* http://www.fairtrade.org.uk (visited on Aug. 31, 2015). American consumers' awareness of 'fair trade' grew up to 27 % in 2007 from 12 % in 2004. In the American coffee market, FTC occupied 3.3 % in 2006, eight times more than the level in 2001. *Fair Trade in Bloom*, N.Y. Times, Oct. 2, 2007. Organic food sales grew by 17–20 % annually during the past few years compared to 2–3 % annual sales growth of conventional foods. Around 4 % of total agricultural land was dedicated to organic food production in the EU. Even Cuba converted the whole country agricultural production to organic and many of pesticides are not permitted to be used by law. Alexander and Anderson (1984), at 31–41.

[247]IISD & UNCTAD (2003), at 12 footnote 33.

[248]U.S. Department of Agriculture (USDA) develops organic food standards under its regulations and accredits certifying agents to certify producers. European Commission controls farmers, processors and trades under strict requirements, e.g., Council Regulation (EC) (No. 834/2007), for organic food certification. Brazil, Chile, Japan, Thailand, and other countries followed the path.

through diversification.[249] A relatively high price of labeled products, boosted by the fair reward policy and license as well as the inspection fee, might result in difficulty in attracting consumers sensitive to such high prices. The studies need to reflect diverse perspectives of multistakeholders. For example, the ICoA of 2007 led members' efforts to a way for developing a market and for promoting the quality of products and consumption including information campaigns, research, capacity-building, and studies regarding coffee production and consumption.[250] ICoO opened the room for multistakeholders by allowing voluntary finance from nonmembers, other organizations, and the private sectors.[251]

A forum for cooperation among private entities, and both exporting countries and importing countries, along with the representatives of NGOs reflecting the voices of SPOs, can play an important role in the successful progress of eco-labels. The prosperity of the label system largely relies on the level of consumers' purchase affected by commercial strategies more likely to come through discussion among private entities with expertise in marketing and public entities in charge of trade conditions. An ICA consisting of exporting and importing countries, with the participation of private sectors and representatives of smallholders, will be an appropriate vehicle to carry out the cooperative work.

(4) Analysis

As Art. XX(h) of GATT, as a general exception provision, approved the adoption of state measures pursuant to obligations under any ICA, ICAs could have operated diverse market-intervening measures, e.g., supply control, buffet stock, and compensatory scheme. However, the past demise of ICAs indicated that the market-intervening measures cost much regarding their operation from both perspectives of finance and internal dispute settlement. In light of the above-mentioned new proposals, ICAs should place focus more on cooperation on diversification and productivity increase through fair benefit-sharing[252] than on the cost-demanding market-intervening measures. As market-adaptive measures, the development of diversified products, the cultivation of their markets, and research on productivity increase should have initiatives among other policies in ICAs. The participation of the private sectors with superior capacities in the area of product diversification, market cultivation, and the research is very desirable for the successful functioning of the market-adaptive measures. As the market-adaptive measures are intended not to control markets but to promote market supply, internal conflicts regarding the

[249] Article 1(7) and (9) of 2007 ICoA. *See* IISD & UNCTAD (2003), at 12. It addresses the development of a consumer market for fair trade labeled coffees as a effective response to macroeconomic conditions of global coffee market.

[250] Article 25(1) and (2) of the ICoA of 2007.

[251] Article 25(3) and (4).

[252] *See* Sucharitkul (2006), at 14. Sucharitkul mentioned, generally, that cooperation is most needed in equitable sharing of shared resources and conserving of endangered species, thereby contributing to the maintenance of sustainable development.

measures will, if ever, rarely result in such disputes as would result in the demise of ICAs.

When the policy for a fair benefit share is pursued, the policy should consider protection of intellectual property for new techniques, effective commercialization in markets, e.g., eco-label, and the necessity of special treatment for LDCs. Growing genetic plants can be developed with stable investment only when its techniques can secure fair rewards under strong intellectual property regime. Under the auspice of trademark regime, the eco-labels have contributed to the goal of fair benefit-sharing. Still, further research to improve the quality of products is necessary to cultivate their markets in light of their relatively high price. SDT for LDCs, CDDCs, and low income food deficit countries (LIFDCs) should be incorporated into ICAs so that poor farmers in the countries can subsist on their products.

C. The Roles of ICAS in Food Trade

A market-based trade is acknowledged to be an important and effective method to foster world food security by world leaders and experts.[253] Governmental interventions through subsidies and export and import tariffs have been major targets which DDA tried to reduce or eliminate as culprits distorting free international food trade. However, food has been treated more as an object of important international human rights than commodity under free trade regime. The sudden extension of a market-oriented trade regime to cover food commodity looks not to comply with the accumulated international laws that have treated food from the human rights perspective.

Since the Universal Declaration on Human Rights (UDHR) and the International Covenant on Economic, Social and Cultural Rights (ICESC) had in common the right to a standard of living adequate for the health and well-being of the people, including right to food, international laws, e.g., 2008 Rome Declaration of WFS, have perceived food as an object of human rights.[254] On the other hand, international laws, such as WFS Plan of Action and ITPGRFA, have acknowledged that farmers have the right to earn a fair return from their labor and management.[255]

---

[253]Rome Declaration, at eighth and tenth para.; Commitment Four of the World Food Summit Plan of Action, para. 37; The World Food Summit, Declaration of World Food Security (WFS): Five Years Later, para. 12 (2002). *See* Beattie, *Making Hay: As food costs rise, farmers cling to their subsidies*, FT, May 14, 2008, at 7; para. 6.(d) and 7.(e), Declaration of the High-Level Conference on WFS: the Challenges of Climate Change and Bio-energy (2008 Rome Declaration on WFS) (June 5, 2008).

[254]*See* Art. 25(1) of UDHR, and Art. 11(1)(2) of ICESC. Subsequent international laws are para. 1 of Universal Declaration on the Eradication of Hunger and Malnutrition, UN World Food Conference, UN Doc. E/CONF.65/20 (1974), para. 1 of Rome Declaration on WFS, The World Food Summit, W3613/E (1996), and para. 2 of UN GA Resolution on the Right to Food, GA Res. 56/155, UN Doc. A/Res/56/155 (2002); Para. 1 and 3 of 2008 Rome Declaration on WFS.

[255]World Food Summit Plan of Action, W3613/E, Commitment Two, Objective 2.1 (d) (1998); ICESC, Art.11(2)(a) (1967). The Biodiversity Convention and the ITPGRFA protect farmers' right as breeders of plant genetic resources and biological resources from intellectual property perspective.

Although more focus has been placed on people's right to food from the food security perspective, the right to food should not ignore farmers' right to fair remuneration. International cooperation between them throughout the ups and downs of food supply has been urged in order to ensure an equitable distribution of world food supplies in relation to need.[256]

On the contrary to a widely acknowledged international consensus in the human rights perspective, the expansion of a free trade regime to international food trade has achieved a low level of consensus. Long standstill of DDA reflects the low consensus due to internal political reasons from individual countries.[257] Food price surge in 2008 seemed to drive countries complying with the free food trade regime, e.g., Philippines and India, back to the stage of autarky. Through enduring the food crisis, the countries grew not to trust open competition of the world food market any more but want a sufficient domestic food supply from the food security perspective.

In light of the circumstances, a modified or hybrid type of commodity trade regimes will be a more appropriate institution for the international food trade. Efforts to establish an international free 'food' trade regime[258] should go with complimentary measures fulfilling human right perspectives and the needs of CDDCs and LIFDC. Concrete measures include research for the productivity increase, emergency aid, crop insurance,[259] technical and financial assistances, and SDT for LDCs and LIFDC. For example, the GATT Decision on Measures Concerning the Possible Negative Effects of the Reform Programme on Least-Developed and Net Food-Importing Developing Countries addressed possible detrimental impacts of the free food trade regime on LDCs and LIFDC, and suggested such institutional supports as a forum to offer an appropriate level of food aid, guidelines to ensure the provision of basic foodstuffs to LDCs, access to international financial institutions, and technical and financial assistance for improving agricultural productivity. Moreover, the Agreement on Agriculture under WTO Agreement limited food export prohibition or restriction in light of the effect of such measures on the food security of importing countries.[260] Furthermore, the

---

[256]*See* ICESC, Art.11(2)(b). Universal Declaration on the Eradication of Hunger and Malnutrition, Rome Declaration, UN GA Resolution on the Right to Food, and Declaration of WFS placed emphasis right to food as fundament human right.

[257]Beattie, *Trade Deal hopes fade as G4 talks fall apart*, FT, June 22, 2007, at 1.

[258]For the alternatives, refer to Grant Aldonas, *A Fresch Free Trade Agenda for DOHA*, FT, Jul.13, 2007, at 9.

[259]Malawi and the World Bank will pilot a crop insurance against adverse weather. Beattie, *Malawi cultivates cash gains for its farmers*, FT, June 10, 2008, at 3.

[260]UR Ministerial Decision, para. 5; Agreement Establishing the World Trade Organization (WTO Agreement), Apr. 15, 1994, Annex 1A: Agreement on Agriculture (AA), Part VI, Art.12, para. 1 (a) and (b).

GATT Decision and the WTO Agreement approved differential treatment for LDCs and net food-importing developing countries.[261]

ICAs have a potential as important cooperators to a new free trade regime. ICAs can operate a kind of pool arrangement[262] requiring for major producers to reserve a small percentage of production, from which net importing countries can draw an indispensable amount in times of urgent need. It does not cost as much as buffer stock system because it does not interrupt price mechanisms in markets but temporarily stores foods in each country. Emergency aid may be provided with the pool arrangement. An ICA can offer more chances for member countries to participate in the research for raising productivity of a particular crop than any institutional vehicle.

Price surge of staple foods as well as agricultural products, e.g., in 2008, from increasing demand and stagnated production along with other factors, was not a problem which could work out in a short time with a free trade system. Although such free trade regime might reduce distortion in markets, it is not likely to solve mistrust toward agricultural policies among nations and poor people's starvation issue in LIFDC.[263] International organizations led by the UN FAO have contributed their efforts to proposing aids with broad coverage, as 2008 Rome Food Security Summit announced.[264] However, the reform of ICAs toward the ones with the roles of a reserve pool and a research center for raising productivity should accompany the global free trade regime and assistances from international organizations. An ICA with concentrated focus on a particular food product is in better position to produce the most appropriate and in-detailed measures with accumulated expertise. Operation of international organizations, e.g., UN, CFC, and FAO, will be more efficient when they focus only on overall management of each ICA's works, and other comprehensive issues, e.g., the limitation of biofuel.

---

[261]The Uruguay Round Agreements (UR) Ministerial Decision, Measures Concerning the Possible Negative Effects of the Reform Programme on Least-Developed and Net Food-Importing Developing Countries, para. 4 (1993–1994); WTO Agreement, Annex 1A: AA, Part XII, Art.20 (c).

[262]Beattie, *Malawi cultivates cash gains for its farmers*, FT, June 10, 2008. Beattie introduced a global food bank, suggested by Joachim von Braun, as a concept of coalition for the caring. Dr. von Braun argued that the Group of Eight rich countries with some of big food exporters establish it. As an interim step, Dr. von Braun suggested a rice-pooling arrangement in Asia.

[263]*See id.* Dr. von Braun agreed with the limitation of free trade regime.

[264]Para. 5, 2008 Rome Declaration on WFS; UN FAO, Renewed Financial Effort in Fight on Hunger: Countries Increase Commitment at Rome Food Summit (June 5, 2008), *at* http://www.fao.org/newsroom/en/news/2008/1000858/index.html (visited on June 15, 2008). Newly announced financial commitments during the Rome Food Security Summit amount to US$ 18.36 billion, including U.S.A.'s US$ 5 billion, and France's US$ 1.5 billion.

6.7 Conclusion

International communities have strived for achieving a binding multilateral cartel regulation for quite a long time since the Havana Charter included cartel regulation under a chapter for competition law distinguished from a chapter for commodity law, but failed in obtaining sufficient ratifications to be effective. However, the efforts have produced little success except a recent nonbinding multilateral agreement among industrialized countries, the 1998 OECD Recommendation. This chapter examined the inherent limitations of respective international agreements as binding agreements.

First, a bilateral agreement has proved to be an improper method in achieving a binding international cartel regulation. The bipartisan structure of a bilateral agreement reveals too large of transaction costs to achieve the effect which a multilateral agreement can achieve. Dissimilar cartel regulations under diverse levels of economic development and a different legal system have worked as impediments in spreading bilateral agreements. Insufficient trust between reciprocal cartel authorities makes a country with relatively developed cartel practice hesitant to reach a cooperative agreement with a country with less developed cartel practice. Even most bilateral agreements do not have binding characteristics but recommendatory ones, particularly due to conflicts of national interest.

Second, the reasons why past efforts toward a binding multilateral agreement have faced a deadlock are analyzed as the following points: the lack of an international consensus, insufficient institutions, and diversified interests within developing countries (DCs). While competition, which a cartel aims at restricting, strengthens national economies by promoting competitive sectors and economic efficiency, quite a few DCs fear that their weak economic foundations may be undermined or fractured by eradicating domestic cartels. Besides their economic development, legal institutions, political system, and the level of economical research in a majority of DCs are not sufficiently mature to adopt international cartel law. Growing diversification and subsequent different voices within the DCs, along with the weakened power of NIEO, let industrialized countries with advanced economies succeed in reaching nonbinding agreements regulating cartels with a small number of developing countries.

The multilateral agreement itself has inherent limitations although it has some advantages, e.g., leading to uniform international law, as currently effective international trade law of the WTO agreement came from the Uruguay Round as a multilateral agreement. It usually takes much time and costs to reach the agreement with unanimous consent as the requirement under art. 11 of Vienna Convention on the Law of Treaties. The cartel law has proved to be a disputed area in light of immature domestic competition law practice, less awareness of cartel-causing damages, and domestic fear against competition. Even the U.S., with the strictest cartel practice in the world, has demonstrated its unwillingness to accede to a binding international cartel law as its business community has objected to it and as its competition law experts do not want to restrict with the law their jurisdictional power capable of reaching a foreign cartel, and strong enforcement against cartels. In light of the divergent interests, the fact that the DDA dropped competition policy out of its negotiation agenda is not surprising.

Third, the current widespread of free trade rule under WTO and the rapid development of emerging economies and transitional markets signal severe competition and tend to tempt companies, which are supposed to compete, to collude under a secret cartel agreement, which causes huge consumers' damages in overall markets. The necessity for a binding international cartel law will continue to grow. To successfully address the necessity, rather than a multilateral agreement, a plurilateral agreement, either through the expansion of a regional or a bilateral agreement, e.g., FTA, or an internal agreement within a international organization, is a more appropriate way to achieve a binding multilateral agreement as to cartels. So far diverse levels of economic developments, legal systems, political development, and economic research have hindered a binding multilateral agreement of competition policy from being reached. It would be better to start from procedural cooperation and convergence and then to reach a point of substantial convergence as procedural cooperation can attract more countries with less burdens on sovereignty. In the same line, international relationship theories support the argument that an international agreement can be made better within a group of states with similar interests rather than between groups with different interests, e.g., between the North and the South.

Both short-term and long-term approaches are suggested for a binding multilateral agreement. Under the short-term approach that the coverage of international cartel agreement needs to be narrowed down sufficiently to achieve member countries' consensus, the book suggests bid-rigging as the initial object for cartel regulation because bid-rigging causes damages to public revenue important to any country, either industrial or developing. Price-fixing, output restriction, and market allocation are the next objects. Such main categories are categorized as cartels causing clearest anticompetitive damages according to accumulated researches and case laws. The other horizontal agreements usually with the incidental effect of competition restriction should be under the long-term approach covering the whole competition policy as they invoke discussion of pro- and anti- competitive effects. The exemption provisions which exonerate cartels with proof of outweighing public interests are needed because development-related exemptions, e.g., R&D cartel, depression cartel, SME cartel, and industrialization cartels, can attract DCs' accession to the agreement. The exemptions can reduce DCs' concerns about economic development. However, the exemptions should be regularly reviewed by an independent panel with the participation of competition experts under a transparent standard so as not to be abused. An export cartel will be under one of the exemptions under the narrow approach as industrialized countries representing net exporting countries want to add it for its national interests and as the narrow approach requires the accession of the industrialized countries. However, it is to be reviewed under the same strict screening standard.

The long-term approach comes from the experiences of under enforcement of cartel regulation in countries, where the whole competition law was not enacted.[265] Activating the effective cartel regulation needs to be parallel with operating the national competition regime. However, in order to reduce the huge cost for the full harmonization of international competition law due to gaps of competition law development, principle-based international law is better than concrete-provisioned law. In light of a wide range of countries adopting or considering the adoption of competition law, SDT in favor of LDCs and low or mid income DCs should be acknowledged. Moreover, international competition law procedures, comprising compliance-securing procedures, harmonized procedures, and coordinated procedures, should be established in priority over concrete substantive rules. Most of the procedural differences can be reduced more easily as they are less related to national interest than substantive rules. In addition, an international system for securing confidential information, e.g., an international merger report system, is needed.

Discussion for adopting international criminal law as to cartels has been immature at this moment when binding international cartel law does not exist and the accumulation of successful criminal cartel cases was limited to only a few countries, e.g., the U.S., the UK, and Canada. The competition or consumers' welfare maximized through the competition is not yet acknowledged as the interest worthy of protection through international criminal law. Commercial ethics in the market is not sufficiently widespread enough to form criminal culmination against cartels, let alone the necessity of international criminalization against cartels. Activating private actions along with public sanctions, either administrative sanction, or criminal penalty, can invoke public awareness of the criminalization of cartels.

As primary commodities have such unique characteristics different from artificial products, as the inelasticity of production, state involvement, and significant importance to the economies of CDDCs, it is neither possible nor proper to apply cartel regulation in competition law. Commodity production is related to several issues, such as hunger, national intervention, equitable development between exporting countries and importing countries, and environmental protection. The complicated interests generated diverse international commodity agreements (ICAs) in order to regulate production and trade with respect to each commodity. The ICAs should balance conflicting interests between producers and consumers in terms of development and hunger, and between current generations and future generations in terms of environmental protection.

However, most ICAs have grown defunct, except a few examples, under internal conflicts among members as well as under market-interrupting mechanisms since mid-1980s. Inner political disputes regarding the operation of the quota system weakened the operation of ICAs because the ICAs could not harmonize various

---

[265]France and Germany before the WWII, and developing countries before the adoption of sophisticated competition law on the foundation of economic, political and legal development as well as economical research, e.g., Mexico before 1994, South Africa before 1998, and South Korea before 1992 demonstrated the under-enforcement of price-fixing regulation.

interests among member states within their operating tools. The huge cost of operating a buffer stock system resulted in the disruption of other ICAs. On the contrary to the demise of ICAs, market-management tools, e.g., PRMs, have drawn attention. In addition, the structural policies, e.g., production diversification in CDDCs, have gained momentum.

The necessity of protecting the environment during the process of economic development invoked the international community to create the concept of 'sustainable development.' 'Sustainable development' urges states to protect the ability of future generations while pursuing economic development. In international commodity law, 'sustainable development' has more room to be applied as the competitive exploitation of primary commodities can endanger the protection of natural resources and equitable food production and distribution. International law on 'sustainable development' should be developed more. It is cooperation among producers for further production and environmental protection as one of the concrete policies that international commodity law needs to address.

As a main vehicle for the cooperation, an ICA, formerly defunct, should be reformed so as to work effectively under international commodity law. A main point of an ICA's reform plan is to use market-adaptive measures, e.g., commercialization through diversification, rather than to depend on former market-interrupting measures. Concretely, two models for reforming ICAs are to be introduced: ①productivity-focused model and ②multilateral cooperation model. The first model is for productivity increase and fair benefit-sharing from the increased productivity. It includes public or both public and private investment in technology and scientific research and the protection of intellectual property. The other one is for the promotion of multilateral cooperation. The latter model intends to reflect opinions of, particularly, private actors and smallholder producers on the activities of an ICA in the commodity market. As the SCI, established under the auspice of international organizations, e.g., the UNCTAD, has a plan to promote cooperation between the public and private sectors for pursuing sustainable development in international commodity market, the SCI's coworks with ICAs fall under the category of the second model. The model is expected to generate several benefits, such as the reform of governance structure reflecting voices from SPOs, benevolent financial and technical assistance to smallholder farmers, and the improvement of commodity production and supply chains through the participation of the private sector.

A noticeable example on which a reformed ICA may focus is an eco-label system. The eco-label system falls on the harmonized approach which makes use of both the first and second models, respectively, representing incorporation of fair benefit-sharing into the commodity market and cooperation with private sectors for 'sustainable development.' Through accepting the entities ignored under conventional ICAs, a reformed ICA is expected to become a forum to discuss the ways of productivity increase and fair distribution, which can reflect multistake holders' opinions.

Particularly, regarding food commodities, international law has acknowledged right to food as a fundamental human right. On the other hand, farmers' right to have fair reward for the agricultural commodity has been developed in light of farmers' disadvantaged living conditions. Although the expansion of free trade regime is acknowledged as an effective measure to eliminate distortions in international food trade, the blind application of free trade law to food commodities without respect to the two rights cannot produce a desirable result. As the free trade agenda with respect to food does not achieve as much consensus as the two rights mentioned above, a modified commodity trade regime should be studied. Concrete measures functioning as supplements to a free commodity trade regime are the offering of financial aid in the short term, and research for productivity increase and the facilitation of related institutions for agricultural business in the long term. ICAs with special expertise in each commodity are expected to play important roles in realizing the goals both in the short term and the long term. A pool arrangement for producing countries to reserve an amount of production for a temporary period can be an institution for offering assistance to food-importing countries in times of emergency food shortages.

References

Books

American Bar Association (ABA) Section of Antitrust Law (2007) Federal Statutory Exemptions from Antitrust Law, ABA Pub., Illinois U.S.

Araim AS (1991) Intergovernmental commodity organizations and the new international economic order, Praeger, New York, U.S.

Bassiouni MC (1998–1999) International criminal law, 2nd edn. Ardsley

Bassiouni MC (1987) A draft international criminal code and draft statute for an international criminal tribunal. Martinus Nijhoff Pub.

Dabbah MM (2003) The internationalisation of antitrust policy. Cambridge

Huh C-H (2002) Korea's monopoly restraint and fair trade act [MRFTA] and cartel regulation [공정거래법과 카르텔규제]. Bi-Bong Pub., Seoul, Korea

Kwon O-S (1999) Economic law [경제법], Bubmoon-sa, Seoul, Korea

Peritz R (1996) Competition policy in America: history, rhetoric, law, Rev. edn. Oxford Univ. Pr., Oxford, U.K.

Scherer FM (1994) Competition policies for an integrated world economy. Brookings Inst., Washington D.C., U.S.

Sell S (1998) Power & ideas: North-South politics of intellectual property and antitrust, State Univ. of N.Y. Pr., New York, U.S.

Taylor M (2006) International competition law: a new dimension for the WTO? Cambridge Univ. Press, Cambridge, U.K.

U.N. (2007) Model law on competition, UN Doc TD/RBP/CONF.5/7/Rev.3, Sales No. E.07.II.D.7

Articles, Papers

Agritrade B (2007) Executive brief. http://agritrade.cta.int/en/layout/set/print/content/view/full/2505

Alexander R, Anderson PK (1984) Pesticide use, alternatives & workers' health in Cuba. Int J Health Serv 14(1):31–41

Baranski M et al (2014) Higher antioxidant and lower cadmium concentrations & lower incidence of pesticide residues in organically grown crops: a systematic literature review and meta-analyses. Br J Nutr 1–18. http://foodpolitics.com

Brown B (1994) Developing Countries in the International Trade Order, 14 N Ill UL Rev 347:347–380

Common Fund for Commodities (CFC) (2006) Current trends & the new development role of commodities. http://www.cfc.org

Connor JM, Helmers CG (2007) Statistics on modern private international cartels: 1995–2005. American Antitrust Institute (AAI) Working Paper No. 07-01

Connor J, Lande R (2005) American Antitrust Institute symposium: thinking creatively about remedies: how high do cartels raise prices. Implications for optical cartel fines. Tul L Rev 80:513

Consumer International (CI) (2007) Consumers and competition: a consumer welfare analysis of three retail markets in 14 EU member states. http://www.consumerinternational.org

Drexl J (2003) Comments on Harry First: decentralized antitrust enforcement and the evolution of an int'l common law of antitrust. In Drexl J (ed) The future of transnational antitrust-from comparative to common competition law, vol 53. Staempfli Pub., Berne, Switzerland

First H (2003) Evolving toward what? The development of international antitrust. In: Drexl J (ed) The future of transnational antitrust-from comparative to common competition law. Staempfli Pub., Berne, Switzerland, pp 42–43

Fiebig A (1999) Crisis cartels and the triumph of industrial policy over competition law in Europe. Brooklyn J Int L 25:607

Fingleton J, Girard M-B, Williams S (2007) The fight against cartels: is a 'mixed' approach to enforcement the answer? In: Hawk B (ed) Annual proceedings of the Fordham Corporate Law Institute: International Antitrust Law and Policy (hereinafter IALP). FLI, NY, U.S.

Guzman A (1998) Is international antitrust possible? NYU Rev 73:1501

Hawk BE (2007) Criminal enforcement of antitrust law-roundtable. In: IALP. FLI, NY, U.S.

Immenga U (1999) Conflicts between competition policy and industrial policy: a comparative view on potential responses. In: Zaech R (ed) Towards WTO competition rules: key issues and comments on the WTO report on trade and competition, Kluwer Law Int'l

International Institute of Sustainable Development (IISD) & UNCTAD (2003) Sustainability in the coffee sector: exploring opportunities for international cooperation. http://www.iisd.org

International Coffee Organization (ICoO) (2006) Grounds for change. http://www.oxfam.de

Kahn TJ (1980) The protection of trading interests act of 1980: Britain's response to US extraterritorial antitrust enforcement. Nw J Int L Bus 2:476–498

Kennedy KC (2001) Symposium: global trade issues in the New Millennium: foreign direct investment and competition policy at the WTO, 33 Geo. Wash Int Rev 585–650

Lee SH (2008–2009) Effective strategies for an international agreement regulating cartels. Int Trade Law 87:149–185

Levenstein M, Suslow V (2005) The changing int'l status of export cartel exemptions. Am U Int L Rev 20:785–828

OECD (2001) GFC: contribution from China. CCNM/GF/COMP/WD(2001)10. 2 Oct 2001

OECD (2002) Report on the nature and impact of hard core cartel and sanctions against cartels under national competition laws. DAFFE/COMP(2002)7

Potts J (2004) Building a sustainable coffee sector using market-based approaches: the role of multi-stakeholder cooperation. IISD. http://www.iisd.org

Quill E (1994) The failure of int'l commodity agreements: forms, functions, and implications. Denv J Int L Pol 22:503
Reinert E (2007) How rich countries got rich … and why poor countries stay poor. Constable & Robinson Ltd., London, U.K.
Rosenthal DE (1998) Jurisdiction and enforcement: equipping the multilateral trading system with a style and principles to increase market access Geo Mason L Rev 6:543
SCI (2007) SCI rationale and road-map: 2008–2011. http://www.iisd.org/pdf/2007/sci_roadmap.pdf. Visited on 5 Feb 2008
Sucharitkul S (2006) A just world under law, vol 14. Unpublished manuscript, on file with the Golden Gate Univ. School of Law Library
Waller SW (1997) The internationalization of antitrust enforcement. Boston Univ L Rev 77:343

Chapter 7
General Conclusion: Summary and Prospect

Abstract While the international community has struggled to operate a binding multilateral international agreement on cartels, its efforts to understand differences of political, economic, and social foundations of law and economy between the North and the South have been made insufficiently from competition law and policy perspective. The academic investigation on the history of international law regarding competition and commodity indicates that there are distinctive characteristics of both areas for regulation although such distinction has lessened. Realistic strategies-short-term and long-term- are suggested for solving the current standstill of multilateral negotiation on international trade issues, particularly competition law including cartel regulation. International agreement on cartels needs to be initiated centering on bid-rigging while international commodity agreement needs to be dealt in the separate area.

Keywords International competition law · A cartel · A binding multilateral international agreement on cartels · International commodity agreement · International commodity law

7.1 Compendium of Research

In summary, this study argued that a multilateral binding international cartel regulation, desirable for furthering economic development, can be achieved by using two strategies and that an intergovernmental commodity agreement (ICA) in distinction with an international cartel should adopt reform projects, focusing on either productivity-enhancement or allow the participation of multistakeholders, or both, in order to continue to function effectively in the international commodity market. This book has developed verifiable academic and practical foundations for these arguments.

A cartel is defined in the narrow way for the purpose of achieving international cartel law through Chap. 2. The reason is that it is very difficult to reach an international consensus regarding the law when the definition of a cartel covers

J.S. Lee, *Strategies to Achieve a Binding International Agreement on Regulating Cartels*, DOI 10.1007/978-981-10-2756-7_7

broad aspects of competition-related activities. The typical aspects of hard core cartels, such as price-fixing, outputrestriction, market allocation, and bid-rigging, are widely acknowledged to bring about huge damages, both direct and indirect. From the regulatory perspective in international law, the definition of a cartel needs to be confined in "an agreement for or merely collusive acts, which cause anti-competitive impact on related markets, among independent entrepreneurs competing in the same line of business for obtaining extra-profits." With the definition, concentrating on the typical aspects of cartels, widely considered as negative, will be an efficient way to create international cartel law.

It is true that cartels sometimes generate benevolent effects, such as preventing waste of financial and personal resources, cooperative investment on research and development, the securing of reasonable regulation in professional associations or by industry itself, and the prevention of extreme price fluctuation. Each country places a different level of weight on a cartel's benevolent effects in comparison to its accompanying anticompetitive effects in light of economic and political situations, and legal development. However, historically, most advanced countries have adopted quite a few exceptions to their strict cartel regulations. Therefore, some exceptions to cartel regulations with verifiable net pro-competitive impact or significant public interest should be acknowledged in international cartel law.

An ICA has been acknowledged under international commodity law, in distinction with a cartel under international competition law, because a commodity in distinction with an artificial product has unique characteristics from the economic, political, and legal perspective. Although commodity trade is a significant factor which determines national income in CDDCs, commodity supply, and demand are inflexible, thereby making commodity price unstable. As a result, states have been deeply involved in commodity production and made restrictions on its trade. The characteristics distinguish primary commodities from artificial products, thereby having developed commodity law in distinction with competition law under international law. An intergovernmental producers' association (IPA), although restricting competition more severely than an ICA, is regulated, along with an ICA, under international commodity law as it deals with a commodity.

According to the statistical research, a private international cartel caused damages in the amount of around US$ 2.6 billion. It was formed in a highly concentrated market with a few competitors where entry barriers existed, to which the markets in developing countries (DCs) are more similar than those in advanced countries. However, as the international vitamin cartel and electrode graphite cartel cases indicated, the level of cartel enforcement in DCs was much lower than that in advanced countries. In order to overcome such weak enforcement, international supports for cartel regulation in DCs are needed. Particularly, a binding multilateral international cartel law can facilitate active cartel enforcement in DCs.

Chapter 3 reviewed, in order, legal characteristics of international cartels, three exemplary international organizations under doubt of being an international cartel, and the development of international cartel law and commodity law. Before figuring out the legal characteristics of a cartel, two types of international cartels should be categorized: an agreement among competitors, and a loose association established by the agreement among competitors. While the agreement-type cartel has no legal personality similar to an international agreement, the association-type cartel can work as an international organization with a legal personality. ICAs and IPAs under the broadest definition of the cartel fall under the category of an international organization.

Among international organizations under the suspicion of an international cartel, OPEC, ITU, and IATA were analyzed. The OPEC, as one of the most effective and long-standing IPAs, is not a private cartel under cartel regulation. An intergovernmental producers' agreement (IPA) consisting of sovereign states, the status of oil as a nonrenewable natural resource, the absence of penalties against cheating, and the necessity of sustainable development distinguish the OPEC as an IPA from an international private cartel. Similarly, the activities of the ITU as a standard-setting organization mostly of sovereign states possess fewer characteristics of an international cartel. Its rate-setting practices necessary for accommodating several public interests, e.g., equity, universality, and static efficiency, have resulted in price decrease. The RFS allocation is an inevitable regime for effective cross-border broadcasting at the current technical level. On the contrary, the IATA can fall under the category of an international cartel because the association of competing private airlines provides such practices as the setting of passenger rates or air cargo fees. In addition, its interlineable fare system has effectively settled fares to the same level in spite of a nonbinding recommendation. On the other hand, slot allocation and airport scheduling are considered as necessary procedures for reducing congestion in airports unless they unfairly exclude new comers in favor of existent large slot holders.

Although there were prohibitions of profiteering through hard core cartel activities from the ancient to the modern ages, sophisticated cartel regulations were developed centering on industrialized countries in the late twentieth century. In response to the emergence of international cartels, centering around popular bilateral or regional agreements, international competition law produced several multilateral nonbinding agreements, led by international organizations, e.g., UNCTAD, UN, and OECD. The level and scope of cartel regulations have been improved and widened by regulatory development. Unfortunately, however, recent efforts to adopt cartel regulation and competition policy in the Doha negotiation for binding multilateral agreements under the WTO were collapsed by strong objection from the majority of DCs and LDCs.

ICAs, separate from private international cartels, have been under international commodity law because commodities have unique characteristics which should be treated under a rule different from competition law. Regarding ICAs, international organizations have issued resolutions, declarations, and made treaties registered.

Although bilateral agreements have unique advantages, such as low cost and can the negotiation on specific issues, bilateral agreements can not replace multilateral agreements because the bilateral agreements, as foundation of international law, have certain natural limitations, e.g., narrow membership. Developed amongst industrialized countries, the bilateral agreements had difficulty in improving the overall level of cooperation among competition authorities. The multilateral agreement in light of former failures needs to reduce conflicts of opinion between a majority of DCs and advanced countries.

Chapter 4 discussed concrete ways to reduce conflicts between DCs and industrial countries. The 2003 Cancun WTO Ministerial Conference revealed that a unilateral market-oriented competition regime under DDA, supported by industrialized countries, would not be welcomed by DCs even though competition law provides legal guidelines to business activities among competing companies and proffers much benefit in consumers' welfare and efficiency in DCs markets. Enacting a competition regime unfamiliar to DCs in their economies causes a fear that less competitive domestic companies might collapse in the presence of competitive multinational corporations.

In light of the concern, the effective enforcement of competition law in DCs, including cartel regulations, needs substantial time, the development of legal institution and market economies, and enforcement techniques. Before and during the time, the developed world needs to persuade DCs that competition policy can benefit their economic development and to provide technical supports and know how to enforce cartel regulation actively.

Reflection of international development law into the international competition regime is the other solution for development-oriented international competition law. The nonreciprocal principle, SDT, and governmental intervention should be adopted in competition law in light of the wide gap between advanced and developing countries. However, the main rules of GATT/WTO, e.g., MFN, national treatment, may not be damaged by the international competition law.

State-operating cartels or statutory exemptions of cartels can be approved in the context of economic development. A research and development (R&D) cartel, a crisis cartel, small and middle-sized enterprises cartel, a cartel for efficiency-increasing technical standard, and a cartel which rationalizes production and distribution may be exemplary cases. However, those cartels should not be abused but be screened regularly.

A roadmap to a binding multilateral international cartel regulation was proposed. In order to overcome the lack of international consensus regarding cartel regulation, the international community should strive to disseminate competition systems to DCs. Establishing competition law which adopts economic development as an objective of competition policy can help create a permissive mood. The effective activation of domestic cartel regulations in DCs, however, needs external aids from advanced cartel enforcers besides internal institutional improvement. Bilateral agreements and regional agreements for operating effective cartel enforcement can work as building blocks for a multilateral cartel agreement. The expansion of such regional cartel agreements will ultimately result in a multilateral cartel agreement, as the Treaty of EU with competition law included finally created the 1998 OECD Hard Core Cartel Recommendation. A plurilateral competition agreement can be a connector between nonbinding and binding multilateral agreements as it induces countries to voluntarily accede. Then, a narrow approach in a confined topic would be the first type of a binding multilateral international cartel law. As the continuous active cartel enforcement needs a whole competition regime, a broad approach of promoting multilateral competition law should follow the narrow approach.

Chapter 5 analyzed development of competition regimes, respectively, in four advanced countries, such as the U.S., UK, France, and Germany, and four DCs including Mexico, South Africa, China, and South Korea. Based upon the analysis, it focused on c for cartel enforcement with respect to economic development, and proposed institutional supports for adopting cartel regulations, particularly sanctions, leniency program, and bounty system. Finally, it argued that DCs should have international cooperation in order to develop their cartel regulation.

The analysis of advanced competition regimes indicated that the development of cartel law has been facilitated by four conditions: (i) the development of market economy under an open trade policy, (ii) political support under a democratic power system, (iii) the development of legal institutions which can produce competition jurisprudence, and (iv) economic research which can support cartel regulations. The competition regimes in the U.S., UK, and Germany have been developed on the basis of these four elements while France's competition regime and cartel regulation have been promoted by its integration to the EU and the global trade regime. In addition, the analysis demonstrated that cartel enforcement had not been effective until it worked with the activation of a whole competition regime.

The comparative analysis of competition laws in DCs demonstrated that, when the DCs had such four categories of support as (i) an open market economy, (ii) political democratization, (iii) a sophisticated legal system, and (iv) economic research on competition. The enforcement of their competition regime and cartel regulations could be seriously pursued. Their cartel regulation and competition regime started to be seriously enforced after they opened their domestic markets to foreign companies. In order to reduce objections against the serious enforcement, political support was a key ally which could provide institutional, financial, and public assistance. Moreover, a substantial part of competition law development was due to legal systems which could issue rules through sophisticated judicial and administrative decisions. Support from economic research would play important roles in preventing political influence from distorting competition policy.

Even though industrial policy in a strict meaning conflicts with competition policy, inefficiency inherent in governmental policy will need competition policy in the private sector in order to achieve economic development in the long term. As continuous economic development requires competition policy and cartel regulation is the maxim of competition policy, the active enforcement of cartel regulation is an important legal institution on the way toward economic development. However, the immediate and general adoption of a whole competition regime should be approached cautiously because economic situations in DCs usually consist of less competitive indigenous companies and severe competition with competitive multinational companies might lead to the collapse of the domestic companies as the Mongolia and Peru cases indicated. Before enacting a whole competition regime, DCs need to place their emphasis on the four institutional conditions for competition policy to work actively.

International competition law and cartel regulation need to acknowledge the function of public policies within international competition law, thereby reducing DCs' concerns about adopting a competition regime. As a countermeasure to prevent the arbitrary abuse of the function, the degree to which the function can contribute to public interests or economic development should be analyzed in comparison to efficiency enhancement through competition. Exemptions from cartel regulations can work as concrete institutions reflecting public policies. The exemptions may allow some cartels which promote long-term competition or which have public interests outweighing the restriction of competition. Some of the control measures which prevent their abuse are an independent panel consisting of competition experts, transparent decision-making, and regular review regarding the appropriateness of the exemptions.

Competition policy needs advocacy from the public and experts so that competition policy may be firmly positioned among the whole economic policy, through political regime shifts. In order to have such support, the effective enforcement of cartel regulations is necessary to create the public support by raising public awareness of damages caused by cartels.

The main institutions which activate cartel enforcement are the following: leniency programs and bounty systems. Leniency programs and bounty systems provide much help to secure important information for cartel investigation. Several concrete measures can help such institutions work in a more positive way, e.g., limited conditions for leniency beneficiaries and bounty recipients, and exclusion of information obtained through coercive or fraudulent measures.

In order to build the capacities of nascent or young competition authorities, practical aids from advanced competition authorities and international organizations are necessary. Besides unilateral practical aids, a bilateral agreement between countries with similar levels of competition law under close economic relationships will help to achieve more than an agreement between countries with different levels of competition law. It is because the countries with similar levels of competition law can cooperate well under the mutual understanding of respective competition policy. Several following hurdles have impeded bilateral agreements in competition law compared to the agreements in other areas: the imbalance of power between advanced and developing competition authorities, concern about confidentiality due to reciprocal mistrust, and the importance of business information in competition law to national interests. Institutional reforms, e.g., differential coverage of information which can be shared between advanced and developing competition authorities, and the creation of a system securing confidentiality, can reduce the wide gap of enforcement power. Through leveling the playing field in competition law, international cooperation in cartel regulation can provide more benefits to each country and strengthen the foundation for a binding multilateral cartel agreement.

Chapter 6 suggests two tactics to achieve a multilateral binding cartel-regulatory agreement, and reform-projects for effective ICAs. The first strategy under the short-term approach is to narrow down an object of multilateral international cartel agreement for inducing a sufficient number of countries to accede. Bid-rigging can be an initial object for invoking consensus for international regulation because it causes huge damages to public revenue and it is punished with criminal penalty by many countries. Price-fixing, output restriction, and market allocation can be the next items of international cartel regulation. The other horizontal collusive agreements, usually with the incidental effect of competition-restriction, might as well be under the long-term approach because they generate in-detail economic analysis regarding pro- and anti-competitive effects.

On the other hand, the long-term approach argues, on the basis of experiences in countries where cartel regulation had been underenforced, that activating effective cartel regulations is possible only when it goes with operating the whole competition law system. The long-term approach suggests that efforts to pursue international cartel regulation should be with those for international competition law. Principle-based international law can reduce conflicts in some areas where divergences in competition law in each country have impeded reaching international law. Competition law procedure with less relationship with national interests than substantive law is an area where international law can induce supports from the business community by reducing business transaction costs and from competition authorities by facilitating practical cooperation. An international institution effectively protecting confidential information is needed in order to reduce the concerns of individual country in cooperation.

The possibility that international criminal law applies to hard core cartels is weak at this moment because consumers' welfare or efficiency, best protected by competition, is considered by a few as an international interest significant enough to constitute an international crime. The public culpability against an international cartel has not grown yet in many DCs as the public have not been made aware of the damages which a cartel causes and there have been a few international cartel cases that were revealed to cause huge damages in those countries and punished by themselves.

ICAs, which balanced conflicting interests between exporting and importing countries and regulated the primary commodities trade, have grown defunct with a few exceptions. The main reason for the demises of most ICAs is, among other things, because the market-intervening measures of ICAs to regulate the commodities trade caused political disputes among members with different interests and huge operational costs. Using market adaptive measures, particularly, price-risk management, can help to avoid the disputes and the costs. An ICA model for productivity-enhancing and benefit-sharing will function through technical assistances and exchange of information. The other model for facilitating multistakeholders' participation will contribute to operating market adaptive measures and finding out concrete measures for research and planning on productivity-increase through allowing participation from the private sector. There can be a hybrid model with the advantages of both models. An ecolabel is a good example in which cooperation between the public and private entities created a market adaptive measure with focus on sustainable development and fair benefit sharing.

Food has been seriously treated more as an object of international human rights, including right to food and farmer's right to earn a fair return, rather than as a commodity under free trade by international law. Current endeavors to apply the free trade regime for the international food trade should adopt measures reflecting the human right perspectives, preferential treatment for LIFDC and LDCs, emergency aid, and research and assistance for productivity-increase, thereby shifting toward a new modified regime. ICAs for food commodities, faced by the challenge of a new free trade regime, can play complimentary roles, e.g., a pool arrangement preparing for urgent needs, or a research center for the productivity-increase. As an ICA has expertise in a specific food commodity, it can create more appropriate measures in light of the commodity market situations than other international organizations. International organizations, e.g., UN and FAO, need to regulate and manage activities of each ICA and provide supports to the productivity-increase project.

7.2 Moderation of Distinction Between International Competition Law and International Commodity Law

Distinctive development between international competition law and international commodity law under the realm of international law had distinguished international cartels from intergovernmental commodity agreements (ICAs) or intergovernmental producers' associations (IPAs). However, author's suggests that public policies or economic development perspectives should be considered in existent efficiency-oriented competition law, and that an ICA or an IPA should use market-adjusting measures and focus on structural policy, e.g., marketing through diversification, can diminish the distinction between the two international law areas. The following picture illustrates the relationship between international commodity law and international competition law and the suggestions of this thesis.

On the two standards of market efficiency and fair distribution, including the level of state involvement into distribution system,[1] international competition law has had more dependency on market efficiency while international commodity law has relied upon fair distribution. International competition law has refined its objective of improving the market efficiency under the leadership of advanced countries. Cartel activities, which fall on (A) in the picture, occupy a part of the objects of int'l competition law. Some activities of the IATA fall under the category of (A), as IATA, including private airlines, restricts competition in air fare or cargo fee, and its practices in slot allocation, e.g., historical precedence, influences fair distribution negatively. Meanwhile, under the realm of international commodity law, an IPA has less interest in both fair distribution and market efficiency than an ICA because an IPA consisting of producers keeps the position of demanding

[1]State involvement is emphasized in terms of fair distribution so that the division between int'l commodity law and int'l competition law can be made clearly. As a result, an IPA and an ICA with high evaluation in fair distribution are placed above a cartel in the picture. As fair distribution has deep relationship with public interest, state involvement under public policy is inevitable in most countries.

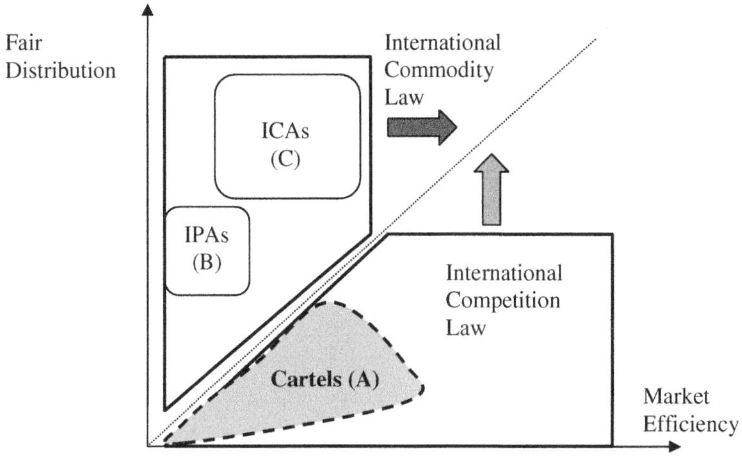

Fig. 7.1 Relationship between Int'l competition law and Int'l commodity law

unilateral reward for their productions even at the cost of market efficiency and consumers' fair share. OPEC, as the representative example of an IPA, falls under this category of (B) of (Fig. 7.1). An ICA, comprising hybrid members ranging from producing countries to consuming countries, is more concerned about fair distribution than an IPA. However, its activities reflect the market efficiency perspective less than those of other private entities under international competition law. ITU, even though telecommunication service is arguably less considered as commodity, has been contributed to fair distribution and market efficiency. In addition, its main members are countries. In light of the characteristics, ITU can be located in the realm of (C).

The argument of this study that international competition law should adopt a development-oriented approach and absorb the function of public policy, particularly economic development, through cartel exemptions, lifts the efficiency-oriented international competition law up to the middle line, as showed by the arrow in the (Fig. 7.1). With the shift, international cartels that contribute to public policy or economic development to an extent outweighing market inefficiency should be approved as legitimate as long as their positive effects exist.

The other argument that an ICA with its focus on productivity-improvement should use market-adaptive policies along with participation from the private sector rather than market-manipulative policies suggests that the emphasis of int'l commodity law on fair distribution among producers should be changed. The focus should move from fair distribution toward the market efficiency-increasing direction, which is illustrated with the shift toward the right in Fig. 7.1.

The possibility that the two international laws under different developmental paths may meet each other and be fully integrated is low because states have enjoyed different treatments from private companies under international law and because primary commodities, in distinction from artificial products under competition law, have unique characteristics and more interests to be harmonized. However, the past failures of ICAs and their current demise teach a lesson that an ICA should be reformed in line with market friendly measures through abandoning costly and inefficient market-interrupting measures. Meanwhile, in order to achieve a consensus sufficient for a binding multilateral cartel regulation, international competition law should inevitably adopt a development perspective or at least reflect the function of public policy in competition policy. If such shifts take place, it will abate distinguish of international cartel regulations from international commodity law regulating ICAs or IPAs.

Index

B
Bid-rigging, 15, 18, 23, 34, 53, 154, 157, 186, 208, 212, 217, 237, 253, 255, 265, 266, 271, 272, 294, 318, 326
Binding international agreement, 146, 153, 260
Binding international cartel regulation, 5, 21, 255
Bounty system, 236, 237

C
Cartel enforcement, 5, 53, 55, 60, 102, 103, 130, 133, 137, 157, 158, 161, 165, 182, 193, 205, 206, 215, 219, 222, 225, 232, 245, 246, 248, 254, 262, 267, 292, 326, 328–330
Competition authorities, vii, 3, 4, 7, 20, 23, 53, 56, 102, 103, 114, 121, 124, 128, 133, 135, 137, 139, 140, 154, 157, 160–164, 166, 176, 178, 179, 182, 184, 185, 193, 210, 213, 214, 218, 219, 233, 235, 236, 239–249, 259, 261, 262, 264, 265, 267, 276, 284, 286, 290, 292, 295, 327, 330, 331
Consensus-building, 7, 20, 50, 193, 194, 204, 270, 329

D
DDA, 3–5, 7, 19, 113, 130, 140, 146, 147, 149–151, 153, 226, 241, 254, 257–259, 265, 270, 271, 291, 307, 314, 315, 318, 328
Development approach, 179, 180

H
Hard core cartel, 1, 5, 151

I
IATA, 63, 65, 88–96, 140, 143, 327, 332
ICA, 22, 25, 26, 29, 38, 39, 42, 43, 45, 46, 49, 50, 59, 66, 107–114, 117, 118, 140, 175, 255, 296–298, 300–302, 306, 308–311, 313, 314, 316, 319–321, 326, 327, 330–333
International cartel, 5–7, 9, 14, 21, 25, 26, 34, 50–53, 55, 56, 58–60, 63–65, 67, 68, 74, 100–103, 120, 128, 134, 138–141, 143, 145, 146, 154–156, 166, 167, 177, 185, 186, 189, 194, 213, 216, 229, 231, 236, 240, 244–246, 253–256, 258, 259, 262, 263, 265, 267, 269, 273, 274, 278–280, 286, 291, 292, 294, 296, 317–319, 325–328, 330–334
International cartel law, 5, 7, 166, 186, 326, 328
International competition law, 3, 7, 11, 18, 20, 47, 63, 64, 74, 125, 126, 132, 139, 140, 145, 173, 176, 177, 179, 186–188, 194, 256, 281–285, 307, 319, 326–328, 330–334
International cooperation, 6, 56, 102, 103, 106, 112, 133, 151, 168, 188, 193, 243, 247, 249, 261, 267, 286, 302, 308, 309, 329, 330
International development law, 7, 145, 153, 171, 172, 188, 284, 328
IPA, 22, 25, 39, 42, 49, 50, 59, 66, 74, 109, 111, 112, 114, 139, 140, 254, 296, 300, 302, 306, 326, 327, 332–334

K
Keywords
- hard core cartel, 1, 2, 11, 12, 15–21, 26, 50, 59, 104, 118, 128, 140, 146, 179, 186–188, 195, 208, 217, 235, 254, 259, 264–272, 280, 294, 326–328, 331
- IPA, 22
- UNCTAD, 3, 18, 20, 22, 27, 43, 103, 109, 116, 121–124, 146, 152, 164, 167, 170–173, 177, 240, 254, 255, 269, 279, 284, 303, 309, 320, 327
- UN Set, 121

J.S. Lee, *Strategies to Achieve a Binding International Agreement on Regulating Cartels*, DOI 10.1007/978-981-10-2756-7

L
Leniency program, 54, 138, 193, 206, 212, 215, 231, 236–239, 242, 244–246, 249, 329, 330
Long-term approach, 266, 280

N
Non-reciprocal principle, 171

O
OPEC, 2, 10, 31, 36, 39, 42, 48, 49, 63, 65, 68–71, 73, 74, 111, 114, 118, 140, 164, 168, 170, 257, 296, 300, 327, 333

R
Regulatory development, 193, 327

S
Short-term approach, 265, 271
Special and differential treatment, 46, 284

U
UNCTAD, 151
UN Set, 3, 17, 18, 26, 50, 103, 118, 121–124, 132, 140, 146, 150, 151, 166, 169, 170, 173, 177, 179, 240, 254, 257–259, 291

The manufacturer's authorised representative in the EU is Springer Nature Customer Service Centre GmbH, Europaplatz 3, 69115 Heidelberg, Germany. If you have any concerns regarding our products, please contact ProductSafety@springernature.com

Printed and bound by CPI Group (UK) Ltd, Croydon, CR0 4YY
30/09/2026
02225444-0014